T0321991

Trends, Applications, and Challenges of Chatbot Technology

Mohammad Amin Kuhail
Zayed University, UAE

Bayan Abu Shawar
Al-Ain University, UAE

Rawad Hammad
University of East London, UK

A volume in the Advances in Web
Technologies and Engineering
(AWTE) Book Series

Published in the United States of America by
    IGI Global
    Engineering Science Reference (an imprint of IGI Global)
    701 E. Chocolate Avenue
    Hershey PA, USA 17033
    Tel: 717-533-8845
    Fax: 717-533-8661
    E-mail: cust@igi-global.com
    Web site: http://www.igi-global.com

Library of Congress Cataloging-in-Publication Data

Names: Kuhail, Mohammad Amin, 1982- editor. | AbuShawar, Bayan, 1972-
   editor. | Hammad, Rawad, 1981- editor.
Title: Trends, applications, and challenges of chatbot technology / edited
   by Mohammad Amin Kuhail, Bayan AbuShawar, Rawad Hammad.
Description: Hershey, PA : Engineering Science Reference, [2023] | Includes
   bibliographical references and index. | Summary: "This book will provide
   novel research content as well as reviews of the state of the art in
   chatbot technology. The book will cover a variety of theoretical and
   practical topics in various domains such as human-computer interaction,
   natural language processing, education, cybersecurity, and more. Such
   content could be highly beneficial to researchers aiming at developing
   chatbots that are usable, accurate, effective, and secure. Further, the
   book sheds light on challenges and open questions in chatbots, and
   possible research directions"-- Provided by publisher.
Identifiers: LCCN 2022043763 (print) | LCCN 2022043764 (ebook) | ISBN
   9781668462348 (h/c) | ISBN 9781668462386 (s/c) | ISBN 9781668462355
   (eISBN)
Subjects: LCSH: Chatbots. | Expert systems (Computer science) | Virtual
   humans (Artificial intelligence) | Question answering systems.
Classification: LCC QA76.76.C52 T74 2023 (print) | LCC QA76.76.C52
   (ebook) | DDC 005--dc23/eng/20221214
LC record available at https://lccn.loc.gov/2022043763
LC ebook record available at https://lccn.loc.gov/2022043764

This book is published in the IGI Global book series Advances in Web Technologies and Engineering (AWTE) (ISSN: 2328-2762; eISSN: 2328-2754)

British Cataloguing in Publication Data
A Cataloguing in Publication record for this book is available from the British Library.

All work contributed to this book is new, previously-unpublished material.
The views expressed in this book are those of the authors, but not necessarily of the publisher.

For electronic access to this publication, please contact: eresources@igi-global.com.

Advances in Web Technologies and Engineering (AWTE) Book Series

ISSN:2328-2762
EISSN:2328-2754

Editor-in-Chief: Ghazi I. Alkhatib The Hashemite University, Jordan David C. Rine George Mason University, USA

MISSION

The **Advances in Web Technologies and Engineering (AWTE) Book Series** aims to provide a platform for research in the area of Information Technology (IT) concepts, tools, methodologies, and ethnography, in the contexts of global communication systems and Web engineered applications. Organizations are continuously overwhelmed by a variety of new information technologies, many are Web based. These new technologies are capitalizing on the widespread use of network and communication technologies for seamless integration of various issues in information and knowledge sharing within and among organizations. This emphasis on integrated approaches is unique to this book series and dictates cross platform and multidisciplinary strategy to research and practice.

The **Advances in Web Technologies and Engineering (AWTE) Book Series** seeks to create a stage where comprehensive publications are distributed for the objective of bettering and expanding the field of web systems, knowledge capture, and communication technologies. The series will provide researchers and practitioners with solutions for improving how technology is utilized for the purpose of a growing awareness of the importance of web applications and engineering.

COVERAGE

- Data analytics for business and government organizations
- Case studies validating Web-based IT solutions
- Quality of service and service level agreement issues among integrated systems
- IT readiness and technology transfer studies
- Security, integrity, privacy, and policy issues
- Virtual teams and virtual enterprises: communication, policies, operation, creativity, and innovation
- Web systems performance engineering studies
- Information filtering and display adaptation techniques for wireless devices
- Software agent-based applications
- Human factors and cultural impact of IT-based systems

IGI Global is currently accepting manuscripts for publication within this series. To submit a proposal for a volume in this series, please contact our Acquisition Editors at Acquisitions@igi-global.com or visit: http://www.igi-global.com/publish/.

Titles in this Series

For a list of additional titles in this series, please visit:
www.igi-global.com/book-series/advances-web-technologies-engineering/37158

Strategies and Opportunities for Technology in the Metaverse World
P.C. Lai (University of Malaya, Malaysia)
Engineering Science Reference • © 2023 • 390pp • H/C (ISBN: 9781668457320) • US $270.00

Supporting Technologies and the Impact of Blockchain on Organizations and Society
Luís Ferreira (Polytechnic Institute of Cávado and Ave, Portugal) Miguel Rosado Cruz (Polytechnic Institute of Viana do Castelo, Portugal) Estrela Ferreira Cruz (Polytechnic Institute of Viana do Castelo, Portugal) Helder Quintela (Polytechnic Institute of Cavado and Ave, Portugal) and Manuela Cruz Cunha (Polytechnic Institute of Cavado and Ave, Portugal)
Engineering Science Reference • © 2023 • 310pp • H/C (ISBN: 9781668457474) • US $270.00

Architectural Framework for Web Development and Micro Distributed Applications
Guillermo Rodriguez (QuantiLogic, USA) and Mario G. Beruvides (Texas Tech University, USA)
Engineering Science Reference • © 2023 • 320pp • H/C (ISBN: 9781668448496) • US $250.00

3D Modeling Using Autodesk 3ds Max With Rendering View
Debabrata Samanta (CHRIST University, India)
Engineering Science Reference • © 2022 • 291pp • H/C (ISBN: 9781668441398) • US $270.00

Handbook of Research on Gamification Dynamics and User Experience Design
Oscar Bernardes (ISCAP, ISEP, Polytechnic Institute of Porto, Portugal & University of Aveiro, Portugal) Vanessa Amorim (ISCAP, Polytechnic Institute of Porto, Portugal) and Antonio Carrizo Moreira (University of Aveiro, Portugal)
Engineering Science Reference • © 2022 • 516pp • H/C (ISBN: 9781668442913) • US $380.00

For an entire list of titles in this series, please visit:
www.igi-global.com/book-series/advances-web-technologies-engineering/37158

701 East Chocolate Avenue, Hershey, PA 17033, USA
Tel: 717-533-8845 x100 • Fax: 717-533-8661
E-Mail: cust@igi-global.com • www.igi-global.com

Table of Contents

Section 3
Chatbots in Business: Overview and Challenges

Section 4
Chatbot Algorithms and Privacy Concerns

Chapter 12
Conversational AI Chatbots in Digital Engagement: Privacy and Security
Uma S., Hindusthan College of Engineering and Technology,
Coimbatore, India

Detailed Table of Contents

Section 1
Chatbot Design and Usability Considerations

Chatbots are rapidly growing and becoming prevalent in many applications, including healthcare, education, and consumer services. As such, it is crucial to design chatbots with usability in mind. Traditional usability heuristics call for error prevention, consistency, and task efficiency. The heuristics are suited for all types of user interfaces, including chatbots. However, chatbots have their unique challenges, and thus, recently, some researchers have developed sets of usability guidelines specifically for chatbots. However, there is a shortage of studies that summarize the latest advances in chatbot usability design and assessment. As such, this chapter covers the existing general and chatbot-specific usability heuristics and examples of usage. Moreover, the chapter presents the recent developments in chatbot design techniques and challenges.

Chatbots are efficient artificial intelligence tools employed frequently across various industries such as healthcare, tourism, entertainment, and education, to assist in performing repetitive activities requiring a conversation, thereby facilitating humans to focus on more innovative tasks. This chapter reviews the design challenges of two types of chatbots classified based on their interaction modes: dyadic chatbots interacting with one individual at a time; and polyadic chatbots interacting with multiple individuals simultaneously. Further, the chapter identified the associated challenges in the chatbots, namely: engagement, trust, and human likeliness based on personality types - at a higher level in the chatbot design, together with the impact of each challenge on the user behavior. The authors review the literature in the relevant areas to pinpoint the research gaps requiring more focus within each area of challenge. The research community can address these identified research areas, which will eventually promote a more efficient human-machine collaboration.

Chapter 3

Alice Ashcroft, Lancaster University, UK
Angela Ashcroft, University of Central Lancashire, UK

The majority of chatbots are built, by default, as women. In doing so, dangerous stereotypes and behaviors are perpetuated by those responsible for designing the chatbots, and ultimately the users. It is therefore crucial that gender identity and expression are well understood by all those involved in designing the chatbots. This chapter explores this alongside a literature survey regarding feminist methodologies, anthropomorphism, and authenticity to put forward three recommendations. That those responsible for building chatbots should keep up to date with research, look to widen the diversity of their own team, and to integrate ethics in their design processes. Only in doing so will chatbots that are fit for purpose be built.

Section 2
Chatbots in Education: Overview, Applications, and Challenges

Chapter 4

Masood Ghayoomi, Faculty of Linguistics, Institute for Humanities and Cultural Studies, Tehran, Iran

This chapter mainly concerns the application of artificial intelligence (AI) based chatbots in education (in the general sense). Three general applications of such systems are studied: a) language learning, b) teaching a course, and c) assistive for educational purposes (in the narrow sense). There are advantages and disadvantages for using chatbots in education. Their interaction with the students, human-like conversation simulation, 24/7 availability, and easy accessibility are some of the key advantages of using AI-based chatbots in education. The main disadvantage of such systems is their knowledge-bases (KB) requirement. A KB plays as the brain of a chatbot. However, their development is labor intensive and expensive in terms of time and effort. In this chapter, the main research studies on chatbots for the educational domain are reviewed and general construction of a chatbot as well as the evaluation metrics of chatbots are explained; and the available chatbot tools and systems used in education, in the general sense, are collected.

Chapter 5

The rapid technological developments have revolutionised approaches toward learning. The adoption of eLearning technologies such as chatbots has been increasing in the past few years, as there are various opportunities that can be identified to integrate educational chatbots with online learning process. For example, chatbots in education can provide various services such as personal tutoring, personal support, assessment and evaluation, etc. Iissues in remote learning—such as real-time assistance, feedback, and support—can be addressed by deploying educational chatbots. Yet, there are various challenges associated with chatbot technologies in education, e.g., novelty effect, cognitive load, the readiness of students and teachers, etc. This study reviews the various opportunities and challenges associated with educational chatbots in learning. These findings would help future researchers and designers to identify the core functionality and design aspects of educational chatbots, and also aids future research by the recommendations of research propositions.

Chapter 6

Chatbots have offered numerous useful applications to a range of market industries due to their absolute benefit of saving costs and eliminating unneeded work for employees. This state had a greater impact on other features than on itself. With the aid of chatbots, the efficiency, competency, and productivity of labor and processes have been maximized on a scale that transcends human capabilities. As a result of such a profitable conclusion for firms and businesses, which stimulates additional skills of both humans and machines, it is argued that chatbots are not only a useful tool but also motivational agents.

Rawad Hammad, University of East London, UK
Mohammed Bhaja, University of Birmingham, UK
Jinal Patel, University of East London, UK

Recently, chatbots have been used in various domains including health care and entertainment. Despite the impact of using chatbots on student engagement, there is little investment in how to develop and use chatbots in education. Such use of advanced technologies supports student learning, both individually and collaboratively. The effective use of chatbots in education depends on different factors, including the learning process, teaching methods, communications, etc. In this paper, the authors focus on the systematic utilization of chatbots in education. A proof of concept has been developed and tested using two MSc module, i.e., cloud computing and software engineering. The authors have used AWS Services to build the backend of Chatbot and integrate it with Facebook Messenger to allow students to learn via an additional venue, i.e., social media. The use of EDUBOT proved that chatbot can improve student learning and engagement especially at the time of COVID-19 where higher education is moving towards online teaching. Extending EDUBOT framework will help to support students' admin and other queries.

Elsayed Issa, University of Arizona, USA
Michael Hammond, University of Arizona, USA

Chatbot technology is a subfield of Artificial Intelligence (AI) that deals with text-based or speech-based conversational agents. In general terms, a chatbot enables a user to have a conversational interaction with a computer. Chatbots have applications in several fields including trade, tourism, customer care, health services, education, et cetera. This chapter describes two chatbot systems that we are developing for learning Arabic as a foreign language. KalaamBot is a speech-based chatbot that converses with learners and teaches them the language in a conversational setting. KalimaBot is a text-based personal vocabulary assistant that enables students to search for the meaning of words, synonyms, antonyms, and word usage in context. This chapter provides extensive discussion of the several challenges second language researchers and chatbot practitioners encounter when designing chatbots for language learning. Then, it concludes with recommendations and future research.

Section 3
Chatbots in Business: Overview and Challenges

Chapter 9

   Syed Jawad Hussain Shah, University of Missouri-Kansas City, USA

Artificial intelligence (AI)-driven chatbots have established themselves as standard front-line solutions for companies looking to update consumer experiences while maximizing client engagement. Chatbots have become a crucial component of a company's customer-centric operations because of their fast replies, round-the-clock assistance, and ability to comprehend user inquiries. This chapter will describe the function of chatbots as customer service representatives and some of the benefits they offer to organizations. There will also be a discussion of the present difficulties facing the industry in integrating these conversational bots.

Chapter 10

   Marta Ferreira, University of Porto, Portugal
   Belem Barbosa, University of Porto, Portugal

The main objectives of this chapter are to provide an overview of chatbot personality dimensions and to analyze the expected impacts on user behavior. To accomplish these objectives, the chapter provides a detailed review of the main contributions in the literature regarding this topic. It highlights the chatbot personality characteristics that are expected to foster user satisfaction, trust, loyalty, and engagement. This information is useful for both practitioners and researchers, particularly related to customer service, as it provides clear guidance on what characteristics to incorporate in chatbots and on what factors need to be further studied in the future.

Section 4
Chatbot Algorithms and Privacy Concerns

Chapter 11

   Guendalina Caldarini, University of Sunderland, UK
   Sardar Jaf, University of Sunderland, UK

Intelligent conversational computer systems, known as chatbots, have always been at the forefront of artificial intelligence. They are made to sound like humans in order for machines to communicate with humans. Because of the rising benefits of chatbots, numerous sectors have adopted them to give virtual support to clients. They are also used as companions and virtual assistants. Natural language processing and deep learning are two artificial intelligence disciplines that are used in chatbots. This chapter will examine current advancements in chatbot algorithms, approaches, and technologies that use artificial intelligence and/or natural language processing.

Chapter 12
> *Uma S., Hindusthan College of Engineering and Technology,*
> *Coimbatore, India*

Digital transformation and globalisation have taken the online business to the next frontier, embracing the customer engagements with conversational artificial intelligence or chatbots. Chatbots are deployed across several industries ranging from e-commerce to healthcare. While the advantages of using chatbots are enormous, chatbots also introduce certain pitfalls. A lack of diversity among creators may result in biased responses from the chatbot. Though chatbots are widely used, not all of their security issues are satisfactorily resolved. It causes significant security issues and risks, which needs immediate attention. Many chatbots are built on top of social/messaging platforms, which has its own set of terms and conditions governing data collection and usage. This work gives a detailed analysis of security considerations in the context of communication with bots. This chapter has the potential to spark a debate and draw attention to the issues surrounding data storage and usage of chatbots to protect users.

Preface

Chatbots are set to be the most disruptive technology of this decade. The chatbot market globally is projected to be 1.25 billion dollars in 2025 (Statista 2023). Two decades ago, Abu Shawar and Atwell asked, "Chatbots: are they really useful?" (Abu Shawar & Atwell 2007) and found a variety of example applications. However, these pioneering systems were limited in various ways. They were restricted by computing power and learning algorithms available at the time. They were either for general conversation without specialized domain knowledge (e.g., ALICE) or for answering questions on a pre-specified topic, based on a hand-crafted knowledge base of question patterns and responses. A new generation of chatbots is coming, based on neural pattern-matching algorithms which can learn from huge volumes of raw text and are pre-trained to capture the knowledge of the entire World Wide Web. Online neural network chatbots such as ChatGPT can harness huge cloud computing power to process any question and generate a sophisticated, impressive answer in real-time and in flawless English, drawn from knowledge anywhere on the internet. For example:

Me: What are the main differences between chatbots in 2007 and today's chatbot systems?

ChatGPT: *There have been many advances in chatbot technology since 2007, and today's chatbot systems are much more sophisticated and capable than those of the past. Some of the main differences between chatbots in 2007 and today's chatbots include:*

Capability: Chatbots in 2007 were often limited in their capabilities and could only perform a few specific tasks. Today's chatbots, on the other hand, are much more capable and can perform a wide range of tasks, from answering simple questions to engaging in complex conversations.

Natural language processing: Chatbots in 2007 often had difficulty understanding and interpreting natural language input from users. Today's chatbots, however, have much better natural language processing capabilities and can understand and respond to a wide range of inputs.

Personalization: Chatbots in 2007 were often one-size-fits-all and could not personalize their responses to individual users. Today's chatbots, on the other hand, can be customized and personalized better to meet the needs and preferences of individual users.

Integration: Chatbots in 2007 were often standalone systems that were not easily integrated with other systems or platforms. Today's chatbots, on the other hand, can be easily integrated with a wide range of systems and platforms, making it easier to build custom chatbot applications.

Availability: Chatbots in 2007 were less widespread and were not as widely available as they are today. Today, chatbots are an integral part of many companies' customer service and support systems, and there is a wide range of chatbot platforms and tools available to developers.

Overall, the main differences between chatbots in 2007 and today's chatbots are the increased capabilities, improved natural language processing, ability to personalize responses, ease of integration, and wider availability. . . ." (ChatGPT, personal communication, 2023)

Despite their recent popularity, chatbots have been around for over half a century. The first chatbot, ELIZA, used pattern matching to mimic a psychotherapist interacting with a patient (Weizenbaum, 1966). As the technology evolved, chatbot developers started using artificial intelligence (AI) to provide accurate responses to user input using a knowledge base (Abu Shawar & Atwell, 2015). The rapid advances in AI enabled improved recognition of text and human speech (Shankar, 2018), enabling the growth of chatbots in different domains.

This book introduces the design methodologies and usability issues of chatbots, covering a variety of trends, applications, and challenges of chatbots in many domains, including education and business. The book also covers chatbot algorithms and privacy concerns.

With respect to design and methodologies, new approaches to the design and validation of chatbots have emerged. For instance, usability heuristics specific to chatbot design have been proposed (Murad et al., 2019; Sugisaki & Bleiker, 2020). The heuristics cover a range of conversational issues. They can be mapped to generic usability guidelines by Shniderman et al. (2016) and Nielsen (1994), emphasizing visibility, consistency, and recognition rather than recall.

In the field of education, chatbots are being increasingly adopted as they can engage students and personalize learning (Kuhail et al., 2022). Over the past decade, chatbots have been used to perform a variety of educational tasks, such as serving as tutors, coaches, and learning companions (Haake et al., 2009). Additionally, chatbots can fulfill various roles, such as motivation and learning by teaching (Kuhail et al., 2022). Chatbots can also help with educational needs, including answering questions (Feng, 2006), and language assistance (Heffernan & Croteau, 2004).

In business, chatbots have been harnessed to improve customer experience by cost-effectively offering customer support. Chatbots have also been used to automate help desks, allowing customers to inquire about product or service information without waiting for a human agent to become available. Chatbots have reportedly improved response time and sales.

Several algorithms have been utilized to allow chatbots to provide accurate answers to users' input. For instance, some algorithms rely on detecting users' intent based on certain words, concepts, actions, verbs, and more, while other algorithms utilize deep learning to understand users' overall messages and generate a matching answer.

BOOK OVERVIEW

Section 1 introduces the readers to chatbots, and the various design methodologies needed to ensure a human-centric chatbot. The section covers the impact of various design configurations on user behavior and the influence of the chatbot's gender on behavior. Chapter 1 presents generic usability heuristics, including error prevention, task efficiency, and consistency, besides the chatbot-specific heuristics catering to the conversational nature of chatbots. The chapter reviews the recent developments in design methodologies and usability considerations and challenges. Chapter 2 reviews the challenges in designing two types of chatbots, dyadic (one-on-one) and polyadic (one-on-many) chatbots. The chapter presents key challenges in designing chatbots, such as developing chatbots to achieve engagement, trust, and human likeness. Chapter 3 tackles the issue of chatbot gender. The chapter discusses recommendations that integrate ethics into the design process of chatbots while maintaining anthropomorphism and authenticity.

Section 2 introduces the applications of chatbots in the educational domain. This section covers a range of theories, concepts, and tools stretching from the pedagogy of learning through technological applications. It also highlights the impact of chatbots on education, such as improving students' engagement. Chapter 4 focuses on the general application of chatbots in education, in (1) language teaching, (2) generic teaching skills, and (3) supporting education. The chapter considers the time and effort required to develop such tools. Chapter 5 presents educational chatbot opportunities and challenges, applied to specific purposes such as personal tutoring, assessment, support, and evaluation. Chapter 6 highlights the impact of using chatbots in education to improve learners' motivation. This chapter adopts a pedagogical-based approach to analyze learning characteristics, including focus span, learning techniques, and learner behavior. Chapter 7 introduces a novel framework for a chatbot in education: Edubot. This chapter provides a walkthrough to guide educators on the best way to develop educational chatbots, including requirements, design, implementation, and evaluation. The Edubot framework is connected to social media platforms such as Facebook messenger. Chapter 8 describes a chatbot system for learning Arabic as a foreign language with a speech-based interface, KalaamBot, that converses with learners and teaches them the language in a conversational setting; and a text-based personal vocabulary assistant. Further, KalimaBot enables students to search for the meaning of words, synonyms, antonyms, and word usage in context. The chapter discusses the challenges that second language researchers and chatbot practitioners encounter when designing chatbots for language learning.

Section 3 discusses the role that chatbots play in business and customer support and how anthropomorphism can affect and enhance that role. Chapter 9 reviews how chatbots can function as customer service agents and perform various tasks deemed beneficial to organizations. The chapter also discusses the challenges of applying chatbots in such environments. Chapter 10 introduces the concept of chatbot personality and how it impacts user behavior. The chapter shows that certain personality traits improve user satisfaction and engagement, and discusses the impact of chatbot personality on practitioners in the domain of customer service.

Section 4 provides an overview of chatbot algorithms and privacy concerns. Chapter 11 describes a range of chatbot algorithms, starting from rule-based algorithms in which answers are based on matching users' input with text in collected or recorded corpora, to machine learning and deep learning algorithms where new answers can be learned or generated based on understanding the users' input. Several machine learning techniques are reviewed, including sequence to sequence, Encoder to Decoder, and Bert. Based on the algorithm, chatbots can be classified into retrieval-based or generative-based. Chapter 12 investigates the necessity of protecting customer privacy and security issues while using chatbots; applying machine-learning techniques, chatbots can learn from conversations that may contain sensitive information. The chapter reviews a range of security mechanisms, such as using biometric authentication, two-factor authentication, or time-based authentication, to allow only registered users to use the chatbot.

To illustrate the power of deep-learning chatbots based on large language models, I asked ChatGPT to summarize the above:

This book presents an overview of recent developments, applications, and challenges in the field of chatbots. The first section covers chatbot design and usability considerations, including recent methodologies, design challenges, and the gendered nature of chatbots. The second section focuses on chatbots in education, discussing their applications, opportunities and challenges, and their role as motivational agents. The third section explores the use of chatbots in business and customer support, and the fourth section delves into the algorithms and technologies behind chatbots, as well as the privacy and security concerns surrounding their use. We hope that this book will provide a comprehensive and informative overview of the current state of chatbots and their potential impact on various domains. (ChatGPT, personal communication, 2023)

Eric Atwell
University of Leeds UK

REFERENCES

Abu Shawar, B., & Atwell, E. (2007). Chatbots: Are they Really Useful? *Journal for Language Technology and Computational Linguistics*, *22*(1), 29–49. https://jlcl.org/article/view/88

Abu Shawar, B., & Atwell, E. (2015). Alice chatbot: Trials and outputs. *Computación y Sistemas*, *19*(4), 625–632.

Alobaidi, O. G., Crockett, K. A., O'Shea, J. D., & Jarad, T. M. (2013). Abdullah: An intelligent Arabic conversational tutoring system for modern Islamic education. In *Proceedings of the World Congress on Engineering* (*Vol. 2*). Academic Press.

Feng, D., Shaw, E., Kim, J., & Hovy, E. (2006). An intelligent discussion-bot for answering student queries in threaded discussions. *Proceedings of the 11th International Conference on Intelligent User Interfaces*.

Haake, M., & Gulz, A. (2009). A look at the roles of look & roles in embodied pedagogical agents— A user preference perspective. *International Journal of Artificial Intelligence in Education*, *19*, 39–71.

Heffernan, N. T., & Croteau, E. A. (2004). Web-based evaluations showing differential learning for tutorial strategies employed by the Ms. Lindquist tutor. *Proceedings of the International Conference on Intelligent Tutoring Systems*.

Kaczorowska-Spychalska, D. (2019). Chatbots in marketing. *Management*, *23*(1).

Kuhail, M. A., Alturki, N., & Alramlawi, S. (2022). Interacting with educational chatbots: A systematic review. *Educ Inf Technol*. doi:10.1007/s10639-022-11177-3

Murad, C., Munteanu, C., Cowan, B. R., & Clark, L. (2019). Revolution or evolution? Speech interaction and HCI design guidelines. *IEEE Pervasive Computing*, *18*(2), 33–45. https://doi.org/10.1109/MPRV.2019.2906991

Nielsen, J. (1994). Enhancing the explanatory power of usability heuristics. In *Proceedings of the SIGCHI Conference on Human Factors in Computing Systems (CHI '94)* (pp. 152–158). ACM. doi:10.1145/191666.191729

Shankar, V. (2018). How Artificial Intelligence (AI) is Reshaping Retailing. *Journal of Retailing*, *94*(4), VI–XI.

Shneiderman, B., Plaisant, C., Cohen, M., Jacobs, S., & Elmqvist, N. (2016). *Designing the user interface: Strategies for effective human-computer interaction* (6th ed.). Pearson.

Statista.com. (2023). *Size of the chatbot market worldwide in 2016 and 2025*. https://www.statista.com/statistics/656596/worldwide-chatbot -market/

Sugisaki, K., & Bleiker, A. (2020). Usability guidelines and evaluation criteria for conversational user interfaces - a heuristic and linguistic approach. In *MuC'20: Proceedings of the Conference on Mensch Und Computer* (pp. 309–319). ACM.

Weizenbaum, J. (1966). Eliza – a computer program for the study of natural language communication between man and machine. *Communications of the ACM*, *9*(1), 36–45.

Section 1
Chatbot Design and Usability Considerations

Chapter 1
Recent Developments in Chatbot Usability and Design Methodologies

Mohammad Amin Kuhail
iD https://orcid.org/0000-0002-0000-0989
Zayed University, UAE

Shahbano Farooq
Zayed University, UAE

Shurooq Almutairi
Princess Nourah bint Abdulrahman University, Saudi Arabia

ABSTRACT

Chatbots are rapidly growing and becoming prevalent in many applications, including healthcare, education, and consumer services. As such, it is crucial to design chatbots with usability in mind. Traditional usability heuristics call for error prevention, consistency, and task efficiency. The heuristics are suited for all types of user interfaces, including chatbots. However, chatbots have their unique challenges, and thus, recently, some researchers have developed sets of usability guidelines specifically for chatbots. However, there is a shortage of studies that summarize the latest advances in chatbot usability design and assessment. As such, this chapter covers the existing general and chatbot-specific usability heuristics and examples of usage. Moreover, the chapter presents the recent developments in chatbot design techniques and challenges.

DOI: 10.4018/978-1-6684-6234-8.ch001

INTRODUCTION

Chatbots, also known as conversational agents, facilitate the interaction of humans with computers using natural language by applying natural language processing (NLP) (Bradeško & Mladenić, 2012). Chatbots are rapidly becoming prevalent as they imitate human conversations and thus automate service, and they are now utilized in various areas, including healthcare (Oh et al., 2017), consumer services (Xu et al., 2017), education (Kuhail et al., 2022), and academic advising (Kuhail et al., 2022).

Despite the popularity of chatbots in various fields and a plethora of studies on chatbots in academia, there is a lack of studies summarizing the recent development of chatbots' usability and user experience in terms of design and usability evaluation. In essence, usability assesses how easy a user interface is to use (Nathoo et al., 2019). Traditionally, Schneiderman et al. (2016), Sugisaki and Bleiker (2020), and Nielsen and Molich (1990) identified generic usability heuristics as useful for guiding and evaluating user interfaces. However, since they are generic, the usability heuristics are susceptible to different interpretations by designers (Sugisaki & Bleiker, 2020), especially for conversational interfaces, which have unique characteristics such as sequential communication and freedom of interaction and initiative (Shneiderman et al., 2016). Consequently, various researchers contributed usability heuristics to guide the design and assessment of conversational user interfaces (Bos et al., 1999) (Murad et al., 2019) (Sugisaki & Bleiker, 2020). These heuristics are established on the generic usability heuristics together with particularity connected to conversation and language studies. Other techniques and strategies have been used for evaluating chatbots, including log analysis and observations (Kawasaki et al., 2020) and surveys (Xiao et al., 2020).

In addition to usability heuristics, a few studies have contributed several methodologies guiding the design and development of chatbots. For instance, Pricilla et al. (2018) based their chatbot design on understanding user goals and tasks, while other studies based their design on interviews with users (Zheng et al., 2022) and eliciting scenarios (Kuhail et al., 2022). Nevertheless, there is a lack of studies that provide an overview of the existing approaches to designing and evaluating chatbots. Concerning design techniques, there are several design techniques presented in the literature. For instance, a rule-based approach uses predefined rules to generate responses (Agarwal & Mani, 2020; Thorat & Jadhav, 2020). Other approaches use information retrieval, including Word-level Vector space models with a cosine distance, to find the best match Q-A pair (Mnasri, 2019). Moreover, machine learning techniques commonly employ a different set of features. Sequence-to-sequence learning and reinforcement learning are the most used machine learning models (Mnasri, 2019). Thus, this study aims to bridge the gap by summarizing, analyzing, and reflecting on the latest attempts to design and evaluate the usability of chatbots. This chapter is structured as follows. First, we cover the usability guidelines and criteria, including general usability criteria and those specific to chatbots. Thereafter, we cover the general chatbot design methodologies and provide reflections on the suitability of the design approaches in various contexts.

USABILITY GUIDELINES AND EVALUATION

Various platforms are rapidly incorporating chatbots to improve user experience (Moriuchi et al., 2021), while educators are using artificially intelligent digital assistants to teach, assist, or mentor students to enhance student learning and experience (Wollny et al., 2021). With the application of conversational agents in various domains, evaluating their quality with respect to user experience is essential. The focus of this section is to provide an overview of evaluation methods used for determining the usability of a conversational agent in the context of the education domain, referred to as pedagogical conversational agents (Hobert, 2019).

User experience (UX) focuses on using research methods during the design process to ensure that systems such as chatbots are easy and pleasant to use. The field has adapted and invented many research methods to gather and incorporate usability requirements iteratively during design, such as; usability testing, competitive analysis, A/B testing, and walkthroughs that can help determine the objective usability of the interface. Objective usability refers to how easy it is for the user to perform tasks or meet goals (Bevan et al., 2016). Therefore, the number of encountered problems and task performance can be used to measure the system's usability objectively. Research methods such as focus groups, interviews, questionnaires, and heuristic evaluations are used in UX to help access the system's subjective usability or the user's attitude toward the interface. Moreover, satisfaction, motivation, and preference are qualitative measures of accessing subjective usability. Based on empirical evidence, there is a strong correlation between objective and subjective usability. In other words, users are more likely to perceive a system as usable if it provides better utility. (Nielsen & Levy, 1994). According to Schneiderman, "The design of excellent tools depends upon understanding how they will be used; therefore, usability is a pre-requisite for successful utility" (Grinstein et al., 2003). The following section provides an overview of various usability criteria used to access usability.

Usability Criteria

Usability criteria are common practical quality criteria for creating better design and avoiding common pitfalls based on the guidelines of existing experts in the field.

Recent reviews on the state of research on chatbots for education have identified the use of heterogeneous usability criteria for evaluating the quality of the technology. For example, some studies accessed objective usability, such as learning gain and performance, while others used subjective usability criteria, such as satisfaction, motivation, affection, and accessibility. The most cited and generalized usability criteria or heuristics applied to access usability irrespective of the context were introduced by (Nielsen, 1994):

- *Learnability:* The system should be easy to learn.
- *Efficiency*: The system should allow the user to perform tasks efficiently
- *Memorability*: The system allows users to remember how to perform previously learned tasks.
- *Few Errors*: The system should allow users to make minimal errors and allow them to overcome their mistakes.
- Satisfaction: The system should be pleasant to use.

Another frequently referenced criteria is the quality of use criteria outlined by the ISO 9241-11 standard, which are based on the definition of usability: "the extent to which a system, product or service can be used by specified users to achieve specified goals with effectiveness, efficiency and satisfaction in a specified context of use" (Bevan et al., 2016). The ISO standard expects product designers to decompose the quality criteria, effectiveness, efficiency, and satisfaction into measurable secondary attributes for the specific context and evaluate and reduce potential risks. A recent review on voice assistants indicates that although many of the secondary criteria used by current research fall under effectiveness, efficiency, and satisfaction, specific but relevant voice assistant-related criteria do not fall under the scope of ISO 9241-11, such as attitude, machine voice, and cognitive load (Dutsinma et al., 2022). Therefore, it is difficult to conform to one standard set of usability criteria when conducting usability studies on conversational agents.

Ben Schneiderman proposed 8 usability criteria or heuristics widely recognized and applied to website and application design, which are: consistency, universal usability, informative feedback, dialogues to yield closure, error prevention, permitting easy reversal of actions, keeping users in control, and reducing short term memory load (Shneiderman et al., 2016). In human centered-AI, Schneiderman cites reliability, safety, and trust as important criteria for artificially intelligent systems to ensure the appropriate use of human control versus computer control in the particular context of AI use (Shneiderman, 2020).

The above-mentioned widely accepted usability criteria have been customized to fit the needs of emerging technologies and the context in which they are used, for example; virtual environments (Sutcliffe & Gault, 2004), customer service

Table 1. General usability heuristics

	Usability Criterion	**Description**
1.	Visibility/feedback of the system status.	Users should be informed using appropriate feedback quickly
2.	Mapping between system and the real world.	The interface should use a language familiar to the user
3.	User control and freedom	Users should be able to control when to start and end communication with the system
4.	Consistency	Conventions, standards, and terminology should be followed consistently.
5.	Recognition rather than recall	The system shall reduce the user's cognitive load by making the functionality and information visible
6.	Flexibility and efficiency of use	The system should allow for shortcuts to expedite the interaction for experienced users
7.	Aesthetics and minimalism in design and dialogue	The interface should only contain essential elements
8.	Error prevention	A good user interface eliminates error-prone conditions.
9.	Allowing users to recognize and recover from errors	Error messages should be displayed in understandable. language and a constructive message to help users recover from the error
10	Help and documentation	It is ideal if the system does not need additional documentation. However, it may be needed to help users understand the system's functionality

conversational agents on social media (Xu et al., 2017) and game interfaces for playability (Desurvire et al., 2004). A recent study on a pedagogical conversational agent for advising combined usability criteria from ISO (Bevan et al., 2016), (Nielsen, 1994), and (Shneiderman et al., 2016) to propose a generalized set of 10 heuristics applicable to pedagogical conversational agents illustrated in Table 1 (Kuhail et al., 2022). The researchers followed the user experience design process applying the given heuristics to guide their design. These heuristics can be used for formative evaluation of the conversational agent during the design process.

The following section provides an overview of the recent reviews that have explained common research methods and usability criteria used for summative evaluation of conversational agents in education.

Usability Evaluation Methods

UX designers take an iterative approach and apply formative usability evaluations throughout the design process to incorporate usability with functionality from the project's inception (Nielsen, 1994). However, recent reviews on pedagogical conversational agents, recognize that most researchers focus on summative evaluations at the end of the interface design to evaluate the conversational agent's usability (Kuhail et al., 2022) (Hobert, 2019), (Pérez, 2020), (Hwang & Chang, 2021). Moreover, researchers mostly rely on common research methods used by the scientific community, such as formal experiments, evaluation studies, surveys/questionnaires, focus groups, and interviews.

A review on 25 pedagogical conversational agents (Hobert, 2019) acknowledged the interdisciplinary nature of this technology, resulting in the use of domain-specific evaluation methods by the researchers and a limited but blended set of usability criteria. As a result, the review proposed a comprehensive and clear categorization of evaluation criteria for pedagogical conversational agents and their applicability to various research methods. The research methods were categorized into formative procedures and summative measurements. The formative procedures identified in the review are Wizard of Oz studies, controlled laboratory studies, field studies, and technical validation. In comparison, the most widely used summative measurement was quantitative questionnaires, besides qualitative interviews, an analysis of the conversation, and the technical log file.

Similarly, a comprehensive review of 80 conversational agents identified questionnaires as the most common research method to attain learners' subjective usability or perceived learnability (Pérez, 2020). The review acknowledged that the research community used different quality criteria to evaluate chatbots in education. For example, a few papers used objective measures to evaluate chatbot effectiveness and performance, while others used various subjective quality criteria formulated based on effective teaching, human-like personality, or quality conversations. The review recognized that conversation-related criteria and established usability criteria are all important to emulate an effective human-like conversation.

According to another review of 29 conversational agents, researchers found that most evaluations used quantitative measures to gather empirical evidence of learning effectiveness (Hwang & Chang, 2021). Although the paper provides different types of quantitative analysis, interviews are the only qualitative method identified. ANCOVA/MANCOVA, t-tests, ANOVA/MANNOVA, correlation, and descriptive statistics were used to provide statistical evidence of the positive impact of conversational agents in education. However, it is not presented whether the purpose of each quantitative method was to determine learning gain (objective measure) before and after the intervention or whether the purpose was to determine perceived learnability (subjective measure).

Findings from the most recent review of 36 conversational agents in education (Kuhail et al., 2022) indicate that 36.11% were formal experiments under controlled environments accessing one variable to gather statistically significant results, while

27.77% of the research used evaluation studies involving a small sample of the population using the pre and post-test method to gain variable insights into chatbot use, including objective usability such as task completeness and learning gain, as well as subjective preference, such as motivation, satisfaction, engagement and perceived learning. Questionnaires were used equally as much as the evaluation studies. Focus groups is another research method used to involve a small group and observe user behavior towards the chatbot to identify usability concerns or collect subjective preference. Focus groups were used in a limited amount of research papers (8.22%). Table 1 provides an overview of various evaluation methods mentioned by recent literature reviews (Hobert, 2019) (Pérez, 2020) (Hwang & Chang, 2021) (Kuhail et al., 2022). Table 2 illustrates the usability criteria used in the design and evaluation of chatbots based on recent literature reviews (Hobert, 2019) (Pérez, 2020) (Hwang & Chang, 2021) (Kuhail et al., 2022)

Based on the above reviews, the research on pedagogical conversational agents does not conform to standard usability evaluation criteria. Therefore, we found that most researchers in this area rely on widely accepted measurement instruments, such as heuristics and questionnaires, as a benchmark for effective usability evaluations.

Table 2. Types of Evaluation methods used to support better design of chatbots based on recent literature reviews on pedagogical conversational agents (Hobert, 2019) (Pérez, 2020) (Hwang & Chang, 2021) (Kuhail et al., 2022).

	Wizard of Oz Studies	Laboratory experiments or study	Field Study	Technical validation (Test Cases)	Interviews	Questionnaires	Conversation Analysis	Focus Groups
(Hobert, 2019)	x	x	x	x	x	-	x	-
(Pérez, 2020)	-	x	-	-	-	x	x	-
(Hwang & Chang, 2021)	x	x	x	-	x	x	-	-
(Kuhail et al., 2022)	-	x	x	-	-	x	-	x

Measurement Instruments

The UX research community and internal standards have been proposing and updating design frameworks and usability criteria to keep up with the pace of evolutionary technologies, such as recommender systems, autonomous cars, conversational agents, and augmented reality applications (Kuhail et al., 2022), (Shneiderman et al., 2016), (Shneiderman, 2020), (Novak & L. Hoffman, 2019), (Rubio-Tamayo et al., 2017), (Bevan et al., 2016). Despite the variety of proposed usability criteria, developers of emerging technologies rely on generalized criteria that can be easily adapted to

Table 3. Important usability criteria for chatbots compiled and adapted from the recent literature reviews (Hobert, 2019) (Pérez, 2020) (Hwang & Chang, 2021) (Kuhail et al., 2022)

Objective Measures	Subjective Measures			
Common Quantitative Criteria	Common Psychological Criteria	Chatbot Criteria Human-Like Quality	Chatbot Criteria Conversation Quality	Pedagogical Criteria Teaching Quality
Performance (Task accomplishment and Dialog efficiency) (Hobert, 2019) (Pérez, 2020) (Hwang & Chang, 2021) (Kuhail et al., 2022)	Motivation or Engagement (Hobert, 2019) (Pérez, 2020) (Hwang & Chang, 2021) (Kuhail et al., 2022)	Chatbot Physical Persona (facial features and gestures) (Hobert, 2019) (Pérez, 2020) (Kuhail et al., 2022)	Dialog quality (Relevance) (Hobert, 2019) (Pérez, 2020) (Kuhail et al., 2022)	Mimicking Roles to support Pedagogical Practice (Teaching agent in an experiential or constructivist environment, or a peer agent to provide adequate support) (Pérez, 2020) (Kuhail et al., 2022)
Increase in Learning (Hobert, 2019) (Pérez, 2020) (Hwang & Chang, 2021) (Kuhail et al., 2022)	Usefulness and ease-of-use (Hobert, 2019) (Pérez, 2020) (Kuhail et al., 2022)	Chatbot Personality (Friendly, humorous, affectionate, charismatic, professional, informal) (Pérez, 2020) (Kuhail et al., 2022)	Building a Relationship (Building common ground, and creating trust) (Pérez, 2020) (Kuhail et al., 2022)	Effective use of Teaching Practices (Supporting accessibility, providing feedback, and encourage task completion) (Pérez, 2020) (Kuhail et al., 2022)
	Perceived Increase in Learning (Hobert, 2019) (Pérez, 2020) (Hwang & Chang, 2021) (Kuhail et al., 2022)			

take the first step toward usability evaluation. Therefore, most researchers adopt widely accepted measurable instruments for time-efficient usability testing. These measurable instruments can be used as heuristic evaluations early in the design phase to gather expert ratings, post-test to evaluate subjective usability, or pre and post-intervention, to provide empirical evidence of subjective preference. As a result, the measurement instruments discussed is this section can be easily adapted to various inspection and evaluation methods of pedagogical conversational agents.

System Usability Scale (SUS):

The system usability scale (SUS) measures usability and learnability. It is the most widely used, reliable, 10-question survey to determine a system's general usability quickly. Questions 4 and 10 access learnability, and all others access ease of use. User ratings are taken on a 5-point Likert scale and need to be normalized to create a percentile ranking (Brooke, 1996).

Technology Acceptance Model (TAM):

Another widely accepted and reliable survey is the TAM questionnaire used to access two subjective criteria: perceived usefulness and perceived ease of use. It comprises 12 questions on a 7-point Likert scale. (Davis, 1989).

Computer System Usability Questionnaire (CSUQ):

The computer system usability survey measures system usefulness, information, and interface quality. It is also a widely accepted survey developed around the same time as SUS. It consists of 16 positively constructed questions on a 7-point Likert scale with an NA option outside the scale. (Lewis, 1995)

User Engagement Scale (UES-SF):

The user engagement scale -short form is a relatively new survey compared to SUS, CSUQ, and TAM (O'Brien & G. Toms, 2010). However, it is widely accepted for evaluating user engagement, a significant factor in education. The questions are based on four criteria: focused attention, feeling immersed, perceived usability, aesthetic appeal, and reward. It consists of 12 questions rated on a 7-point Likert scale for reliability.

Chatbot Usability Questionnaire (CUQ):

A usability survey has been specifically designed to evaluate chatbots for post-intervention. CUQ consists of 16 questions on a 5-point Likert scale measuring chatbot personality, onboarding, user experience, and error handling. (Holmes et al., 2019).

CHATBOT DESIGN METHODOLOGIES

A chatbot's primary task is to generate a response based on natural language input presented by the user. Several approaches to eliciting that response efine the modeling mechanism of a chatbot (Agarwal & Mani, 2020). However, according to (Cebrián et al., 2021), several factors must be considered before deploying chatbots as a communication channel between users. These factors are: (1) The task and the level of complexity that chatbots perform, in addition to the customer's needs, demands, and characteristics. (2) The use of available solutions while evaluating performance, computational costs, and time. (3) Examining the quantity and quality of training data and resources for the domain and language. (4) Create the best interactions with the chatbot based on the users' environment, and finally, acknowledge and resolve any ethical issues.

General Structure of Chatbots

Initially, designing a system entails identifying the constituent parts according to a standard so that a modular development approach can be followed (Ramesh et al., 2017). This design principle can be applied to chatbot development. A chatbot system can be divided into three significant parts, shown in Figure 1, which are described as follows:

1) **Responder:** This component interfaces between the chatbot's main methods and the user. The Responder's responsibilities include transferring data from the user to the Classifier and controlling the input and output.
2) **Classifier:** It is the link that connects the Responder and the Graphmaster. This layer's functions include filtering and normalizing the input, segmenting the user's input into logical components, transferring the normalized sentence into the Graphmaster, processing the Graphmaster's output, and handling database syntax instructions (e.g., AIML).
3) **Graphmaster:** The pattern-matching component. It acts as the brain of the chatbot, and its tasks include organizing the brain's contents and storing and holding the pattern-matching algorithms.

Chatbots Design Approaches

Chatbots are based on a complex development platform and a knowledge base. Therefore, building chatbots requires programming skills and experienced developers, and mostly it requires an extensive database and must provide reasonable responses to

Figure 1. The general structure of a chatbot

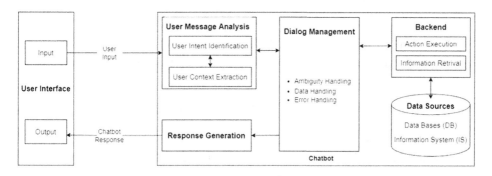

all interactions. (Pereira & Luisa, 2013; Abdul-Kader & John, 2015). Fundamentally, there are different types of chatbots. However, as a general rule, the types of chatbots can be divided into two main categories: Rule-based chatbots or AI (Machine learning, Deep learning etc.). According to (Hussain et al., 2019; Ramesh et al., 2017; Chen et al., 2017; Masche & Le, 2017; Abdul-Kader & John, 2015; Mathur & Singh, 2018; Bradeško & Mladenić, 2012), several approaches have been explored for chatbot development, and each of the main types can employ these approaches. The next part takes a broad look at each of these approaches.

Parsing

Parsing is a technique that takes text as input and converts it into a set of simpler strings that can be easily stored and manipulated using several NLP functions, for example, trees in Python Natural Language ToolKit (NLTK). First, it is used to determine the grammatical structure of a sentence. After that, an abstract syntax tree is constructed, and the lexical structure can be validated to see if it forms an allowed sentence according to the language rules (syntactical parsing). A simplistic parsing technique only checks if recognizable keywords provided by the user as input were present in the corpus or not to find the appropriate response to the user. An example of this type of parsing would be the ELIZA chatbot (Hussain et al., 2019; Ramesh et al., 2017).

Pattern Matching

It is a widely used technique in most Chatbots. It is popular in question-answer systems that depend on matching types, such as natural language inquiries, simple statements, or semantic meaning of inquiries (Abdul-Kader & John, 2015; Ramesh et al., 2017; Meffert, 2006). It classifies the user input as a "pattern" and generates a suitable response for the user stored in a " template." These "pattern" and "template" pairs are manually made (Hussain et al., 2019). The complexity of pattern-matching approaches varies, but the basic idea remains the same. Earlier chatbots such as ELIZA and PC Therapist used the most basic patterns (Bradeško & Mladenić, 2012).

AIML

AIML stands for Artificial Intelligence Mark-up Language. It is XML-based (Extensible Mark-up Language). AIML is designed to assist chatbots in creating conversational flow. It is an open standard made up of data objects known as AIML objects. These objects, also known as AIML elements, are composed of units known as topics and categories. The topic is an optional top-level element with a name attribute and a set of related categories. At the same time, categories are the most fundamental unit of knowledge. A category must include at least two more elements "pattern" and "template." Each category represents a rule for converting input to output. The "pattern" is used to match the user input, and the "template" is used to generate the chatbot's response. AIML is influential in designing chatbots' conversational flow, which is flexible and straightforward, but it requires some natural language processing and programming expertise (Hussain et al., 2019).

Chatscript

It is a technique that can be used when there are no matches in AIML. It focuses on the best syntax for constructing a reasonable default answer. It provides a set of features such as variable concepts, facts, and logical and/or (Abdul-Kader '& John, 2015). It is a rule-based engine in which rules are written in program scripts using a technique known as dialog flow scripting. These scripts can be saved as text files. Machine learning tools can also be used to mine user conversation logs to improve dialog flows. Concepts are used in chatscript, and it is possible to create a concept that includes all nouns and adverbs. There is an existing database of approximately 2000 predefined concepts, and scripters can quickly write their concepts (Hussain et al., 2019).

Ontologies

They are also known as semantic networks and are a collection of related and hierarchically connected concepts. The goal of incorporating ontologies into a chatbot is to compute the relationship between these concepts, such as synonyms, hyponyms, and other natural language concept names. The connections between these concepts can be represented in a graph, allowing the computer to search using specific reasoning rules (Abdul-Kader & John, 2015). The main benefit of using domain ontology in a chatbot is that it cannot only explore the concept nodes of an ontology to establish the relationship between concepts used in conversation, but it can also imply new reasoning. However, using ontologies in chatbots is still quite limited (Hussain et al., 2019).

Markov Chain Model

A Markov chain model is a probabilistic model that attempts to simulate the model probabilities of state transitions over time. The key idea behind this model is that given the current state, there is a fixed probability that it will go to one or more states next. When a chatbot employs this method, it generates an output corresponding to the state transition. This enables the chatbot to construct sentences for responses that are more likely to be appropriate probabilistically while being different each time but more or less coherent. Furthermore, the starting state can be determined by user input, making the response more relevant. Markov Chains are famous for creating chatbots that mimic simple human conversation for entertainment purposes. A simple Markov chains model is simple to program and can be summarized in a matrix (Hussain et al., 2019).

Recurrent Neural Networks (RNNs)

When making decisions, our thoughts consider the earlier background and conversational knowledge before making a choice. This ability to examine the conversational past is not present in conventional neural networks. Recurrent neural networks are helpful in this situation because they can maintain information across time (Ramesh et al., 2017). A loop in the RNN allows information to be transmitted from one stage of the network to the next by feeding the neurons with an input (Xt) and details from the previous conversation if we unroll the loop in the recurrent neural network.

RNNs can be viewed as different iterations of the same network, each of which transmits information about the current state of the conversation to its successor. Each cell in the RNN model analyzes a word and determines the probabilities of the likely words that will follow it in a phrase. When used to solve problems in areas like speech recognition, language modeling, translation, and picture captioning, RNNs have seen tremendous success in recent years (Ramesh et al., 2017).

Long Short-Term Memory Networks (LSTMs)

Long-term dependencies can be learned using Long Short-Term Memory networks (LSTMs), a particular RNN (Ramesh et al., 2017). In LSTMs, memory cells and gates are added, enabling the cells to retain the previously learned information for extended periods. Similar to data in a computer's memory, these memory cells may store information, write new information, and read information from them. The usage of input gates, forget gates, and output gates regulate the flow of information (Hussain et al., 2019).

Compared to a conventional RNN, an LSTM network is the best choice for experience-based learning. RNNs are no longer the industry standard for this job; LSTM networks are. Even when there is a long period with gaps of undetermined magnitude between significant events, a well-trained LSTM network can do superior categorization, processing, and prediction of time series. These features demonstrate the superior performance of the LSTM in comparison to other RNNs, hidden Markov models, and other sequence learning techniques employed in several applications. Due to their propensity to constantly refer to a piece of distant knowledge in time, LSTMs are thus shown to be quite helpful in constructing chatbots (Hussain et al., 2019; Ramesh et al., 2017).

Sequence to Sequence Neural Model

The Seq2Seq model is based on RNN architecture, which consists of two RNNs: an encoder for processing input and a decoder for producing output. The model can be fed with input sentences of different lengths using both the encoder and decoder. It was initially proposed in 2014 as a modification of Ritter's generative model that maximizes accuracy by utilizing recent developments in deep learning. The decoder decodes the "status" or input sentence after the "status" has been encoded and produces the required "response." The model is most frequently applied to language translation, such as statistical machine translation, where the input sentence is written in one language, and the translated sentence is written in a different language. In addition, chatbots can use this paradigm to translate between input "status" and output "response." This model is now the most popular and effective method for generating responses (Hussain et al., 2019).

Chatbots Design Classification

Most commercial chatbots are designed to serve as a communication channel between businesses and users to solve a specific problem or task. For example, they provide information about the company or product, collect data from the user to redirect them to the appropriate human agent, or solve repetitive but simple tasks such as scheduling, purchasing tickets, or playing music or videos. These task-dependent chatbots are typically implemented using a reasonable number of rules, i.e., rule-based or decision-tree systems or information retrieval approaches the use of regular expressions to extract relevant information from user responses and some predefined and specific dialog flow structure (Cebrián et al., 2021). In contrast, when the task requires a more unconstrained interaction, such as answering open questions, chit-chat, or handling complaints, or when many possible situations, domains, or topics must be handled, reasonable solutions are currently available through deep learning algorithms or hybrid approaches (combining rules, information retrieval, and deep learning models) (Cebrián et al., 2021)

Various criteria can be used to categorize chatbots, and the design methods generally used to create these agents depend on the criteria listed below. These criteria may include the fundamental design principles of conversational agents, the degree to which context needs to be kept and taken into account when understanding the dialogue, or the nature and goal of the conversation for which the chatbot needs to be developed. In this book, we explore two different approaches (rule-based and data-driven)

Rule-Based

The classical approach can be called rule-based. This chatbot system uses predefined rules to generate responses (Agarwal & Mani, 2020; Thorat & Jadhav, 2020). Over time, these rules have become more complex and sophisticated. They are highly effective when the conversation is focused on a single topic or task and the conversation's domain is closed. However, the effectiveness of rule-based techniques decreases as the input becomes more natural or the domain becomes more open. Writing rules can be made by AIML, a language designed for classical chatbots (Ramesh et al., 2017).

According to (Cebrián et al., 2021), the following reasons are the primary justifications for choosing a ruled-based approach: (a) minimal training data with annotations to produce a more sophisticated solution (a typical situation when creating a chatbot from scratch for a new domain or task), (b) they are more predictable in terms of the prompts presented to the user and the actions to be taken following each interaction, (c) it is a preliminary solution for data collection and detecting essential user needs and expressions, (d) it can safely draw the attention of users to the new communication channel, (e) it is capable of completing particular tasks, and (f) after gathering information and keywords, it is simple to redirect the interaction to a human agent.

The basic idea behind the rule-based chatbot approach is that the bot contains a knowledge base with documents containing a "pattern" and "template." When the chatbot receives an input that matches the "pattern," it responds with the message stored in the "template." For example, the "pattern" could be a phrase like "What is your name?" or a pattern like "My name is *," where the star is a regular expression. These "pattern" and "template" pairs are typically handcrafted (Cahn, 2017). The programmer's main challenge is selecting an algorithm for pattern matching between the input sentence and the documents in the data corpus. Consider this the nearest neighbor problem to define the distance function and retrieve the closest document to the input sentence.

Data-Driven

Data-driven chatbots are the most recent and widely used approach. The availability of text datasets in general, and conversational datasets in particular, enabled data-driven approaches to text to be applied. While rule-based approaches use handcrafted rules to generate answers or questions, data-driven approaches use existing human-human or bot-human conversations and/or narrative documents to generate bot utterances. To leverage existing conversational data, either Information Retrieval (IR) or Machine Learning (ML) can be used. The next part takes a broad look at each of these approaches.

Information Retrieval-based Chatbots

CleverBot was one of the first IR chatbots. Rollo Carpenter created it in 1988 and published it in 1997. CleverBot responds to questions by analyzing how a human responded to a similar question in a conversation database. CleverBot, despite its simplicity, was widely used. Information retrieval chatbot models function similarly to search engines, with the query representing the user's turn and the search result representing the chatbot's answer. With a Q-R1 pairs dataset and a question Q, the IR-based conversational model will search the Q-R dataset for the best matching pair (Q',R') and return R as an answer to Q. This can be thought of as a method of mirroring the training data. Many retrieval baseline models have been proposed to accomplish these tasks. Word-level Vector space models with a cosine distance have been widely used to find the best match Q-A pair (Mnasri, 2019).

Other studies concentrated on retrieval models based on the term frequency - inverse document frequency (TF-IDF). Galitsky and Ilvovsky proposed a chatbot for customer support and product recommendation to assist users in quickly navigating to the exact expected answer. To that end, they propose modeling the generalization or specification relations between possible answers using discourse trees and, particularly, Rhetorical Structure Theory. WikiAnswers2, Yahoo Answers3, and Twitter conversations are among the most popular open-domain datasets for generalist IR-based chatbots Some researchers have extended the IR approach beyond these datasets and applied it to narrative text datasets such as Wikipedia (Mnasri, 2019).

Machine Learning-based Chatbots

Recently, the problem of generating human-like conversations has been modeled as the problem of mapping a human turn to the target to be predicted machine turn. Most recent work has focused on applying deep learning models, but each formulates the problem differently and employs a different set of features. Sequence-to-sequence learning and reinforcement learning are the most commonly used machine learning models (Mnasri, 2019). Sequence-to-sequence is described above.

Reinforcement learning allows machines to learn like humans do by interacting with their surroundings. The learning process seeks to maximize the concept of cumulative reward. Following each interaction, the agent observes the outcomes of its actions and receives a reward, which can be positive or negative. End users use the chatbot to train a dialogue system with reinforcement learning as it becomes more efficient throughout the conversations. Before neural networks, the problem of dialogue systems was modeled as Markov Decision Processes (MDPs) to use reinforcement learning. The system is represented by a set of states that correspond to the entirety of the dialogue and actions that represent the system's responses. The goal is to maximize the reward for completing user requests. An SLU (Speech Language Understanding) component precedes this dialogue manager, and an NLG (Natural Language Generation) component follows it.

Partially Observed Markov Decision Processes (POMDPs) were later used to model dialogue systems. This method assumes that the dialogue begins in state s_0. A transition probability $p(s_t \mid s_{t-1}, a_{t-1})$ is used to model succeeding states, where s_t is the state at time t and a_t is the action taken at time t. The state st is partially observable to account for the error rate of the language understanding framework. To that end, the user input is converted to observation with probability $p(o_t \mid s_t)$ at each turn, where o_t is the observation at time t (Mnasri, 2019).

The dialogue model M represents the transition and observation probability stochastic functions. Another stochastic model encoding the policy P is used to delegate the possible system actions. During the dialogue, a reward is assigned to the system at each utterance in order to favor the dialogue system's ideal behavior. The dialogue and policy models are optimized by adding up the cumulative rewards during the dialogue. The best policy is learned through a reward system in reinforcement learning. This procedure can be learned online or offline (Mnasri, 2019).

CONCLUSION

This chapter has summarized the design and usability assessment strategies used for assessing and guiding the usability of chatbots. Moreover, the chapter presented the recent developments in chatbot design techniques and challenges. In terms of usability guidelines, the traditional usability heuristics defined by Schneiderman and Nielsen, including visibility of the system status, mapping between system and the real world, user control and freedom, consistency, recognition rather than recall, flexibility and efficiency of use, aesthetics and minimalism in design and dialogue, error prevention, allowing users to recognize and recover from errors, and documentation. The traditional usability heuristics are still valid in the context of chatbots. However, new usability guidelines have recently emerged that are specifically designed to accommodate the conversational nature of chatbots. The chapter also reviewed the evaluation methods used to evaluate the usability of chatbots, including questionnaires, experiments, field studies, technical validation, interviews, Conversation Analysis, and focus groups. Moreover, several standard tests are used to evaluate the chatbot's usability such as System Usability Scale, Technology Acceptance Model, Computer System Usability Questionnaire, User Engagement Scale, and Chatbot Usability Questionnaire.

The chapter presented the common design techniques used to develop chatbots such as parsing, pattern matching, and the usage of machine learning. Moreover, the chapter has also presented design approaches to chatbots such as rule-based, data-driven, information-retrieval, and machine-learning-based chatbots.

ACKNOWLEDGMENT

This work was funded by Zayed University, UAE, under the RIF research grant number R20131

REFERENCES

Abdul-Kader, S. A., & John, W. C. (2015). Survey on chatbot design techniques in speech conversation systems. *International Journal of Advanced Computer Science and Applications*, 6(7).

Agarwal, R., & Mani, W. (2020). Review of state-of-the-art design techniques for chatbots. *SN Computer Science*, 1(5), 1–12. doi:10.100742979-020-00255-3

Bevan, N. (2016). New ISO standards for usability, usability reports and usability measures. *In International conference on human-computer interaction*, 268-278.

Bos, J., Bohlin, P., Larsson, S., Lewin, I., Matheson, C, & Milward, D. (1999). Survey of existing interactive systems. Technical Report, Task Oriented Instructional Dialogue. *Gothenburg University.*

Bradeško, L., & Mladenić, D. (2012). A survey of chatbot systems through a loebner prize competition. *Proceedings of Slovenian language technologies society eighth conference of language technologies*, (pp. 34–37). Semantic Scholar.

Brooke, J. (1996). SUS-A quick and dirty usability scale. *Usability evaluation in industry, 194*(189), 4-7.

Cahn, J. (2017). *CHATBOT: Architecture, design, & development.* University of Pennsylvania School of Engineering and Applied Science Department of Computer and Information Science.

Cebrián, J., Martínez-Jiménez, R., Rodriguez, N., & D'Haro, L. F. (2021). Considerations on creating conversational agents for multiple environments and users. *AI Magazine, 42*(2), 71–86. doi:10.1609/aimag.v42i2.7484

Chen, H., Liu, X., Yin, D., & Tang, J. (2017). A survey on dialogue systems: Recent advances and new frontiers. *Acm Sigkdd Explorations Newsletter, 19*(2), 25–35. doi:10.1145/3166054.3166058

Davis, F. D. (1989). Perceived usefulness, perceived ease of use, and user acceptance of information technology. *Management Information Systems Quarterly, 13*(3), 319–340. doi:10.2307/249008

Desurvire, H., Caplan, M. & Toth, A. J. (2004). Using heuristics to evaluate the playability of games. *CHI '04.*

Dutsinma, F. L. I., Pal, D., Funilkul, S. & H. Chan, J. (2022). A Systematic Review of Voice Assistant Usability: An ISO 9241–11 Approach. *SN Computer Science 3*(4), 1-23.

Grinstein, G. (2003). *Which comes first, usability or utility?* IEEE Computer Society. doi:10.1109/VISUAL.2003.1250426

Hobert, S. (2019). *How are you, chatbot? Evaluating chatbots in educational settings–results of a literature review.* DELFI.

Holmes, S. (2019). Usability testing of a healthcare chatbot: Can we use conventional methods to assess conversational user interfaces? In *Proceedings of the 31st European Conference on Cognitive Ergonomics (ECCE 2019)*. ACM. 10.1145/3335082.3335094

Hussain, S., Omid, A. S., & Nedal, A. (2019). A survey on conversational agents/chatbots classification and design techniques. *Workshops of the International Conference on Advanced Information Networking and Applications*. Springer.

Hwang, G.-J., & Chang, C.-Y. (2021). A review of opportunities and challenges of chatbots in education. *Interactive Learning Environments*, 1–14.

Kawasaki, M., Yamashita, N., Lee, Y.-C., & Nohara, K. (2020). Assessing Users' Mental Status from their Journaling Behavior through Chatbots. *Proceedings of the 20th ACM International Conference on Intelligent Virtual Agents (IVA '20)*, (pp. 1–8). ACM. 10.1145/3383652.3423870

Kuhail, M. A., Al Katheeri, H., Negreiros, J., Seffah, A., & Alfandi, O. (2022). Engaging Students With a Chatbot-Based Academic Advising System. *International Journal of Human-Computer Interaction*, 1–27. doi:10.1080/10447318.2022.2074645

Kuhail, M. A., Alturki, N., Alramlawi, S., & Alhejori, K. (2022). Interacting with educational chatbots: A systematic review. *Education and Information Technologies*. Advance online publication. doi:10.100710639-022-11177-3

Lewis, J. R. (1995). Computer system usability questionnaire. *International Journal of Human-Computer Interaction*.

Masche, J., & Le, N.-T. (2017). A review of technologies for conversational systems. *International conference on computer science, applied mathematics and applications*. Springer.

Mathur, V. & Singh, A. (2018). *The rapidly changing landscape of conversational agents*. Cornell University.

Meffert, K. (2006). Supporting design patterns with annotations. In *13th Annual IEEE International Symposium and Workshop on Engineering of Computer-Based Systems (ECBS'06)*. (pp. 8). IEEE.

Mnasri, M. (2019). *Recent advances in conversational NLP: Towards the standardization of Chatbot building*. Cornell University.

Moriuchi, E., Landers, M., Colton, D., & Hair, N. (2021). Engagement with chatbots versus augmented reality interactive technology in e-commerce. *Journal of Strategic Marketing*, 29(5), 375–389. doi:10.1080/0965254X.2020.1740766

Murad, C., Munteanu, C., Cowan, B. R., & Clark, L. (2019). evolution or Evolution? Speech Interaction and HCI Design Guidelines. *IEEE Pervasive Computing*, *18*(2), 33–45. doi:10.1109/MPRV.2019.2906991

Nathoo, A., Gangabissoon, T., & Bekaroo, G. (2019). Exploringthe use of tangible user interfaces for teaching basic java programming concepts: A usability study. 2019 conference on next generation computing applications. NextComp.

Nielsen, J. (1994). *Usability Engineering*. Academic Press.

Nielsen, J., & Levy, J. (1994). Measuring usability: Preference vs. performance. *Communications of the ACM*, *4*(37), 66–75. doi:10.1145/175276.175282

Novak, T. P., & Hoffman, L. (2019). Relationship journeys in the internet of things: A new framework for understanding interactions between consumers and smart objects. *Journal of the Academy of Marketing Science*, *2*(47), 216–237. doi:10.100711747-018-0608-3

O'Brien, H. L., & Toms, G. (2010). The development and evaluation of a survey to measure user engagement. *Journal of the American Society for Information Science and Technology*, *61*(1), 50–69. doi:10.1002/asi.21229

Oh, K. J., Lee, D., Ko, B., & Choi, H.-J. (2017). *A chatbot for psychiatric counseling in mental healthcare service based on emotional dialogue analysis and sentence generation*. doi:10.1109/MDM.2017.64

Pereira, M. J. & Luisa, C. (2013). *Just. Chat-a platform for processing information to be used in chatbots*. Semantic Scholar.

Pérez, J. Q. T. D. J. M. M. P., Daradoumis, T., & Puig, J. M. M. (2020). Rediscovering the use of chatbots in education: A systematic literature review. *Computer Applications in Engineering Education*, *28*(6), 1549–1565. doi:10.1002/cae.22326

Ramesh, K., Ravishankaran, S., Joshi, A., & Chandrasekaran, K. 2017. A survey of design techniques for conversational agents. In *International conference on information, communication and computing technology,* (pp. 336-350). Springer. 10.1007/978-981-10-6544-6_31

Rubio-Tamayo, J. L., Gertrudix Barrio, M., & García García, F. (2017). Immersive environments and virtual reality: Systematic review and advances in communication, interaction and simulation. *Multimodal Technologies and Interaction*, *4*(1), 21. doi:10.3390/mti1040021

Shneiderman, B. (2016). *Designing the user interface: strategies for effective human-computer interaction*. Pearson.

Shneiderman, B. (2020). Human-centered artificial intelligence: Reliable, safe & trustworthy. *International Journal of Human-Computer Interaction*, *36*(6), 495–504. doi:10.1080/10447318.2020.1741118

Sugisaki, K., & Bleiker, A. 2020. Usability guidelines and evaluation criteria for conversational user interfaces: a heuristic and linguistic approach, 309--319. ACM. doi:10.1145/3404983.3405505

Sutcliffe, A. & Gault, B., 2004. Heuristic evaluation of virtual reality applications.. *Interacting with computers, 16*(4), 831-849.

Thorat, S. A., & Jadhav, V. (2020). A review on implementation issues of rule-based chatbot systems. *Proceedings of the International Conference on Innovative Computing \& Communications (ICICC).* SSRN. 10.2139srn.3567047

Xiao, Z., Zhou, M. X., Liao, Q. V., Mark, G., Chi, C., Chen, W., & Yang, H. (2020). Tell Me About Yourself: Using an AI-Powered Chatbot to Conduct Conversational Surveys with Open-ended Questions. *ACM Transactions on Computer-Human Interaction*, *27*(3), 1–37. doi:10.1145/3381804

Xu, A. (2017). A new chatbot for customer service on social media. *Proceedings of the 2017 CHI conference on human factors in computing systems*, (pp. 3506–3510). ACM. 10.1145/3025453.3025496

Zheng, Q. (2022). UX Research on Conversational Human-AI Interaction: A Literature Review of the ACM Digital Library. *Proceedings of the 2022 CHI Conference on Human Factors in Computing Systems (CHI '22).* ACM. 10.1145/3491102.3501855

KEY TERMS AND DEFINITIONS

Heuristic Evaluation: An application is assessed using a set of rules by one or more usability experts during a heuristic evaluation.

Artificial Intelligence (AI): A field in computer science that in working towards creating systems that can simulate human like qualities such as speech recognition systems and self-driving cars.

Artificial Neural Networks (ANN): They are based on the concept of neurons in the brain and are a set of nodes connected together through weighted edges that help in recognizing patterns to develop artificially intelligent systems.

Artificial Intelligence Markup Language (AIML): An easy to use open standard mark-up language used for developing chatbots.

Ease of use (EOU): A usability criteria that determines how easy it is for a user to accomplish a task. For example, is it easy for a user to place an order in a few clicks without having to watch a tutorial or take a tour on how to place an order.

Heuristic Evaluation: An application is assessed using a set of rules by one or more usability experts based on a set of usability criteria or heuristics.

Lexical Structure: The syntax or grammatical structure of a language. For example, nouns, verbs, adjectives, and adverbs make up a sentence or lexical structure in the English language.

Long Short-Term Memory Network (LSTM): A type of recurrent neural network that takes sequence of data as input to generate insights and predictions, such as real-time speech. It is the most used neural network used in the field of artificial intelligence.

Machine Learning (ML): It is a sub field of artificial intelligence that identifies patterns in human conversations and can be used to create chatbots.

Natural Language Processing (NLP): Applying linguistics, computer science and artificial intelligence to develop systems that can process and analyze natural languages, such as Arabic and English, and be able to understand the content and context of the provided text or speech, to generate insights.

Recurrent Neural Networks (RNN): Artificial neural networks that use deep learning for sequential data or time-series data are known as recurrent neural networks. They make use of memory to store past data or context to improve future results.

Usefulness: A usability criteria that determines whether the features and tasks provided by the system are useful to the user in getting intended work done.

Usability Criteria: A set of quality criteria provided by experts in the field to help guide better design of products and services.

Chapter 2
Chatbot Design Challenges and the Effect on User Behavior

Shurooq Almutairi
Princess Nourah bint Abdulrahman University, Saudi Arabia

Sana A. Khan
Zayed University, UAE

Mohammad Amin Kuhail
https://orcid.org/0000-0002-0000-0989
Zayed University, UAE

Imran Taj
Zayed University, UAE

ABSTRACT

Chatbots are efficient artificial intelligence tools employed frequently across various industries such as healthcare, tourism, entertainment, and education, to assist in performing repetitive activities requiring a conversation, thereby facilitating humans to focus on more innovative tasks. This chapter reviews the design challenges of two types of chatbots classified based on their interaction modes: dyadic chatbots interacting with one individual at a time; and polyadic chatbots interacting with multiple individuals simultaneously. Further, the chapter identified the associated challenges in the chatbots, namely: engagement, trust, and human likeliness based on personality types - at a higher level in the chatbot design, together with the impact of each challenge on the user behavior. The authors review the literature in the relevant areas to pinpoint the research gaps requiring more focus within each area of challenge. The research community can address these identified research areas, which will eventually promote a more efficient human-machine collaboration.

DOI: 10.4018/978-1-6684-6234-8.ch002

INTRODUCTION

Chatbots have become prevalent in various industries, including tourism, education, healthcare, and education, as they can simulate a uniquely human activity, conversation. Recent advances in artificial intelligence gave rise to natural language processing (NLP) which accelerated the growth of chatbots. For example, chatbots can now comprehend language and analyze emotions. As such, researchers are increasingly developing more human-like chatbots. However, despite the rise in chatbot adoption and recent advances in its design, many challenges remain open for researchers to tackle. The dyadic chatbots involve one-on-one conversations with a human user (Kim et al., 2019), and several issues and concerns have emerged in the literature. For instance, to design empathetic chatbots, various researchers developed frameworks that incorporate context and use emotion sampling and imitation (Majumder et al., 2020), while other researchers developed machine learning techniques that enhance intent prediction and language processing (hum et al., 2018).

For polyadic chatbots, conversational agents that mediate human-human conversations and involve multiple parties, various challenges have been reported in the literature (Tegos et al., 2015). For instance, such chatbots are often ignored or mistreated by the users, or even worse, they may be considered intrusive (Tegos et al., 2015). Moreover, various researchers raised the concern that several polyadic chatbots need to use social cues to be accepted by human users (Liu et al., 2018). Nevertheless, building a chatbot with full comprehension capacity is still challenging. As such, researchers continue to explore modeling empathetic conversation, memory, and knowledge, to improve the quality of chatbots. Researchers have also explored the effect of chatbot design on human behavior, in particular, user engagement, usage intention, trust, and perceived authenticity. For example, research shows that there is a positive relationship between trust and anthropomorphism of chatbots (Lee et al., 2021). Similar relationships can be found for other behavioral aspects. Moreover, the effect of chatbot personality has also been assessed (Kulkarni et al., 2015), with the results showing that users favor agreeable chatbots.

This chapter sums up the design challenges of dyadic and polyadic chatbots and how the chatbot design configuration affects user behavior. The first section of this chapter provides a succinct overview of the research design challenges in dyadic and polyadic chatbots, while the second section summarizes the latest research on chatbot design's impact on user behavior. Finally, we conclude by providing the main insights of the chapter.

DESIGN CHALLENGES OF DYADIC CHATBOTS

Conversational Styles /Intelligence

In Social Penetration Theory, relationship formation is understood as driven by self-disclosure, that is, "the act of revealing personal information about oneself to another" (Altman & Taylor, 1973). Different studies have shown that self-disclosure between chatbots and humans improves relationship formation (Kjuve et al., 2022). Chatbots have the potential to be a powerful, affordable tool to support people's self-disclosure. Lee et al. (2020) built a chatbot with self-disclosure capabilities that engage in informal talk with individuals. Results suggest that users' self-disclosure behavior can be impacted by chatbots' conversational styles, but it may also depend on users' expectations of the kind of discussion they will have. To inform users that a certain kind of dialogue is taking place and, more specifically, that their self-disclosure will be encouraged, conversational designs for chatbots should consider if sensitive questions would be included in the chat script. On the other hand, if the chatbot's goal is to gather some relatively innocuous data (such as journaling), its conversational design might include casual small talk. According to the "Similarity attraction theory" by Naas et al., humans favor engaging with machines having personalities similar to their own (Nass et al., 1995). Kim et al. (2019) investigated whether respondents' responses and survey experiences are influenced by the conversational style (formal vs. casual). Users of the chatbot survey exhibit less satisfied behavior when using an informal conversational approach as opposed to a formal style, but not users of the web survey. By providing participants with interaction, the chatbot survey may aid in overcoming the socio-emotional shortcomings of static online surveys. The inability to change an answer was one of the drawbacks of the chatbot survey interface that this study identified. The personality of a chatbot should reflect its domain, according to Jain (Jain et al., 2018). Participants anticipated that the news chatbot would use formal language, whereas they anticipated the shopping chatbot to use informal and amusing language. Depending on the platform, chatbot capabilities, target audience, and usage environment, the interaction style should change (Piccolo et al., 2019).

Empathy

Empathy is a fundamental human characteristic that reflects the ability to identify and comprehend the emotions of those with whom we interact (Majumder et al., 2020). Chatbots started to mimic this trait only in the past few years due to the complexity of this behavior. Earlier research proves the overall advantage of using empathy in chatbots response, such as diminishing users' negative emotions (Hu et al., 2018), reducing stress (Prendinger & Ishizuka, 2005), and improving user trust and engagement (Brave et al., 2005). So naturally, emotion recognition has attracted much interest in customer service due to the enormous impact of enhancing customer satisfaction, improving word-of-mouth activity, and improving user attitude toward the brand (Hu et al., 2018).

Though chatbots are ostensibly made for practical tasks like customer service, some agents, such as mental health applications, are also built to respond to the user's emotional condition (Morris et al., 2018). For instance, chatbots have been utilized for various purposes, including giving psychiatric tests and psychoeducational materials, in commercially available products like Woebot, 7Cups, and Koko (Morris et al., 2018). For some agents, such as those primarily intended for transactional interactions, the empathy trait might be excused, but it becomes essential when automated systems are more frequently used to support healthcare applications, particularly those dealing with mental health.

To produce replies that are acceptable and empathetic for positive or negative comments, Majumder, et al (2020) proposes a new method for an empathetic generation that incorporates context and emotions and uses emotion stochastic sampling and emotion imitation. Positive feelings typically follow positively charged remarks, though they can also be ambivalent. Conversely, in response to negative statements, it is necessary to use a composite emotion that shares the user's feelings while also trying to provide some consolation in the form of optimism or finding the bright side. This study made the mistake of assuming that the feelings of surprise and anticipation were positive, yet one might be both pleasantly and negatively astonished (ambiguous polarity). Even though machine learning techniques have improved intent prediction and natural language understanding, chatbot interaction is still prone to misunderstandings that lead to conversational breakdowns (Porcheron et al., 2018). However, a chatbot's empathic expressions may be perceived slightly differently than a human. Expressed empathy is likely a skill that will never be possible for a robot to execute as well as a human (Morris et al., 2018; Medeiros et al., 2021).

Identity

The design characteristics of chatbots can be different according to the task that needs to be performed by the chatbot. However, chatbots' social cues are essential to the design aspects and, thus, relevant design dimensions that encourage the user to interact with the chatbot socially (Benke et al., 2020). According to (Feine et al., 2019), the social traits of chatbots can be categorized into verbal, visual, auditory, and invisible characteristics. Using these conceptual underpinnings (Benke et al., 2020), three key design aspects in developing chatbots are identified, in their participatory design study. These aspects are the chatbot's appearance representation and messages, the chatbot's behavior, and the interaction patterns that are tied to an invisible behavior.

Although (Feine et al., 2019) adhered to established procedures and made an effort to maintain a high level of accuracy to develop a taxonomy of social cues, not all taxonomy categories will be equally important to all researchers. As a result, future research could broaden the taxonomy by incorporating additional social cues. Moreover, (Guo et al., 2021) suggest that future designs should make the identification information more obvious. It is easy to reveal information to a chatbot by treating it like a real person. According to Jain et al. (2018) and Gnewuch et al. (2017), one of the chatbot design criteria is to give new users an introductory message that describes the capabilities of the chatbots.

DESIGN CHALLENGES Of POLYADIC CHATBOTS

Persistent Intervention

Tegos et al. investigated the impact of a linking contributions (LC) intervention mode implemented by a conversational agent. They reported that the group learner will occasionally overlook and mistreat polyadic chatbots (Tegos et al., 2015). The authors discovered that students gave hurried responses to the tutor agent and occasionally preferred to focus more on the learning questions than the agent's facilitation. As a result of them being "too frequent," "not context sensitive," and distracting, participants also felt that task reminder chatbots were intrusive or bothersome (Toxtli et al., 2018). The outcomes could possibly backfire if chatbots are persistent in their intervention (Zheng et al., 2022). Benke et al. (2020) also draw the conclusion that chatbots for managing emotions in group conversation should be social and humanistic in design. Interactive patterns must be used to support the design. Increasing emotion regulation and behavioral concessions within teams are all benefits of expanding stimulated awareness. However, a careful configuration is needed to balance chatbots acting as helpful instructors versus monitoring micromanagers. It might be crucial that consumers maintain control over the functionalities that are activated. Autonomy could be undermined, and the appearance of surveillance could be created by too sociable and intrusive behavior.

To add emojis to text messages, ReactionBot analyzes users' facial expressions (Liu et al., 2018). Although it helped people become more conscious of their affect and facial expressions, there was a noticeable rise in worry about emotional spillover. Instead of good emotional leaking, participants were more worried about negative emotional leakage.

Depending on the nature of the assignment, chatbots should be used appropriately in group conversations (Kim et al., 2020). Teams may manage their work with TaskBot from the communication platforms they already use (Toxtli et al., 2018). The study found that the inability of TaskBot and other bots to manage multiple ongoing conversations at once is one of their biggest issues (Handling multi-threaded conversations).

Building a social chatbot with intelligence that can fully comprehend humans and the actual environment in which they live and meet their needs would be incredibly difficult. It calls for innovations in a wide range of cognitive and conscious AI fields, including the modeling of empathic conversation, modeling of knowledge and memory, interpretable and controllable machine intelligence, deep neural-symbolic reasoning, cross-media, and continuous streaming AI, and modeling and calibration of emotional or intrinsic rewards reflected in human needs. These are open challenges in AI (hum et al., 2018).

IMPACT OF CHATBOT DESIGN ON USER BEHAVIOR

This section addresses the recent literature on user behavior toward different chatbot designs regarding engagement, trust, and human-likeness.

Engagement

Researchers have been studying the social interactions between humans and computers for decades. However, the interaction between users and chatbots still endures a lack of engagement, even when people treat computers like humans (Reeves & Nass, 1996).

In their participatory design study of 2020, Benke et al. (Benke et al., 2020) created three different chatbot designs, SocialBot (SBT), ActionBot (ABT), and NeutralBot (NBT), in order to manage the emotions of distributed teams of tools like Slack or Microsoft Teams. The SBT chatbot incorporates anthropomorphic and social design features. Meanwhile, the ABT chatbot operates as a live moderator who actively intervenes. In contrast, the NBT chatbot demonstrates a neutral design. All three designs exhibit improved emotional awareness and communication efficiency among team members. However, the users' engagement is magnified when the chatbot is in a social and interactive form. For example, in the first two chatbots, SBT and ABT significantly provoked emotion regulation strategies within the team members. As opposed to NBT that reduced members' emotional competence and was neglected. The first two designs were personalized, humanized, and subjective, which helped in higher acceptance.

Other research has shown that when users recognize a chatbot as a human, they believe the conversation is more engaging and has better outcomes (Lee et al., 2021; Medeiros et al., 2021). According to the study by (Lee et al., 2021), focused on designing two different chatbots with (HC) and without (OC) human support that guide people to practice journaling skills. Their findings showed that HC participants followed the guidance more accurately and had a substantially higher engagement and trust in the chatbot system than the other participants. This is consistent with the finding of (Medeiros et al., 2021), that investigated the potential of chatbots for providing humans with online emotional support tailored to stressors. In addition, the study results show that the "human" condition produces the best results, while the "computer" condition produces the worst.

On the other hand, when users recognize chatbots as a human, it is not always an indication that the conversation will be more engaging or even have better outcomes. For example, at the end of the experiment (Lee et al., 2020), participants were asked if they would like to share their self-disclosed conversations with a mental health professional. They discovered that some participants edited their self-disclosed content before sharing it with the professional. While (Medeiros et al., 2021), they discovered that the OC participants practiced journaling skills far more than the HC participants. Furthermore, time influences people's self-disclosure interactions with chatbots. As a result of (Lee et al., 2020), the study findings highlight the significance of time in human self-disclosure and the development of human-chatbot relationships.

Additionally, studies focusing on multi-user engagement found that communication efficiency with chatbots is increased (Benke, Knierim, & Maedche, 2020; Wang et al., 2021). Furthermore, Chatbots influence and encourage humans to participate in social support for community members on the internet, not only in chat rooms, which is emphasized by Wang et al. findings (Wang et al., 2021). However, some gaps related to human engagement in recent studies need to be addressed. For example, the team's emotional understanding was unaffected by chatbot designs, and some negative effects were reported that caused disturbance or confusion to users, such as contextual factors, too obtrusive interventions, and too neutral messages. On the negative side, some designs showed partial surveillance and loss of control due to intervention. As a result, a combination of advantageous design features should catalyze positive effects while mitigating disadvantages.

Trust

Researchers have developed a variety of approaches to evaluating conversational systems. One of these approaches is assessing subjective human experience, such as measuring users' trust in a chatbot (Han et al., 2021). The willingness of chatbot users to share information is affected by trust, while human trust is influenced by realistic user expectations, the relevance and timeliness of chatbot responses, and the chatbot's personality, transparency, and social interaction style (Kulkarni et al., 2015; Setlur & Melanie, 2022). Specifically, a higher level of trust is often correlated to establishing a relationship in dealing with self-disclosure to chatbots. However, this kind of relationship takes time (Lee et al., 2020). The authors of (Lee et al., 2020) demonstrated how people's trust in a chatbot interacted with their trust in the doctor, as well as with their self-disclosure behavior. The chatbot was used as a mediator for collecting sensitive self-disclosure content and sharing it with real mental health professionals. The chatbot first interacted with the participants before gradually introducing a professional image (doctor) via technology. As a result, participants provided the doctor with the same level of self-disclosure data. This finding implies that an effective chatbot design has the potential to transfer people's trust in the chatbot to their trust in a health service provider introduced by the chatbot.

Moreover, other findings showed that users had a substantially higher trust in the chatbot system with human support than the other designs (Lee et al., 2021; Medeiros et al., 2021). Interesting findings of (Benke et al., 2020) support previous studies that obtrusive chatbot appearance was perceived as a source of confusion or disturbance. As a result, we propose precisely tuning the triggering mechanism to the task, conversation flow, and individual preference. However, we report that the implications are not as obvious as they appear because the chatbot messages still require additional explanations to bridge potential gaps in human emotion comprehension. Aside from optimizing the mechanism, one method is to provide explanations about the derived behavior and learn chatbots through regular check-backs.

Human Likeness

In the studies where individuals or multi-users are involved, participants reported that chatbot felt more human-like. The authors acknowledged several reasons that might influence this impression. These reasons could be the chatbot moderation in emotions, which implies some human characteristics, graphical visualization of the chatbot, the use of emojis and GIF, finally the chatbot's casual conversational style (Benke et al., 2020; Kim et al., 2019).

Furthermore, when it comes to providing emotional support, not just one message but an entire dialogue may play a role. This implies that there should be room for non-stressful small talk. Furthermore, human peers have memories and can ask stressed friends about problems from the past. Finally, multiple interaction modalities, such as voice messages and pictures, may be present in a human-like conversation. As a result, we argue that future versions of computer-generated emotional support should include mechanisms to cover these aspects to create a more realistic simulation of a supportive human peer, and it is necessary to conduct further research on how users with different backgrounds interact differently with various chatbots design (Medeiros et al., 2021; Kim et al., 2019).

CONCLUSION

In today's world, chatbots are essential stakeholders of our modern workforce that automate the recurring chats, thereby reshaping the employment structure. In that regard, this chapter has reviewed the latest design challenges—requiring more focus—in dyadic and polyadic chatbots. The reviewed challenges for dyadic chatbots include the design for empathy, and self-disclosure; whereas for polyadic counterparts include intrusiveness, being ignored, and mistreated by users. We also analyzed the impact of chatbot design settings on user behavior - engagement, trust, usage intentions, and perceived authenticity. While the identified issues are being tackled by the research community, more effort is required in developing chatbots with social cues, so that they are more acceptable for human users. The indepth persuasion of the identified design challenges, in this chapter, together with their impact on user behavior will multipy the opportunities for modern workforce, eventually leading to a fully autonomous and inclusive society (Holroyd, 2020). Such a society will see chatbots as empathetic and trustworthy collaborators that would facilitate to live comfortably on one's own.

ACKNOWLEDGMENT

This work was funded by Zayed University, UAE, under the RIF research grant number R20131

REFERENCES

Altman, I., & Taylor, D. A. (1973). Social penetration: The development of interpersonal relationships. Holt, Rinehart & Winston.

Benke, I., Knierim, M. T., & Maedche, A. (2020). Chatbot-based Emotion Management for Distributed Teams: A Participatory Design Study, p. 30. Association for Computing Machinery. doi:10.1145/3415189

Brave, S., Nass, C., & Hutchinson, K. (2005). Computers that care: Investigating the effects of orientation of emotion exhibited by an embodied computer agent. *International Journal of Human-Computer Studies*, *62*(2), 161–178. doi:10.1016/j.ijhcs.2004.11.002

Feine, J., Gnewuch, U., Morana, S., & Maedche, A. (2019). A taxonomy of social cues for conversational agents. *International Journal of Human-Computer Studies*, *132*, 138–161. doi:10.1016/j.ijhcs.2019.07.009

Gnewuch, U., Morana, S. & Maedche, A. (2017). *Towards Designing Cooperative and Social Conversational Agents for Customer Service.* AIS eLibrary (AISeL).

Guo, J. (2021). Shing: A Conversational Agent to Alert Customers of Suspected Online-payment Fraud with Empathetical Communication Skills, pp. 1-11. Association for Computing Machinery.

Han, X., Zhou, M., Turner, M. J., & Yeh, T. (2021). Designing effective interview chatbots: Automatic chatbot profiling and design suggestion generation for chatbot debugging. *In Proceedings of the 2021 CHI Conference on Human Factors in Computing Systems*, (pp. 1-15). ACM. 10.1145/3411764.3445569

Holroyd, C. (2020). Technological innovation and building a 'super smart' society: Japan's vision of society 5.0. *Journal of Asian Public Policy*, 1–14.

Hu, T. (2018). Touch your heart: A tone-aware chatbot for customer care on social media, pp. 1-12. ACM.

Hum, H., He, X., & Li, D. (2018). From Eliza to XiaoIce: Challenges and opportunities with social chatbots. *Frontiers of Information Technology & Electronic Engineering*, *19*, 10–26.

Jain, M., Kumar, P., Kota, R., & Patel, S. N. (2018). *Evaluating and Informing the Design of Chatbots.* Association for Computing Machinery.

Jain, M., Kumar, P., Kota, R., & Patel, S. N. (2018). *Evaluating and Informing the Design of Chatbots.* . Association for Computing Machinery.

Kim, S. (2020). *Bot in the Bunch: Facilitating Group Chat Discussion by Improving Efficiency and Participation with a Chatbot.* . Association for Computing Machinery.

Kim, S., Lee, J., & Gweon, G. (2019). *Comparing Data from Chatbot and Web Surveys: Effects of Platform and Conversational Style on Survey Response Quality.* Association for Computing Machinery.

Kjuve, M., Følstad, A., Fostervold, K. I. & Brandtzaeg, P. B. (2022). A longitudinal study of human--chatbot relationships. *International Journal of Human-Computer Studies, 168*, 102903.

Kowatsch, T. (2017). *Text-based Healthcare Chatbots Supporting Patient and Health Professional Teams: Preliminary Results of a Randomized Controlled Trial on Childhood Obesity.* Paper presented at the Persuasive Embodies Conference on Intellifent Cirttual Agents. Stockholm, Sweeden.

Kulkarni, C. E., Bernstein, M. S., & Klemmer, S. R. (2015). PeerStudio: rapid peer feedback emphasizes revision and improves performance. *In Proceedings of the second ACM conference on learning@ scale,* (pp. 75-84). ACM.

Lee, Y. C., Yamashita, N., & Huang, Y. 2020. Designing a chatbot as a mediator for promoting deep self-disclosure to a real mental health professional. *Proceedings of the ACM on Human-Computer Interaction*, (pp. 1-27). ACM.

Lee, Y. C., Yamashita, N., & Huang, Y. 2021. Exploring the Effects of Incorporating Human Experts to Deliver Journaling Guidance through a Chatbot. *Proceedings of the ACM on Human-Computer Interaction*, (pp. 1-27). ACM.

Lee, Y.-C., Yamashita, N., Huang, Y., & Fu, W. (2020). *"I Hear You, I Feel You": Encouraging Deep Self-disclosure through a Chatbot.* Association for Computing Machinery.

Liu, M. (2018). *ReactionBot: Exploring the Effects of Expression-Triggered Emoji in Text Messages.* . Association for Computing Machinery.

Majumder, N. (2020). MIME: MIMicking Emotions for Empathetic Response Generation. *arXiv preprint arXiv:2010.01454.*

Medeiros, L., Bosse, T., & Gerritsen, C. (2021). Can a Chatbot Comfort Humans? Studying the Impact of a Supportive Chatbot on Users' Self-Perceived Stress. *IEEE Transactions on Human-Machine Systems*, 343–353.

Morris, R., Kouddous, K., Kshirsagar, R., & Schueller, S. (2018). Towards an artificially empathic conversational agent for mental health applications: System design and user perceptions. *Journal of Medical Internet Research, 20*(6), e10148.

Nass, C. (1995). *Can computer personalities be human personalities?* Association for Computing Machinery.

Piccolo, L., Mensio, M., & Alani, H. (2019). Chasing the Chatbots. In S. S. Bodrunova (Ed.), *Internet Science.* (pp. 157–169). Springer International Publishing.

Porcheron, M., Fischer, J. E., Reeves, S., & Sharples, S. (2018). Voice Interfaces in Everyday Life. Human Factors in Computing Systems (CHI '18), pp. 1-12.

Prendinger, H., & Ishizuka, M. (2005). The Empathic Companion: A Character-Based Interface That Addresses Users' affective States. *Applied Artificial Intelligence, 19*(3-4), 267–285.

Reeves, B. & Nass, C. (1996). The media equation: How people treat computers, television, and new media like real people. *Cambridge, UK, 10,* 10.

Setlur, V., & Melanie, T. (2022). How do you Converse with an Analytical Chatbot? Revisiting Gricean Maxims for Designing Analytical Conversational Behavior. *In CHI Conference on Human Factors in Computing Systems*, (pp. 1-17). ACM.

Tegos, S., Demetriadis, S., & Karakostas, A. (2015). Promoting academically productive talk with conversational agent interventions in collaborative learning settings. *Computers & Education, 87,* 309–325.

Toxtli, C., Monroy-Hernández, A., & Cranshaw, J. (2018). *Understanding Chatbot-mediated Task Management.* . Association for Computing Machinery.

Toxtli, C., Monroy-Hernández, A., & Cranshaw, J. (2018). *Understanding chatbot-mediated task management.* . Association for Computing Machinery.

Wang, L. (2021). Cass: Towards building a social-support chatbot for online health community. *Proceedings of the ACM on Human-Computer Interaction*, (pp. 1-31). ACM.

Zheng, Q. (2022). *X Research on Conversational Human-AI Interaction: A Literature Review of the ACM Digital Library.* . Association for Computing Machinery.

Chapter 3
The Gendered Nature of Chatbots:
Anthropomorphism and Authenticity

Alice Ashcroft
Lancaster University, UK

Angela Ashcroft
University of Central Lancashire, UK

ABSTRACT

The majority of chatbots are built, by default, as women. In doing so, dangerous stereotypes and behaviors are perpetuated by those responsible for designing the chatbots, and ultimately the users. It is therefore crucial that gender identity and expression are well understood by all those involved in designing the chatbots. This chapter explores this alongside a literature survey regarding feminist methodologies, anthropomorphism, and authenticity to put forward three recommendations. That those responsible for building chatbots should keep up to date with research, look to widen the diversity of their own team, and to integrate ethics in their design processes. Only in doing so will chatbots that are fit for purpose be built.

INTRODUCTION

This chapter outlines a review of existing literature pertaining to gender and anthropomorphism in chatbots. Anthropomorphism is referred to in this work as the attribution of human characteristics to inanimate objects, animals, or others (Duffy, 2003). chatbots, by default, are frequently designed to present as women or female

DOI: 10.4018/978-1-6684-6234-8.ch003

(Fortunati, 2022). On the surface, this may not appear problematic; it could be argued that these decisions are random. But with many of the major voice interfaces being built to present as women, consideration must be given to both the reason for this, and the potential impact this might have. There is an inherent tension between designing chatbots anthropomorphically, as users will always see a chatbot through a gendered lens, and in a current default gender or aim for gender neutrality. This tension will be discussed at length throughout this chapter.

Using feminist theories (De Hertogh et al., 2019) and existing research pertaining to both gendered language and the design of chatbots in a software development process, this chapter will outline many potential areas where gender stereotyping may cause issues when it comes to chatbots, their use and the perpetuation of stereotypes, as well as provide recommendations to reduce the impact this can have. Using the example of marketing, and aligning this with how the brand's personality which fits with the user's self-image, or, self-brand congruence (Grohmann, 2020), this chapter suggests that the gender expression of a designed chatbot should be intentional, not presumed, and could in fact be a tool for brands and those building the chatbots. Three recommendations are derived from this (see the section entitled, 'Recommendations') and should be considered by anyone who is involved in the design and creation of chatbots. Firstly, that chatbot creators should keep up to date with current research. Secondly, that they should work not only on widening the diversity of their own team, but work more closely with stakeholders, for example users and marketing. Thirdly, teams should make ethics a part of their design process.

FEMINIST CHATBOTS

Before the impact of gender regarding chatbots (from the beginning through to their use) can be understood, there must first be an acknowledgement of the feminist methodologies and theories which already exist. In doing so, chatbot designers and creators can make full use of existing understandings that allow for equality. Furthermore, there should be an acknowledgement of Intersectionality, not as simply the overlapping of characteristics, but as a product of Black feminist theory (De Hertogh et al., 2019).

Feminist methodologies, generally, but also when applied to HCI, are built and operate on the understanding that gender will have an impact on anything built or researched previously, due to being built as part of a patriarchal society and will have an impact on anything being built going forwards (Ashcroft, 2022a; Sprague, 2016). With chatbots increasing in popularity (Seaborn et al., 2022), it should be considered where the responsibility lies to ensure that they are built for purpose, and therefore are able to be used by as much of the population as possible, without detrimentally affecting those who have designed and built them, and supporting those who use them, without perpetuating any dangerous stereotypes. With any innovation, or adaptation of technology, all potential implications should be considered, and chatbots are no exception to this. If anything, they carry particular relevance when it comes to these issues within HCI, as it is no longer simply regarding the interaction between human and computer, but a human and a computer mimicking a human. When HCI research is being carried out, even when gender is not the focus of the research, it is important to consider feminist methodologies (Ashcroft 2022b; Morris, 2007; Schlesinger 2017). The existing literature regarding feminist methodologies and HCI (Bardzell & Bardzell, 2011) rarely seems to focus on the impact of gender when gender is not the focused area of research, which in the case of this book is chatbots. This will have particular prevalence when developing any system but particularly when designing chatbots, as feminist methodologies refer to the theory of knowledge and understanding, and in this instance, it is not only the subjects of research that will 'have gender' (for example, participants or users) but it could be argued and has been shown in existing chatbots, that they too are often designed around 'having gender' (for example, Amazon's Alexa or Apple's Siri (Costa & Ribas, 2019) and proven by Feine et al. (2019)).

In the creation of chatbots, one of the main targets is seemingly that of 'appearing human' (Go and Sundar, 2019), with the justification that if users anthropomorphise the chatbot, this encourages users to engage with them (Blut et al., 2021) and the implications for this will be discussed through a feminist lens later in this chapter. However, what should also be considered are the gendered issues that may then be extrapolated from society and then placed onto the chatbots being created. If the aim is to appear human and represent society through anthropomorphism, then it could be argued that the chatbots being created should represent society's views on gender. These authors believe that this should not be the aim when it comes to issues of gender, race or any characteristics which are currently used against people in society. Surely, the aim of creating technology is to ensure it is inclusive, and meets the needs of all who use it, without the perpetuation of dangerous stereotypes.

The feminist methodologies, which underpin the data collection used to support Feminist Epistemology, acknowledge gender and intersectionality (Fuller, 2020). When it comes to chatbots, however, this needs to be explored in further detail. This chapter begins to make some assertions from existing literature and an understanding of the development of chatbots, but what remains to be seen is the observation and practical research regarding the impact of gender on the creation of chatbots in practice.

Only by understanding the world in which chatbots have been and are being created, can they be built to be fit for purpose and without detriment to the team building them; users are so often the focus of any research, it is important to consider the impact of gender on those building the chatbots too. Feminism and feminist methodologies should be considered in each stage of the chatbots lifecycle, as this is merely an example of a software development lifecycle (Ashcroft, 2022b), and the implications for gender on this are potentially vast. In short; how can feminism be considered to help ensure that chatbots are fit for purpose without the perpetuation of any gendered stereotypes?

CHATBOTS EVERYWHERE

To fully understand the impact of gender and chatbots, there needs to be a more universal understanding of *why* chatbots are being built, as the purpose of any software should be implicit in its design (Sommerville, 2016). This is equally as important as the *how* chatbots are built, as the purpose itself should also be feminist, as this will impact how they are designed and built. This Section delves further into the 'why' and poses potential areas of research regarding anthropomorphism with regards to gender, and how this itself ties into industry relevance and authenticity. Only by combining the understanding of these areas, can the pervasiveness of chatbots, and the implications of this, be fully understood and harnessed to be used as a tool in the process of building them.

Why are chatbots Being Built?

Despite initial difficulties with understanding and user reluctance (Coniam, 2014), chatbots have become widely used by organisations across digital spaces such as websites and social media platforms (Borau et al., 2021). They are used in a variety of fields such as education, business, healthcare and e-commerce and are used for a wide range of purposes such as information retrieval or amusement (Shawar & Atwell, 2007). The main rationale and justification for their prevalence is to make the lives of customers easier and more efficient (Brandtzaeg & Følstad, 2017). chatbot creators have established a concept of best practice in encouraging users to anthropomorphise the chatbots by using social cues such as names and pictures that are supposed to represent the 'person' the user is chatting with (Feine et al., 2020). While early research encouraged the view that representing a chatbot with a woman's name and avatar would encourage use, this has since been shown to be severely problematic in terms of stereotyping and perceived effectiveness. This has brought about concerns about dishonest anthropomorphism and the perpetuation of gender stereotypes that bring harm to sections of society (UNESCO, 2019). The four most popular voice assistants, Apple's Siri, Google Assistant, Microsoft's Cortana and Amazon's Alexa, all have feminized personas and women's voices by default and apart from Google, have feminine names (Andrienko, 2020). Despite denying they hold a gender, they have been described as problematic in terms of perpetuating the idea of women as submissive assistants (UNESCO, 2019). The harm that stereotypes bring is a long-established field of research (Appel & Weber, 2021). Examples of this include media that portrays women as less able at maths, causing women to achieve less well at maths (Davies et al., 2002), affecting their life choices. To give another example, when home computers became more affordable, many more were bought by fathers for young boys than girls, also impacting on career choices (UNESCO, 2019). Gender inequality is linked to a country's economic growth (Todaro & Smith, 2009). With such far-reaching effects, any potential gender stereotyping in chatbots is especially worrying with the size of the chatbot market forecasted to rise to 1.25 US Dollars by 2025 (Thormundsson, 2022). Best practice in terms of chatbot representation should be informed by up-to-date research and evolve before any more harm is done (Garousi et al., 2016).

The rising use of social media has driven users to see chatbots on such platforms as a convenient way to contact organisations (Xu et al., 2017). Twitter users send companies millions of requests in the US alone (Xu et al., 2017). In 2013, 53% of users expected a response within an hour (Lee, 2013). However, with the average response taking six and half hours, platforms began to allow organisations to use chatbots for customer service queries. In the twelve months from their launch in spring 2016, 30,000 chatbots were launched on Facebook Messenger (Brandtzaeg & Følstad, 2017). Although early bots often proved to be disappointing to the user, chatbots' conversation skills have improved (Brandtzaeg & Følstad, 2017). The convenience of mobile messaging apps, such as WhatsApp and Facebook Messenger are seen as the perfect platform for chatbots (Kühnel et al., 2020) and the instant interaction a chatbot provides between brand and customer, reduces barriers and the need for brand awareness, which in turn influences customers' purchase intention (Lo Presti et al., 2021).

Advancements in technology have also led to chatbots becoming more popular on websites (Hari et al., 2021). These chatbots can be updated automatically and regularly, and are a simple way for users to initiate a conversation with the organisation. They are generally placed on homepages or on any page where a user might want to engage and are especially useful for helping a visitor to navigate a website (Ehrenpreis & DeLooper, 2022). A main advantage is that they can fulfil different roles according to the website. For example, a university webpage chatbot may be able to help with administrative tasks, giving academic staff more time (Cunningham-Nelson, 2019), in healthcare, scheduling appointments or locating the clinic (Palanica et al., 2019) or in a library, help with finding resources or opening hours (Ehrenpreis & DeLooper, 2022).

From this, it is easy to see how and why organisations see chatbots on websites and social media as an extremely useful customer relationship tool, for example, at different stages of a buyer journey (Murtarelli, 2021). They are available 24 hours a day, respond instantly, answer simple queries, and help businesses be more effective (Balakrishnan & Dwivedi, 2021). By 2020, 80% of marketing leaders included chatbots as part of their strategy for customer experience and chatbots responded to 85% of customer service interactions (Todorov, 2021). In the prepurchase and purchase stage, chatbots can provide information and recommendations (Roggeveen & Sethuraman, 2020). In the post purchase stage chatbots can give a personalised service to follow up tasks (Pawlik, 2022). It is clear from this that an appropriate chatbot saves organisations money and should give the customer a better customer service. The use of chatbots is expected to grow over coming years (Balakrishnan & Dwivedi, 2021).

Why Anthropomorphise and How Does This Tie into Gender?

While chatbots were a recent development it was perhaps understandable why designers encouraged users to imagine that chatbots had human qualities to encourage acceptance (Borau et al., 2021), although some have suggested an influence of female automaton in science fiction (Adams, 2019). Giving a chatbot a face, users will see the bot as more approachable and put more trust in the new technology (Leong & Selinger, 2019). A face will trigger the instinctive human trait of anthropomorphising the bot and so users see the bot as more approachable and feel more trust towards it (Leong & Selinger 2021). This trust can cause users to reveal personal information about themselves, which can be stored and aggregated for later use (Murtarelli et al., 2021), which could in itself be morally questionable. Creators can also use identity cues such as a name or conversational human language (Go & Sundar, 2019). Over recent years the seemingly natural conversation of modern chatbots can be so realistic that it can lead the user to question whether they are talking to a human or a piece of software (Murtarelli et al., 2021). Whilst chatbots can enhance customer service, they have no empathy or discretion; they make decisions based on algorithms not judgement (Murtarelli et al., 2021). They may have intelligence, but not compassion (Borau et al., 2021). If the chatbot is given such cues that the user believes themselves to be conversing with a human, there could be privacy issues surrounding information gathering. The debate about ethics and the collection of data by encouraging anthropomorphism is beyond the scope of this work, but for more information see Murtarelli et al. (2021). The social cues that creators embed in chatbots not only suggest the chatbot to be human, but it has been taken as best practice for chatbot creators to encourage anthropomorphism (Go & Sundar, 2019) and especially gender, by giving chatbots a female appearance and name (Feine et al., 2020).

On many corporate websites, the chatbot is also often represented by a young, attractive woman (De Angeli & Brahnam, 2006). There has been research to suggest that users who view a chatbot as a woman, expect the chatbot to hold stereotypical female attributes such as warmth and empathy and therefore the chatbot might be seen as holding the two aspects of humanity, traditionally most prized, intelligence and warmth; the intelligence of technology and the warmth of a stereotypical woman (Borau et al., 2021). Encouraging anthropomorphism and the expression of gender identity as a woman, then, may seem to work in the favour of the organisation initially, raising the user's intent to use the chatbot and expected performance of the chatbot (Pawlik, 2022). Humans are, however, likely to categorise and stereotype individuals or objects according to their labels (Ashforth & Humphrey, 1997). The same stereotyping, therefore, that leads to acceptance of the chatbot continues to be a lens through which users judge the chatbot during and after use (Stroessner & Benitez, 2018). Feine et al. (2020) also explore the substantial research that suggests that the social cues of chatbots such as avatars or names lead humans to apply gender stereotypes. This is especially unhelpful if the chatbot proves to be less than satisfactory and could continue to perpetuate harmful stereotypes.

Industry Relevance

A further difficulty lies with chatbots used by different industries and whether they are linked stereotypically to a male or female gender. McDonnell and Baxter (2019) stated that chatbots were found to be more satisfactory when the portrayed gender of the chatbot was in line with the stereotype of the subject area, for example, women and everyday childcare (McDonnell & Baxter, 2019). McDonnell and Baxter (2019) also state that a chatbot with no gender assigned to it received higher satisfaction ratings in all subject areas. This brings into question the desirability of assigning a gender to a chatbot to encourage use at all when chatbots are so prevalent throughout the digital space. With virtual assistants such as Alexa and Google Assistant in our homes and Siri or Cortana on our phones (McLean et al., 2021), people are comfortable with using artificial intelligent agents in their everyday lives (Guzman, 2019). Not only is the practice of pretending chatbots are human needless, but actually damaging to the perceived usefulness of the chatbot (McDonnell & Baxter, 2019).

The prevalence of chatbots created by AI teams mostly made up of men (World Economic Forum, 2018), being portrayed as women, answering simple questions confirms the stereotype of women's role as an assistant who is available on demand (UNESCO, 2019). UNESCO also states that once such decisions are set by development teams early in the development of AI, and established as best practice, they are difficult to counteract. Furthermore, the developments that have been made in the offline environment in gender equality are at risk of being undermined by the digital space (UNESCO, 2019). With chatbots portrayed as female receiving significantly more sexual conversation by the user than male or non-gendered chatbots (De Angeli & Brahman, 2006) it may be suggested that what has developed as best practice should be adapted according to new research and knowledge from other, related fields.

The position of chatbots now being firmly placed in the area of customer relationship management (Todorov, 2021), how they represent a brand or organisations should be considered from a marketing perspective. The stereotyping of women in marketing media has a long history of study (O'Driscoll, 2019). Dealing with diverse topics such as the objectification of women, gender roles or self-objectification, research has shown how media upholds stereotypes. Stereotypes emphasize differences between groups and minimize variability within a group (Bordalo et al., 2016). If stereotypes are already established in society, humans will look only for information that confirms their beliefs, or, confirmation bias. To change or replace a stereotype, however untrue it may be, can take substantial evidence (Bordalo et al., 2016). If chatbot creators have exploited established stereotypes to encourage usage, they are surely responsible for confirming those stereotypes by example (Sherman, 1996). The consistent example of a female, on-demand assistant, who performs below an expectation created by anthropomorphism of the chatbot will confirm the stereotypes that society has made some strides to dispel (Neale et al., 2016). The harm of using stereotypes in advertising is well understood (Ross et al., 2011, p. 2) and those who create any type of representative media, including chatbots, should understand that responsibility.

How chatbots represent an organisation is linked to another established area of research in marketing, that of branding. Organisations take a great deal of care to manage how their brand image is perceived (Essamri et al., 2019). Brands are described in advertising as having attributes such as friendliness or youthfulness and also gender; these are different to benefits such as price or performance (Sirgy et al., 1997). Brand identity is a concept that has been long discussed in marketing (Plummer, 1984) and it can have a dramatic impact on how a brand is perceived. Attention, sales and loyalty are all impacted by the fit between the consumer's self-concept and the brand's image, known as self-brand congruence (Wijnands & Gill, 2020). An individual's self-concept consists of who the individual feels they are and their ideal self, their aspirations and goals (Japutra et al., 2019). By triggering a consumer's need for self-consistency and self-esteem, a consumer feels a high self-brand congruity when they perceive the product to match their self-image (Sirgy et al., 1997). As gender identity is an important part of an individual's self-concept, the gender identity of a brand is an important factor in self-brand congruence (Neale et al., 2016).

There may be some arguments, therefore, for a chatbot to be represented in a way that fits with this self-brand congruence. It has been shown that chatbots are used differently by different people. Merritt (2018) reports that women use chatbots more than men and use them for different purposes. This picture only, however, shows a binary picture, which does not represent the population, where 6.9% of the UK population identifies *"as having a gender that was neither exclusively that of a man nor a woman"* (Government Equalities Office, 2019). Advertising has tried to move towards using masculine and feminine traits in branding; however, this still brings difficulties. Neale et al. (2016) found that consumers with a masculine or androgynous gender had a strong positive reaction to brand personality that reflected their own. Consumers with a gender expressed as feminine were more accepting of a brand personality that differed to their own (Neale et al., 2016). With gender, as opposed to sex, being more important (Neale et al., 2016), there is clearly more research needed in this area. There is also research that suggests users prefer certain personality traits for different chatbot tasks (Lee et al., 2018). This may be one way for a chatbot to more clearly represent a brand and align with a user's self-concept.

One example of a chatbot that is represented in an honest way is Woebot (Woebot Health, 2022). Woebot helps the user with cognitive behavioural therapy and although it uses anthropomorphic language, it never deceives the user about its non-human nature (Leong & Selinger, 2021). Woebot's witty examples and pretence at reminiscing could be seen as experiencing the personality of the chatbot through actions as opposed to its description, described by Ryan Calo as visceral notice (2012). Woebot makes clear its nature by how it behaves and what it says, for example, when introducing itself to users, Woebot states that while it may seem human, it is not capable of understanding the needs of the user (Fitzpatrick et al., 2017). Winning several awards, Woebot is considered to be one of the most successful chatbots (Kent, 2021). Furthermore, research shows that it is the open and authentic chatbot nature of Woebot that encourages users to develop a therapeutic bond (Darcy et al., 2021). Whilst Woebot does not give cues such as avatars or a name to encourage anthropomorphism or gender, it does, for example, express sympathy for loneliness (Fitzpatrick et al., 2017). This visceral notice then might encourage anthropomorphism, even with the inclusion of the openness perceived by users. This clearly demonstrates the concept of computers as social actors outlined by Nass et al. (1994), that in chatbots a social response is not a result of a conscious belief that the system is human, or human-like. A user may simultaneously anthropomorphise a chatbot and believe it to be authentic while knowing it is a computer programme.

Authenticity

The authenticity with which brands represent themselves is becoming more of a key concept in brand management (Uggla, 2020). Affecting aspects such as customer preference, loyalty, and repurchase, how a brand is perceived is crucial to the customers' decision-making. Furthermore, authenticity is seen as more important in purchasing decisions than quality (Morhart et al., 2015). This would suggest that if a brand seeks to represent itself by using technology, this should be no less authentic. Several authors confirm that perceived authenticity is extremely important to acceptability in terms of chatbots (Neururer et al., 2018; Kuhail et al., 2022). Whilst this work is in agreement that social skills, learning and use of natural language all add to the user experience, it argues that authenticity in terms of honesty about who a customer is talking to might also add to user experience. The example of Woebot shows that honesty about the nature of who a user is talking to need not be a barrier to intended use. Users enjoy the personality, the humour and skills of Woebot, although they are aware that they are conversing with a chatbot and are clearly willing to accept the chatbot in conversation (Fitzpatrick et al., 2017). This work suggests that it is not always necessary to disguise the technological nature of a chatbot and that a more authentic portrayal or description can in fact be a benefit to user experience. This is the definition of authenticity that this chapter refers to.

Pawlik's research, (2022), found that for chatbots with no gender assigned, the expectation for performance was lower. This, however, should not be dismissed as a negative and fits with the work of Leong and Selinger (2021) who found that dishonest anthropomorphism can cause users to exaggerate their perspective of what a chatbot can do. Go and Sundar (2019) also found that improved service can compensate for a chatbot without anthropomorphic visual cues. This would certainly suggest that allowing users to recognise a chatbot as just that, would give them a more realistic expectation and therefore be less disappointed with the chatbot's performance.

How Does This Affect Building for Purpose and Gender?

It can be seen from this exploration, that the need to encourage anthropomorphism is not only unnecessary to encourage users to communicate with chatbots but can cause users to be disappointed, by an overestimation of the chatbot's capabilities (Crolic et al., 2022). Furthermore, the perceived best practice of portraying chatbots as women in an assistive capacity, on-demand, who may also disappoint users, perpetuates gender stereotypes of women as assistive and low-agency (UNESCO, 2019). By exemplifying a stereotype of women in this way it perpetuates an association of these traits with women in the users' minds (Sherman, 1996). If organisations want their representation to be perceived as authentic, they would be better served by showing a non-gendered avatar more appropriate to a chatbot. This would reduce the encouragement of stereotyping and allow the brand to be revealed in a visceral, or active way through its conversation, personality and effectiveness. With the use of chatbots expected to grow substantially in the coming years (Balakrishnan & Dwivedi, 2021), the damage done by what has been thought of as best practice needs to be stemmed and new examples of best practice sought. This will contribute to building authenticity and personality more in congruence with the user, enable users to be served more satisfactorily and begin to curb the stereotyping of women by artificial intelligence.

This area affords a great deal of scope for future research as the development of chatbots becomes more established, and they become more able to give the user a satisfactory experience. If, as the above research suggests, chatbots can be more useful to consumers and brands, and not be detrimental in perpetuating stereotypes, more research will build new concepts of best practices that benefits all parties involved. As indicated by the UNESCO (2019) report, however, there are several issues that have contributed to the problem of gendered anthropomorphism in chatbots, including, a low level of diversity in artificial intelligence teams and the use of systems such as data sets that contain gender bias to create chatbots. How the team that creates the chatbot construct the language it uses and how it interacts with the user is central to a chatbot's effectiveness and so it is important to explore how this and gender interrelate.

LANGUAGE AND INTERACTION

chatbots converse with users in natural language and so it is essential to explore what impact the design and language will have on the conversation, as well as how they are built. As discussed above, anthropomorphism has been encouraged to motivate users to use chatbots and gendering with social cues has become considered best practice. This, however, brings many difficulties as outlined above. 'More on Anthropomorphism' will explore whether portraying a chatbot as gendered is the only way to encourage a user to feel they are being listened to and what other strategies might be used. Using theories from linguistics and gendered language (see the Section entitled 'Gendered Language') provides a deeper exploration of how language stereotypes can impact interaction. This leads to an examination of how the gender bias of the chatbot users and creators can lead to abusive interactions and possible harm to society.

More on Anthropomorphism

Humans have the ability, from an early age, to pretend that inanimate objects such as bricks and boxes have human qualities, even when the human is fully aware that an object is simply an object (Airenti, 2015). As has been shown above, humans need very little in the way of cues to anthropomorphise a chatbot. Being perceived as a helper is enough for humans to attribute mental attitudes to an object. In the anthropomorphism in human play, though, all the implied qualities are bestowed by the human when interaction begins, and not pretended to by the object. Airenti (2015) suggests that when an object signifies qualities such as empathy, it can be unsettling to the user because humans know that chatbots do not possess emotions or human minds. Whilst limited forms of empathy may be useful in enabling a user to feel more comfortable in using a chatbot, care should be taken that this is when the interaction has been established so it does is does not feel unnatural to the user (Airenti, 2015).

Pelau et al. (2021) also suggest that AI devices can be perceived as a threat if implemented incorrectly; however, carefully suggesting empathetic characteristics can improve interaction quality. Liu-Thompkins et al. (2022) also state that user experience can be impacted through the use of artificial empathy by amplifying positive emotions. Despite gender stereotypes, research in the field of empathy would appear to show that whilst both men and women experience and demonstrate empathy, although it may be directed or exhibited in different ways (Christov-Moore et al., 2014) or affected by self-reporting biases (Baez et al., 2017). Empathy has also been a pillar of marketing, one of the main purposes of chatbots for many years (McBane, 1995); and understanding the customer's position has been recognised to be invaluable in gaining the trust of the customer when providing relevant products or services (Pedersen, 2020). Empathy has been described as a type of 'social glue' (Pedersen, 2020) that increases cooperation and improves relationship quality (Ndubisi & Nataraajan, 2018). It is, therefore, appropriate to suggest that a chatbot might be designed with empathy implied in the language and tone it uses in conversation. There is growing interest in research for empathetic chatbots (Lahoz-Beltra & Lopez, 2021; Wang et al., 2021; Yalcin and DiPaola, 2018; Zhou et al., 2020), but this is not the only way that a chatbot's language and interaction can add to the user's experience without stereotyping. Further research on the users' anthropomorphism of empathetic chatbots, created to be gender neutral, might also provide knowledge on whether the empathy causes the anthropomorphism to be gendered.

In terms of usability, a clear advantage of chatbots is that users can communicate using natural language, whether it be spoken or written. The user cannot, however, see the customer service agent raise their eyebrow, smile in sympathy or looked puzzled. These paralingual expressions, or, everything other than the words in a conversation, need to be conveyed textually in a chatbot (Luangrath, 2017). Textual paralanguage contributes to anthropomorphism as perceiving a chatbot as having a mind. This gives more meaning to having a conversation with it and a stronger feeling of presence, or, being co-located with their partner in conversation (Lee et al., 2020). As text-based media continues to innovate and evolve, it may offer options that might enhance a text-based conversation (Schandorf, 2013). Paralinguistic cues that have developed online include the repetition of letters, for example, *'cooooll'* (Pavalanathan & Eisenstein, 2015) and predefined pictographic characters such as emojis. Emojis include a standard round face showing different emotions with, for example, tears or hearts. These are increasingly popular in social media (Pavalanathan & Eisenstein, 2015) and text-based messaging (Luangrath et al., 2017). With social presence leading to greater trust and purchase intention it is clear that textual paralinguistic cues could be useful (Hayes et al., 2020) when designing chatbots. Whilst the use of emojis on Twitter may increase engagement (McShane et al., 2021) care should be taken for appropriateness in, for example, a customer relations context (Sidi et al, 2021).

Lee et al. (2020) also found a greater sense of both parties being present in the conversation by using more subtle paralinguistic cues such as repeated exclamation marks and question marks, and also, in using encouraging words such as hmm, aha and okay, known as backchanneling. Repeating the user's phrases also encouraged a feeling of social presence (Lee et al., 2020). The use of such paralinguistic cues also needs to be approached with care, though, as Chen et al. (2018) found that although there is a great deal of overlap, emojis were shown to be used slightly differently by gender. For example, women are more likely to use positive and face-related emojis such as a smiling face for happiness and men are more likely to use heart emojis (Chen et al., 2018). If an organisation seeks to suggest a gender for their chatbot for reasons of brand congruence, or remain gender neutral, this should be a consideration. Other language features that might be relevant to providing a positive experience without gender, include the chatbot using I to describe itself (Nass et al., 1994) and ensuring the chatbot adheres to appropriate polite language (Looi & See, 2012). Just as with using avatars, however, these features should not be adhered to as best practice, but could be starters for exploration of the best natural language to enhance brand-self congruence in a chatbot that represents an organisation. chatbots are used by people of different genders, with reports of women using chatbots more than men and with different gender identities using them for different purposes (Merritt, 2018). Each user and use case will be different and organisations should be wary of using a chatbot without exploring the needs and personas of those who might come into contact with it.

The research and reporting of who encounters chatbots and how they interact with them should have an impact on the design, development, testing and implementation of future chatbots. As Aylett et al. (2019) stated about voice assistants, however, mimicry of humanity alone cannot produce the creative artistry required for conversation and that mimicry is based on a perception of humanness. If the perception of a chatbot's conversation is based on a stereotype of humanity, there is still more research to be carried out and listened to. If a development team generally made up of white men (Sey and Hafkin, 2019) creates their chatbot persona from a biased perception of women, it is not surprising that the interaction has difficulties because of the design of interactions or the language it uses (UNESCO, 2019). Gendered language itself is a well-researched area, and as research regarding chatbots emerges, it would be reminiscent not to consider the potential implications of these areas of research overlapping.

Gendered Language

Gendered language is a well-established field of linguistics (Eckert & McConnell-Ginet, 2003; Stokoe & Weatheral, 2002). As discussed in the Section entitled chatbots Everywhere, designers often use social cues to suggest a chatbot has a gender and the language a chatbot uses can be one of these cues (Go & Sundar, 2019). As chatbot creators seek to suggest a gender for the chatbot, it is important that they do not use stereotypically 'feminine language'. Lakoff (1975) asserted that women's speech is trivial, powerless and without a strong feeling of expression, typified by words such as charming and lovely (Quina et al., 1987). Since the work of Lakoff (1975) there has been a great deal of research overlapping such subjects as linguistics, psychology, discourse and gender studies that now shows that how language is used is much more complex. There is little evidence that language is used differently by women and men, but language is performed differently by different people in different situations (Weatherall, 2016).

Discourse research explores, for example, different versions of masculinity, not all of which identify with the stereotypes of strength, aggression or non-emotionality (Weatherall, 2016). This research expands into the postfeminist feminine identity which includes a sexist element of highly sexualised self-identity (Weatherall, 2016). As with using avatars or names, the choice of language for a chatbot should not be taken lightly. Using stereotypically feminine language can bring difficulties when creators try to give users confidence in their chatbot by suggesting agency, or competence. Moradbakhti et al. (2022) found an artificially intelligent assistant that did not conform to stereotypes, for instance, a high-agency female assistant, gave less satisfaction to men than a low-agency female. This is not to suggest that designers should perpetuate users' bias by creating chatbots that conform to a low-agency female stereotype, as discussed, but confidence in a chatbot's abilities leads to intent to use the chatbot (Borau et al., 2021). This may be further evidence that chatbot designers should research their users from a marketing or customer service perspective before designing any persona or choice of language. The impact of gender identity on consumer variables has been researched for nearly four decades (Palan, 2001). Any bias on the part of the user should be taken into consideration not only so biases are not perpetuated but so the chatbot is more effective.

User bias is shown in the language individuals adopt when using artificially intelligent agents (Fossa & Sucameli, 2022). In their research on interactions with different styles of chatbots, Brahnam and De Angeli (2012) found that the chatbot presenting as a woman was subjected to more sexually explicit content than chatbots presenting as men. This talk revolved around sexual stereotypes involving prostitution, sexual insults and violence. Brahnam and De Angeli (2012) report that 11% of interactions mention hard-core sex. Some researchers liken the discussion around this topic to being similar to that of computer games, with the concern that if people are violent towards women in computer games, or verbally violent towards a chatbot presenting as a woman, they may be more likely to carry out such behaviour in real life (Whitby, 2008). This is based on the parallel of abusing a virtual simulation of a human. Whilst Whitby (2008) argues that the trend in evidence would suggest that regular involvement in virtual violence does desensitize users to violence in real life, others suggest the picture is more complex (Ferguson et al., 2022; Hilgard et al., 2019). In terms of sexist, violent games Gabbiadini et al. (2016) found that a lack of empathy for women victims of violence was affected by the user's identification with the violent male game character. This comparison is not altogether satisfactory as the violent and sexist nature of some games is inherent in their design (Gabbiadini, et al., 2016).

Considering this, media attention in recent years regarding digital assistants that '*peddle stereotypes of female subservience*' with concerns that the assistant's responses help '*entrench sexist tropes through their passivity*' (Fessler, 2017) may not be unfounded. Curry and Reiser (2018) used real-life examples of abuse chatbots had received to test the responses of popular, existing chatbots. chatbot responses included collaborating with the user, but as user requests became more offensive, chatbots refused to engage. Other chatbot responses were ungrammatical and incoherent but also flirtatious. Curry and Rieser (2018) also estimate that approximately 4% of conversations with chatbots are sexually charged but that current systems are only evaluated using customer satisfaction ratings, and so are ineffective. Evaluation and hate speech detection will be explored further in the development section, but the question of moral obligation is not defined at present. There are issues of bias that need to be considered carefully; bias on the part of the user, and whether this should be used to advantage or encouraged, and bias on the part of the chatbot's design and behaviour.

Lee et al. (2019) outline three ways in which gender bias already impacts chatbots, and perhaps the most relevant measure they use in their study is that of a "comparison with human baseline". What should be considered here is whether or not this is an appropriate measure or something that could cause more issues than it raises. If society is, intrinsically, patriarchal, then the comparative "human baseline" will also contain bias, and thus a chatbot is being measured for gender bias against a system which itself contains gender bias. This has been proven by Borau et al. (2021), in their discovery of "female" coded chatbots being perceived as "more human". As stated above, gender differences in language are already a well-researched area within the field of Linguistics, with much attention being given to ideas of taking up space (Talbot, 2019) and how language is used (Weatherall, 2016). This, in combination with how conversations are designed with chatbots, leaves room for gender to have a significant impact on not only what is 'said' by the chatbot, but how this is perceived. Therefore, what should be considered by all those involved in the creation of chatbots, is the impact that their patriarchal bias and the gendered nature of language can have in both the process of creating the chatbot and the conversations which are designed.

Furthermore, the impact that gendered language can have on the software development itself, with interactions affecting decisions that are made in each stage of the development process, cannot be understated (Ashcroft, 2022b), and it could be argued that chatbots are no exception to this. Aligning with the recommendation given by Feine et al. (2019), the gender diversity of the team creating the chatbot will of course have an impact on this, and should be addressed. It could be argued that the team should not need to be diverse to create a product that is fit for its purpose, although this would be better for many other reasons. But what should be considered is what self-reflective practices and learnings team members should be carrying out to uncover any unconscious biases they hold and the impact that they can have on the chatbots that are being created.

Personalisation

With the widespread use of chatbots across many different industries (Skjuve et al., 2019), encouraging use must be done ethically, so that the chatbot provides a quality experience for the user and causes no harm to society. More recently there has been some research into combining personalisation algorithms with chatbots to give a more personal service to the user (Kim et al., 2021; Sardella et at., 2019). A chatbot that greets the user by name and gives personal recommendations based on previous purchases is likely to become more commonplace and of more use to the consumer (Richardson, 2022). This would be of great benefit in terms of chatbot-user congruence. If this prediction is true, then describing usage statistics in binary terms of "male" or "female" will be poor segmentation as organisations move towards first-party data (Richardson, 2022) and further perpetuates the outdated view of gender as a binary. Humans are more complex than simple 'male' or 'female' as a UK government report stated that 6.9% of the population identify "as having a gender that was neither exclusively that of a man nor a woman" (Government Equalities Office, 2019).

Therefore, the interaction between a user and chatbot can not only be influenced by the creator of the chatbot but also by the beliefs and attitudes of the user. More research is needed into whether portraying a chatbot as a woman does suggest warmth and compassion, or whether research is missing any unconscious bias of participants as women being seen as weaker and more amenable. Whilst encouraging an impression of empathy might be useful in some use cases, it is not essential to suggest gender or to use stereotypically feminine language to suggest warmth or empathy. Techniques such as textual paralinguistics can suggest a sense of presence in the conversation and research is ongoing to create a more realistic impression of empathy. Presenting a chatbot explicitly or implicitly as a woman can lead to more incidents of harsh verbal abuse and hard-core sexual suggestion (De Angeli & Brahnam et al., 2006) which would suggest that organisations designing their chatbot need to know their users well. UNESCO (2019) state that chatbots are too tolerant of sexual abuse and respond provocatively, whereas they should at least respond with a flat discouragement. This is supported by Young (2017) who states that during the design phase, chatbot creators should consider the language the chatbot should use and how it might deal with any abusive incidents. Winkle et al. (2021) state that an aggressive response may be considered inappropriate for a chatbot portrayed as a woman as it may not be considered a fit with the traditional concept of women's politeness. This is in itself seemingly problematic, in that gender constraints still bind chatbots that do not truly have gender. While Winkle et al. (2021) found that reasoned arguments did counter user bias, more research is needed in this area to a broader range of situations before ideas of best practice can be formed. It would be of more benefit to negate the need for these as much as possible in design before the need arises and so chatbot creators need to understand their users and any potential bias as much as possible.

Language and Interaction – A Summary

Rather than using gender to encourage anthropomorphism, it may be more effective to encourage the characteristics that users really look for in an assistant, such as empathy (Airenti, 2015). Care should be taken, however, that this is introduced appropriately. Other devices that could encourage a feeling of presence include the use of textual paralinguistics. This is increasingly used to good effect in other areas of marketing and might also encourage user confidence (Chen et al., 2015; Lee et al., 2020). As most Artificial Intelligence teams are made up of white men (Sey & Hafkin, 2019), there is a danger that any bias they hold is reflected in the chatbot. For example, stereotypes of gendered language should be avoided and designers should explore more carefully who their users are, to suggest the most appropriate personality for the chatbot. This is a practice well researched in marketing (Palan et al., 2001). The use of stereotyping chatbots also has an impact on the way users interact with chatbots, with an estimated 4% of conversations with chatbots having an inappropriate sexual nature (Curry & Rieser, 2018). It is also important to point out that this figure is suggested by a baseline that will itself contain gender bias. It has been demonstrated that gender bias affects the development and use of chatbots from the side of the creator, but also the side of the user. As the responsibility falls to those who create the chatbots, the following Section will explore more deeply the impact of gender bias in the design and development of chatbots.

DESIGN, DEVELOPMENT AND DELIVERY

To understand the impact that gender can have on the final product, what must first be considered is design. Therefore, it must be understood how current HCI design paradigms and Feminist Methodologies align with the practice of building chatbots. Considering the feminist methodologies outlined above, all considerations throughout the design, development, and delivery of a chatbot should be considered through a feminist lens. From why the chatbot is being built, all the way through to its release and maintenance, all areas leave themselves open to perpetuating or supporting existing patriarchal bias. Even if all efforts are made to break down gender barriers, and expectations, it could be argued that if these chatbots are being built using technology that was also made in a patriarchal society, then the chatbots will never truly be feminist. Of course, this is an extreme example, and not one that is unique to chatbots in comparison to other software, but one that should be considered, and one that is explored within this Section.

Furthermore, when it comes to the language used and the personas given to chatbots, these currently expose themselves to be particularly affected by gender, given the nature of gendered language. This includes issues such as team diversity, the design process and the team's involvement in testing (Ashcroft, 2021). The personality attributed to a chatbot can be affected by gender in a multitude of ways, including language construction and tone of voice, and this will of course be impacted by the team who is building each component of this. With the software development lifecycle being broken down into five stages (Sommerville, 2016), and each of these stages susceptible to gender bias through language (Ashcroft, 2022b), care must be given to understand the potential impact of this when chatbots are the software in question. The first of these stages, outlined by Ashcroft (2022b), is the need for software – also known as the use case.

The use case for chatbots being built can be many and varied, from human resources (Honnavalli et al., 2022) to customer services (Sheehan et al., 2020). The need for software, in this case chatbots, can be brought forward through a number of methods from project proposals, problems with existing processes, through to an innovation process (Ashcroft, 2022b). When it comes to how chatbots themselves are affected by gendered language in these processes remains to be seen, and requires research to uncover any potential impacts. Similar to other software, if the need for the chatbot to be built is only adhered to when the language used to present it is more 'masculine' then the chatbot itself is already biased. It could also be suggested that the way in which the need for these chatbots is brought forward will vary by industry. It is therefore important to consider that the industry that the chatbot is built for and within may have an impact on the way in which they are built. chatbots can be found for example, on websites, social media applications and in smart speakers. Alongside this, chatbots now perform many different functions, providing challenges for developers (Yao, 2017). chatbots belonging to Beauty companies can recommend tutorial videos and browse gift boxes. Fashion companies' chatbots offer personalized recommendations and insurance companies' chatbots can give quotes and advice (Yao, 2017). Covering a wide range of industries, the most common use for chatbots is customer service (Sheehan et al., 2020). The relationship between the customer and the organisation is at the centre of most modern definitions of customer relationship management and each interaction has a critical role in shaping the customer's perception of the organisation (Shukla & Pattnaik, 2019). Specifically, Youn and Jin (2021) found the user's relationship with a chatbot to have an impact on perceived brand personality. It is clear that if an organisation wants its brand to be perceived in a certain way, therefore, their chatbot should also be aligned with this. One example of where creators have constructed chatbots in line with the organisation is on the websites of academic libraries in the United States of America. While this sector has been slow to embrace chatbots, most of those in use are gender neutral by design (Brown, 2022) with gender neutral names such as Bizzy and Panther. These names and personalities are however, in line with the character of the university they represent and their mascots. With ambiguous or agender avatars, they are designed in a way to avoiding alienating a significant proportion of users with sexist stereotypes whilst being in line with the brand persona of the organisations.

Organisations often construct a brand personality, or a set of characteristics associated with the organisation (Lieven et al., 2014). The personality of the brand and how it reflects the consumer's self-image, or, self-brand congruence is an important consideration (Grohmann, 2009) and research continues to develop

(Lieven et al., 2014). It has also been established that the correspondence between the brand gender and the consumers' identity can have a positive effect on trust, loyalty and recommendations (Lieven et al., 2014). In their study on brand equity, or, the perception of the brand that allows it to position itself, Lieven et al. (2014) found that higher levels of masculinity and femininity were found to have higher equity than undifferentiated brands. Brand androgyny, or, high levels of both masculinity and femininity had a negative impact on brand equity (Lieven et al., 2014). Although stereotyping assistants as women by default is inappropriate (UNESCO, 2019), attempting to design a gender-neutral chatbot might also not be in the best interests of an organisation.

Solis expressed concerns in 2010 that the then new forms of digital media caused organisations to reach and connect with markets in ways that might not adhere to the voice or personality of the brand. This concern might be seen to be reflected in the continued use of portraying chatbots as young women (Feine et al., 2020). The scales and definitions of personality, or identity used for chatbots may be outdated and could be accused of characterizing different genders of certain fundamental characteristics and, gender and sex are often conflated (Hearn & Hein, 2015). As suggested in above, the use of stereotyping women as warm, compliant assistants is outdated, damaging to society and possibly off-brand. Furthermore, the way women are portrayed and treated in media is likely to become more of a concern with 65% of young people in a survey reported by Chahal (2015) believing that how brands depict women is too sexualised. Furthermore, 72% agree that feminism is important. It should be helpful, therefore, to examine why those responsible for marketing are not more involved in the designing of chatbots. If most chatbots are designed and constructed by white, male, computer experts, with any conscious or unconscious bias that they hold, there may be a gap in collaboration.

Kozinets and Gretzel (2020) suggest that difficulties may arise because marketers are themselves consumers of and not creators of artificial intelligence. While digital and technological systems are valuable and useful to marketers, they are often not involved in the design or development of the systems. Furthermore, Kozinets and Gretzel (2020) explain that systems such as chatbots can become a barrier or disconnection between the marketer and the consumer. Marketers often have an understanding and discernment that artificial intelligence might not and any learning a system creates can be lost if it is not transferable or explainable (De Bruyn et al., 2020). Taj and Jhanjhi (2022) discussed the concept of more explainable algorithms, or, explainable artificial intelligence with the aim of more productive human-machine collaboration. As artificial intelligence systems such as chatbots become more commonplace, collaboration will become more important, especially if chatbots are to represent organisations in an appropriate way. As this field develops, research is likely to show whether this collaboration is between humans and machines, or, interdepartmental.

The design itself of the chatbot should fall into the specification and development stages of the Software Development Life-cycle process. As discussed throughout this chapter, there are a number of ways in which gender, and gendered language, should be considered in the design of the chatbot, both in the language "given" to the chatbot through intents and responses, but also in how those involved in the process talk to one another. As discussed, the way in which ideas are presented, sometimes as an opinion when a fact, or as a fact when they are an opinion (Ashcroft, 2022b), has potential to lead to bias in Software Development. Therefore, each stage of the chatbot design process should not only be feminist in its practices and methodologies as they are built, but in the discussion which take place in which decisions are made. For example, in designing chatbots, decisions are made in the interpretation of what is said to the chatbot, in the understanding attributed to the language, and in the response it gives. Gender must be considered in each of these stages, both in how these are designed and built. For example, how is gender expressed in the conversation? If self-brand congruence is truly a technique that should be deployed when designing chatbots, then perhaps gender is not something to be avoided but a tool to further assist the user; but the potential impact of this should be understood and designed for. One potential solution for this may be a combination of feminist methodologies (De Hertogh et al., 2019) and User Centred Design (UCD) (Monk, 2000).

Many technology teams are aware of the need to centre the design of their product around the user (LeRouge et al., 2016). When designing a chatbot, all the responsibility for the interaction is based on understanding the natural language of the user and the ability to respond in an appropriate way. While developments in natural language processing have been substantial in recent years (Wang et al., 2019), not only does the language understood need to be domain specific, but the chatbot needs to understand users from a variety of backgrounds. For example, in 2020-21, 605,130 international students studied in the United Kingdom; a significant implication for a chatbot in higher education. Elsner (2017) recorded 33% of respondents in a survey report that chatbots give incorrect answers and 29% do not understand them. Issues of gender bias in natural language processing are well reported (Honnavalli et al., 2022). In systems that associate gender with certain professions or traits associated with seniority, for example, the impact on a human resources chatbot is clear (Honnavalli et al., 2022). It could be argued that in the design of the chatbot, the solution to gendered issues is simple; design a gender neutral chatbot. Efforts have even been made to design a simulated voice that itself is gender neutral (Brahnam & De Angeli, 2012). Whether or not a chatbot can ever really be gender neutral, as gender is so embedded in the current state of 'being', should also be considered. For example, if a gender neutral chatbot was ever truly built, would the gendered lens of the user cause them to see the chatbot as gendered anyway? Furthermore, as discussed above, if the aim of most chatbots is to represent the user (Wijnands & Gill, 2020), then this would surely include gender, as this is a major contributing factor when it comes to identity (Faye, 2021). Following this, what should be understood with further research, is how the gender identity of the team building the chatbot, may impact on its design and development. That is not to say that only men can design chatbots for men, or women can only design chatbots for women, an argument that Dourish (2006) makes clear more generally, but that the potential impact should be understood by all those involved in the development process. With gendered language affecting how software design teams function (Ashcroft, 2022b), through to differences in coding between men and women (May et al., 2019), there are many ways in which software development can be affected by gender before chatbots are even considered.

Furthermore, there is still a great deal of difficulty in terms of gender in the text that is used to train the machine learning models that many chatbot platforms are built upon (Ferrer et al., 2020). It could be suggested, and will be discussed in this chapter, how development teams potentially open up the floor to even more stereotyping based on gender, due to the gendered language that is likely to be used during their development, and how linguistic techniques are leveraged to turn intents into actions and how these are presented back to the user. This analysis of gendered language and Natural Language Processing (NLP) Models within the context of chatbots, is vital to consider. Examples of this failing when it comes to gender and other underrepresented characteristics in other areas of technology are varied (Virginia, 2012). Training data carries a risk of perpetuating stereotypes present in society, for example, identifying phrases that refer to the same identity, known as coreference resolution, may link pronouns to occupations dominated by the gender of the pronoun (Rudinger et al., 2018; Zhao et al., 2018;). Whilst some developers blame copyright law and the access they have to suitable material (Leentz, 2021), there is research to try to remove or at least mitigate these problems (Bolukbasi et al., 2016). In 2016 Microsoft released a chatbot with the name Tay on Twitter. Designed to imitate a millennial girl from the United States of America, Microsoft removed Tay's account within 24 hours (Bridge et al., 2021). The chatbot's account had tweeted over 93,000 racist and sexist statements and there is a great deal of controversy about whether the chatbot copied what was said to it by an asserted attack or simply reflected the society it was in (Zemcik, 2020). Whilst such online learning methods can help a chatbot's conversational abilities improve, it clearly leaves opportunities for corruption (Chai et al., 2020). Whilst there has been research in the area of hate speech detection (Ravi and Ravi, 2015; Zhang et al., 2018), there is clearly more to be done. Although Tay is an extreme example, chatbots are likely to discriminate against women unless deliberate actions are taken (Sey & Hafkin, 2019). It is important, therefore, that those involved in creating chatbots learn from up-to-date research and take deliberate steps to minimise possibilities of harm.

Considering all of the above, the main consideration regarding gender and chatbots at the moment is seemingly the persona given to chatbots, and how they 'have gender'. As discussed above, particular attention needs to be given to the anthropomorphic nature of chatbots, and how this pertains to industry relevance and their perceived authenticity. These topics should be explored by individual organisations with stakeholders and how they relate to their situation and explored by further research. Only by doing so, can the impact of this field of study, be measured.

SOLUTIONS AND RECOMMENDATIONS

The previous sections of this chapter have explored several areas of difficulty that face chatbot creators at the present time and each has highlighted areas that need further research. This section outlines recommendations based around three areas and the reasons why these are important. chatbot creators should keep up to date with current research. They should work not only on widening the diversity of their own team, but work more closely with stakeholders, for example, users and marketing. Creation teams should also make ethics a part of their design and evaluation process.

Keeping Up-to-Date

With the development of chatbot technology developing at great speed over recent years (Borau et al., 2021) and computing experts being left to develop their own ideas of best practice, it is unsurprising that what is considered best practice will need to develop as new research emerges (Fossa & Sucameli, 2022). The prevalence of chatbots in our digital society now negates the need for chatbot creators to try to entice users to use the new technology. With Siri and Alexa in homes and phones, and the number of messages organisations on social media receive, it is clear that users are comfortable with the technology. They view it as a quick and easy way to reach an organisation and hopefully get a swift response (Balakrishnan & Dwivedi, 2021). The exploration in this chapter, however, demonstrates that designing chatbots with social cues to encourage users to anthropomorphise the chatbot can be self-defeating. Users will naturally anthropomorphise a chatbot by the nature of it wanting to help and communicating in natural language. This chapter also demonstrates that the use of cues such as women's names and pictures of young attractive women (De Angeli & Brahman, 2006) as avatars perpetuates the stereotype that women are subservient, always waiting to help and quite often incompetent if the chatbot fails to perform

(Crolic et al, 2022; UNESCO, 2019). Designers do not need to sacrifice ethics for user intent, a chatbot can demonstrate social presence by replying promptly, understanding the user's language and using appropriate textual paralinguistic devices (Lee et al., 2020). The chatbot can demonstrate agency and warmth by being able to help the user with their requests, having domain knowledge and being polite (Looii & See, 2012). Whether the chatbot is given gendered cues should be considered carefully with stakeholders, with a full understanding of an organisation's brand personality. Rather than following the tide of gender stereotyping with chatbots, creators now have an opportunity and responsibility to follow the research that shows that chatbots can be effective and welcomed without always being portrayed as women.

Using the Knowledge of Others

When chatbot designers develop a personality for their chatbot, they may better serve their organisation by taking advantage of work that others may have done in developing a brand personality (Udas, 2020). Many digital development teams are comfortable with concepts such as user-centred design and participatory design (Spinuzzi, 2005) and these are particularly suited to designing and developing a chatbot. While many development teams are still struggling to become more diverse (Fey & Hafkin, 2019), they can endeavour to understand the chatbot user and their context (Young, 2017). While context is a fluid and developmental concept (Dourish, 2004), and each user will have their own backstory for using the chatbot, designing a chatbot can be helped, for example, by role-playing conversations, and interviewing various stakeholders (Strömberg et al., 2004). Digital development teams are often familiar with gathering requirements, however, when designing a chatbot, written or spoken language is the dominant form of communication and this is constructed and negotiated in communities that may or may not contain people of similar gender (Eckert & McConnel-Ginet, 2003, p. 57).

The language of chatbot users should never be assumed (Young, 2017); for example, in a higher education setting, a café bar might be referred to by one name by staff and another name by students, or a small group of students with a diverse gender. Users might have different gender identities and accents, and so training and testing a chatbot needs to be carried out by more than a development team that might all have a similar gender. There is no universal user and it would be inappropriate to have a universal chatbot (Young, 2017). Design teams should also consider whether users themselves might hold stereotypes and how design choices might prompt people to behave inappropriately and whether reminding users that they are conversing with a robot regularly might minimise this (Fossa & Sucameli, 2022). While genderless chatbots might not always be appropriate, and may not even be truly possible, there are choices that need to be explored before development starts.

Ethics as Part of the Process

As this chapter has explored, there are several areas of difficulty facing chatbot creators (Gustavsson, 2005). Major considerations include, what personality should be reflected by the chatbot, and whether it should be portrayed as a woman, what systems creators can use so as not to perpetuate bias contained in them, through to how the chatbot should deal with sexual abuse. Even if the chatbot is intended as gender neutral, anthropomorphism might still cause users to envisage a gender for the chatbot (Fossa & Sucameli, 2022) and creators should establish how the chatbot should respond. If the chatbot fulfils the requirements for agency and warmth, and performs well, it would be difficult to justify a weak response to abuse for reasons of system credibility. Furthermore, aligning the chatbot persona to take advantage of user-brand congruence should help to minimise these occurrences. This is an area where the knowledge and experience of creation teams can contribute to new research. Reporting on what has worked well, without triggering difficulties such as abuse can help to develop new ideas of best practice.

Developers should seek to not only dispel stereotypes by design but also seek to use systems and data that do not contain any bias prevalent in society (Zhao et al., 2018). As the previous Section ('Design, Development and Delivery') explores, this is not only ethically difficult to justify but can also be detrimental to organisations, for example, a human resources chatbot that only suggests managerial positions to men (Honnavalli et al., 2022), or a Twitter account that repeats sexist and racist comments (Bridge et al., 2021).

Gender bias in chatbots is part of a wider issue with a lack of diversity in technology and artificial intelligence specifically (UNESCO, 2019). The longer digital tools are designed and built by men, the more gendered the field becomes and for women to enter the field becomes even more difficult. Whilst there are more recommendations suggested by various organisations for readdressing the wider problem (UNESCO, 2019; Sey & Hafkin, 2019), the chatbot creators of today strive to build a useful product that users will enjoy and that do not perpetuate any harmful stereotypes. The research explored throughout this work suggests that the benefits of social presence and warmth can be achieved without resorting to perpetuating stereotypes. chatbot creators should strive to be better informed about how the organisations personality should be best represented, take a firm stance on not condoning sexual abuse of the chatbot and ensuring systems and data used for the creation are ethical. This might, for example, instigate difficult but necessary conversations about user personas that might themselves hold any bias. Further research is needed on how self-brand congruence in chatbots might affect their perceived usability and the level of sexual harassment of the chatbot.

Recommendations Summary

This work is not recommending that chatbots should never be portrayed as women. It is recommending that they should not be portrayed as young attractive women by default. As with many fields in computing, the field of chatbots is developing quickly and as this work shows, new findings are published often. The recommendations above also encourage more collaboration between chatbot creation teams and stakeholders, so skilled teams can build chatbots they and their stakeholders will be proud of. It also makes recommendations for ethics to be part of the design, development and evaluation process so teams can make informed decisions about what systems their chatbots should be based on and how it should be portrayed, speak and behave in difficult situations. It could be argued, of course, that ethical design is a recommendation that should be followed regardless of the topic, and this is true. However, this recommendation it seems is still rarely followed so stands as a recommendation in this paper until it is standardised practice.

CONCLUSION

In understanding feminist issues, there is hope for building chatbots that will benefit not only users, and the teams that create them, but society as a whole. As discussed in above, chatbots are everywhere. Despite being built for different purposes, they are becoming more and more prevalent (Araujo, 2018) in day-to-day society, and users are willing to adopt them. However, there are a number of issues listed in this chapter which must still be addressed through feminist research and practices. With regards to industry relevance, one of the main considerations when choosing how to present gender in a chatbot may be resolved through understanding and implementing the established understanding of self-brand congruence (Grohmann, 2020), which may lead to a higher level of authenticity, not only in the chatbots but in the brands they represent. This could further be established with the language given to them. Gendered language, as discussed above, is a well-established area of research, and ties into the themes of anthropomorphism discussed throughout this chapter. This is important to understand when it comes to supporting or breaking down stereotypes, in this case, that women do not just have to be servants (Gustavsson, 2005). How individual or brand identity is expressed through language will be gendered; as discussed above, gender and language are a part of 'being' and a major part of how people express themselves – should a chatbot be any different? This also holds alignment with how the chatbots themselves are treated. If stereotypes are perpetuated by the allowing of chatbots presented as women to be subject to abuse with little or no consequence, it could be argued that the chatbots are doing more harm than good to society. This is an important consideration regardless of industry or the sector the chatbot is being built for.

When it comes to the design, development and delivery of the chatbot, as discussed in 'Design, Development and Delivery', gendered language must be considered once again. Gendered language not only has the potential to affect what is being built, but it affects how they are built and the people building them. What should also be considered is the use case with once again self-brand congruence perhaps holding more relevance than a default 'female bot'. This aligns with existing principles in UCD, where it is the users that are designed for, instead of arbitrary decisions based on existing assumptions and stereotypes. Feminist methodologies would appear to support this, as well as the need to explore and breakdown gendered issues in any NLP models that are used in development. It could be argued that NLP models need map linked words and represent language as it is actually used, but this would simply perpetuate stereotypes and, as this chapter suggests, do more harm than good. In addition to this further research is required through the observation and analysis of teams designing chatbots to uncover how and if gender is discussed, as well as how the make-up of the team, with regards to gender, may impact decisions that are made.

This chapter has broken down the existing research with regards to feminist methodologies, the pervasive nature of chatbots and their industry relevance, the need to be authentic when it comes to anthropomorphism and how this can affect perceptions. Therefore, the three recommendations that this chapter has made, should be considered by anybody involved in any stage of a chatbots creation. Firstly, current research should be consistently explored and adopted to enable equality within chatbot creation. The responsibility for this lies within the hands of those involved in the process. In line with Black Feminist Theories, it should not be the responsibility of those disadvantaged, in this case women, to educate those in the positions of power. Secondly, continued consistent effort should be made to increase the diversity of any team involved in the creation of chatbots. As this is not always possible, effort should be made, using principles of UCD, to work more closely with stakeholders (which could be anybody from teams throughout the organisation in question – for example, marketing, through to the users themselves), to ensure a chatbot which is more representative of the user themselves. This recommendation stems from the importance of self-brand congruence, and merely applies this to chatbots. The third and final recommendation is to ensure that teams hold themselves to a high standard of ethics when it comes to gendered biases and stereotypes. Once again, it is the responsibility of those building chatbots to understand the impact they could have, therefore a high standard of ethics is crucial.

If these recommendations are followed, a hopeful outlook may be adopted when it comes to the impact of chatbots on society as a whole.

ACKNOWLEDGMENT

This research received no specific grant from any funding agency in the public, commercial, or not-for-profit sectors.

The authors would like to thank Dr Emily Winter and Dr Mark Rouncefield for their thoughts and guidance on the chapter, as well as the reviewers for their helpful comments and feedback.

REFERENCES

Adams, R. (2019). Helen A'Loy and other tales of female automata: A gendered reading of the narratives of hopes and fears of intelligent machines and artificial intelligence. *AI & Society*, *35*(3), 569–579. doi:10.100700146-019-00918-7

Airenti, G. (2015). The Cognitive Bases of Anthropomorphism: From Relatedness to Empathy. *International Journal of Social Robotics*, *7*(1), 117–127. doi:10.100712369-014-0263-x

Andrienko, O. (2020). *Leveraging Voice Search for Local Businesses.* Semrush. www.semrush.com. https://www.semrush.com/blog/voice-search-local-seo/

Appel, M., & Weber, S. (2021). Do mass mediated stereotypes harm members of negatively stereotyped groups? A meta-analytical review on media-generated stereotype threat and stereotype lift. *Communication Research*, *48*(2), 151–179. doi:10.1177/0093650217715543

Araujo, T. (2018). Living up to the chatbot hype: The influence of anthropomorphic design cues and communicative agency framing on conversational agent and company perceptions. *Computers in Human Behavior*, *85*, 183–189. doi:10.1016/j.chb.2018.03.051

Ashcroft, A. (2021). Do I Belong Here?: An exploration of meeting structure and language, alongside gender and a sense of belonging. Paper presented at the *OzCHI '21*. ACM. 10.1145/3520495.3520514

Ashcroft, A. (2022a). Feminist Thematic Discourse Analysis in CS. Paper presented at the *15th International Conferences ICT, Society, and Human Beings 2022*, (pp. 281-284). Lancaster University.

Ashcroft, A. (2022b). I think" Hedging" could be a Feminist Issue in Software Engineering. Paper presented at the *Proceedings of 20th European Conference on Computer-Supported Cooperative Work*. ESSET.

Ashforth, B. E., & Humphrey, R. H. (1997). The Ubiquity and Potency of Labeling in Organizations. *Organization Science (Providence, R.I.), 8*(1), 43-58. doi:10.1145/3520495.3520514

Aylett, M., Cowan, B., & Clark, L. (2019). Siri, Echo and Performance: You have to Suffer Darling. Paper presented at the *CHI Conference on Human Factors in Computing Systems.* CHI. doi:10.1371/journal.pone.0179336

Baez, S., Flichtentrei, D., Prats, M., Mastandueno, R., García, A. M., Cetkovich, M., & Ibáñez, A. (2017). Men, women…who cares? A population-based study on sex differences and gender roles in empathy and moral cognition. *PLoS One, 12*(6), e0179336. doi:10.1371/journal.pone.0179336

Balakrishnan, J., & Dwivedi, Y. K. (2021). Role of cognitive absorption in building user trust and experience. *Psychology and Marketing, 38*(4), 643–668. doi:10.1002/mar.21462

Bardzell, S., & Bardzell, J. (May 2011). Towards a feminist HCI methodology: social science, feminism, and HCI. Paper presented at the *SIGCHI Conference on Human Factors in Computing Systems*, (pp. 675-684). ACM. 10.1145/1978942.1979041

Blut, M., Wang, C., Wünderlich, N. V., & Brock, C. (2021). Understanding anthropomorphism in service provision: A meta-analysis of physical robots, chatbots, and other AI. *Journal of the Academy of Marketing Science, 49*(4), 632–658. doi:10.100711747-020-00762-y

Bolukbasi, T., Kai-Wei Chang, Zou, J., Saligrama, V., & Kalai, A. (2016). *Man is to Computer Programmer as Woman is to Homemaker? Debiasing Word Embeddings.* Cornell University Library.

Borau, S., Otterbring, T., Laporte, S., & Fosso Wamba, S. (2021). The most human bot: Female gendering increases humanness perceptions of bots and acceptance of AI. *Psychology and Marketing, 38*(7), 1052–1068. doi:10.1002/mar.21480

Bordalo, P., Coffman, K., Gennaioli, N., & Shleifer, A. (2016). Stereotypes. *The Quarterly Journal of Economics, 131*(4), 1753–1794. doi:10.1093/qje/qjw029

Brahnam, S., & De Angeli, A. (2012). Gender affordances of conversational agents. *Interacting with Computers, 24*(3), 139–153. doi:10.1016/j.intcom.2012.05.001

Brandtzaeg, P. B., & Følstad, A. (2017). *Why People Use chatbots. Internet Science.* Springer International Publishing. doi:10.1007/978-3-319-70284-1_30

Bridge, O., Raper, R., Strong, N., & Nugent, S. E. (2021). Modelling a socialised chatbot using trust development in children: Lessons learnt from Tay. *Cognitive Computation and Systems*, *3*(2), 100–108. doi:10.1049/ccs2.12019

Brown, L. M. (2022). Gendered Artificial Intelligence in Libraries: Opportunities to Deconstruct Sexism and Gender Binarism. *Journal of Library Administration*, *62*(1), 19–30. doi:10.1080/01930826.2021.2006979

Chahal, M. (2015). Why marketing should take a stance on feminism. *Marketing Week*. https://www.marketingweek.com/why-marketing-should-take-a-stance-on-feminism/

Chen, Z., Lu, X., Ai, W., Li, H., Mei, Q., & Liu, X. (2018). Through a Gender Lens: Learning Usage Patterns of Emojis from Large-Scale Android Users. Paper presented at the *World Wide Web Conference*. ACM. 10.1145/3178876.3186157

Christov-Moore, L., Simpson, E. A., Coudé, G., Grigaityte, K., Iacoboni, M., & Ferrari, P. F. (2014). Empathy: Gender effects in brain and behavior. *Neuroscience and Biobehavioral Reviews*. *Neuroscience and Biobehavioral Reviews*, *46*(4), 604–627. doi:10.1016/j.neubiorev.2014.09.001 PMID:25236781

Coniam, D. (2014). The linguistic accuracy of chatbots: Usability from an ESL perspective. *Text & Talk*, *34*(5). doi:10.1515/text-2014-0018

Costa, P., & Ribas, L. (2019). AI becomes her: Discussing gender and artificial intelligence. *Technoetic Arts: a Journal of Speculative Research*, *17*(1-2), 171–193. doi:10.1386/tear_00014_1

Crolic, C., Thomaz, F., Hadi, R., & Stephen, A. T. (2022). Blame the Bot: Anthropomorphism and Anger in Customer–chatbot Interactions. *Journal of Marketing*. *Journal of Marketing*, *86*(1), 132–148. doi:10.1177/00222429211045687

Cunningham-Nelson, S., Boles, W., Trouton, L., & Margerison, E. (2019). A Review of chatbots in Education: Practical Steps Forward. Paper presented at the *30th Annual Conference for the Australasian Association for Engineering Education (AAEE 2019): Educators Becoming Agents of Change: Innovate, Integrate, Motivate,* (pp. 299-306). QUT. https://eprints.qut.edu.au/134323/1/AAEE2019_SCN_WB_LT_EM.pdf

Curry, A. C., & Rieser, V. (2018). #metoo alexa: How conversational systems respond to sexual harassment. Paper presented at the *Proceedings of the Second Acl Workshop on Ethics in Natural Language Processing,* (pp. 7-14). ACL. 10.18653/v1/W18-0802

Darcy, A., Daniels, J., Salinger, D., Wicks, P., & Robinson, A. (2021). Evidence of Human-Level Bonds Established With a Digital Conversational Agent: Cross-sectional, Retrospective Observational Study. *JMIR Formative Research. JMIR Formative Research*, *5*(5), e27868. doi:10.2196/27868 PMID:33973854

Davies, P. G., Spencer, S. J., Quinn, D. M., & Gerhardstein, R. (2002). Consuming Images: How Television Commercials that Elicit Stereotype Threat Can Restrain Women Academically and Professionally. *Personality and Social Psychology Bulletin*, *28*(12), 1615–1628. doi:10.1177/014616702237644

De Angeli, A., & Brahnam, S. (2006). Sex Stereotypes and Conversational Agents. Paper presented at the *Proc. of Gender and Interaction: Real and Virtual Women in a Male World*. Semantic Scholar.

De Bruyn, A., Viswanathan, V., Beh, Y. S., Brock, J. K., & von Wangenheim, F. (2020). Artificial Intelligence and Marketing: Pitfalls and Opportunities. *Journal of Interactive Marketing*, *51*(1), 91–105. doi:10.1016/j.intmar.2020.04.007

De Hertogh, L. B., Lane, L., & Ouellette, J. (2019). "Feminist Leanings:" Tracing Technofeminist and Intersectional Practices and Values in Three Decades of Computers and Composition. *Computers and Composition*, *51*, 4–13. doi:10.1016/j.compcom.2018.11.004

Dourish, P. (2004). What we talk about when we talk about context. *Personal and Ubiquitous Computing*, *8*(1), 19–30. doi:10.100700779-003-0253-8

Dourish, P. (2006). Implications for design. Paper presented at the *Proceedings of the SIGCHI Conference on Human Factors in Computing Systems*, (pp. 541-550). ACM. 10.1145/1124772.1124855

Duffy, B. R. (2003). Anthropomorphism and the social robot. *Robotics and Autonomous Systems*, *42*(3), 177–190. doi:10.1016/S0921-8890(02)00374-3

Eckert, P., & McConnell-Ginet, S. (2003). *Language and gender*. Cambridge University Press. doi:10.1017/CBO9780511791147

Ehrenpreis, M., & DeLooper, J. (2022). Implementing a chatbot on a Library Website. *Journal of Web Librarianship*, *16*(2), 120–142. doi:10.1080/19322909.2022.2060893

Elsner, N. (2017). *KAYAK Mobile Travel Report: chatbots in the UK*. KAYAK. https://www.kayak.co.uk/news/mobile-travel-report-2017/

Essamri, A., McKechnie, S., & Winklhofer, H. (2019). Co-creating corporate brand identity with online brand communities: A managerial perspective. *Journal of Business Research*, *96*, 366–375. doi:10.1016/j.jbusres.2018.07.015

Faye, S. (2021). *The transgender issue: An argument for justice.* Penguin UK.

Feine, J., Gnewuch, U., Morana, S., & Maedche, A. (2019). A Taxonomy of Social Cues for Conversational Agents. *International Journal of Human-Computer Studies*, *132*, 138–161. doi:10.1016/j.ijhcs.2019.07.009

Feine, J., Gnewuch, U., Morana, S., & Maedche, A. (2020). Gender Bias in chatbot Design. Paper presented at the *International Workshop on chatbot Research and Design*, (pp. 79-93). Springer. 10.1007/978-3-030-39540-7_6

Ferguson, C. J., Gryshyna, A., Kim, J. S., Knowles, E., Nadeem, Z., Cardozo, I., Esser, C., Trebbi, V., & Willis, E. (2022). Video games, frustration, violence, and virtual reality: Two studies. *British Journal of Social Psychology. British Journal of Social Psychology*, *61*(1), 83–99. doi:10.1111/bjso.12471 PMID:34114247

Ferrer, X., Tom, v. N., Jose, M. S., & Criado, N. (2020). *Discovering and Categorising Language Biases in Reddit.* Cornell University Library.

Fessler, L. (2017). We tested bots like Siri and Alexa to see who would stand up to sexual harassment. *Quartz.* https://qz.com/911681/we-tested-apples-siri-amazon-echos-ale xa-microsofts-cortana-and-googles-google-home-to-see-which-p ersonal-assistant-bots-stand-up-for-themselves-in-the-face-o f-sexual-harassment/

Fitzpatrick, K. K., Darcy, A., & Vierhile, M. (2017). Delivering Cognitive Behavior Therapy to Young Adults With Symptoms of Depression and Anxiety Using a Fully Automated Conversational Agent (Woebot): A Randomized Controlled Trial. *JMIR Mental Health. JMIR Mental Health*, *4*(2), e19. doi:10.2196/mental.7785 PMID:28588005

Fortunati, L., Edwards, A., Edwards, C., Manganelli, A. M., & de Luca, F. (2022). Is Alexa female, male, or neutral? A cross-national and cross-gender comparison of perceptions of Alexa's gender and status as a communicator. *Computers in Human Behavior*, *137*, 107426. doi:10.1016/j.chb.2022.107426

Fossa, F., & Sucameli, I. (2022). Gender Bias and Conversational Agents: An ethical perspective on Social Robotics. *Science and Engineering Ethics*, *28*(3), 23. doi:10.100711948-022-00376-3 PMID:35445886

Fuller, K. (2020). The "7 Up" Intersectionality Life Grid: A Tool for Reflexive Practice. *Frontiers in Education*, *0*, 77. doi:10.3389/feduc.2020.00077

Gabbiadini, A., Riva, P., Andrighetto, L., Volpato, C., & Bushman, B. J. (2016). Acting like a tough guy: Violent-sexist video games, identification with game characters, masculine beliefs, & empathy for female violence victims. *PloS One. PLoS One*, *11*(4), e0152121. doi:10.1371/journal.pone.0152121 PMID:27074057

Garousi, V., Petersen, K., & Ozkan, B. (2016). Challenges and best practices in industry-academia collaborations in software engineering: A systematic literature review. *Information and Software Technology*, *79*, 106–127. doi:10.1016/j. infsof.2016.07.006

Go, E., & Sundar, S. S. (2019). Humanizing chatbots: The effects of visual, identity and conversational cues on humanness perceptions. *Computers in Human Behavior*, *97*, 304–316. doi:10.1016/j.chb.2019.01.020

Government Equalities Office. (2019). *National LGBT Survey: Summary report*. GOV.UK. https://www.gov.uk/government/publications/national-lgbt-survey-summary-report/national-lgbt-survey-summary-report

Grohmann, B. (2009). Gender Dimensions of Brand Personality. *JMR, Journal of Marketing Research*, *46*(1), 105–119. doi:10.1509/jmkr.46.1.105

Gustavsson, E. (2005). Virtual servants: Stereotyping female front-office employees on the internet. *Gender, Work and Organization*, *12*(5), 400–419. doi:10.1111/j.1468-0432.2005.00281.x

Guzman, A. L. (2019). Voices in and of the machine: Source orientation toward mobile virtual assistants. *Computers in Human Behavior*, *90*, 343–350. doi:10.1016/j. chb.2018.08.009

Hari, H., Iyer, R., & Sampat, B. (2021). Customer Brand Engagement through chatbots on Bank Websites– Examining the Antecedents and Consequences. *International Journal of Human-Computer Interaction*, 1–16. doi:10.1080/10447 318.2021.1988487

Hayes, J. L., Britt, B. C., Applequist, J., Ramirez, A. Jr, & Hill, J. (2020). Leveraging Textual Paralanguage and Consumer-Brand Relationships for More Relatable Online Brand Communication: A Social Presence Approach. *Journal of Interactive Advertising*, *20*(1), 17–30. doi:10.1080/15252019.2019.1691093

Hearn, J., & Hein, W. (2015). Reframing gender and feminist knowledge construction in marketing and consumer research: Missing feminisms and the case of men and masculinities. *Journal of Marketing Management*, *31*(15-16), 1626–1651. doi:10. 1080/0267257X.2015.1068835

Hilgard, J., Engelhardt, C. R., Rouder, J. N., Segert, I. L., & Bartholow, B. D. (2019). Null Effects of Game Violence, Game Difficulty, and 2D:4D Digit Ratio on Aggressive Behavior. *Psychological Science. Psychological Science*, *30*(4), 606–616. doi:10.1177/0956797619829688 PMID:30843758

Honnavalli, S., Parekh, A., Ou, L., Groenwold, S., Levy, S., Ordonez, V., & William, Y. W. (2022). *Towards Understanding Gender-Seniority Compound Bias in Natural Language Generation*. Cornell University Library.

Japutra, A., Ekinci, Y., & Simkin, L. (2019). Self-congruence, brand attachment and compulsive buying. *Journal of Business Research*, *99*, 456–463. doi:10.1016/j.jbusres.2017.08.024

Kent, C. (2021, -05-21T08:00:01+00:00). Mental health chatbots might do better when they don't try to act human. *Medical Device Network*. https://www.medicaldevice-network.com/analysis/mental-health-chatbot/

Kim, S., Lee, S., & Lee, J. (2021). Male, Female, or Robot?: Effects of Task Type and User Gender on Expected Gender of chatbots. *Journal of Korea Multimedia Society*, *24*(2), 320–327. doi:10.9717/kmms.2020.24.2.320

Kozinets, R. V., & Gretzel, U. (2021). Commentary: Artificial Intelligence: The Marketer's Dilemma. *Journal of Marketing*, *85*(1), 156–159. doi:10.1177/0022242920972933

Kuhail, M. A., Thomas, J., Alramlawi, S., Shah, S. J. H., & Thornquist, E. (2022). Interacting with a chatbot-Based Advising System: Understanding the Effect of chatbot Personality and User Gender on Behavior. Paper presented at the *Informatics, 9*(4) 81.

Kühnel, J., Ebner, M., & Ebner, M. (2020). chatbots for Brand Representation in Comparison with Traditional Websites. *International Journal of Interactive Mobile Technologies*, *14*(18), 18–33. doi:10.3991/ijim.v14i18.13433

Lahoz-Beltra, R., & López, C. C. (2021). Lenna (Learning emotions neural network assisted): An empathic chatbot designed to study the simulation of emotions in a bot and their analysis in a conversation. *Computers (Basel)*, *10*(12), 170. doi:10.3390/computers10120170

Lakoff, R. T. (1975). *Language and woman's place*. Harper and Row.

Lee, A., Kim, S., Lee, G., & Lee, J. (2018). Robots in Diverse Contexts: Effects of Robots Tasks on Expected Personality. Paper presented at the *ACM/IEEE International Conference*. ACM, IEEE. 10.1145/3173386.3176989

Lee, J. (2013). Brands Expected to Respond Within an Hour on Twitter [Study]. *Search Engine Watch*. https://www.searchenginewatch.com/2013/11/01/brands-expected-to-respond-within-an-hour-on-twitter-study/

Lee, N., Madotto, A., & Fung, P. (2019). Exploring Social Bias in chatbots using Stereotype Knowledge. Paper presented at the *Wnlp@ Acl,* (pp. 177-180). ACL.

Lee, S., Lee, N., & Sah, Y. J. (2020). Perceiving a Mind in a chatbot: Effect of Mind Perception and Social Cues on Co-presence, Closeness, and Intention to Use. *International Journal of Human-Computer Interaction, 36*(10), 930–940. doi:10.1080/10447318.2019.1699748

Leentz, A. (2021). Garbage in, garbage out: is AI discriminatory or simply a mirror of IRL inequalities? *Universal Rights*. https://www.universal-rights.org/blog/garbage-in-garbage-out-is-ai-discriminatory-or-simply-a-mirror-of-irl-inequalities/

Leong, B., & Selinger, E. (January 2019). Robot Eyes Wide Shut: Understanding Dishonest Anthropomorphism. Paper presented at the *Conference on Fairness, Accountability, and Transparency*, (pp. 299-308). ACM. 10.1145/3287560.3287591

LeRouge, C., Ma, J., Sneha, S., & Tolle, K. (2011). User profiles and personas in the design and development of consumer health technologies. *International Journal of Medical Informatics (Shannon, Ireland). International Journal of Medical Informatics, 82*(11), e251–e268. doi:10.1016/j.ijmedinf.2011.03.006 PMID:21481635

Lieven, T., Grohmann, B., Herrmann, A., Landwehr, J. R., & van Tilburg, M. (2014). The Effect of Brand Gender on Brand Equity. *Psychology & Marketing. Psychology and Marketing, 31*(5), 371–385. doi:10.1002/mar.20701

Liu-Thompkins, Y., Okazaki, S., & Li, H. (2022). Artificial empathy in marketing interactions: Bridging the human-AI gap in affective and social customer experience. *Journal of the Academy of Marketing Science, 50*(6), 1198–1218. doi:10.100711747-022-00892-5

Lo Presti, L., Maggiore, G., & Marino, V. (2021). The role of the chatbot on customer purchase intention: Towards digital relational sales. *Italian Journal of Marketing, 2021*(3), 165–188. doi:10.100743039-021-00029-6

Looi, Q. E., & See, S. L. (March 2012). Applying politeness maxims in social robotics polite dialogue. Paper presented at the *7th ACM/IEEE International Conference on Human-Robot Interaction (HRI)*, (pp. 189-190). ACM, IEEE. 10.1145/2157689.2157749

Luangrath, A. W., Peck, J., & Barger, V. A. (2017). Textual paralanguage and its implications for marketing communications. *Journal of Consumer Psychology*, *27*(1), 98–107. doi:10.1016/j.jcps.2016.05.002

May, A., Wachs, J., & Hannák, A. (2019). Gender differences in participation and reward on Stack Overflow. *Empirical Software Engineering: An International Journal*, *24*(4), 1997–2019. doi:10.100710664-019-09685-x

McBane, D. A. (1995). Empathy and the salesperson: A multidimensional perspective. *Psychology & Marketing. Psychology and Marketing*, *12*(4), 349–370. doi:10.1002/mar.4220120409

McDonnell, M., & Baxter, D. (2019). chatbots and Gender Stereotyping. *ITNow*, *61*(4), 66. doi:10.1093/itnow/bwz119

McLean, G., Osei-Frimpong, K., & Barhorst, J. (2021). Alexa, do voice assistants influence consumer brand engagement? – Examining the role of AI powered voice assistants in influencing consumer brand engagement. *Journal of Business Research*, *124*, 312–328. doi:10.1016/j.jbusres.2020.11.045

McShane, L., Pancer, E., Poole, M., & Deng, Q. (2021). Emoji, Playfulness, and Brand Engagement on Twitter. *Journal of Interactive Marketing*, *53*(1), 96–110. doi:10.1016/j.intmar.2020.06.002

Merritt, A. (2018). Here's what people are really doing with their Alexa and Google Home assistants. *Venture Beat*. https://venturebeat.com/2018/11/17/heres-what-people-are-really-doing-with-their-alexa-and-google-home-assistants/

Monk, A. (2000). User-centred design. Paper presented at the *International Conference on Home-Oriented Informatics and Telematics*, (pp. 181-190). Springer. 10.1007/978-0-387-35511-5_14

Moradbakhti, L., Schreibelmayr, S., & Mara, M. (2022). Do Men Have No Need for "Feminist" Artificial Intelligence? Agentic and Gendered Voice Assistants in the Light of Basic Psychological Needs. *Frontiers in Psychology*, *13*, 855091. doi:10.3389/fpsyg.2022.855091 PMID:35774945

Morhart, F., Malär, L., Guèvremont, A., Girardin, F., & Grohmann, B. (2015). Brand authenticity: An integrative framework and measurement scale. *Journal of Consumer Psychology*, *25*(2), 200–218. doi:10.1016/j.jcps.2014.11.006

Morris, M., & Bunjun, B. (2007). *Using intersectional feminist frameworks in research*. Canadian Research Institute for the Advancement of Women.

Murtarelli, G., Gregory, A., & Romenti, S. (2021). A conversation-based perspective for shaping ethical human–machine interactions: The particular challenge of chatbots. *Journal of Business Research, 129,* 927–935. doi:10.1016/j.jbusres.2020.09.018

Nass, C., Steuer, J., & Tauber, E. R. (1994). Computers are social actors. Paper presented at the *Proceedings of the SIGCHI Conference on Human Factors in Computing Systems,* (pp. 72-78). ACM.

Ndubisi, N. O., & Nataraajan, R. (2018). Customer satisfaction, Confucian dynamism, and long-term oriented marketing relationship: A threefold empirical analysis. *Psychology and Marketing, 35*(6), 477–487. doi:10.1002/mar.21100

Neale, L., Robbie, R., & Martin, B. (2016). Gender identity and brand incongruence: When in doubt, pursue masculinity. *Journal of Strategic Marketing, 24*(5), 347–359. doi:10.1080/0965254X.2015.1011203

Neururer, M., Schlögl, S., Brinkschulte, L., & Groth, A. (2018). Perceptions on Authenticity in Chat Bots. *Multimodal Technologies and Interaction, 2*(3), 60. doi:10.3390/mti2030060

O'Driscoll, A. (2019). From sex objects to bumbling idiots: Tracing advertising students' perceptions of gender and advertising. *Feminist Media Studies, 19*(5), 732–749. doi:10.1080/14680777.2018.1506943

Palan, K. M. (2001). Gender identity in consumer behavior research: A literature review and research agenda. *Academy of Marketing Science Review, 10,* 1–31.

Palanica, A., Flaschner, P., Thommandram, A., Li, M., & Fossat, Y. (2019). Physicians' Perceptions of chatbots in Health Care: Cross-Sectional Web-Based Survey. *Journal of Medical Internet Research. Journal of Medical Internet Research, 21*(4), e12887. doi:10.2196/12887 PMID:30950796

Pavalanathan, U., & Eisenstein, J. (2015). *Emoticons vs. Emojis on Twitter: A Causal Inference Approach.* Cornell University Library.

Pawlik, P. (2022). Design Matters! How Visual Gendered Anthropomorphic Design Cues Moderate the Determinants of the Behavioral Intention Towards Using chatbots. *Lecture Notes in Computer Science, 13171,* 192-208. Springer. https://link.springer.com/chapter/10.1007/978-3-030-94890-0_12

Pedersen, C. L. (2021). Empathy-based marketing. *Psychology and Marketing, 38*(3), 470–480. doi:10.1002/mar.21448

Pelau, C., Dabija, D., & Ene, I. (2021). What makes an AI device human-like? The role of interaction quality, empathy and perceived psychological anthropomorphic characteristics in the acceptance of artificial intelligence in the service industry. *Computers in Human Behavior*, *122*, 106855. doi:10.1016/j.chb.2021.106855

Pine, J. I. I., & Gilmore, J. H. (2008). Keep it real. *Marketing Management (Chicago, Ill.)*, *17*(1), 18.

Plummer, J. T. (1984). How Personality Makes a Difference. *Journal of Advertising Research*, *24*(6), 27.

Quina, K., Wingard, J. A., & Bates, H. G. (1987). Language style and gender stereotypes in person perception. *Psychology of Women Quarterly*, *11*(1), 111–122. doi:10.1111/j.1471-6402.1987.tb00778.x

Richardson, S. (2022). *How and why to take your customer engagement strategy 'back to the future'.* Marketing Week. https://www.marketingweek.com/how-and-why-to-take-your-customer-engagement-strategy-back-to-the-future/

Roggeveen, A. L., & Sethuraman, R. (2020). Customer-Interfacing Retail Technologies in 2020 & Beyond: An Integrative Framework and Research Directions. *Journal of Retailing*, *96*(3), 299–309. doi:10.1016/j.jretai.2020.08.001

Ross, S. D., & Lester, P. M. (2011). *Images that injure: pictorial stereotypes in the media*. Praeger.

Rudinger, R., Naradowsky, J., Leonard, B., & Benjamin, V. D. (2018). *Gender Bias in Coreference Resolution*. Cornell University Library, arXiv.org.

Ryan Calo, M. (2012). Against notice skepticism in privacy (and elsewhere). *The Notre Dame Law Review*, *87*(3), 1027–1072.

Sardella, N., Biancalana, C., Micarelli, A., & Sansonetti, G. (2019). An Approach to Conversational Recommendation of Restaurants. Paper presented at the *HCI International 2019,* (pp. 123-130). Springer. 10.1007/978-3-030-23525-3_16

Schandorf, M. (2013). Mediated gesture: Paralinguistic communication and phatic text. *Convergence (London, England)*, *19*(3), 319–344. doi:10.1177/1354856512439501

Schlesinger, A., Edwards, W. K., & Grinter, R. E. (2017). Intersectional HCI: Engaging identity through gender, race, and class. Paper presented at the *Proceedings of the 2017 CHI Conference on Human Factors in Computing Systems*, (pp. 5412-5427). ACM. 10.1145/3025453.3025766

Seaborn, K., Miyake, N. P., Pennefather, P., & Otake-Matsuura, M. (2022). Voice in Human–Agent Interaction: A Survey. *ACM Computing Surveys, 54*(4), 1–43. doi:10.1145/3386867

Sey, A., & Hafkin, N. (2019). *Taking stock: Data and evidence on gender equality in digital access, skills and leadership*. United Nations University.

Shawar, B. A., & Atwell, E. (2017). chatbots: Are They Really Useful? *Ldv Forum, 22*(1), 29-49.

Sheehan, B., Jin, H. S., & Gottlieb, U. (2020). Customer service chatbots: Anthropomorphism and adoption. *Journal of Business Research, 115*, 14–24. doi:10.1016/j.jbusres.2020.04.030

Sherman, J. W. (1996). Development and Mental Representation of Stereotypes. *Journal of Personality and Social Psychology, 70*(6), 1126–1141. doi:10.1037/0022-3514.70.6.1126 PMID:8667161

Shukla, M. K., & Pattnaik, P. N. (2019). Managing Customer Relations in a Modern Business Environment: Towards an Ecosystem-Based Sustainable CRM Model. *Journal of Relationship Marketing (Binghamton, N.Y.), 18*(1), 17–33. doi:10.1080/15332667.2018.1534057

Sidi, Y., Glikson, E., & Cheshin, A. (2021). Do You Get What I Mean?!? The Undesirable Outcomes of (Ab)Using Paralinguistic Cues in Computer-Mediated Communication. *Frontiers in Psychology, 12*, 658844. doi:10.3389/fpsyg.2021.658844 PMID:34054662

Sirgy, M. J., Grewal, D., Mangleburg, T. F., Park, J., Chon, K. S., Claiborne, C. B., Johar, J. S., & Berkman, H. (1997). Assessing the predictive validity of two methods of measuring self-image congruence. *Journal of the Academy of Marketing Science, 25*(3), 229–241. doi:10.1177/0092070397253004

Skjuve, M., Haugstveit, I. M., Følstad, A., & Brandtzaeg, P. B. (2019). Help! Is my chatbot falling into the uncanny valley? An empirical study of user experience in human-chatbot interaction. *Human Technology, 15*(1), 30–54. doi:10.17011/ht/urn.201902201607

Solis, B. (2010). The social-media style guide: Eight steps to creating a brand persona. *Advertising Age, 81*(19), 16.

Sommerville, I. (2016). *Software engineering*. Pearson Education.

Spinuzzi, C. (2005). The Methodology of Participatory Design. *Technical Communication (Washington). Technical Communication (Washington), 52*(2), 163–174.

Sprague, J. (2016). *Feminist methodologies for critical researchers: Bridging differences.* Rowman & Littlefield.

Stokoe, E. H., & Weatheral, A. (2002). Gender, language, conversation analysis and feminism. *Discourse & Society, 13*(6), 707–713. doi:10.1177/0957926502013006751

Stroessner, S. J., & Benitez, J. (2018). The Social Perception of Humanoid and Non-Humanoid Robots: Effects of Gendered and Machinelike Features. *International Journal of Social Robotics, 11*(2), 305–315. doi:10.100712369-018-0502-7

Strömberg, H., Pirttilä, V., & Ikonen, V. (2004). Interactive scenarios - Building ubiquitous computing concepts in the spirit of participatory design. *Personal and Ubiquitous Computing, 8*(3-4), 200–207. doi:10.100700779-004-0278-7

Taj, I., & Zaman, N. (2022). Towards Industrial Revolution 5.0 and Explainable Artificial Intelligence: Challenges and Opportunities. *International Journal of Computing and Digital Systems, 12*(1), 295–320. doi:10.12785/ijcds/120128

Talbot, M. (2019). *Language and gender.* John Wiley & Sons.

Thormundsson, B. (2022). Global chatbot market 2025. *Statista.* https://www.statista.com/statistics/656596/worldwide-chatbot -market/

Todaro, M. P., & Smith, S. C. (2009). *Economic development.* Pearson Education.

Todorov, G. (2021). 65 Artificial Intelligence Statistics for 2021 and Beyond. *Semrush Blog.* https://www.semrush.com/blog/artificial-intelligence-stats

Udas, R. (2020). "A chatbot Should Have A Personality," Says Magnus Revang, Gartner. *Express Computer,* Uggla, H. (2020). Research Challenges for Brand Authenticity. *IUP Journal of Brand Management, 17*(1), 17–20.

UNESCO. (2019). *I'd blush if I could: closing gender divides in digital skills through education.* UNESCO. https://unesdoc.unesco.org/ark:/48223/pf0000367416.page=1

Virginia, F. K. (2012). Social Networking Ties and Low Interest, Underrepresentation and Low Status for Women in Information Technology Field. *Sex Roles, 66*(3-4), 253–255. doi:10.100711199-011-0072-8

Wang, A., Singh, A., Michael, J., Hill, F., Levy, O., & Samuel, R. B. (2019). *GLUE: A Multi-Task Benchmark and Analysis Platform for Natural Language Understanding*. Cornell University Library.

Wang, W., Cai, X., Chong, H. H., Wang, H., Lu, H., Liu, X., & Peng, W. (2021). *Emily: Developing An Emotion-affective Open-Domain chatbot with Knowledge Graph-based Persona*. Cornell University Library.

Weatherall, A. (2016). *Discourse and Gender*. Wiley Online Library. doi:10.1002/9781118663219.wbegss150

Whitby, B. (2008). Sometimes it's hard to be a robot: A call for action on the ethics of abusing artificial agents. *Interacting with Computers*, 20(3), 326–333. doi:10.1016/j.intcom.2008.02.002

Wijnands, F., & Gill, T. (2020). 'You're not perfect, but you're still my favourite.' Brand affective congruence as a new determinant of self-brand congruence. *Journal of Marketing Management*, 36(11-12), 1076–1103. doi:10.1080/026725 7X.2020.1767679

Winkle, K., Melsion, G. I., McMillan, D., & Leite, I. (2021). Boosting Robot Credibility and Challenging Gender Norms in Responding to Abusive Behaviour: A Case for Feminist Robots. Paper presented at the *HRI '21 Companion,* (pp. 29-37). ACM. 10.1145/3434074.3446910

Woebot Health. (2022). *Woebot Health*. Woebot Health. https://woebothealth.com/

World Economic Forum. (2018). *The Global Gender Gap Report 2018*. World Economic Forum. https://www3.weforum.org/docs/WEF_GGGR_2018.pdf

Xu, A., Liu, Z., Guo, Y., Sinha, V., & Akkiraju, R. (2017). A new chatbot for customer service on social media. Paper presented at the *Proceedings of the 2017 CHI Conference on Human Factors in Computing Systems*, (pp. 3506-3510). ACM. 10.1145/3025453.3025496

Yalcin, Ö. N., & DiPaola, S. (2018). A computational model of empathy for interactive agents. *Biologically Inspired Cognitive Architectures*, 26, 20–25. doi:10.1016/j.bica.2018.07.010

Yao, M. (2017). *100 Best Bots, chatbots, and Voice Experiences For Brands & Businesses*. TOPBOTS. https://www.topbots.com/100-best-bots-brands-businesses/

Youn, S., & Jin, S. V. (2021). "In A.I. we trust?" The effects of parasocial interaction and technopian versus luddite ideological views on chatbot-based customer relationship management in the emerging "feeling economy". *Computers in Human Behavior, 119*, 106721. doi:10.1016/j.chb.2021.106721

Young, J. (2017). *Feminist Design Tool.* Feminist Internet & Josie Young. https://drive.google.com/file/d/1AxWWPb76Lk2_71GIkqLqJW9a17x B5a5P/view

Zemcik, T. (2020). Failure of chatbot Tay was evil, ugliness and uselessness in its nature or do we judge it through cognitive shortcuts and biases? *AI & Society, 36*(1), 361–367. doi:10.100700146-020-01053-4

Zhao, J., Wang, T., Yatskar, M., Ordonez, V., & Kai-Wei Chang. (2018). *Gender Bias in Coreference Resolution: Evaluation and Debiasing Methods.* Cornell University Library.

Zhou, L., Gao, J., Li, D., & Shum, H. (2020). The Design and Implementation of XiaoIce, an Empathetic Social chatbot. *Computational Linguistics - Association for Computational Linguistics, 46*(1), 53-93. doi:10.1162/coli_a_00368

KEY TERMS AND DEFINITIONS

Agency: A person's ability to make decisions that affect the context and situation they are in.

Anthropomorphism: Attributing human characteristics to a non-human. Users may ascribe human characteristics to a chatbot.

Authenticity: How consumers perceive that an organisation or chatbot is faithful to itself and to its consumers.

Design: The process of decision making leading to the final outcome of what has to be built. With chatbots this pertains to how they will be built as well as the how the conversations will take place through intents and responses.

Diversity: The process of inclusion of a variety of people regardless of race, gender, socio-economic background, and any other characteristic.

Development: The process of building software, normally through programming.

Gender: The identity of a person expressed however they choose to, examples of this include but are not limited to; 'man,' 'woman,' 'trans,' 'non-binary.'

Self-brand Congruence: The relationship between a brand's personality and how the consumer perceives themselves, and the extent to which these two are in harmony.

Sex: The biological makeup of an organism pertaining to chromosomes, genitalia (internal and external), and hormones (production and reception).

Section 2

Chatbots in Education: Overview, Applications, and Challenges

Chapter 4
Applications of Chatbots
in Education

Masood Ghayoomi
Faculty of Linguistics, Institute for Humanities and Cultural Studies, Tehran, Iran

ABSTRACT

This chapter mainly concerns the application of artificial intelligence (AI) based chatbots in education (in the general sense). Three general applications of such systems are studied: a) language learning, b) teaching a course, and c) assistive for educational purposes (in the narrow sense). There are advantages and disadvantages for using chatbots in education. Their interaction with the students, human-like conversation simulation, 24/7 availability, and easy accessibility are some of the key advantages of using AI-based chatbots in education. The main disadvantage of such systems is their knowledge-bases (KB) requirement. A KB plays as the brain of a chatbot. However, their development is labor intensive and expensive in terms of time and effort. In this chapter, the main research studies on chatbots for the educational domain are reviewed and general construction of a chatbot as well as the evaluation metrics of chatbots are explained; and the available chatbot tools and systems used in education, in the general sense, are collected.

INTRODUCTION

Language is a means of communication to convey a message from the speaker (producer) to the listener (recipient) through an information channel. This tool makes it possible for people in society to have dialogues or conversations with each other. In 1950, Turing (1950) raised a question whether machines can think, and Turing Test was created. In 1966, Wiesenbaum (1983) developed the first system

DOI: 10.4018/978-1-6684-6234-8.ch004

at the MIT lab, called ELIZA, to open a dialogue with. This system operated in such a way that it first recognized the keywords or phrases from the input data to reproduce a response using those keywords based on the predefined responses. The dialogue was predefined to illustrate machinery understanding. In 1972, Kenneth Colby developed a computer program, called Parry, to model the behavior of a paranoid schizophrenic.[1] Rollo Carpenter developed Jabberwocky[2] chatbot in 1981 to "simulate natural human chat in an interesting, entertaining and humorous manner." In 1985, the Tomy Chatbot, a wireless robot toy, was created. This toy repeated any message recorded on its tape.[3]

It was almost in 1992 when a revolution in developing chatbots happened such that the chatbots were empowered with Artificial Intelligence (AI). Since then, the speed of developing various chatbots for research or commercial purposes has increased. In early 1992, Dr. Sbaitso, speech synthesis software, was released by the Creative Labs in Singapore within the MS-DOS environment. This software, which was an ELIZA-like chatbot, was able to converse with a user as a psychologist in a digitized voice.[4] In 1994, Michael Mauldin created Julia[5] and Verbot. Mauldin coined the word "chatterbot", which is later known as "chatbot". This word is derived from the term "verbot" which is constructed from "verse" and "robot" to mean "talking robot". In 1995, Richard Wallace developed an artificial-based chatbot, called ALICE which is the acronym of Artificial Linguistic Internet Computer Entity. This chatbot used heuristic patterns instead of static rules based on human's input. In 1996, Jason Hutchens developed Hex, which was another ELIZA-like chatbot and won the prize in the Loebner contest.[6] In 2001, the SmarterChild chatbot was developed at ActiveBuddy Inc.[7] It could access real-time news and information and could do tasks, like looking up the weather, storing notes, triggering timed instant message reminders, calculating, converting measures and scales, and generally answering any kinds of questions, like "What's the population of Indonesia?" or "What movies are playing near me tonight?". This chatbot became the cornerstone of the current well-known chatbots, namely Siri[8], Google Assistant[9], and Alexa[10], from 2010 to 2014. In 2015, Microsoft developed Cortana[11], and in 2016, Facebook created Messenger[12]. In 2017, Woebot, an automated conversational agent that helps to monitor mood and to learn about yourself, was developed.[13] This chatbot was a combination of natural language processing (NLP) techniques and psychological expertise. Endurance, an open-source chatbot, was created in 2018.[14] In 2019, Insomnobot was developed to be used for people who have insomnia.[15] Nowadays, conversational chatbots that use NLP methods are developing. Figure 1 represents the evolution timeline of chatbots.

Research and development of chatbots have become a hot topic since early 2000, and it has increasingly caught researchers' attention (Caldarini et al., 2022). Chatbots have various applications in different fields, from health (Crisseyb et al.,

Figure 1. Evolution timeline of chatbots

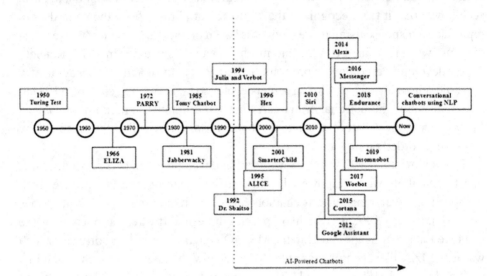

2019; Dharwadkar & Deshpande, 2018; Dharmapuri et al., 2022; Fadhil, 2018; Fadhil & Gabrielli, 2017; Naveen Kumar et al., 2016; Ni et al., 2017;), to fintech and business management (Athota et al., 2020; Eren, 2021; Heo et al., 2018; Ko & Lin, 2018), cultural heritage (Lombardi et al., 2019), tourism (Verasius et al., 2018), accommodation (Cheng et al., 2022), agriculture (Suebsombut et al., 2022), and customer service (Nuruzzaman & Hussain, 2018).

There are different educational technologies used in education. One is dialogue systems and pedagogical conversational agents (Lester et al., 1997), which simulates a natural conversation with a partner and uses NLP techniques for providing feedback. Another educational technology is the intelligent tutoring system (Graesser et al., 2001) which provides a computerized learning environment along with user's feedback according to the learning progress. The other one is learning analytics, which focuses on tracing the learning progress of students to improve their learning skills. This technique can be used by instructors as well to assess students' efforts (Duval & Verbert, 2012; Greller & Drachsler, 2012).

A chatbot is a subtype of a dialogue system. One of its progressive applications, among all, is in education and language learning. This means that a student interacts with a machine in the target language for language practice (Fryer et al., 2017), answering questions related to language learning (Xu et al., 2021), or assessment of the language skill and providing feedback (Jia et al., 2012). This approach in digital learning is different from the traditional e-learning approach, where there exists no interaction between the user and machine.

One main advantage of chatbots that makes them popular is their high capacity for personalization. This means that a chatbot as an assistant tool uses NLP algorithms along with AI-based machine learning methods to analyze the user's input and to interact with him. Automatic understanding of a user's information need or his readability level and adapting the provided information based on the user's profile or style are two examples of personalization properties.

There are two ways to make the chatbots applicable: one is a web-based application that is accessible through the web from several computers, and the other one is a stand-alone application that runs on electronic devices, such as a single computer, a smartphone, or a tablet. The primary reason that has made chatbots so favorite and popular, in addition to the existing interactive atmosphere, is their accessibility via such electronic devices. According to the study by Brooks and Pomerantz (2017: 5-6), at least 95% of undergraduate students own a laptop or a smartphone; and 30% of the students own all electronic devices. In this study, 75% of the students said that smartphones are moderately important for them. Moreover, the majority of students have said that using technology, such as a search tool, has enhanced their learning, and the collaborative technology tools have encouraged them to use the tools. They suggested, like their instructors, to use more technology in the classes. Additionally, they prefer to have online courses rather than the traditional face-to-face courses. In another study by Adams Becker et al. (2017), 67% of students use smartphones for studying, and 73% of the smartphone owners use voice commands to interact with their smartphones. The popularity of electronic devices, especially smartphones, and learning enhancement through collaborative technology tools are strong reasons to have special attention to using chatbots in education and to see the strong motivation to increase the demand for making their usage popular.

In this chapter, we merely focus on utilizing chatbots for educational purposes, and discuss their properties. The structure of the chapter is as follows. After the introduction, the general properties of chatbots are described. The next section reviews the application of chatbots in education. Two applications of chatbots are discussed, either for learning a course or educational purposes, such as a student help desk at the university. After reviewing the literature, we discuss the advantages and disadvantages of using chatbots in education. Then, a general structure of a chatbot and the related modules are introduced. The evaluation metrics are introduced in the next section. Then, a list of chatbot tools and systems developed in industry or academia used in education are introduced. The paper will be over with the concluding remarks, challenges, and the future direction of this topic.

GENERAL PROPERTIES OF CHATBOTS

A chatbot is, in fact, a dialogue system that algorithmically communicates with a human by using natural language in the form of text, speech, or both. Chatbots are different from the task-oriented dialogue systems, such as Siri, Alexa, Microsoft Cortana, or Google Assistant. As stated by Jurafsky and Martin (2021, Ch 24, p. 2), chatbots are "set up to mimic the unstructured conversations or 'chats' characteristics of human-human interaction, mainly for entertainment, but also for practical purposes like making task-oriented agents more natural". Because of the complexity of human conversations and their characteristics, developing a dialogue system that performs natural machine-human conversations is not an easy task. Chatbots are the simplest version of the dialogue systems that process natural language inputs and mimic human-human interactions.

There are two general approaches to develop chatbots (Jurafsky and Martin, 2021, Ch 24, p. 7): a) rule-based, b) corpus-based. In the former approach, such as ELIZA (Weizenbaum, 1983), a set of predefined rules to proceed with the conversation are written by experts. While, in the latter approach, a large volume of human-human conversations as a corpus is processed, either to find the most relevant response from the corpus by using information retrieval techniques, or to generate a response according to the input utterance. Switchboard corpus of American English telephone conversations (Godfrey et al., 1992) and movie dialogues (Danescu-Niculescu-Mizil and Lee, 2011; Ghandeharioun et al., 2019; He et al., 2021; Lison and Tiedemann, 2016; Roller et al., 2021) are examples of the datasets used in corpus-based chatbots.

CHATBOTS IN EDUCATION

Utilizing chatbots in education are divided into two major categories: a) chatbots for language learning purposes; and b) chatbots for related topics in education, such as a course, administrating, or scheduling. In the following, the studies on using chatbots in education are reviewed.

Chatbots for Language Learning

Rollo Carpenter developed another chatbot, called Cleverbot. It was used as a tool for language learning in 1986, and it became available online in 1997. According to the reports, most students enjoyed using this chatbot (Fryer and Carpenter, 2006).

Jia (2003, 2004) studied the utilization of a web-based chatbot to teach English and German as foreign languages. The developed system was, in fact, a keyword-based dialogue system. According to the findings, short dialogues interacted between the human and the machine, and the machinery responses were mostly repeated, and had irrelevant topics. This means the system has not understood the language at all, and the tool cannot function as a teaching assistant program in learning a foreign language.

Heller et al. (2005) developed a chatbot, called Freudbot, for psychology students to interact with. They utilized the AI Mark-up Language (AIML; Wallace, 2001) which is an open-source architecture to develop chatbots. In their research, 53 students participated in two sets of studies to have a 10-minute chat with Freudbot. Then, a questionnaire was used to provide feedback based on their experience.

Graesser et al. (2001) developed a dialogue system that simulated a conversation in natural language between the machine and a language learner, called AutoTutor. This system could answer challenging questions that a paragraph response is required to answer. Language learners might give a sentence as an answer to the question. However, the interaction between the learner and the systems for the answer enhances to improve the language knowledge and skill of the learner. To make the system more interactive, a three-dimensional interaction was simulated to increase the learner's engagement. Moreover, adaptation to the emotion or the learner's knowledge was another advantage of the system (Graesser ct al., 2005).

Haristiani (2019) developed an AI-based chatbot for language learning, called Gengobot, as a tool for autonomous learning. The target language in this research was Japanese to learn the grammar of this language based on the grammar and the dictionary of the Japanese proficiency test at the N3 level (Haristiani and Rifai, 2021), N4 and N5 levels (Haristiani et al., 2019). Gengobot was developed within the CodeIgniter framework, and it was easily accessible via the LINE social media. The questionnaire-based results showed that the application of this tool improved the Japanese grammar skill for the intermediate level (Haristiani and Rifai, 2021).

Shin et al. (2021) studied using an AI-based chatbot as a conversation partner for second language learners. To this end, an accessible chatbot, called Mitsuku, was used for the language learning task. The chatbot was not task-oriented. In this study, 53 participants who learned English in Korea (27 high school students and 26 college students) were involved in the study and used the text-based chatbot. The system backed up users' activities, and used the collected information for qualitative and quantitative studies, including the quantity activity of the user, the vocabulary level, the number of turns in the conversation between the user and the chatbot, the rate of success in the task, and the feeling of conversing with a chatbot. One of the additional findings in this study was topic shifting when the chatbot has not understood the utterance and responded irrelevantly. The other finding was fine-tuning of the chatbot to use the vocabulary level based on the students' language proficiency level. High school students had more positive feelings about using the chatbot system than college students; because wrong or inappropriate answers annoyed college students.

Mageira et al. (2022) designed and implemented a chatbot for education, called AsasaraBot. This chatbot contributed to the simultaneous learning of the cultural content of English and French languages in two private language schools in Greece. The system was used by students aged 12 to 18 years old without teacher intervention. The cultural content was about the Minoan Civilization, more specifically on the Minoan Snake Goddess. Two types of messages were used in the conversations: a) questions to reflect the chatbot's cognitive and linguistic capabilities; b) praise and encouragement to keep students motivated. In this chatbot, 52 interactions were defined based on the needs. The experimental results have shown that the proposed simultaneous learning method is effective.

Lee and Hwang (2022) studied the impact of three variables for using AI-based chatbots to teach English as a foreign language to Korean students at Jeonju University. In this research, 58 students participated in 16 experimental trials. They found out that the impact of using chatbots increases when the students belong to the lower school level. Moreover, the impact of using chatbots before the eighth week of usage was more beneficial. Additionally, the experimental results showed that specific task-oriented chatbots have more significant impact than general chatbots. This research concluded that using chatbots in education improved the quality, the equity, and the efficiency of education, and they optimized students to reach their goals.

Chatbots for Education

Heller et al. (2005) developed a chatbot for distance education, called Freudbot. This chatbot was built for psychology students. In this study, 53 students participated and interacted with Freudbot over the Web for 10 minutes. They completed a questionnaire and provided information about their experience. The results indicated a high proportion of on-task behavior.

Mondal et al. (2018) developed a conversation-based chatbot in education. To initialize the model, they collected around 1500 educational conversations from an educational organization. After preprocessing, the data reduced to 1000 conversations. Then, features, such as term frequency and inverse document frequency, noun and verb categories, along with semantic features, including synonymy or hyponymy from WordNet, the number of words in questions, and the question type, were extracted from the text data. The semantic features played a significant role in identifying the keywords in the response. The contextual features from the questions helped to use this knowledge in answers. These features trained a model to extract a response to a question from the data. In their research, the user was simulated and the primary evaluation metrics, such as precision, recall, and f-score, were used to compute the performance.

Chun Ho et al. (2018) developed a conversational advising chatbot, called EASElective, which helps students to select elective courses. The chatbot interacted with students based on the topics from introductory official courses to informal students' opinions. This chatbot was enhanced with an intent detection method and a recommendation method to personalize the answers to help students for making correct decisions on selecting the appropriate courses.

Colace et al. (2018) developed a chatbot for educational purposes to help students to learn specific subjects, including the Fundamental of Computer Science and Computer Networks courses. NLP techniques for intent detection and in-domain KBs were used for selecting the answers. Two groups of experimental and control were used for the two courses. The total number of students who participated in the courses was 167 and 124 students, respectively. All students had access to the chatbot, but after filtering them via a test, a questionnaire was emailed to the students. The correct suggestions of the chatbot to the users were used for the evaluation. The result showed a high percentage of correct suggestions (71.13%) by the chatbot.

Debnath and Agarwal (2020) described the appropriateness of chatbots used in educational institutes. They proposed the architecture of an AI-based chatbot framework for multi-uses, including answering frequently asked questions.

Lee et al. (2020) studied the general properties of chatbots and the importance of social chatbots. They classified the chatbot-based language-related activities into three categories. According to this study, a crucial role of chatbots was practicing the language skills, such as speaking and listening. Practicing the reading and writing skills in assistive chatbots on a specific subject was another achievement. The other achievement was that problem-solving tasks in chatbots, such as finding a place, increased the interaction between the user and chatbot, and it could help practicing the language skill.

Abdelhamid and Katz (2020) used a chatbot, called Alpha, as an intelligent teaching assistant tool for first-year engineering students in the Introduction to Information Systems course. This AI-based chatbot contained AI algorithms, cloud-based databases, speech recognition techniques, and web services. Before developing the chatbot, they investigated whether students are familiar with chatbots, the required properties of chatbots as teacher assistants, the role of chatbots in their education, and the expected features of chatbots. Among the 42 participants, 48% of them were female, and the rest (52%) were male. The findings were:

a)   80% of students used text chatting, and 75% used chatbot services;
b)   25% of students used chatbot for learning or searching for a topic;

c)   50% of students asked teacher assistants for help, but 71% of students said they have difficulty to meet the teacher assistants.

d)   95% of students found chatbots helpful in answering some of their questions;

e)   80% of students believed that chatbots improve their language learning skills;

f)   65% of students found chatbots useful to find key terms and information quickly rather than search engines.

According to the experimental results obtained through a questionnaire, it was found that the students considered the chatbot system highly usable and easy to learn.

Deveci Topal et al. (2021) studied the effect of AI-based chatbots for only one lesson of the Science course in the 5th grade. The Dialogflow and the Telegram instant messaging programs were used to develop the chatbot. In this study, a group of 41 participants cooperated, including 20 participants in the experimental group and 21 students in the control group. According to the experimental results, in terms of academic achievements, no significant results were found. However, students found chatbots helpful in learning outside the classroom. To compare the experimental and control groups, the Wilcoxon test was used.

Vanichvasin (2021) developed and evaluated a chatbot at a Thai university, for two courses, namely Business, and Computer Education, to study the effectiveness of chatbots in education. To increase the applicability of the chatbot, a recommendation system was used to increase and improve students' knowledge and to make personalized learning better. To quantify the research, a questionnaire was used such that the answers to the questions were scored from 1 to 5. For evaluation, common statistical metrics, such as mean, standard deviation, content analysis, and t-test, were utilized. The system asked for feedback from the user. The suggestions for improvements were as follows: adding research content and being more interactive, adding more examples and graphics to make chatbots more interesting, and leaving a hyperlink for unanswered questions.

Mateos-Sanchez et al. (2022) developed a chatbot as a mobile application, called CapacitaBOT, which was used for people with disabilities to train them with social skills. The chatbot aimed to be developed for this group of people who have been deeply affected by the COVID-19 crisis and social distance. This chatbot used speech recognition and speech synthesis systems developed by IBM Watson. A deductive logical method for a conversation was used to translate input for Watson. Different types of linguistic information, including intention, named entities, category, and conversation structure, were extracted from the data, and used as input for Watson to adapt it for the task.

Essel et al. (2022) studied the impact of chatbots on students' learning in Ghanaian higher education. In their experiments, 68 undergraduate students, who were randomly allocated, participated in this study. The students were divided into experiment and

Table 1. Summary of the resources using chatbots in education

Resource	Chatbot Application
Heller et al. (2005)	Specific course(s)
Mondal et al. (2018)	General
Chun Ho et al. (2018)	To select the elective courses
Colace et al. (2018)	Specific course(s)
Debnath and Agarwal (2020)	General (FAQ)
Abdelhamid and Katz (2020)	Specific course(s)
Lee et al. (2020)	General
Deveci Topal et al. (2021)	Specific course(s)
Vanichvasin (2021)	Specific course(s)
Mateos-Sanchez et al. (2022)	Social skills for people with disabilities
Essel et al. (2022)	General

control groups. One variable that should be taken care of is the pre-existing knowledge of users. This variable has a direct impact on both the performance and evaluation. To control this variable, they designed and implemented pre-tests and post-tests. According to the results, the students who interacted with the chatbot performed better than those who interacted with the course tutor. The qualitative analysis determined the positive impact of utilizing chatbots for academic performance and student satisfaction. In this study, providing feedback at different times without any delays had a significant impact on motivating students to use chatbots. Furthermore, the impacts of other variables on using chatbots were studied, including gender, age, previous experience with Whatsapp, academic performance, and post-test scores. According to the findings, these variables indicated no significant impact on the students to use chatbots for learning.

Table 1 summarizes the research studies on using chatbots for educational purposes. As it can be seen, most of the studies have focused on a particular course or lessons of a course. That means the developed KBs are very limited and specific to the subject.

In the literature, several articles reviewed the research on the field systematically. The main points concerned in the reviews are mentioned. Smutny and Schreiberova (2020) reviewed educational chatbots for the Facebook Messenger to support learning. They evaluated 47 educational chatbots that have used Facebook Messenger and classified them based on four criteria, including the quality attributes of teaching, humanity, affect, and accessibility. The study showed that the chatbots which are part of Facebook Messenger are still far away from becoming an AI teaching assistant tool.

Okonkwo and Ade-Ibijola (2021) reviewed 53 papers systematically focused on the application of chatbot in education. In the review process, they had four research questions, and put an effort to answer the questions. The questions focused on the recent status of the research for chatbots in education, the benefits of using chatbots in this domain, the facing challenges in implementation, the future direction of education, and the obtained benefits of using chatbots. To this end, they collected data by crawling online article archives, such as IEEE and Scopus, and extracted the required information to address the questions. They defined five quality evaluation metrics to compare the papers. The papers in the domain of using chatbots for education were classified into five categories based on their topics, including:

a) Teaching and learning (66%);
b) Research and development (19%);
c) Assessment (6%);
d) Administrative tasks in education (5%);
e) Advisory to make decisions on academic activities (4%).

The primary benefits of using chatbots in education were as follows:

a) Integration of the specific contents from different sources by the instructor;
b) Keeping students motivated and engaged in using online platforms;
c) Quick access of chatbots to educational information;
d) Allowing multiple users;
e) Immediate assistance of chatbots by receiving rapid replies.

The challenges of using chatbots for education included the following:

a) Ethical issues for user privacy, personalization, and security;
b) Evaluation issues such as the engagement of the chatbot in their learning activities along with the significant evaluation in a large population;
c) User attitude issue for adaptation of the software based on the user's behavioral intention;
d) Programming issue of a chatbot to use NLP techniques and have an appropriate answer to the question at a proper time;
e) Supervision and maintenance issues for correct input and output, checking system's performance based on the planned objectives, and keeping the databases and KBs updated.

For the future direction of chatbots, the following issues were mentioned:

a) Technical advancements to cover challenges and to improve the models;
b) Developing ethical principles;
c) Usability testing of chatbots for the learning abilities of the students.

Wollny et al. (2021) also did another systematic review of chatbots in education. In this review, among 2678 publications on chatbots, 74 papers focused on the application of chatbots in education. The papers were selected to be reviewed. In this review, five major questions were asked:

a) The objectives that are taken into consideration in the implementation process of chatbots, including skill improvement, the efficiency of education, and students' motivation;
b) The pedagogical role of chatbots, including a supporting learning role, an assisting role, and a mentoring role;
c) The application scenarios for mentoring students, including the mentoring method and topic;
d) Adaptability of chatbots for personalization, including student discussions, talking to the chatbot, self-assessment and providing feedback, using user's knowledge level to provide feedback, and system adaptation based on psychological features;
e) The domains of the so-far developed chatbots in education, including learning chatbots, assisting chatbots, and mentoring chatbots.

Pérez et al. (2020) reviewed 80 papers systematically within a framework called Preferred Reporting Items for Systematic Reviews and Meta-Analyses (PRISMA; Moher et al., 2009). PRISMA contains a set of 27 predefined criteria and a four-phase flowchart to help researchers with the systematic review to increase clarity and transparency in the analysis. In this review, five questions were raised:

a) The type of educational environment of chatbots;
b) Their influence on student learning or service improvement;
c) The type of technology used in the chatbots;
d) The usefulness of chatbots to help learners compared to the condition using human tutors;
e) The methods to evaluate the quality of the chatbots.

Kuhail et al. (2022) reviewed 36 papers from 7 dimensions, including the platform that chatbots operate on, the educational field of the chatbots, the role of chatbots when interact with students, the supported interaction styles of the chatbots, the principles used in the chatbots, the method to validate the chatbots, and the challenges to use chatbots in classrooms as a real application. The following results were derived from the papers:

a)   The chatbots are mainly web-based rather than phone-based applications;

b)   They are used to teach computer science, engineering, mathematics, language, and general education.

c)   More than half of the chatbots are used as human teachers to present instructions, to illustrate examples, and to ask questions. In contrast, almost one-third of the chatbots are used as students' learning mates within a learning path. The students who interact with a human teacher obtain more knowledge than the latter approach, where the students are guided through a predefined conversational path.

d)   More than half of the chatbots are flow-based that follow a predetermined learning path. One-third of the chatbots use the pattern-matching method for pre-made responses, and almost one-tenth of the chatbots are AI-powered.

e)   Almost one-third of the chatbots use personalized learning approach, which adapts to the students' learning needs. In contrast, other chatbots use the experimental learning approach, the social dialogue approach, the collaborative learning approach, the affective learning approach, the learning by teaching approach, and the scaffolding approach.

f)   There exist four types of evaluation methods, namely a) the experimental method, when one variable is tested at a time based on a hypothesis (36%), b) the evaluation method, which examines specific parameters without a prior hypothesis (28%), c) using questionnaires (28%), and d) evaluating a small group (8%).

g)   The following challenges are found in the reviewed paper. The main issue concerns the insufficient or inadequate datasets to train the models. The other one addresses to the designing process of the chatbots when students are involved in the development process. Decreasing interest in using such services over time, lack of a mechanism to evaluate the feedback from the user side, and distracting users by external links and popup suggestions are the other challenges.

The other direction of the research field on using chatbots in education is implementing the teaching principles in abstract models. Gonda et al. (2019) evaluated an educational chatbot developed based on the principles for good teaching of university students. Five out of seven principles were implemented in their system. The most challenging part of the development was training the chatbot for responses.

ADVANTAGES AND DISADVANTAGES OF USING CHATBOTS IN EDUCATION

Advantages

There are several advantages using chatbots in education:

- The primary advantages of chatbots in education are playing as intelligent tutors by presenting educational material, stimulating dialogue, and providing feedback to students.
- Chatbots guide in a 24/7 time span (Mageira et al., 2022) which is impossible for human tutors. It is possible to practice language skills at any time with chatbots (Haristiani, 2019; Winkler & Soellner, 2018).
- When it comes to second or foreign language learning, the teachers are overwhelmed with the questions of many students to interact with and give an answer to them. A chatbot can help (Huang et al., 2022) to reduce overwhelmedness.
- Chatbot systems can reduce or diminish the shyness feeling of students during language practice or communication with a human partner (Fryer & Carpenter, 2006).
- Chatbots can improve communication between the learner and the teacher (Sjöström et al., 2018), and provide an individualized learning experience for students (Benotti et al., 2017; Cunningham-Nelson et al., 2019; Okonkwo & Ade-Ibijola, 2021).
- Chatbots can provide broader information about the target language compared with the human partners that might not have more extra knowledge about the language in terms of expressions, and vocabularies (Fryer et al., 2019).
- Experimentally, it has been found out that chatbots can be a significant help to students for memory retention and learning outcomes in comparison with students who use search engines (Abbasi & Kazi, 2014).
- Chatbots are also helpful in a pandemic situation and distance learning, such as COVID-19 pandemic that in late 2019 the disease became spread in almost all countries on the planet, governors decided to lockdown the cities, and social distance was emphasized to control the epidemic.
- Chatbot-based e-learning systems can be a help for students in less privileged areas, and also rural areas, where it is difficult to provide all learning facilities, including libraries, or expert teachers in a specific field. This advantage provides an ideal situation to make educational justice come true.
- Although, according to the transactional distance theory proposed by Moor (1993), there is no psychological and face-to-face interaction between the

tutor and the learner in distance learning, chatbots can reduce the transactional distance problem due to creating a sort of interactive, dialogic status between the learner and the content (Huang et al., 2022).

- Chatbots can bring positive results in learning by increasing the learning rates and intelligent monitoring of the user's performance by checking the log file of a chatbot and finding out the user's weaknesses and problems that had been questioned (Shawar & Atwell, 2007). In this way, the teacher will be aware of the problems, and he will design a teaching material to cover and reduce the students' problems.

Disadvantages

There are general challenges and limitations for chatbots:

- One major challenge is the limitations in existing knowledge-bases (KB) and dialogue-based processing models to analyze a natural language, and to recognize the information need. Because chatbots' KBs, as their brains, are fixed, and they contain the knowledge that is already stored (Carlander-Reuterfelt et al., 2020; Dahiya, 2017; Huang et al., 2018; Krassmann et al., 2019; Leonhardt et al., 2007; Ranoliya et al., 2017). Usually, the KB of a chatbot is domain-specific, such as education, and it is limited to an external source, which is not enough to cover all information needs of a user (Hussain & Athula, 2018). AI-based chatbots (conversational/ collaborative chatbots) can reduce this shortcoming algorithmically.
- Manual development of a chatbot's KB is difficult, time-consuming, and labor-intensive. It requires the knowledge of engineers and experts in the field (Carlander-Reuterfelt et al., 2020; Dahiya, 2017; Ranoliya et al., 2017). Automatic development of the KBs can be a solution (Zhang et al., 2017; Bhatia and Pinto, 2021), but the quality of such a source cannot be guaranteed.
- It is a fact that language and human environment change, and human knowledge extends by passage of time. This means that the developed KBs should not remain static, and developing and updating KBs as the brain of chatbots should be considered as an ongoing process.
- Difficulty of the systems in dealing with unknown sentences (Neves et al., 2006) and their inability to answer complex or unexpected questions (Kleoniki et al., 2012) are other disadvantages of chatbots. The lack of correct understanding of the question might result in an inappropriate answer, and it may make the user upset and reduce his interest in further using of the chatbots. However, AI-based chatbots can reduce the effect of these problems on performance and quality.

- To be informative, chatbots might provide additional information, such as links and popup messages (Qin et al., 2020), that is relevant to the topic, but not necessary. This distracts users from the necessary information (Inostroza et al., 2012; Kuhail et al., 2022) and confuses them by adding more questions and uncertainties.
- Another challenge of chatbots is related to social media harms. Chatbots can be used to spread rumors and misinformation, or attack people for their posted thoughts and opinions (Radziwill & Benton, 2017).

CHATBOT ARCHITECTURE AND TECHNIQUES USED IN EDUCATION

Edwards and Wegerif (1994: 143) proposed a three-part information exchange structure in the talks in the classroom: a) initiation, b) response, and c) feedback. Wegerif (2004) added one more element to this structure: the collaborative discussion. The chatbots developed for educational applications should simulate the classroom information extended exchange structure, including initiation, response, feedback, and discussion. Strijbos et al. (2004) introduced two views on designing the instruction of the courses for group-based learning: One view, which is the casual design, uses the knowledge world to design the required learning environment of a determined skill for a learner. In this view, the outcome and the learning goals are important. The other view, which is the probabilistic design, uses the learning world to design the required learning environment of either a determined skill, partial skill, or unforeseen skill. In this view, the learning process is important, and no attention is given to the predefined goals. While using chatbots in education, either of the views can be implemented; but the probabilistic design is preferred.

Figure 2 illustrates the general abstract architecture of a chatbot. As it can be seen, chatbots contain two major components: a) front-end; and b) back-end. The front-end is, in fact, the user interface that makes it possible for the user to interact with the system, either via a web page, or an application. Front-end has a graphical view, and it should be designed in such a way that it makes the user enthusiastic about engaging to use the tool. The main challenge of a chatbot concerns the back-end, where processing input and a response to the query is provided. The back-end contains four main modules: a) NLP components, b) Databases (DBs), c) KBs, and d) the Natural Language Generation (NLG) components. The modules are described in the following.

Back-end

NLP Components

The NLP component contains specific algorithms to process language, and to provide the required information used in the NLG module and query search in DBs and KBs. NLP techniques construct the core of the system. The techniques include the models trained by different corpora. According to Adams Becker et al. (2017) who said that voiced commands are popular among smartphone users, the speech processing techniques can be used in chatbots to increase the interaction between the chatbot and students in real applications. To this end, two types of speech processing methods are required, including speech recognition that takes the speech of the user as a query and converts it into a text, and speech synthesis that converts the text-based query results into a normal speech as the output of the chatbot.

After converting the sound data format into a text data format, text-processing algorithms are used to provide a deep language understanding. The basic NLP techniques used for text processing include recognizing the named entities in the queries, sentiment analysis of the query, and information extraction from the query.

It is essential to recognize the intent of the user's query. Because it has a direct influence on finding the in-domain, relevant response to the user's query. For instance, in the domain of education, it is vital to recognize the user's intent correctly: whether he asks questions about the rules and regulations at a school, in a class, a semester, or course calendar, or he asks content questions about a course (Cunningham-Nelson et al., 2019, pp. 299–306), such as language learning, literature, chemistry, physics, etc., questions and answers related to the assignments (Sinha et al., 2020), frequently asked questions related to university (Ranoliya et al., 2017), evaluation criteria (Benotti et al., 2017; Durall & Kapros, 2020), deadlines for assignment, education advice (Ismail & Ade-Ibijola, 2019), aiding for campus path direction of visitors for locating venues (Mabunda & Ade-Ibijola, 2019), providing services for administrative and learning support (Hien et al., 2018, pp. 69–76; Rohrig and Heβ, 2019), or academic advising (Chun Ho et al., 2018).

The slot-filling component is primarily used in pattern-based responses, where the user asks a question, and the chatbot extracts the required information from the user's query and uses the information to fill up a pattern-based response. In Example (1), the user introduces himself, and then the chatbot uses the name in the response. In this example, the named entity recognition component recognizes the entity, say Daniel, and this information is used to fill in the pattern "Hello, NAME.".

(1) **Human**: *My name is Daniel.*

Figure 2. The general architecture of a chatbot

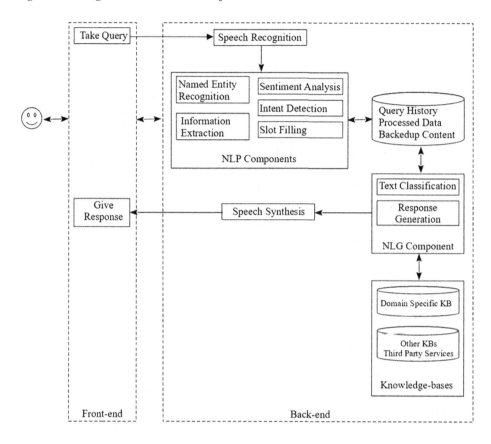

Chatbot*: Hello, Daniel.*

Having all the processed information from the user's query, since the user may ask repeated questions, it is needed to back up the content transformed in the chatbot conversation. The backup retrieves the answer from the frequently asked questions more quickly than searching the data.

Database

There are two types of data sources to be used in chatbots: one is a DB, and the other one is a KB. A DB stores the user's queries and the processed queries. Moreover, the content, i.e., both the queries and the responses, are stored in the database. This information is useful when a teacher checks the backup of the chatbot to find what the problems questioned by the users are, and what the existing difficulties of the course are to improve the syllabus of the course or the teaching methodology.

Knowledge-base

To respond a query in a domain, a chatbot requires a KB. This KB includes almost all relevant information related to a domain. The advantage of AI-based chatbots to rule-based (pattern-based/ retrieval-based) chatbots is that if the system sees a new pattern and cannot find the response from the already stored questions and answers, it finds the most relevant response from the data. This new approach has made the chatbots more robust than the rule-based chatbots. However, it is possible to have out-of-domain queries. To make chatbots more robust, they should have access to other KBs, or other services, such as discussion forums, or API of other services including online libraries and archives.

NLG Components

After applying NLP techniques to the user's query and understanding the information needed, it is required that the chatbot provides an answer to the user. This component is the core of a chatbot. To this end, two NLG techniques can be used: a) using text classification technique to find the most relevant answer from the KB, either in-domain or out-of-domain KBs, b) generating a response when the system is faced with a question that cannot find similar questions, and an answer should be generated. There are two well-known response generation methods: a) template-base, which selects a diverse response from a set of predefined patterns, such as "I do not know." "What do you mean?", or "Please give more explanation!", b) generating a new sentence using a Generative Pre-trained Transformer (GPT) as an autoregressive language model that uses deep learning to generate human-like texts (Brown et al., 2020; Radford et al., 2018).

To return the result of the NLG component to the user, a speech synthesis system can convert the text into speech to make the interaction complete between the system and the user. In addition, the result can also be transformed through text messaging.

Front-end

A multi-purpose chatbot in education requires properties that should be taken into consideration. The user interface of the chatbot should be simple but enthusiastic, and it should keep the users engaged in using the application (Fadhil and Schiavo, 2019). Chatbots that use machine learning methods are preferred over those that search KBs (Abbasi & Kazi, 2014). Using backups from the users' activities, the users' information, and the log file of the chatbot can help teachers to find the problems, and redesign the course syllables (Debnath & Agarwal, 2020).

Instead of developing chatbots from scratch, it is possible to use already-built chatbots, such as Mitsuku, which was used by Shin et al. (2021). Pandorabots is an online hosting platform for developing chatbots. To make it user-friendly, an AIML has been built by Wallace (2001) to work as the brain of the chatbot. AIML is a derivative of XML[16] that enables users to add the required KB to the chatbot (Ross, 2018: 1-2). AIML contains linguistic patterns that are used in daily conversations. Figure 3 represents the AIML of Example (1).[17] The tag <category> in this figure determines the basic unit of knowledge. This tag always contains two other tags, one as the input, called <pattern>, and the other one as the response, called <template>. The <star/> is a variable that can be replaced with any string. Synonymous patterns, such as Hi, Hi there, Hello, and so on, are also defined in AIML.

Figure 3. A simple AIML pattern

```
<category>
  <pattern>MY NAME IS *</pattern>
  <template>Hello, <star/>.</ template>
</category>
```

To develop a chatbot in the Pandorabots platform, it is required to determine a relationship between three entities: a) the chatbot to make the interaction between human and machine possible; b) the botmaster who creates, develops, and maintains the code and the content to develop the chatbot; and c) the client that is the person who interacts with the chatbot. In the platform, log files are recorded for reviewing the chats. The platform contains two pre-processing modules for input data: a) normalizing the data, including replacing written forms in chats, such as "ganna" to "going to", or replacing emojis, such as ":-(" to "SAD", expanding contractions, such as "hasn't" to "has not", and removing extra spaces; b) sentence splitting to split a string into sentences. Sometimes it is possible that a chatbot cannot respond to a query. It is possible to select responses concerning the input patterns randomly. Each random response can be stored in the tag <random>.

EVALUATION METRICS

Chatbots can be evaluated quantitatively (objective evaluation) or qualitatively (subjective evaluation). For objective evaluation, it is possible to evaluate the linguistic quality of the chatbots (Vetter, 2002), syntactically, and/or semantically (Coniam, 2014). Chatbots can be considered as question-answering systems, and the standard metrics, such as precision, recall, and F-measure, can be used to evaluate the performance (Goh et al., 2007). If the chatbot user is simulated, then it is possible to use these basic evaluation metrics (Mondal et al., 2018).

Other statistical metrics with linguistic properties can be used, such as semantic similarity by calculating cosine similarity between the user's query and the chatbot response, average word coherence, extreme word coherence, greedy word coherence between the user's query and the chatbot response, the question query score for cases that the chatbot asks questions. The number of words that users use to give feedback to the chatbot can also be considered as a metric (Ghandeharioun et al., 2019). Shum et al. (2018) used the number of conversation turns per session as a metric to evaluate the lengthy maintenance of the chatbot on a specific topic. Przegalinska et al. (2019) proposed a metric to measure the quality of a chatbot by using the length and the structure of the conversation.

For subjective evaluation, the ISO 9241 concept of 'usability' can be referred which is "the effectiveness, efficiency, and satisfaction with which specified users achieve specified goals in particular environments" (Abran et al., 2003). Effectiveness refers to the accuracy and completeness with which users achieve their specified goals; efficiency refers to how well the resources are benefited to achieve the goals; and satisfaction refers to how well customers are satisfied with the developed tool. These metrics are divided into two groups at a macro level: a) effectiveness and efficiency fall more on the service provider side; and b) satisfaction falls on the user side.

According to the ISO 9241 concept, Shawar and Atwell (2007) proposed the metrics, such as dialog efficiency, dialog quality, and user satisfaction, for evaluating chatbots. Radziwill and Benton (2017) argued that measuring the quality of a chatbot can be objective without considering the type of the chatbot. However, the subjective metrics, such as performance, functionality, and efficiency of chatbots, should be evaluated based on the ISO 9241 concept.

Perception of learning, providing correct or incorrect responses, and the time element in the system can be defined as metrics for quality assessment of chatbots (Kaleem et al., 2016).

Gonda et al. (2019) qualified educational chatbots based on seven principles for good teaching, which are related to the contact between students and the teacher, the cooperation among students, the students' activities in the classroom, providing quick feedback through the tool, the spent time on the tasks, communication, and paying attention to different talents and learning methods.

Kuhail et al. (2022) summarized the evaluation metrics into four categories, including a) the experimental metric when one variable is tested at a time, and the rest variables are remained unchanged; b) the evaluation study that provides insights into specific parameters without an existing prior hypothesis to prove; c) the collected data through questionnaires designed for a specific set of questions; and d) evaluating the characteristics of focus groups when it is impossible to examine all groups.

Mageira et al. (2022) mentioned two general evaluation methods in the experiments related to chatbots: one is chatbot-based learning, and the other one is ICT[18]-based learning. In the chatbot-based learning approach, the participants in the experiments are divided into the control and the experimental groups; and a questionnaire is assigned to them. The experimental group interacts with a chatbot, while the control group does not have access to the chatbot. In this approach, statistical metrics, such as mean, standard deviation, perplexity, BLEU score, *t*-test, Chi-square test, Pearson correlation coefficient, ANOVA test, ANCOVA test, and Wilcoxon test, can be used (Caldarini et al., 2022; Ghandeharioun et al., 2019; Hwang & Chang, 2021; Pears et al., 2021; Vanichvasin, 2021). For the ICT-based learning approach, Google Forms[19] and Padlet[20] are used to create questionnaires.

AVAILABLE CHATBOT TOOLS AND SYSTEMS IN EDUCATION

The task-specific chatbots used in education are divided into two major groups. The first group is commercial. There are various commercial chatbots. The four top chatbots used for higher education are as follows:

- Ivy.ai[21] is used as a student help desk, and it supports 105 languages;
- Mongoose[22] is a text messaging chatbot, and it is used by students, parents, and alumni;
- HubSpot[23] is a web-based chatbot builder, and it is used on the website of schools;
- GeckoEngage[24] is an engagement platform to connect students and staff.

The other group of chatbots is research-based, and they are developed in academia. We list some of the developed systems in this group. One interesting point about the developed chatbots of this group is that some of them are developed for a specific course in different fields, from humanities to engineering, or a specific subject of a course, which means their KBs are too limited. The tools developed in academia are as follows:

- Autotutor: Graesser et al. (2001; 2005) developed Autotutor, which is a conversational AI-based learning chatbot to enhance learners' engagement.
- Freudbot[25]: Heller et al. (2005) developed the Freudbot used as a teaching and learning tool for the educational purposes of students in psychology. The system teaches students the theories, concepts, and biographies of Freud.
- Cleverbot[26]: Carpenter developed this chatbot used in language learning (Fryer and Carpenter, 2006).
- CLIVE: Zakos and Capper (2008) developed a conversational AI-based language practice chatbot that can switch between the world's major languages.
- CSIEC[27]: Jia (2009) developed CSIEC for foreign language learning. The system generates responses based on the user's input, context, user and personality knowledge, common-sense knowledge, and inference knowledge
- Confucius: Hsieh (2011) developed Confucius as an assistive supplement in classrooms.
- NDLtutor: Suleman et al. (2016) developed the NDLtutor chatbot to improve students' engagement in classrooms.
- Jill Watson[28]: Jill Watson chatbot has been the first AI-based chatbot developed at Georgia University for the Computer Science course. The chatbot motivated students in the course and encouraged them to use the chatbot for other courses.
- Chatbot: Benotti et al. (2017) developed Chatbot as an educational chatbot for studying computer science.
- StudyBuddy and SmarterChild: Molnar and Szuts (2018) developed the two chatbots for learning an informal language.
- EASElective: Chun Ho et al. (2018) developed EASElective as an advising chatbot to guide students to select the elective courses in their education.
- Xbot: Auccahuasi et al. (2019) developed a chatbot for high school students to improve skills, including mathematics, programming, and logic.
- Gengobot: Haristiani et al. (2019) developed a chatbot for learning Japanese. The chatbot gives explanations and meanings based on the grammar and dictionary.
- The BookBuddy system: Ruan et al. (2019) developed a chatbot integrated from three other chatbots. The chatbots help children to select the book, which is appropriate for their English language level. It also helps students to comprehend readings by answering vocabulary questions. Moreover, it converses with the children to provide individualized feedback.

- Mondly and Andy English Bot: Lee et al. (2020) developed the two chatbots that propose several possible responses to the learners, and the learners can choose the most relevant response.
- Alpha: Abdelhamid and Katz (2020) developed Alpha as an intelligent teaching assistant chatbot used for first-year engineering students.
- CapacitaBOT: Mateos-Sanchez et al. (2022) developed CapacitaBOT as a mobile application used for people with intellectual disabilities. This application helps them with their social skills.
- AssassaraBot: Mageira et al. (2022) developed AssassaraBot to assist students with their content and language learning objectives of two languages, including English and French.

The existing chatbots used in education can be divided into three main categories, summarized in Table 2. They are used as a) teaching assistant tools to enhance teaching, b) a tutor to teach a course, or c) an assistive tool for language learning, either for learning a language skill or linguistic knowledge.

CONCLUSION AND THE FUTURE DIRECTIONS

In this chapter, we studied the main motivations for using chatbots in education and their influence on education. We described the evolution timeline of chatbots and their widespread applications. One application of chatbots was in the domain of education. Reviewing the papers, three general applications of chatbots in education were found, either for language learning, teaching a course, or assistive for educational purposes. We further described the advantages and disadvantages of using chatbots in education. We proposed the general architecture of chatbots, and described the components of the model. Moreover, the evaluation metrics were introduced.

One finding shared among the research studies is the positive enhancement of using chatbots in education, especially in the early steps. Increasing the knowledge of users at higher levels of education might make the users annoyed and unsatisfied, due to the wrong answers provided in some cases. The future of using chatbots in education may have different directions:

- Using advanced neural network-based models, such as using GPT or transformer models, instead of using traditional methods in chatbots, can increase the performance of the chatbots developed both in industry and academia.

Table 2. Categorizing chatbots in education based on their functionalities

Category	Tool	Resource	Course
Teaching Assistant	Autotutor	Graesser et al. (2001; 2005)	
	Confucius	Hsieh (2011)	
	NDLtutor	Suleman et al. (2016)	
	EASElective	Chun Ho et al. (2018)	
	Alpha	Abdelhamid and Katz (2020)	
	CapacitaBOT	Mateos-Sanchez et al. (2022)	
Teaching a Course	Freudbot	Heller et al. (2005)	psychology
	Jill Watson	Georgia University	computer science
	Chatbot	Benotti et al. (2017)	computer science
	Xbot	Auccahuasi et al. (2019)	mathematics, programming, and logic
Language Learning	Cleverbot	R. Carpenter	
	CLIVE	Zakos and Capper (2008)	
	CSIEC	Jia (2009)	
	StudyBuddy	Molnar and Szuts (2018)	
	SmarterChild	Molnar and Szuts (2018)	
	Gengobot	Haristiani et al. (2019)	Japanese
	The BookBuddy system	Ruan et al. (2019)	English
	Mondly	Lee et al. (2020)	English
	Andy English Bot	Lee et al. (2020)	English
	AssassaraBot	Mageira et al. (2022)	English and French

- Recent development of AI-powered chatbots increased both the performance of the tools and the predictability of the users' actions. This provides a path for future works by advanced personalized chatbots to fit them to the users' requirements

- To personalize AI-powered chatbots, a large amount of personal information is collected based on the users' actions and behavior. This obliges information security. As a result, data security will be a big challenge in the future, and specific attention is required.

- Enriching the models with NLP techniques is another direction for future works. This helps chatbots to understand the users' requests better, and to answer the users' queries more accurately to increase user satisfaction. The consequence of this satisfaction is increasing the motivation and demand to use the tool, and achieving learning effectiveness.

- The evaluation metrics need to be more comprehensive to evaluate the software quality, interface design, learning success, and technology acceptance.
- To make the applications of chatbots widespread, it is required to propose more general and comprehensive models across domains. This means the challenge of the data sparsity problem to train models has to be resolved, and a general system architecture has to be proposed.
- Machinery methods should be used to develop KBs with reliable quality. The so-far developed KBs are built manually, which is labor-intensive and time-consuming, and updating the KBs intensifies the costs and efforts. Manual development of a KB for each lesson of a course magnifies the efforts, and it becomes very time-consuming. Therefore, it is required to rely more on machinery methods in developing a KB. This need will emerge when chatbots are used widespread.
- Innovations and emerging new technologies will open up a new direction to use better technology for human's life. Therefore, new processing models can be proposed to achieve further improvements in the performance of the chatbots.
- To make chatbots popular, an efficient process is required through speeding up the response time, 24/7 availability to answer questions, or clarify the questions.
- Increasing the performance of chatbots and their 24/7 availability bring chatbots into practice to improve the learning experience. This results in economic benefits. Because highly performing chatbots can help human resources and it can reduce employment costs. Its consequence is using chatbots more often than expected in the near future.
- To increase the efficiency of chatbots, the repeated questions should be quickly answered, feedback should be provided, and they should support students who missed one or more lessons.
- Usability of chatbots in education has already been studied. These studies have been done mostly from the technology point of view. The impact of using chatbots on students and teachers can be further studied in the future from the humanities point of view.

ACKNOWLEDGEMENT

Conflict of Interest

The authors of this publication declare there is no conflict of interest.

Funding Agency

This research received no specific grant from any funding agency in the public, commercial, or not-for-profit sectors.

REFERENCES

Abbasi, S., & Kazi, H. (2014). Measuring effectiveness of learning chatbot systems on student's learning outcome and memory retention. *Asian Journal of Applied Science and Engineering*, *3*(7), 57–66. doi:10.15590/ajase/2014/v3i7/53576

Abdelhamid, S., & Katz, A. (2020). Using chatbots as smart teaching assistants for first-year engineering students. In *Conference on First-Year Engineering Experience*. Washington DC, USA.

Abran, A., Khelifi, A., Suryn, W., & Seffah, A. (2003). Consolidating the ISO usability models. In *Proceedings of 11th International Software Quality Management Conference*, (pp. 23-25). Semantic Scholar.

Adams Becker, S., Cummins, M., Davis, A., Freeman, A., Hall Giesinger, C., & Ananthanarayanan, V. (2017). *NMC Horizon Report: 2017 Higher Education Edition*. The New Media Consortium.

Athota, L., Shukla, V. K., Pandey, N., & Rana, A. (2020). Chatbot for healthcare system using artificial intelligence. In *Proceedings of the 8th International Conference on Reliability, Infocom Technologies and Optimization (Trends and Future Directions)*, (pp. 619-622). IEEE. 10.1109/ICRITO48877.2020.9197833

Auccahuasi, W., Santiago, G. B., Núñez, E. O., & Sernaque, F. (2019) Interactive online tool as an instrument for learning mathematics through programming techniques, aimed at high school students. In *ICIT 2018: 6th International Conference on Information Technology: IoT and Smart City*, New York, NY, USA.

Benotti, L., Martinez, M. C., & Schapachnik, F. (2017). A tool for introducing computer science with automatic formative assessment. *IEEE Transactions on Learning Technologies*, *11*(2), 179–192. doi:10.1109/TLT.2017.2682084

Bhatia, A., & Pinto, A. (2021). Automated construction of knowledge-bases for safety critical applications: Challenges and opportunities. In *Proceedings of the AAAI 2021 Spring Symposium on Combining Machine Learning and Knowledge Engineering*. Stanford University.

Brooks, D. C., & Pomerantz, J. (2017). ECAR Study of Undergraduate Students and Information Technology, Research Report. ECAR.

Brown, T. B., Mann, B., Ryder, N., Subbiah, M., Kaplan, J., Dhariwal, P., Neelakantan, A., Shyam, P., Sastry, G., Askell, A., Agarwal, S., Herbert-Voss, A., Krueger, G., Henighan, T., Child, R., Ramesh, A., Ziegler, D. M., Wu, J., Winter, C., & Amodei, D. (2020). Language models are few-shot learners. In *Proceedings of the 34th International Conference on Neural Information Processing Systems*, (pp: 1877–1901). Curran Associates Inc.

Caldarini, G., Jaf, S., & McGarry, K. (2022). A literature survey of recent advances in chatbots. *Information (Basel)*, *13*(1), 41. doi:10.3390/info13010041

Carlander-Reuterfelt, D., Carrera, A., Iglesias, C. A., Araque, O., Sanchez Rada, J. F. S., & Munoz, S. (2020). JAICOB: A data science chatbot. *IEEE Access: Practical Innovations, Open Solutions*, *8*, 180671–180680. doi:10.1109/ACCESS.2020.3024795

Cheng, X., Zhang, X., Yang, B., & Fu, Y. (2022). An investigation on trust in AI-enabled collaboration: Application of AI-Driven chatbot in accommodation-based sharing economy. *Electronic Commerce Research and Applications*, *54*, 101164. doi:10.1016/j.elerap.2022.101164 PMID:35968256

Chun Ho, C., Lee, H. L., Lo, W. K., & Lui, K. F. A. (2018). Developing a chatbot for college student program advisement. In *2018 IEEE International Symposium on Educational Technology*, (pp: 62-56). IEEE.

Colace, F., De Santo, M., Lombardi, M., Pascale, F., & Pietrosanto, A. (2018). Chatbot for e-learning: A case of study. *International Journal of Mechanical Engineering and Robotics Research*, *7*(5), 528–533. doi:10.18178/ijmerr.7.5.528-533

Coniam, D. (2014). The linguistic accuracy of chatbots: Usability from an ESL perspective. *Text & Talk*, *34*(5), 545–567. doi:10.1515/text-2014-0018

Crisseyb, R., Brechemiera, D., Balardya, L., & Nourhashemi, F. (2019). A smartphone chatbot application to optimize monitoring of older patients with cancer. *International Journal of Medical Informatics*, *128*, 18–23. doi:10.1016/j.ijmedinf.2019.05.013 PMID:31160007

Cunningham-Nelson, S., Boles, W., Trouton, L., & Margerison, E. (2019). A review of chatbots in education: Practical steps forward. In *Proceedings of the 30th Annual Conference for the Australasian Association for Engineering Education: Educators Becoming Agents of Change: Innovate, Integrate, Motivate*, (pp: 299-306). AAEE.

Dahiya, M. (2017). A tool of conversation: Chatbot. *International Journal on Computer Science and Engineering*, 5(5), 158–161.

Danescu-Niculescu-Mizil, C., & Lee, L. (2011). Chameleons in imagined conversations: A new approach to understanding coordination of linguistic style in dialogs. In *Proceedings of the 2nd Workshop on Cognitive Modeling and Computational Linguistics*. ACL.

Debnath, B., & Agarwal, A. (2020). A framework to implement AI-integrated chatbot in educational institutes. *Journal of Student Research Fourth Middle East College Student Research Conference*.

Deveci Topal, A., Dilek Eren, C., & Kolburan Geçer, A. (2021). Chatbot application in a 5th grade science course. *Education and Information Technologies*, *26*(5), 6241–6265. doi:10.100710639-021-10627-8 PMID:34177344

Dharmapuri, C. M., Agarwal, A., Anwer, F., & Mahor, J. (2022). AI Chatbot: Application in psychiatric treatment and suicide prevention. *International Mobile and Embedded Technology Conference*. IEEE. 10.1109/MECON53876.2022.9752126

Dharwadkar, R., & Deshpande, N. A. (2018). A medical ChatBot. *International Journal of Computer Trends and Technology*, *60*(1), 41–45. doi:10.14445/22312803/IJCTT-V60P106

Durall, E., & Kapros, E. (2020). Co-design for a competency self-assessment chatbot and survey in science education. In P. Zaphiris & A. Ioannou (Eds.), Lecture Notes in Computer Science: Vol. 12206. *Learning and Collaboration Technologies. Human and Technology Ecosystems* (pp. 13–24). Springer. doi:10.1007/978-3-030-50506-6_2

Duval, E., & Verbert, K. (2012). Learning analytics. *Eleed, 8*(1).

Edwards, A., & Westgate, D. (1994). *Investigating Classroom Talk*. Falmer Press.

Eren, B. A. (2021). Determinants of customer satisfaction in chatbot use: Evidence from a banking application in Turkey. *International Journal of Bank Marketing*, *39*(2), 294–311. doi:10.1108/IJBM-02-2020-0056

Essel, H. B., Vlachopoulos, D., Tachie-Menson, A., Johnson, E. E., & Baah, P. K. (2022). The impact of a virtual teaching assistant (chatbot) on students' learning in Ghanaian higher education. *International Journal of Educational Technology in Higher Education*, *19*(1), 57. doi:10.118641239-022-00362-6

Fadhil, A. (2018). *Can a chatbot determine my diet? Addressing challenges of chatbot application for meal recommendation*. Cornell University.

Fadhil, A., & Gabrielli, S. (2017). Addressing challenges in promoting healthy lifestyles: The AI-chatbot approach. In *Proceedings of the 11th EAI International Conference on Pervasive Computing Technologies for Healthcare*, (pp: 261–265). ACM. 10.1145/3154862.3154914

Fadhil, A., & Schiavo, G. (2019). *Designing for Health Chatbots*. Cornell University. https://arxiv.org/abs/1902.09022

Fryer, L. K., & Carpenter, R. (2006). Bots as language learning tools. *Language Learning & Technology, 10*(3), 8–14.

Fryer, L. K., Nakao, K., & Thompson, A. (2019). Chatbot learning partners: Connecting learning experiences, interest and competence. *Computers in Human Behavior, 93*, 279–289. doi:10.1016/j.chb.2018.12.023

Ghandeharioun, A., Shen, J. H., Jaques, N., Ferguson, C., Jones, N., Lapedriza, A., & Picard, R. (2019). *Approximating interactive human evaluation with self-play for open-domain dialog systems*. In *33rd Conference on Neural Information Processing Systems*, Vancouver, Canada.

Godfrey, J., Holliman, E., & McDaniel, J. (1992). SWITCHBOARD: Telephone speech corpus for research and development. In *Proceedings of the 1992 IEEE International Conference on Acoustics, Speech, and Signal Processing*, (pp. 517-520). IEEE. 10.1109/ICASSP.1992.225858

Goh, O. S., Ardil, C., Wong, W., & Fung, C. C. (2007). A black-box approach for response quality evaluation of conversational agent systems. *International Journal of Computational Intelligence, 3*(3), 195–203.

Gonda, D. E., Luo, J., Wong, Y., & Lei, C. (2019). Evaluation of developing educational chatbots based on the seven principles for good teaching. In *Proceedings of the 2018 IEEE International Conference on Teaching, Assessment, and Learning for Engineering*, (pp: 446-453). IEEE.

Graesser, A. C., Chipman, P., Haynes, B., & Olney, A. (2005). AutoTutor: An intelligent tutoring system with mixed-initiative dialogue. *IEEE Transactions on Education, 48*(4), 612–618. doi:10.1109/TE.2005.856149

Graesser, A. C., VanLehn, K., Rose, C. P., Jordan, P. W., & Harter, D. (2001). Intelligent tutoring systems with conversational dialogue. *AI Magazine, 22*(4), 39–51.

Greller, W., & Drachsler, H. (2012). Translating learning into Numbers: A generic framework for learning analytics. *Journal of Educational Technology & Society, 15*(3), 42–57.

Haristiani, N. (2019). Artificial intelligence (AI) chatbots as language learning medium: An inquiry. *Journal of Physics: Conference Series, 1387*(1), 2020. doi:10.1088/1742-6596/1387/1/012020

Haristiani, N., Danuwijaya, A. A., Rifai, M. M., & Sarila, H. (2019). Gengobot: A chatbot-based grammar application on mobile instant messaging as language learning medium. *Journal of Engineering Science and Technology, 14,* 3158–3173.

Haristiani, N., & Rifai, M. M. (2021). Chatbot-based application development and implementation as an autonomous language learning medium. *Indonesian Journal of Science & Technology, 6*(3), 561–576. doi:10.17509/ijost.v6i3.39150

He, T., Liu, J., Cho, K., Ott, M., Liu, B., Glass, J., & Peng, F. (2021). Analyzing the forgetting problem in the Pretrain-Finetuning of dialogue response models. In *Proceedings of the 16th Conference of the European Chapter of the Association for Computational Linguistics*, (pp. 1121-1133). Association for Computational Linguistics. 10.18653/v1/2021.eacl-main.95

Heller, B., Proctor, M., Mah, D., Jewell, L., & Cheung, B. (2005). Freudbot: An investigation of chatbot technology in distance education. In Proceedings of EdMedia + Innovate Learning. Association for the Advancement of Computing in Education (AACE).

Heo, M., & Lee, K. J. (2018). Chatbot as a new business communication tool: The case of Naver TalkTalk. *Business Communication Research and Practice, 1*(1), 41–45. doi:10.22682/bcrp.2018.1.1.41

Hien, H. T., Cuong, P.-N., Nam, L. N. H., Nhung, H. L. T. K., & Thang, L. D. (2018). Intelligent assistants in higher-education environments: The FITebot, a chatbot for administrative and learning support. In *Proceedings of the 9th International Symposium on Information and Communication Technology*, (pp. 69–76). ACM. 10.1145/3287921.3287937

Hsieh, S. W. (2011). Effects of cognitive styles on an MSN virtual learning companion system as an adjunct to classroom instructions. *Journal of Educational Technology & Society, 14,* 161–174.

Huang, J., Zhou, M., & Yang, D. (2018). *Exctracting chatbot knowledge from online discussion forums.* In 20th International Joint Conference on Artificial Intelligence, Hydera-bad, India.

Huang, W., Hew, K. F., & Fryer, L. K. (2022). Chatbots for language learning - Are they really useful? A systematic review of chatbot-supported language learning. *Journal of Computer Assisted Learning, 38*(1), 237–257. doi:10.1111/jcal.12610

Hussain, S., & Athula, G. (2018). Extending a conventional chatbot knowledge base to external knowledge source and introducing user based sessions for diabetes education. In *Proceedings of the 32nd International Conference on Advanced Information Networking and Applications Workshops*, (pp. 698-703). IEEE. 10.1109/WAINA.2018.00170

Hwang, G. J., & Chang, C. Y. (2021). A review of opportunities and challenges of chatbots in education. [Routledge.]. *Interactive Learning Environments*, 1952615. doi:10.1080/10494820.2021.1952615

Inostroza, R., Rusu, C., Roncagliolo, S., Jimenez, C., & Rusu, V. (2012). Usability heuristics for touchscreen-based mobile devices. In *2012 9th International Conference on Information Technology-New Generations*, Las Vegas, NV, USA, pp. 662–667. 10.1109/ITNG.2012.134

Ismail, M., & Ade-Ibijola, A. (2019). Lecturer's apprentice: A chatbot for assisting novice programmers. In *Proceedings of 2019 IEEE International Multidisciplinary Information Technology and Engineering Conference*, (pp. 1-8). IEEE. 10.1109/IMITEC45504.2019.9015857

Jia, J. (2003). *The study of the application of a keywords based chatbot system on the teaching of foreign languages*. Cornell University.

Jia, J. (2004). *The study of the application of a web-based chatbot system on the teaching of foreign languages*. In the Society for Information Technology & Teacher Education International Conference, Atlanta, GA, USA.

Jia, J. (2009). CSIEC: A computer assisted English learning chatbot based on textual knowledge and reasoning. *Knowledge-Based Systems*, 22(4), 249–255. doi:10.1016/j.knosys.2008.09.001

Jurafsky, D., & Martin, J. (2021). Speech and language processing (3rd ed.). Stanford Press. https://web.stanford.edu/~jurafsky/slp3/

Kaleem, M., Alobadi, O., O'Shea, J., & Crockett, K. (2016). *Framework for the formulation of metrics for conversational agent evaluation*. In RE-WOCHAT: Workshop on Collecting and Generating Resources for Chatbots and Conversational Agents-Development and Evaluation Workshop, Portorož, Slovenia.

Kleoniki, A., Magkitouka, N., Tegos, S., & Demetriadis, S. (2012). Conversational agents in education: Using MentorChat to support students' dialogue. In *8th Pan-Hellenic Conference with International Participation "Information and Communication Technologies in Education"*, Volos, Greece.

Ko, M. C., & Lin, Z. H. (2018). CardBot: A chatbot for business card management. In *Proceedings of the 23rd International Conference on Intelligent User Interfaces Companion*, (pp: 1–2). ACM. 10.1145/3180308.3180313

Krassmann, A. L., Flach, J. M., Grando, A. R. C. D. S., Tarouco, L. M. R., & Bercht, M. (2019). A process for extracting knowledge base for chatbots from text corpora. In *IEEE Global Engineering Education Conference*, (pp. 322-329). IEEE. 10.1109/EDUCON.2019.8725064

Kuhail, M. A., Alturki, N., Alramlawi, S., & Alhejori, K. (2022). Interacting with educational chatbots: A systematic review. *Education and Information Technologies*. doi:10.100710639-022-11177-3

Lee, J. H., Yang, H., Shin, D., & Kim, H. (2020). Chatbots. *ELT Journal, 74*(3), 338–344. doi:10.1093/elt/ccaa035

Lee, J. Y., & Hwang, Y. (2022). A meta-analysis of the effects of using AI chatbots in Korean EFL education. *Studies in English Language & Literature, 48*(1), 213–243. doi:10.21087/nsell.2022.11.83.213

Leonhardt, M., Tarouco, L. M. R., Vicari, R., Santos, E. R., & Da Silva, M. D. S. (2007). Using chatbots for network management training through problem-based oriented education. In *Proceedings of the Seventh IEEE International Conference on Advanced Learning Technologies*, (pp. 845-847). IEEE. 10.1109/ICALT.2007.275

Lester, J. C., Converse, S. A., Kahler, S. E., Barlow, S. T., Stone, B. A., & Bhogal, R. S. (1997). The persona effect: Affective impact of animated pedagogical agents. In *Proceedings of the ACMSIGCHI Conference on Human Factors in Computing Systems*, (pp. 359–366). ACM. 10.1145/258549.258797

Lison, P., & Tiedemann, J. (2016). *Opensubtitles2016: Extracting large parallel corpora from movie and TV subtitles*. In 10th edition of the Language Resources and Evaluation Conference, Portorož, Slovenia.

Lombardi, M., Pascale, F., & Santaniello, D. (2019). An application for cultural heritage using a chatbot. In *Proceedings of the 2nd International Conference on Computer Applications & Information Security*. IEEE. 10.1109/CAIS.2019.8769525

Mabunda, K., & Ade-Ibijola, A. (2019). Pathbot: An intelligent chatbot for guiding visitors and locating venues. In *Proceedings of 2019 IEEE 6th International Conference on Soft Computing & Machine Intelligence*, (pp: 160-168). IEEE. 10.1109/ISCMI47871.2019.9004411

Mageira, K., Pittou, D., Papasalouros, A., Kotis, K., Zangogianni, P., & Daradoumis, A. (2022). Educational AI chatbots for content and language integrated learning. *Applied Sciences (Basel, Switzerland)*, *12*(7), 3239. doi:10.3390/app12073239

Mateos-Sanchez, M., Melo, A. C., Blanco, L. S., & García, A. M. F. (2022). Chatbot, as educational and inclusive tool for people with intellectual disabilities. *Sustainability*, *4*(3), 1520. doi:10.3390u14031520

Moher, D., Liberati, A., Tetzlaff, J., & Altman, D. G. (2009). The PRISMA Group (2009) Preferred reporting items for systematic reviews and meta-analyses: The PRISMA statement. *PLoS Medicine*, *6*(7), e1000097. doi:10.1371/journal.pmed.1000097 PMID:19621072

Molnar, G., & Szuts, Z. (2018). The role of chatbots in formal education. In *Proceedings of the 2018 IEEE 16th International Symposium on Intelligent Systems and Informatics*, (pp. 197-202). IEEE. 10.1109/SISY.2018.8524609

Mondal, A., Dey, M., Das, D., Nagpal, S., & Garda, K. (2018). Chatbot: An automated conversation system for the educational domain. In *Proceedings of the International Joint Symposium on Artificial Intelligence and Natural Language Processing*, (pp. 1-5). IEEE. 10.1109/iSAI NLP.2018.8692927

Naveen Kumar, M., Chandar, P. C. L., Prasad, A. V., & Sumangali, K. (2016). Android based educational chatbot for visually impaired people. In *Proceedings of the IEEE International Conference on Computational Intelligence and Computing Research*, (pp. 1-4). IEEE.

Neves, A. M. M., Barros, F. A., & Hodges, C. (2006). IAIML: A mechanism to treat intentionality in AIML chatterbots. In *Proceedings of the International Conference on Tools with Artificial Intelligence*, (pp. 225-231). IEEE. 10.1109/ICTAI.2006.64

Ni, L., Lu, C., Liu, N., & Liu, J. (2017). MANDY: Towards a Smart Primary Care Chatbot Application. In J. Chen, T. Theeramunkong, T. Supnithi, & X. Tang (Eds.), *Knowledge and Systems Sciences. Communications in Computer and Information Science*. Springer. doi:10.1007/978-981-10-6989-5_4

Nuruzzaman, M., & Hussain, O. K. (2018). A survey on chatbot implementation in customer service industry through deep neural networks. In *Proceedings of the IEEE 15th International Conference on e-Business Engineering*, (pp. 54-61). IEEE. 10.1109/ICEBE.2018.00019

Nurvembrianti, I., Arianti, N., & Noftalina, E. (2022). The use of Telegram chatbot application services as a means of communication in increasing satisfaction and knowledge of mothers who have toddlers. *Galore International Journal of Health Sciences and Research*, *7*(1), 19–25. doi:10.52403/gijhsr.20220103

Okonkwo, C. W., & Ade-Ibijola, A. (2021). Chatbots applications in education: A systematic review. *Computers and Education: Artificial Intelligence*, *2*, 100033. doi:10.1016/j.caeai.2021.100033

Pears, M., Henderson, J., Bamidis, P., Pattichis, C., Karlgren, K., Wharrad, H., & Konstantinidis, S. (2021). Co-creation of chatbots as an educational resource: Training the trainers workshop. In *Proceedings of the 15th International Technology, Education and Development Conference*, (pp. 7808-7815). University of Nottingham.

Pérez, J. Q., Daradoumis, T., & Puig, J. M. M. (2020). Rediscovering the use of chatbots in education: A systematic literature review. *Computer Applications in Engineering Education*, *28*(6), 1549–1565. doi:10.1002/cae.22326

Przegalinska, A. K., Ciechanowski, L., Stróz, A., Gloor, P. A., & Mazurek, G. (2019). In bot we trust: A new methodology of chatbot performance measures. *Business Horizons*, *62*(6), 785–797. doi:10.1016/j.bushor.2019.08.005

Qin, C., Huang, W., & Hew, K. F. (2020). Using the community of inquiry framework to develop an educational chatbot: Lesson learned from a mobile instant messaging learning environment. In *Proceedings of the 28th international conference on computers in education*, (pp. 69-74). APSCE.

Radford, A., Narasimhan, K., Salimans, T., & Sutskever, I. (2018). *Improving language understanding by generative pre-training*. https://s3-us-west-2.amazonaws.com/openai-assets/research-co vers/language-unsupervised/language_understanding_paper.pdf

Radziwill, N., & Benton, M. (2017). Evaluating quality of chatbots and intelligent conversational agents. Cornell University. https://arxiv.org/abs/1704.04579

Ranoliya, B. R., Raghuwanshi, N., & Singh, S. (2017). Chatbot for university related FAQs. In *Proceedings of the International Conference on Advances in Computing, Communications and Informatics*, (pp. 1525-1530). IEEE.

Rohrig, C., & Heß, D. (2019). Omniman: A mobile assistive robot for intralogistics applications. *Engineering Letters*, *27*(4), 893–900.

Roller, S., Dinan, E., Goyal, N., Ju, D., Williamson, M., Liu, Y., Xu, J., Ott, M., Shuster, K., Smith, E. M., Boureau, Y. L., & Weston, J. (2021). Recipes for building an open-domain chatbot. In *Proceedings of the 16th Conference of the European Chapter of the Association for Computational Linguistics*, (pp. 300–325). Association for Computational Linguistics.

Roos, R. (2018). *Chatbots in Education: A Passing Trend or a Valuable Pedagogical Tool?* [Master's Thesis, Uppsala University, Uppsala, Sweden].

Ruan, S., Willis, A., Xu, Q., Davis, G. M., Jiang, L., Brunskill, E., & Landay, J. A. (2019). Bookbuddy: Turning digital materials into interactive foreign language lessons through a voice chatbot. In *Proceedings of the 6th 2019 ACM Conference on Learning at Scale*. ACM. 10.1145/3330430.3333643

Shawar, B. A., & Atwell, E. (2007). Different measurements metrics to evaluate a chatbot system. In *Proceedings of the Workshop on Bridging the Gap: Academic and Industrial Research in Dialog Technologies*, (pp. 89–96). ACM. 10.3115/1556328.1556341

Shin, D., Kim, H., Lee, J. H., & Yang, H. (2021). Exploring the use of an artificial intelligence chatbot as second language conversation partners. *Korean Journal of English Language and Linguistics*, *21*, 375–391.

Shum, H. Y., He, X., & Li, D. (2018). From Eliza to XiaoIce: Challenges and opportunities with social chatbots. *Frontiers of Information Technology & Electronic Engineering*, *19*(1), 10–26. doi:10.1631/FITEE.1700826

Sinha, S., Basak, S., Dey, Y., & Mondal, A. (2020). An educational chatbot for answering queries. In J. Mandal & D. Bhattacharya (Eds.), *Emerging Technology in Modelling and Graphics. Advances in Intelligent Systems and Computing, 937*, 55-60. Springer. doi:10.1007/978-981-13-7403-6_7

Sjöström, J., Aghaee, N., Dahlin, M., & Ågerfalk, P. J. (2018). Designing chatbots for higher education practice. In *Proceedings of the International Conference on Information Systems Education and Research*, (pp. 1-10). Research Gate.

Smutny, P., & Schreiberova, P. (2020). Chatbots for learning: A review of educational chatbots for the Facebook Messenger. *Computers & Education*, *151*, 103862. doi:10.1016/j.compedu.2020.103862

Strijbos, J. W., Martens, R. L., & Jochems, W. M. G. (2004). Designing for interaction: Six steps to designing computer-supported group-based learning. *Computers & Education*, *24*(4), 403–424. doi:10.1016/j.compedu.2003.10.004

Suebsombut, P., Sureephong, P., Sekhari, A., Chernbumroong, S., & Bouras, A. (2022). Chatbot application to support smart agriculture in Thailand. In *Proceedings of Joint International Conference on Digital Arts, Media and Technology with ECTI Northern Section Conference on Electrical, Electronics, Computer and Telecommunications Engineering*, (pp. 364-367). IEEE. 10.1109/ECTIDAMTNCON53731.2022.9720318

Suleman, R. M., Mizoguchi, R., & Ikeda, M. (2016). A new perspective of negotiation-based dialog to enhance metacognitive skills in the context of open learner models. *International Journal of Artificial Intelligence in Education*, *26*(4), 1069–1115. doi:10.100740593-016-0118-8

Turing, A. M. (1950). Computing machinery and intelligence. *Mind*, *59*(236), 433–460. doi:10.1093/mind/LIX.236.433

Vanichvasin, P. (2021). Chatbot development as a digital learning tool to increase students' research knowledge. *International Education Studies*, *14*(2), 44–53. doi:10.5539/ies.v14n2p44

Verasius, A., Sano, D., Imanuel, T. D., Calista, M. I., Nindito, H., & Condrobimo, A. R. (2018). The application of AGNES algorithm to optimize knowledge base for tourism chatbot. In *Proceedings of the International Conference on Information Management and Technology*, (pp. 65-68). Semantic Scholar.

Vetter, M. (2002). Quality aspects of bots. In *Software Quality and Software Testing in Internet Times* (pp. 165–184). Springer Berlin Heidelberg. doi:10.1007/978-3-642-56333-1_11

Wallace, R. (2001). *The Elements of AIML Style*. ALICE A.I Foundation.

Wegerif, R. (2004). The role of educational software as a support for teaching and learning conversations. *Computers & Education*, *43*(1–2), 179–191. doi:10.1016/j.compedu.2003.12.012

Weizenbaum, J. (1983). ELIZA— A computer program for the study of natural language communication between man and machine. *Communications of the ACM*, *26*(1), 23–28. doi:10.1145/357980.357991

Winkler, R., & Soellner, M. (2018). Unleashing the potential of chatbots in education: A state-of-the-art analysis. In *Academy of Management Annual Meeting Proceedings*. Academy of Management. 10.5465/AMBPP.2018.15903abstract

Wollny, S., Schneider, J., Di Mitri, D., Weidlich, J., Rittberger, M., & Drachsler, H. (2021). Are we there yet? - A systematic literature review on chatbots in education. *Frontiers in Artificial Intelligence*, *4*, 654924. doi:10.3389/frai.2021.654924 PMID:34337392

Zakos, J., & Capper, L. (2008). CLIVE—An artificially intelligent chat robot for conversational language practice. In *SETN 2008: Artificial Intelligence: Theories, Models and Applications* (pp. 437–442). Springer. doi:10.1007/978-3-540-87881-0_46

Zhang, C., Ré, C., Cafarella, M., De Sa, C., Ratner, A., Shin, J., Wang, F., & Wu, S. (2017). Deepdive: Declarative knowledge base construction. *Communications of the ACM*, *6*(5), 93–102. doi:10.1145/3060586

ENDNOTES

[1]   https://www.computerhistory.org/internethistory/1970s/
[2]   http://www.jabberwacky.com/
[3]   http://www.theoldrobots.com/chatbot.html
[4]   https://classicreload.com/dr-sbaitso.html
[5]   http://www.lazytd.com/lti/julia/
[6]   https://homepage.kranzky.com/hex/How.html
[7]   https://yakbots.com/chatbot-history-what-is-smarterchild/
[8]   https://www.apple.com/siri/
[9]   https://assistant.google.com/
[10] https://developer.amazon.com/en-US/alexa
[11] https://www.microsoft.com/en-us/cortana
[12] https://www.messengcr.com
[13] https://woebothealth.com/
[14] https://roboticsandautomationnews.com/2016/12/10/endurance-robots-launches-open-source-chatbot-platform/9043/
[15] https://insomnobot3000.com/
[16] eXtensible Markup Language (XML)
[17] https://pandorabots.com/docs/building-bots/tutorial/
[18] Information and Communication Technology (ICT)
[19] https://www.google.com/forms/about/
[20] https://padlet.com/
[21] https://ivy.ai
[22] https://www.mongooseresearch.com

23   https://www.hubspot.com/products/crm/chatbot-builder
24   https://www.geckoengage.com/
25   https://psych.athabascau.ca/html/Freudbot/Freudbot.html
26   https://www.cleverbot.com/
27   http://www.csiec.com/
28   https://pe.gatech.edu/blog/meet-jill-watson-georgia-techs-first-ai-teaching-assistant

Chapter 5

Opportunities and Challenges in Educational Chatbots

Rawad Hammad

ⓘ https://orcid.org/0000-0002-7900-8640
University of East London, UK

Mohammed Bahja
University of Birmingham, UK

ABSTRACT

The rapid technological developments have revolutionised approaches toward learning. The adoption of eLearning technologies such as chatbots has been increasing in the past few years, as there are various opportunities that can be identified to integrate educational chatbots with online learning process. For example, chatbots in education can provide various services such as personal tutoring, personal support, assessment and evaluation, etc. Iissues in remote learning—such as real-time assistance, feedback, and support—can be addressed by deploying educational chatbots. Yet, there are various challenges associated with chatbot technologies in education, e.g., novelty effect, cognitive load, the readiness of students and teachers, etc. This study reviews the various opportunities and challenges associated with educational chatbots in learning. These findings would help future researchers and designers to identify the core functionality and design aspects of educational chatbots, and also aids future research by the recommendations of research propositions.

INTRODUCTION

Chatbots are software applications, which are used for automating conversations

DOI: 10.4018/978-1-6684-6234-8.ch005

or interactions through messaging platforms. The conversations can be modeled through text or speech or a combination of both with a human agent. The main purpose of chatbots or conversational agents is to reduce human interventions to minimize costs by providing automated conversations to address the queries of users in different fields. Chatbot (ELIZA) was first created in 1966 at MIT to mimic human conversation for engaging patients in psychotherapy clinical treatment (Shawar & Atwell, 2007). Eliza was designed using keyword spotting and pattern matching algorithm for selecting the appropriate responses from a pre-defined set, in response to the inputs from the patients. Since then, more advanced chatbots were developed such as Parry, Alice for facilitating human-like conversations in various contexts (Yadav et al., 2019). With the advances in artificial intelligence (AI) and machine learning (ML) technologies, the use of chatbots has gained momentum, especially in the commercial sector. Chatbots are used for various purposes, such as facilitating healthcare education (Yadav et al., 2019), managing team events (Slack, 2022), weather updates (Kik, 2022), customer service (Chatbotguide, 2022), etc.

Nowdays, chatbots can be identified among all digital platforms and social media applications. In addition, conversational applications such as Google Home, and Amazon Alexa are specifically designed not only to address any queries raised by the users but also to perform various tasks such as switching on fans/lights, playing music, and searching for information from the internet. Facebook, for instance, launched its bot development platform for developers in 2016, which recorded over 30,000 chatbot applications within a year of launch (Lunden, 2016), and currently recorded over 300,000 chatbots (Hutchinson, 2019). Due to their socialization feature, chatbots come with the added advantage of making their presence in various contexts and come with various opportunities. For instance, the Mitsuku chatbot in China has got popular which is designed to entertain users by telling stories, jokes, or by playing songs (Mims, 2014). Similarly, the Microsoft Xiaoice chatbot has gained popularity for its unique feature of entertaining users according to their mood cues (Hornigold, 2019).

Chatbot technology is rapidly developing in line with the technologies that can support chatbots. Firstly, the underlying technologies of chatbots, which include AI, ML, and natural language processing. Chatbots can be divided into two categories. In the first category, chatbots function on a pre-set script, where users can respond by selecting the buttons, instead of voice/texts. These types of chatbots are easy to implement, and can still have a major impact on service delivery. The second category of chatbots are intelligent bots that can learn over time and uses advanced technologies such as AI, ML, and NLP. Integrating these technologies can have various advantages such as AI-enables can sell leads to boost revenue, as they automatically take customers through the sales funnel based on their needs and mood; delight them with a new high-tech experience; reduce customer support costs; extract and export useful data that can be used in various decision-making processes; and helps in connecting with more users (Chatfuel, 2022).

Moreover, the integration of ML techniques enables these chatbots to learn from previous and ongoing conversations allowing them to evolve and improve with time by developing a sense of emotional intelligence with the use of NLP technologies. This would make chatbots more human while interacting with users (Mnasri, 2019). NLP technology is at the core of AI-driven chatbots which can process the input text/voices by interpreting, inferring, and determining the meaning, based on which a series of appropriate actions are suggested. NLP includes five steps for processing data: Lexical analysis (identifying and analysing word structures); syntactic analysis or parsing (analysing grammar and arranging words); semantic analysis (drawing exact meaning by mapping syntactic constructions); discourse integration and pragmatic analysis (final interpretation of the real message in text) (Mnasri, 2019). Secondly, interoperability is another emerging concept that allows various chatbots to communicate with each other, which would increase the ease of use. For instance, a user can chat with a bot on WhatsApp to browse some products; and then talk to smart speakers such as Amazon Alexa to order (Rybakova, 2020). Further discussions about this are presented by Bahja et al (2019) in the Talk2Learn framework which is designed to set the scene for educational chatbots development.

Supporting technologies like AI, NLP, ML have led to an increase in the efficiency and effectiveness of chatbot applications in enabling human-like interactions, as a result of which they have been used in various sectors. A recent market research study by Mordor intelligence (2022) estimated the value of chatbot market at $17.17 billion in 2020 and projected the value would reach $102.29 billion by 2026, reflecting a CAGR of 34.75%. Similarly, according to an Insider Intelligence report, consumer retail spending through chatbot conversations is projected to increase from $2.8 billion in 2019 to $142 billion in 2024 (Yuen, 2022). In line with these predictions, chatbots have been used extensively in various industries. According to Salesforce company, chatbots are preferred by 69% of consumers because of its speed and efficiency in communicating with a brand.

In a review by MIT, it was identified that 90% of businesses experienced faster complaints resolution using chatbots. Accordingly, they are used in various industries. For instance, an AI-based chatbot (YES ROBOT) developed by Microsoft for YES Bank in India has enabled the bank's customers to easily perform both financial and non-financial transactions using the bot. Furthermore, QliqSoft, a company specializing in providing HIPAA-compliant solutions has launched a chatbot platform called Quincy, using which healthcare providers can build and deploy different chatbots for patients, which can significantly improve patient-centred services and reduce costs. During the Covid-19 pandemic, World Health Organization has launched Facebook Messenger version of the chatbot called WHO Health Alert platform, which offers instant and accurate information about Covid-19 (Mordor Intelligence, 2022). Although the focus of chatbots is largely limited to the commercial sector, they can also be used in areas which can create social impact (Asbjorn et al., 2018).

Due to its unique features such as the ability to reach many people in affordable ways, they can offer services that can empower people living in constrained environments. One such application of chatbots is in the education sector. A recent systematic review of the application of chatbots in education (Perez et al., 2020) has identified that there are different types of chatbots in education, which can be used for student learning or to improve services in various areas related to education. Although there is enormous scope for utilizing the chatbots in education such as providing services (student query resolution, support for admission or any other information), personalized tutors for learning, etc., there are also challenges that affect the effective utilization of chatbot technology such as lack of technical skills among students, the difference in pedagogic techniques or teaching strategies, inability to support all types of queries etc. It is important to understand that these opportunities and challenges change with time, with the development of supportive technologies, the development of student's skills and competencies, and unforeseen circumstances such as the Covid-19 pandemic. Therefore, it is very much essential to review the changing opportunities and challenges at regular intervals to help the chatbot designers in addressing the issues and also the decision-makers for effective integration of chatbot learning in parallel to traditional classroom learning. Considering these factors, this chapter reviews the various opportunities and challenges associated with the use of chatbots in education and provides recommendations or research propositions to aid further research and support decision-makers in the smooth implementation of chatbot technology in education.

OPPORTUNITIES FOR EDUCATIONAL CHATBOTS

There are various opportunities for educational chatbots, which can be used in different contexts. The opportunities may be classified into two different contexts: assistance/advisory; and learning and evaluation. Chatbots can be used in assisting or advise for both students and teachers. Many chatbots were developed for assisting students in the admission process. These chatbots provide 24x7 assistance to students in contrast to traditional approaches where students can only get help during the university opening times. In addition, by integrating chatbots into the university's website, there is an opportunity to convert website visitors into applicants. In addition, integrating chatbots with social media applications such as Facebook and WhatsApp can provide real-time assistance in a more convenient and friendly way. The increase in social media applications can be an added advantage for increasing the reachability of university courses to students across the globe. In addition, chat histories can help students in making accurate decisions after ending the chat; or they can request a call back if they want to know more information from the education counsellors. Chatbots can also help educators to gain deeper insights into the admission process, where the return on investments can be assessed and aid future decisions. For instance, assessing the number of admissions achieved by advertising the bots or selling the leads can help in keeping track of various factors such as engagements of users with chatbots, track costs per lead, cost per application, return on investment (ROI), etc.

Many applications for assisting were developed and evaluated in the recent literature. Dinius Intelligent Assistance (DINA) is one such chatbot developed for providing consultation services to users. DINA is an AI-based chatbot that is trained using the data from the Universitas Dian Nuswantoro guest book. The chatbot was tested using ten random sample questions from 166 intents, and the chatbot achieved 80% accuracy in providing the correct answers, reflecting the opportunity to utilize the chatbot in providing consultation services to the users (Agus Santoso et al., 2018). Another attempt in a similar study for facilitating admission process consultation using the chatbot (developed using the IBM Watson model) resulted in 95.9% accuracy over 221 test cases (Gbenga et al., 2020). Jooka is another chatbot application developed for supporting admission queries from parents and students. However, the unique feature of Kooka is its bilingual feature, as it can understand queries written in both English and Arabic. However, the chatbot only supports text inputs and does not support voice commands/queries (El Hefny et al., 2021).

Similarly, NEU is another chatbot developed for providing consultation services for various processes including daily updates, admissions, and tuition fees for IELTS course at National Economics University, Vietnam. The chatbot was developed using deep learning models, and it detected more than fifty types of questions from students with 97.1% accuracy (Nguyen et al., 2021). NEU chatbot unlike other chatbots integrated various consulting services in addition to admission, indicating the opportunity to provide services to the students before getting admitted, and also after getting admission (curriculum updates, scores, reminders etc.). The chatbots providing support for the common queries raised by students were also called FAQ chatbots and have various advantages, as they aid educators in analysing the users' trends on chatbots, such as the most frequently asked questions. Such data analysis can aid educators in identifying the problem areas for students and enable them in developing plans for effective communication in those areas (Cunningham-Nelson et al., 2019). Chatbots can also aid teachers in assisting with their queries about students or any other academic process, which can significantly reduce the consultation process and improve productivity by saving time. These chatbots have suggested that chatbots can provide various consultation services to students, teachers, and also parents with good accuracy levels enabling educators to increase admission intakes, reduce costs, and make better decisions.

There are many opportunities for utilizing chatbots in the learning process, as they can have many added advantages such as increasing student engagement in learning, providing smart and personalized feedback and support, and aiding teachers in assessments, evaluations, and providing support. Students can get personalised support using intelligent chatbots as they observe students learning trends, inputs, and accordingly provides customized support in learning. In addition, chatbots integrated with virtual technologies can raise interest among learners and actively engage them in learning.

Furthermore, teachers can use chatbots for providing additional assistance to the students. In addition, they can also use the data from the chatbots to analyse students learning behaviours and the types of queries, based on which they can modify the teaching approaches. Furthermore, students can self-evaluate their learning process using evaluation chatbots or quiz chatbots. It may not be possible to get support from educators at all the time. In such cases, chatbots can be very useful, as they provide 24x7 support. Moreover, they can also aid countries or institutions with limited resources, and contribute to improving literacy levels by improving the access to education through e-learning platforms. As there is a rapid increase in the use of mobile phones and the internet, chatbots can aid students in remote learning. It is evident from the Covid-19 pandemic that eLearning techniques play an important role in remote and customized learning, and in this context, chatbots proved to be very effective in offering learning services remotely to students (Naffi et al., 2022).

Studies (Bahja et al., 2020; Benotti et al., 2014) have shown that chatbots can facilitate an improved learning experience through active learning approaches which increases the students' engagement in learning. In a study (Benotti et al., 2014) focused on evaluating the user-centric chatbot and the general chatbot (Alice) for teaching CS concepts such as variables, conditionals, etc., it was identified that the student's engagement and interest levels are high while using the user-centric chatbot compared to Alice. Chatbots provide a personalized user experience, which raises interest among the students as it promotes active learning (instant and smart feedback, real-time performance evaluation), making it more preferred by the students compared to the other modes of learning, thereby increasing the student's engagement in learning (Bahja et al., 2020). Feedback from the teachers helps students to identify important areas of the lectures being taught and enables them to improve the areas where they are lacking. Similarly, feedbacks from students enable teachers to identify the areas where they are lacking and helps them in improving their teaching abilities. This feedback process usually includes a paper-based approach as the students and teachers have to fill out forms. However, chatbots such as Botsify conversational forms (Khan, 2020) can simplify this whole process by using an automated survey at the end of each session. Furthermore, chatbots can also help in the personalized evaluation of students' learning process allowing them to adopt self-evaluation practices to better understand their status in learning. Chatbots can use quizzes or review sessions to evaluate the progress of students, based on which they can effectively plan the learning process for improving the areas that require special attention (Winkler et al., 2018).

Another important opportunity is to facilitate easy learning of complex subjects or courses. Chatbots can be used as personal assistants or tutors for learning various subjects. Studies have shown that chatbots were effective in facilitating the learning of various subjects among students compared to the traditional modes of classroom teaching. Sofia, a chatbot for assisting in teaching mathematics was developed and used at Harvard mathematics department (Shawar & Atwell, 2007). The chatbot was designed to parallelly converse or communicate with users and mathematical agents (e.g., Parti, Mathematica) for helping the students to solve problems in Algebra. In addition, Sofia was also trained with some jokes and movies in which math plays a key role, a feature that makes learning fun and engaging. In another study (Cai et al., 2021), bandit algorithms were used with Mathbot, a chatbot designed to personalize the learning experience of mathematics subject. The student's performance was evaluated using an experiment conducted with two groups: Mathbot group and the eLearning group. The results suggested that personalized chatbot (Mathbot) are more effective than existing online tools for learning mathematics. NLP and deep learning techniques are being used in developing chatbots for subjects such as mathematics which require efficient and effective analysis of text or voice inputs to determine the right answers (Kasthuri & Balaji, 2021).

Various chatbots were developed for learning other subjects such as programming languages (Abbasi & Kazi, 2014), science courses (Deveci Topal, 2021), and English language (Pham et al., 2018), where the relevant chatbots were identified to be effective in facilitating learning. Chatbots were identified to be also effective in providing training in university courses such as nursing training, resulting in enhanced students' academic performance, critical thinking, and learning satisfaction (Chang et al., 2022; Chen & Kuo, 2021). Chatbots were identified to be effective in facilitating learning in social contexts. For instance, Feedpal, a chatbot designed for breastfeeding education (Yadav et al., 2019) was identified to be effective in improving awareness among women in backward and marginalized families, which is not only supporting women's empowerment but also community development through learning. In a different social context, chatbots were identified to be more effective in providing information to patients regarding breast cancer (Bibault et al., 2019). Therefore, chatbots can create opportunities for learning various subjects not only in the courses associated with educational institutions (primary, secondary, and university education) but also in the areas of social learning (creating awareness among the public) for community development.

CHALLENGES FOR EDUCATIONAL CHATBOTS

Chatbots do have challenges in various areas, which can be related to the opportunities discussed in the previous section. Firstly, although chatbots were proving to be effective in delivering learning solutions, the limitations in their technological capability are one of the major challenges that cannot be undermined. Some of the technological challenges include the perceived unnaturalness of the chatbot-generated voice, which was completely in contrast to human voices (Goda et al., 2014), which may lead to a lack of focus and engagement due to the changes in learning settings. Furthermore, it is natural that students may enter inputs in incomplete forms or in natural language, and it may lead to failed communication if chatbots are not effective in analysing such text/voice inputs or provide unrelated outputs (Fryer et al., 2019). Furthermore, there is a lack of technical ability in facilitating the emotional and visible cues during the interactions with the students, as most of the current technologies such as NLP in research studies focused on understanding the emotional content in the inputs but not on presenting the similar emotional cues in replying or presenting the output to the students. As a result of this technical lag, positive affective states such as engagement, and interest among the students may be affected (Gallacher et al., 2018).

Another major challenge is the unpredictability in the direction of conversations. Normal student-teacher interactions may lead to long-duration discussions in the process of addressing a query or a concept, where examples or references from out-of-the-topic contexts may be used to better explain the concept by the teachers or students. Such out-of-context references may not be understood by the chatbots as it is linked to a subject-related database (Yang & Zapata-Rivera, 2010). These limitations in the technology can affect the accuracy of educational chatbots. Educational chatbots such as DINA achieved 80% accuracy (Agus Santoso et al., 2018), while another chatbot resulted in an accuracy of 95.9% (Gbenga et al., 2020). Slight inaccuracies in the results or chatbot responses can have a significant effect on the learning process. Minor misinformation or inaccurate response from a tutor chatbot can misguide the students which can affect the overall learning process, which makes the chatbots unreliable. Therefore, accuracy and reliability are two major challenges associated with educational chatbots which may continue to exist in the long run.

The novelty effect (Increase or decrease in motivation or engagement of the students in the learning process when a new technology is introduced) is another challenge associated with chatbots (Chen et al., 2016). Although users have been aware of the chatbots in a commercial application, they are relatively new in the education sector. The novelty effect was illustrated by Fryer et al. (2017) concerning educational chatbots, in a 16-week experimental study which found that student's interest in the learning process declined after the conversations with chatbot, as they viewed it as novelty rather than a continuing partner in the learning process. Cognitive load is another challenge associated with chatbots. It is known that humans have a limited capacity for cognitive processing, which can influence the cognitive load when using novelty technologies like chatbots. For instance, chatbot learning design may include complex elements such as voice and animation in contrast to the traditional learning models; and this can confuse students in processing task information and allocation of attention.

Nonetheless, students' prior engagement with such technologies and their skills and competencies plays a key role in assessing the cognitive load. For instance, Kim (2016) found that high language proficiency students were more interested in English language teaching chatbots compared to low proficiency students (burdened with higher cognitive load processing). In such contexts, chatbots may become a barrier to learning as high cognitive loads can diminish students' learning outcomes (Fryer et al., 2020). Moreover, in a recent systematic review of 36 articles on educational chatbots, it was identified that only a quarter of the identified studies used a personalised learning approach design that is centred around students' learning needs, reflecting the challenge of inadequate or insufficient dataset training and a lack of reliance on usability heuristics in educational chatbots research (Kuhail et al., 2022b).

One additional limitation is the limited research focusing on educational chatbots. In a recent systematic review on educational chatbots (Wollny et al., 2021), it was identified that there was a mismatch between the objectives of research studies in this area which is educational chatbots and their evaluation. The study has found that most of the evaluation aspects were narrowed to learning factors such as learning success, accuracy, usability, and technology acceptance, undermining other factors such as students' engagement satisfaction, motivation, performance etc. The design of most chatbot-based advising systems is not user-centric, potentially causing a lack of adoption among students (Kuhail et al., 2022a). Furthermore, the chatbots developed so far were not at the same level in relation to the mentoring activities. To take over the mentoring role, the chatbots are required to fulfil three activities: scaffolding (providing direct assistance while learning new skills); recommending (providing supportive information, tools, or other materials while learning); and informing (encouraging students based on their goals, and support them in developing meta-cognitive skills such as self-regulation).

However, the current studies reflected varying levels in relation to these activities (Wollny et al., 2021). Furthermore, the current research on adaption approaches of chatbots is limited. Learners' traits such as interests, knowledge and skills, personal background, attitudes, and traits were least explored in assessing the adaptation capabilities of chatbots (Wollny et al., 2021). Furthermore, the medium of learning is not only English across the world. Different countries use their national language for teaching and learning, especially Russia, China, Saudi Arabia etc. Therefore, the multi-language feature is an essential component of chatbots that needs to be designed for a wide range of applications in learning. However, complex languages such as Arabic associated with morphological features, orthographic ambiguity and inconsistency, and variety of dialects (Almurayh, 2021) possess a challenge to chatbot technologies including AI, ML, and NLP in accurately assessing the meaning of input text/voice and providing the right output.

Privacy is another important challenge associated with educational chatbots. Chatbots make use of various personal information such as learning behaviour, and personal details such as age, gender, course selection, attitudes, goals, etc. for delivering personalized support. Furthermore, this data can be used by educators for assessing and evaluating the students. Therefore, the whole process of chatbots is associated with the use and analysis of personal information, which may be prone to misuse or theft. Therefore, the privacy and security of the personal data of the learners is one of the important challenges that need to be addressed in chatbot implementation (Srivastava et al., 2021).

Apart from the aforementioned challenges, one of the major challenges is that the research on educational chatbots is still in its early stages (Hwang & Chang, 2021), as a result of which no effective and accurate conclusions can be identified about the opportunities and challenges of educational chatbots. However, based on the analysis of the current research trends and literature, different research propositions are recommended in the following section.

RESEARCH PROPOSITIONS

Based on the review of the opportunities and challenges following research propositions are formulated to guide future research to the development and application of chatbots in educational settings.

RP1: Educational Chatbots and Technology Limitations

As identified from the review, there are technical limitations, especially the application of ML, NLP, and deep learning techniques in achieving high accuracy in educational chatbot performance. Studies should focus on developing the ML algorithms that achieve high accuracy levels, and develop efficient datasets for training these algorithms. In addition, NLP technologies have to be used effectively to generate human-like responses so that students may find chatbots more adaptable compared to other eLearning models. Therefore, future research studies should focus on addressing these technological limitations, which can significantly improve the accuracy and adaptability of educational chatbots in the learning process.

RP2: Educational Chatbots and Learners' Psychological Aspects

As identified in the review, existing research studies primarily focused on the student's or chatbot's performance, undermining the relevant student-related factors that influence learning. For instance, ease of use of the chatbot applications, support of chatbots in motivating students, learnability among students while using chatbot applications, and students' attitudes and satisfaction levels in using chatbot applications are a few students-related psychological factors which need to be considered in future research studies to provide a comprehensive view of the impact of chatbot learning on students.

RP3: Privacy and Security in Educational Chatbots

Privacy and security are two important challenges identified to the use of educational chatbots. Unlike FAQ chatbots which operate on pre-determined datasets, intelligent chatbots are designed not only to effectively analyse the semantics and meaning of the input text/voice messages but also to collect data about the student's performance, goals, evaluation remarks, progress, moods, study timings, types of queries raised, types of information requested and processed and many other personal and behavioural data, infringing their privacy. Although this data can be used for assessing students' performance and progress, based on which educators can improve teaching strategies, they may amount to an infringement of personal privacy. Furthermore, the personal data collected by the chatbots may be associated with the risk of theft or misuse, reflecting the security concerns associated with the personal data. However, collecting personal data is essential for enabling chatbots to provide personalized services. Although educational chatbots involve the use of personal data, there is a lack of research on specifying the ethical standards for the use of personal data in chatbot-based education. Therefore, future research studies can focus on enhancing the privacy and security of educational chatbots, and also on developing ethical standards for the use of personal data in the learning process.

RP4: Across the Courses and Subjects

Varying results have been obtained concerning the use of chatbot applications in various subjects or courses such as mathematics, science, English language courses, programming language courses etc. The pedagogy associated with each subject may be different, as different strategies are adopted by the teachers in the classrooms in explaining the concepts in various subjects. In some subjects such as English language learning, out-of-the-subject references such as cultural references are made to explain the grammar or other language-related concepts. Similarly, in other subjects such as science, and history various references are used by the teachers in the classroom, and accordingly the students also use various contexts as a reference for raising their queries or doubts with a specific concept. These unique pedagogic approaches associated with each subject/course increase the complexity of the design and implementation of chatbots. Therefore, future research should focus on designing chatbots by integrating various pedagogic strategies that are relevant to different subjects/ courses.

CONCLUSION

This chapter has reviewed the various opportunities and challenges associated with educational chatbots. The opportunities largely reflected the accessibility (24x7 remote access), promoting self-learning and self-regulation through chatbot monitoring, reducing costs, and their applicability over many courses/ subjects and at all levels of education, including primary secondary, and tertiary education. Furthermore, chatbots were also used in promoting social learning among the public, especially in creating awareness about various issues in society, such as cancer, breastfeeding etc. All the opportunities identified were associated with some sort of challenges in implementation. For instance, lack of reliability and accuracy in the wide-scale implementation of chatbot in the learning process. However, FAQ of inquiry chatbots was not associated with major challenges as they work on pre-defined datasets, and in the extent when it is not able to respond, it provides an option to connect with the real service executive. Whereas, intelligent chatbots are far more complex, as they need to analyze the input in natural language, extract correct meaning, and respond with the right information. Furthermore, technology limitations in chatbots and lack of sufficient research in various aspects related to chatbot technologies are a few other challenges identified in the review. Overall findings illustrated that although chatbots have enormous opportunities in the field of education, many challenges need to be addressed which makes the wide-scale implementation of chatbot learning, a possibility.

These findings can have various implications in theory and practice. Firstly, this chapter contributes to the lack of literature related to the opportunities and challenges surrounding educational chatbots. Secondly, it proposed various research propositions that can guide future researchers in this area. Thirdly, these findings can aid the chatbot designers and developers to focus on the solutions to address the challenges identified. Fourthly, these findings can guide educational institutions in planning the use of educational chatbots, policy making, and developing regulatory standards such as ethical guidelines. There are also limitations identified in this review, as it considered only a few contexts in assessing the opportunities and challenges based on the existing literature. However, both opportunities and challenges change with the changes in marketplaces, especially with the development of innovative technologies, changes in students' attitudes, skills and competencies etc. Therefore, the generalizability of findings in this study has to be done with care by future researchers.

Conflict of Interest

"The authors of this publication declare there is no conflict of interest."

Funding Agency

This research received no specific grant from any funding agency in the public, commercial, or not-for-profit sectors.

REFERENCES

Abbasi, S., & Kazi, H. (2014). Measuring effectiveness of learning chatbot systems on Student's learning outcome and memory retention. *Asian Journal of Applied Science and Engineering*, *3*(7), 57–66. doi:10.15590/ajase/2014/v3i7/53576

Agus Santoso, H., Anisa Sri Winarsih, N., & Mulyanto, E. Wilujeng sarSaswati, G., Enggar Sukmana, S., & Rustad, S. (2018). Dinus Intelligent Assistance (DINA) Chatbot for University Admission Services. *2018 International Seminar On Application For Technology Of Information And Communication*. IEEE. 10.1109/ISEMANTIC.2018.8549797

Almurayh, A. (2021). The Challenges of Using Arabic Chatbot in Saudi Universities. *International Journal of Computational Science*, *48*(1), 1–12.

Asbjorn, F., Petter, B. B., Tom, F., Ese, L. L., Manfred, T., & Ewa, A. L. (2018). Sig:Chatbots for social good. In *Extended Abstracts of the 2018 CHI Conference on Human Factors in Computing Systems*. ACM.

Bahja, M., Hammad, R., & Butt, G. (2020). A User-Centric Framework for Educational Chatbots Design and Development. In C. Stephanidis, M. Kurosu, H. Degen, & L. Reinerman-Jones (Eds.), Lecture Notes in Computer Science (vol. 12424). *HCI International 2020 - Late Breaking Papers: Multimodality and Intelligence. HCII 2020*. Springer. doi:10.1007/978-3-030-60117-1_3

Bahja, M., Hammad, R., & Hassouna, M. (2019). Talk2Learn: a framework for chatbot learning. In *European Conference on Technology Enhanced Learning* (pp. 582-586). Springer.

Benotti, L., Martínez, M., & Schapachnik, F. (2014). Engaging high school students using chatbots. Proceedings Of The *2014 Conference On Innovation &Amp; Technology In Computer Science Education*. ACM. 10.1145/2591708.2591728

Bibault, J., Chaix, B., Guillemassé, A., Cousin, S., Escande, A., Perrin, M., Pienkowski, A., Delamon, G., Nectoux, P., & Brouard, B. (2019). A Chatbot Versus Physicians to Provide Information for Patients With Breast Cancer: Blind, Randomized Controlled Noninferiority Trial. *Journal of Medical Internet Research*, *21*(11), e15787. doi:10.2196/15787 PMID:31774408

Cai, W., Grossman, J., Lin, Z., Sheng, H., Wei, J., Williams, J., & Goel, S. (2021). Bandit algorithms to personalize educational chatbots. *Machine Learning*, *110*(9), 2389–2418. doi:10.100710994-021-05983-y

Chang, C.-Y., Kuo, S.-Y., & Hwang, G.-H. (2022). Chatbot-facilitated Nursing Education: Incorporating a Knowledge-Based Chatbot System into a Nursing Training Program. *Journal of Educational Technology & Society*, *25*(1), 15–27.

Chatbotguide. (2022). Burberry. *Chatbotguide*. https://www.chatbotguide.org/burberry-bot [Accessed: 26 April 2022].

Chatfuel. (2022). How to Build Smarter Bots With AI. *Chatfuel*. https://chatfuel.com/blog/posts/build-ai-chatbots

Chen, J. A., Tutwiler, M. S., Metcalf, S. J., Kamarainen, A., Grotzer, T., & Dede, C. (2016). A multi-user virtual environment to support students'self-efficacy and interest in science: A latent growth model analysis. *Learning and Instruction*, *41*, 11–22. doi:10.1016/j.learninstruc.2015.09.007

Chen, Y., & Kuo, C. (2021). *Applying the Smartphone-Based Chatbot in Clinical Nursing Education*. Nurse Educator, Publish Ahead of Print., doi:10.1097/NNE.0000000000001131

Cunningham-Nelson, Sam, Boles, Wageeh, Trouton, Luke, & Margerison, E. (2019). A review of chatbots in education: Practical steps forward. In *30th Annual Conference for the Australasian Association for Engineering Education: Educators Becoming Agents of Change: Innovate, Integrate, Motivate. Engineers Australia, Australia*, (pp. 299-306). AAEE.

Deveci Topal, A., Dilek Eren, C., & Kolburan Geçer, A. (2021). Chatbot application in a 5th grade science course. *Education and Information Technologies*, 26(5), 6241–6265. doi:10.100710639-021-10627-8 PMID:34177344

El Hefny, W., Mansy, Y., Abdallah, M., & Abdennadher, S. (2021). Jooka: A Bilingual Chatbot for University Admission. In Á. Rocha, H. Adeli, G. Dzemyda, F. Moreira, & A. M. Ramalho Correia (Eds.), *Trends and Applications in Information Systems and Technologies. WorldCIST 2021. Advances in Intelligent Systems and Computing* (vol. 1367). Springer. doi:10.1007/978-3-030-72660-7_64

Fryer, L. K., Ainley, M., Thompson, A., Gibson, A., & Sherlock, Z. (2017). Stimulating and sustaining interest in a language course: An experimental comparison of Chatbot and Human task partners.*Computers inHuman Behavior, 75*, 461–468.

Fryer, L. K., Coniam, D., & Carpenter, R., & Lapus¸neanu, D. (2020). Bots for language learning now: Current and future directions. *Language Learning & Technology*, 24(2), 8–22.

Fryer, L. K., Nakao, K., & Thompson, A. (2019). Chatbot learning partners: Connecting learning experiences, interest and competence. *Computers in Human Behavior*, 93, 279–289. doi:10.1016/j.chb.2018.12.023

Gallacher, A., Thompson, A., & Howarth, M. (2018)."My robot is an idiot!"–Students' perceptions of AI in the L2 classroom. In P. Taalas, J.Jalkanen, L. Bradley, & S. Thouësny (Eds.),Future-Proof CALL: LanguageLearning as Exploration and Encounters: Short Papers from EUROCALL(pp. 70–76). Research-publishing.

Gbenga, L. O., Oluwafunto, O. T., & Oluwatobi, A. H. (2020). An Improved Rapid Response Model for University Admission Enquiry System Using Chatbot. *International Journal of Computer*, 38(1), 121–131.

Goda, Y., Yamada, M., Matsukawa, H., Hata, K., & Yasunami, S. (2014). Conversation with a chatbot before an online EFL group discussionand the effects on critical thinking. *Journal of Information Systems Education, 13*(1), 1–7. doi:10.12937/ejsise.13.1

Habash, F. (2018). Unified guidelines and resources for arabic dialect orthography. In *Proceedings of the Eleventh International Conference on Language Resources and Evaluation*. ACL.

Hornigold, T. (2019). This Chatbot has Over 660 Million Users—and It Wants to Be Their Best Friend. *Singularity Hub.* https://singularityhub.com/2019/07/14/this-chatbot-has-over-660-million-users-and-it-wants-to-be-their-best-friend/

Hutchinson, A. (2019). Facebook Messenger by the Numbers 2019. *Social Media Today.* https://www.socialmediatoday.com/news/facebook-messenger-by-the-numbers-2019-infographic/553809/

Hwang, G., & Chang, C. (2021). A review of opportunities and challenges of chatbots in education. *Interactive Learning Environments*, 1–14. doi:10.1080/10494820.2021.1952615

Kasthuri, E., & Balaji, S. (2021). A Chatbot for Changing Lifestyle in Education. *2021 Third International Conference On Intelligent Communication Technologies And Virtual Mobile Networks (ICICV)*. IEEE. 10.1109/ICICV50876.2021.9388633

Kik. (2022). Poncho the Weathercat. *Kik.* https://www.kik.com/bots/poncho/

Kim, N.-Y. (2016). Effects of voice chat on EFL learners' speaking ability according to proficiency levels. *Multimedia-Assisted Language Learning, 19*(4), 63–88.

Kuhail, M., Al Katheeri, H., Negreiros, J., Seffah, A., & Alfandi, O. (2022a). Engaging Students With a Chatbot-Based Academic Advising System. *International Journal of Human-Computer Interaction*, 1–27. doi:10.1080/10447318.2022.2074645

Kuhail, M., Alturki, N., Alramlawi, S., & Alhejori, K. (2022b). Interacting with educational chatbots: A systematic review. *Education and Information Technologies*. doi:10.100710639-022-11177-3

Lunden, I. (2016). Facebook opens analytics and FbStart to developers of the 34,000 bots on Messenger. *Tech Crunch.* https://techcrunch.com/2016/11/14/facebook-opens-analytics-and-fbstart-to-messengers-34000-bot-developers/

Mims, C. (2014). Advertising's New Frontier: Talk to the Bot. *Wall Street Journal.* https://www.wsj.com/articles/advertisings-new-frontier-talk-to-the-bot-1406493740

Mnasri, M. (2019). *Recent advances in conversational NLP: Towards the standardization of Chatbot building.* Cornell University. https://arxiv.org/abs/1903.09025

Mordor Intelligence. (2022). *Chatbot Market - Growth, Trends, Covid-19 Impact, And Forecasts (2022 - 2027).* Mordor Intelligence. https://www.mordorintelligence.com/industry-reports/chatbot-market

Naffi, N., Davidson, A., Boch, A., Nandaba, B. K., & Rougui, M. (2022). AI-powered chatbots, designed ethically, can support high-quality university teaching. *The Conversation.* https://theconversation.com/ai-powered-chatbots-designed-ethically-can-support-high-quality-university-teaching-172719

Nguyen, T., Le, A., Hoang, H., & Nguyen, T. (2021). NEU-chatbot: Chatbot for admission of National Economics University. *Computers And Education: Artificial Intelligence, 2,* 100036. doi:10.1016/j.caeai.2021.100036

Pérez, J., Daradoumis, T., & Puig, J. (2020). Rediscovering the use of chatbots in education: A systematic literature review. *Computer Applications in Engineering Education, 28*(6), 1549–1565. doi:10.1002/cae.22326

Pham, X., Pham, T., Nguyen, Q., Nguyen, T., & Cao, T. (2018). Chatbot as an Intelligent Personal Assistant for Mobile Language Learning. *Proceedings Of The 2018 2Nd International Conference On Education And E-Learning.* ACM. 10.1145/3291078.3291115

Rybakova, M. (2020). 4 Evolving Technologies That Are Empowering Chatbots. *AI Authority.* https://aithority.com/guest-authors/4-evolving-technologies-that-are-empowering-chatbots/

Shawar, A. B., & Atwell, E. (2007). Chatbots: Are they Really Useful? *LDV-Forum – Band 22*(1), 29-49.

Slack. (2022). *Kyber.* Slack. https://slack.com/apps/A0EP69E58-kyber.

Srivastava, B., Rossi, F., Usmani, S., & Bernagozzi, M. (2020). Personalized Chatbot Trustworthiness Ratings. *IEEE Transactions On Technology And Society, 1*(4), 184–192. doi:10.1109/TTS.2020.3023919

Winkler, R., & Söllner, M. (2018). Unleashing the potential of chatbots in education: A state-of-the-art analysis. *In Academy of Management Annual Meeting.* AOM.

Wollny, S., Schneider, J., Di Mitri, D., Weidlich, J., Rittberger, M., & Drachsler, H. (2021). Are We There Yet? - A Systematic Literature Review on Chatbots in Education. *Frontiers In Artificial Intelligence, 4,* 654924. doi:10.3389/frai.2021.654924 PMID:34337392

Yadav, D., Malik, P., Dabas, K., & Singh, P. (2019). Feedpal: Understanding opportunities for chatbots in breastfeeding education of women in India. *Proceedings of the ACM on Human-Computer Interaction,* (pp. 1-30). ACM. 10.1145/3359272

Yang, H. C., & Zapata-Rivera, D. (2010). Interlanguage pragmatics with a pedagogical agent: The request game. *Computer Assisted Language Learning, 23*(5), 395–412. doi:10.1080/09588221.2010.520274

Yuen, M. (2022). Chatbot market in 2022: Stats, trends, and companies in the growing AI chatbot industry. *Insider Intelligence.* https://www.insiderintelligence.com/insights/chatbot-market-stats-trends/

Chapter 6

Chatbots as Motivational Agents:
Chatbots – The Value of a Digital Tool in Pedagogy

Huong-Tra Le-Nguyen
iD https://orcid.org/0000-0003-4718-8920
Foreign Trade University, Vietnam

Trung Thanh Tran
Pixta, Vietnam

ABSTRACT

Chatbots have offered numerous useful applications to a range of market industries due to their absolute benefit of saving costs and eliminating unneeded work for employees. This state had a greater impact on other features than on itself. With the aid of chatbots, the efficiency, competency, and productivity of labor and processes have been maximized on a scale that transcends human capabilities. As a result of such a profitable conclusion for firms and businesses, which stimulates additional skills of both humans and machines, it is argued that chatbots are not only a useful tool but also motivational agents.

INTRODUCTION

Today, every company relies on information and communication technology (ICT) for efficient service delivery and resource usage. The global chatbot industry is expected to accelerate over the next decade due to increased demand for faster

DOI: 10.4018/978-1-6684-6234-8.ch006

services and acceptance of artificial intelligence (AI)-based solutions by global corporate operations. In the age of artificial intelligence, the chatbot business is booming because more and more people are using smartphones and messaging services. In recent years, the food delivery, finance, and e-commerce businesses have all embraced chatbot technology.

"Education 4.0" is the name for a system of learning that uses artificial intelligence and is centered on the learner. The learner-centered education system advanced from the previous tutor-centered education system. The improvement of education is vital for adapting to changing lifestyles, economies, technology, and student demands. Furthermore, the scarcity of teachers in our educational system has impelled the use of new technologies. According to studies, chatbots will help to resolve some of the current challenges in the education industry. This article investigates the inclusion of chatbots powered by artificial intelligence into the educational system.

Chatbots have been used for educational reasons for quite some time. There are two categories of chatbots: those with educational objectives and those with nothing. Chatbots with no educative goal are used in administrative tasks such as student advising and assistance. The ones built specifically for education are used to promote teaching and learning. They fit under this category because they provide a framework for the learning process, which includes selecting and arranging content to meet the needs and pace of the students, as well as assisting in reflection and learning motivation. These bots work as learning partners, encouraging interaction, cooperation, and reflection. There are also exercise and practice chatbots, which present a stimulus as a question, to which the learner responds with a response that the chatbot evaluates and then delivers feedback. Because they require a communicative conversation between the bot and the student, chatbots augment conversational learning.

On the other hand, those without educational objectives work mainly as consultants to detect, alert, and notify people who earn authority. One of the chatbots with that function is called a motivational agent or psychological assistance. These bots are responsible for diverting their concentration to the mental side of users. They operate through the conversational mechanism or send a random survey to users and gather as much information as possible. Meanwhile, chatbots are also in the form of companions for managers or administrators. Simplifying office work and increasing productivity over a wider time frame, chatbots are useful because of their increased precision and localization. In other words, they follow the procedure smoothly and guide users in the exact steps without taking too much effort from humans.

HOW FUNCTIONS OF CHATBOTS AND EDUCATIONAL NEEDS INTERTWINE

Review Of The Interrelationship Between Chatbots And Education

Why Chatbots Are Helpful

Researchers are looking for resources to study how chatbots support teaching because there has been extensive research in this area. This information indicates people have integrated chatbot technology into the educational sector in a significant way. All of the preparatory work has led to several parts of education using chatbots to help them do their jobs (Cunningham-Nelson et al., 2016; Medeiros et al., 2018; Smutny & Schreiberova, 2020). These capacities include research and development, the relationship between learners and instructors, administrative companionship, feedback and evaluation, and consultation services. The report showed the degree to which the chatbot technology has been implemented in a variety of educational settings, which consists of administrative companionship (5%), feedback and evaluation (6%), consultation (4%), and research and development (19%). The learner and instructor sector accounts for 66% of the total.

Again, this section presents a review of the positive impact of chatbots performing their duties. According to the analysis, implementing chatbot technology in educational settings is causing significant changes to the educational system. Furthermore, implementing chatbots in educational settings can dramatically enhance both the learning outcomes and the level of satisfaction experienced by students (Winkler & Soellner, 2018). However, not many researchers are concluding a successful scenario where chatbots are integral to educational contexts (Durall & Kapros, 2020). Finally, the implications of chatbots enable educational mechanisms to be envisioned in several ways, including:

Integrated Information: The term "content integration" is coined to prove that educators can put topic-related knowledge and information on a digital platform, where it may be accessed without difficulty by students who get granted permission to do so. This content offers a rundown of the studied topics, a schedule for upcoming assignments, tests, and exams, along with aid and support. Users can get help from chatbots in offering individualized information to students. They may keep students informed and more aware of campus activities, in the long run, particularly sports events or simply about things that capture their interest. According to the findings of the research, several of the studies found that making use of chatbots in educational settings made it easier to integrate subject-matter content, making it more readily available to students whenever and wherever they might be (Akcora et al., 2018, pp. 14–19; Wu et al., 2020; Yang & Evans, 2019, pp. 79–83).

Instant Access: One of the advantages of using a chatbot discussed in the article under consideration is that it facilitates the speed of instant registration for users to find the needed information for their learning problems (Ciupe et al., 2019; Murad et al., 2019; Wu et al., 2020). This function is highly time-saving (Ranoliya et al., 2017), optimizing studying. Also, this tool provides needed materials in an easy-to-navigate format (Clarizia et al., 2018, p. 291–302; Murad et al., 2019).

Interests Span: Today's students learn primarily through online platforms. Motivation and engagement are, therefore, fundamental. In other words, intelligent devices are students' most intimate tools whenever they want to log themselves onto the online platform and get the information they need. This ability provides them with a much more exciting way of learning instead of digging deeper into books and related reading materials. In those reviewed articles, evidence showed that with the ability of chatbots, students keep their interest and study commitment enthusiastically, giving them the motivation to learn in an atmosphere that is both fascinating and comfortable for them (Chen et al., 2020; Pham et al., 2018; Rooein, 2019; Troussas et al., 2017). Henceforth, students avoid the boredom of learning with a conversational agent to learn, and they will be able to absorb the lessons with relaxation. Moreover, it leads to the result that educational use of chatbots significantly contributes to an increase in the level of involvement shown by students (Moln'ar & Szuts, 2018; Lam et al., 2018, pages 18–19; Adamopoulou & Moussiades, 2020).

Parallel Users: The capacity of accessing the system at once was found to be a significant benefit of employing chatbots in education through the study of the chosen articles. This ability suggests that numerous students from various locations can communicate uninterrupted with a specific Chatbot and acquire the necessary knowledge. According to Wu et al. (2020), this function is one of the critical advantages of chatbots. A Chatbot can answer many queries at once, freeing up the user's time to do other duties, according to Rooein (2019).

Availability: One of the most important benefits of using chatbots for education is their ability to provide immediate support to students. Scholars and students can use chatbots in education to quickly answer questions and other tasks (Alias et al., 2019, pp. 263–270). Reviews have shown that chatbots can provide instant help during one-on-one coaching (Okonkwo & Ade-Ibijola, 2020). Moreover, they assist students in automating routine tasks like turning in homework and replying to personal emails (Molnar & Szuts, 2018; Murad et al., 2019); they also are responsive to the actions and emotions of learners (Graesser, 2016) and can provide a response to their questions in a short time (Sreelakshmi et al., 2019).

Roles Of Chatbots In Educational Aspects

Elicitor

In an educational setting, chatbots can answer frequently asked questions (FAQs), run simulations, train students in different skills and talents, and give them ways to think about how they learn. At Cardenal Herrera University, a chatbot advises students and answers their inquiries. While chatbots have gone through more improvements to predict students' psychological reactions and help with the learning process, they now act as assistants. Even more, since curiosity is a key part of intrinsic motivation, chatbots can be used to spark students' interest by asking them questions that make them think. The conversational nature of the program makes it easy to get information from students and opens up new ways of looking at the concept (Oudeyer, Gottlieb, & Lopes, 2016).

Tutor

In today's world, when things change quickly, adaptation is essential. With a huge storage capability, chatbots reduce the procedure and the amount of work in imparting knowledge. Although there are many applications for chatbots in tutoring, the following are some of the more widespread ones:

Data Storage: The most common use of chatbot systems is in education, specifically to teach and be taught. Studies have indicated that chatbots, in their capacity as conversational agents that are able to provide accurate information to users, can be utilized to impart instructional material to students through the medium of an online platform (Akcora et al., 2018, pp. 14–19; Chen et al., 2020; Lin & Tsai, 2019; Medeiros et al., 2018; Mor et al., 2018, pp. 94–101; Nguyen et al., 2019; Okonkwo & Ade-Ibijola, 2020; Rooein, 2019). In order for students to gain learning experiences at an interesting pace, educators are beginning to recognize the value of incorporating chatbots into educational environments (Clarizia et al., 2018, pp. 291–302; Hobert, 2019; Sandu & Gide, 2019; Wu et al., 2020) through taking part in a conversation with an agent to get responses (Hiremath et al., 2018; Mikic-Fonte et al., 2018), and get individualized support (Hiremath et al., 2018; Mikic-Fonte et al., 2018; Pham et al., 2018; Sinha et al., 2020; Song et al., 2017; Troussas et al., 2017; de Barce-los). Adapting chatbots to pedagogical learning techniques has made the privacy of learning for students become feasible. Students can access educational resources whenever and wherever they choose. Both Mr. Wartman and Mr. Combs (2018) said that the professional sector is developing at the same pace as changes in education, which necessitates the implementation of Artificial Intelligence (AI) in offline learning. In the setting, a chatbot observes and adapts students' performance through how they communicate to take notice and personally tailor the student's learning experience with enthusiasm (Crockett et al., 2017).

Ashok Goel, a professor of computer science at Georgia Tech, is one of the first instructors to simplify his work in this manner with the assistance of artificial intelligence. He is also one of the first educators to do so by creating a chatbot and gave it the name Jill Watson in which he used the Watson platform from IBM (Lin & Chang, 2020; Murad et al., 2019; Troussas et al., 2017). The bot answers questions that students post on an online forum and gives them information about what will be covered in lectures and classes. The students were under the impression that Jill was one of the teaching assistants. Before the final exam, they didn't notice any difference between the two until the professor told them that they were talking to a computer. All of the responses were favorable. Her classmates praised Jill's skills, and a few of them even said they might nominate her for an award for outstanding work as a teaching assistant. Chatbots are helpful technological advancements that boost students' interest in learning, their ability to acquire cognitive abilities, and overall accomplishment. Even more, chatbots can boost students' confidence by giving them more control over how well they do in school. This event allows students to take more responsibility for their academic success (van der Meij, van der Meij, & Harmsen, 2015).

These bots are adjusted for use as a research tool in addition to their function as educative and teaching aids when working in the library department, in particular, where assistants were required to train patrons on how to use the facility and how to write. In these situations, a chatbot can send students to a subject guide, answer questions about the library's most important services, explain library terms, and link to relevant databases. The UC Irvine Libraries' chatbot, ANTswers, is a good example of this function in action because it shows how the chatbot can improve library instruction by giving students consistent answers and pointing them to resources they may have forgotten how to use ("Ask Alice," n.d.) . Responses can be prepared especially for the student's classes and assigned work. They are of tremendous use in the work that must be done about applying state, national, or international policies in papers. When a student asks the chatbot for policy resources, it can give them suggestions for how to start their research. This response helps the students get a head start.

For a long time, it has been common for reference departments to offer virtual reference services to people on and off campus. For example, the University of California, Irvine Libraries offer research consultations by email, QuestionPoint, instant message, and by appointment using tools like Google+ Hangouts. According to McNeal and Newyear (2013), the most common topic of discussion in chat and instant messaging exchanges are requests for specific items, places, hours, and policies. Customers have the option of providing themselves with self-service when they make the kinds of information inquiries that chatbots can respond to effectively. Using the Internet, they can meet customers wherever they are and meet their needs wherever they are. AIML and chat robot software let librarians push the limits of what they can do to help and train people around the clock without adding a lot of reference services that need help from a person. Given the state of the economy, the fact that library budgets have been cut, and how hard it is to find new employees, it might be helpful to come up with a service that doesn't require a lot of staff help.

Chatbots have been brought to light in many studies. These systems can help students with their academic research and development by giving relevant answers to conversations about academically relevant topics. Postgraduate students have to do research as part of their coursework, and chatbot technology gives them important directions for doing product research. Two authors, Ureta and Riveria designed a Chatbot to instruct students in STEM research principles (Mckie & Narayan, 2019; Ureta & Rivera, 2018). This is when a chatbot finally ease the research work for student from Wikipedia and enhance their training so they may develop practical skills linked to their career.

Evaluation and Comments: (for academic performance and the methodology of teachers) The employment of chatbot systems for student evaluations is evident from the examination of the papers gathered for this study (Durall & Kapros, 2020, pp. 13–24; Ndukwe et al., 2019, pp. 365–368; Sreelakshmi et al., 2019). Chatbots assisted by AI are great tools to automate classroom environment, one in which educators can observe, analyze, and assess students' progress in real time. By recording what students say and how they respond, these chatbots assist professors in determining how well their pupils comprehend a subject. Chatbots supply students with educational materials, examinations, and quizzes like classrooms. After exams are graded, the findings are relayed to teachers via chatbots so they may monitor their students' progress and speed up class time.

Instructor-Learner Relationship: According to Fleming, the rapport between the chatbot and the learner comprises the following components: initiation, response, and feedback (IRF). First, the chatbot starts a conversation in a way that proposes a problem to solve; then, students critically acclaim and try to come up with proper explanations, and it conveys feedback with remarks based on the student's answer (Fleming, 2018). Students can also talk to each other through these chatbots, and this interaction includes a debate (D), which is where the name IDRF comes from.

Below is Table 1, which describes the salient features of traditional and chatbot-mediated systems.

Recently, chatbots for e-learning systems have gained appeal to foster student learning. Chatbot technology is a vital innovation for e-learning; it is the most innovative method for bridging the gap between technology and education. Analogous to one-on-one interactions with teachers, chatbots create an engaging learning environment for students. By evaluating students' behavior and keeping track of their progress, bots contribute significantly to enhancing their talents.

Table 1. Distinguished traits between traditional system and the ai-bot system

Characteristics	Traditional system/ teacher-centered learning	Chatbot-bot system
Focus span	Instructor-focus	Shared between mentors and mentees
Foundation	Found on the basis of the instructor's foundation about language forms and structures	Focuses on the usage purpose of the student
Learning techniques	Passive learning	Combines both active and passive method
Learner-instructor rapport	Teacher-dependent	Teacher-interdependent
Responsibility for academic performance	The tutor is responsible for the student's proficiency	The student is solely responsible for his/her proficiency
Online platforms	Repository areas	Accommodate interaction and experimentation
Level adaptation	Curriculum-centred	Student-centred, based on their profile, learning experiences and needs
Learner behaviors	Default, not affect the pedagogical model	Key factor to modify the teaching model to learners
Learner environment	Not adaptive	Implement various adaptive learning environments

Additionally, frequent reminders and notifications could be essential in motivating students to work. There are numerous additional instances where chatbots can be utilized for e-learning. For instance, it is possible to provide a system for a tailored learning experience: each student earns and absorbs information at a special rate. With chatbots, it is possible to modify the rate at which a student can learn without being unduly demanding. Chatbots can also facilitate social learning; for instance, students from diverse backgrounds can share their opinions and perspectives on a particular topic while the bot adapts to each individual. By providing group projects and group assignments, this technology can increase student engagement and promote connection with their classmates. Chatbots can aid teachers with daily activities such as responding to student inquiries and grading assignments. They are widely used as online assessments: when there are many students in a classroom, it is difficult for teachers to give each student individual attention, but chatbots may work with multiple students and groups at once. With this in mind, they can support teachers by identifying misspellings and grammatical problems, assessing assignments, offering projects, and keeping track of each student's growth and achievements.

Psychological Assistance

A helpful chatbot's educational effectiveness is frequently validated based on literacy settings but not mindset. Most studies focus on how well chatbots perform in learning environments and are undeniably efficacious (Smith-Griffin, CEO, Founder, & AllHere, 2022). However, when considering learning outcomes in a broader context, there will be examples, including psychological and motivational issues. Those are the difficulties pupils face that they cannot overcome or do not know of. It is caused, for instance, by pressure from school, classmates, social relationships, disorders (instability), or, more recently, the isolation of social distance during the Covid-19 epidemic.

Furthermore, students may feel dread or anxiety due to their surroundings, which can harm their performance and well-being (Merchant, 2021). Due to Covid-19 pandemic, various insecurities about life had led people, especially students to struggle with changes. In which, loneliness and social isolation were among the most difficult challenges for extroverted people. However, the majority of people did not feel comfortable seeing a therapist. These issues are not adequately addressed because most students are afraid to disclose their psychological problems publicly or because of a lack of time owing to the excessive educational burden.

Regardless of societal context, up to two-thirds of children in the United States suffer from trauma, yet there are lack of specializing practitioners to ease their mental health problems. Statistically, the national data estimates for about 100,000 youngsters, there are fewer than ten child psychiatrists, which is less than a quarter of the American Academy of Child and Adolescent Psychiatry's recommended staffing level. This figure is especially concerning for black and brown families, who are more likely to suffer from mental health concerns such as anxiety and depression yet are less likely to seek treatment. Thus, it can be attributed to a lack of access to culturally competent healthcare. With increased focus and investment in mental health in schools comes a need to help these children and their families. In short, enormous challenges, limited resources, and low average medical allocation contribute significantly to students' mental health, resulting in poor performance(2022, Smith-Griffin, CEO, Founder, & AllHere).

Some studies describe the mechanism of emotional behaviors on performance to address the issue more clearly. For starters, kids' attitudes and faith in technology are critical. Again, research demonstrated a close relationship between emotions and learning behaviors when using chatbots as a learning aid, known as chatbot-mediated learning. First, students who believe in the utility of chatbots are better satisfied with their academic achievement (Söllner et al., 2017). Second, learning factors such as traits and personality features significantly impact agent-directed emotions throughout the learning process. Students who exhibit characteristic emotions such as anger, fear, or joy during learning, as well as stable personality qualities such as agreeableness, conscientiousness, and neuroticism, have a significant effect (Harley, Carter, Papaionnou, Bouchet, Landis, Azevedo, & Karabachian, 2016). Third,

Chatbots may collect all user inputs and summarize, notify, and inform authorities of the current status of users (Gull, Qureshi, & Syed, 2019).

This aspect of chatbots draws the most attention in the educational area. Consequently, several goods and agents are being developed to provide psychological support to consumers, namely students. According to Bickmore, Schulman, and Sidner (2013), Chatbots have the features needed to be deemed a good tool for mental consultation. To begin with, they offer privacy, anonymity, and simplicity of access, making it simple to handle acute mental health problems. Correspondingly, chatbots cannot only act as companions for persons suffering from mental illnesses, but they can also provide tailored therapy that integrates principles such as Dialectical Behavior Therapy (DBT), evidence-based Cognitive Behavior Therapy (CBT), and guided meditation. In addition, Chatbots provide a non-confrontational, non-judgmental approach for families to seek help, perhaps increasing the number of children receiving the assistance they require ("Young and Depressed? Try Woebot! "The Rise of Mental Health Chatbots in the United States," 2022).

When all of the above were combined, it was discovered that chatbots allow patients to communicate their views when engaging in therapeutic chats. Chatbots carry on a daily lighthearted dialogue with its user, creating an excellent therapeutic experience for young people and graduate students. They critically determine whether to deliver movies or propose other valuable resources based on users' replies to their inquiries. Users can manually enter or select their mood for the day from chatbot options, rate it, and then record how they feel (Merchant, 2021). The agent then asks a series of probing questions in order to comprehend and categorize the user's cognitive processes. It highlights mental flaws such as excessive worrying, emotional reasoning, and generalization. Agents or programs such as Woebots and Moodnotes have been launched and tested in the market (Merchant, 2021).

Several research reviews looked at chatbots employed as medical agents to help students with their medical education or patients with their therapy. Chatbots on mobile devices are frequently utilized in medical education to make learning location and time independent. These chatbots are typically linked to a learning environment, assisting students with exams and instructional content (Alepis & Virvou, 2011). Chatbots, in patient treatment, deliver information and counseling to hospital patients at the time of release and respond to patient inquiries. The goal of these treatments is to give individual assistance to patients in order to help them adhere to their therapy. One research, for example, found that patients with depressive symptoms prefer to receive help from chatbots rather than physicians or nurses. They had a considerably greater therapeutic connection than patients who did not use a chatbot. Patients learn how to help themselves with the assistance of a chatbot, gaining independence from human care (Bickmore et al., 2010). Chatbots in the well-being industry assist students in changing their harmful habits by initiating talks with them. For example, daily talks with a chatbot can increase physical activity and improve fruit and vegetable eating (Bickmore, Schulman, & Sidner, 2013).

Administrative Companion

In several studies given as a result of the evaluation and analysis of the chosen publications, researchers described chatbots as a. informative tool with the capability to optimize administrative duty in academic offices (Hien et al., 2018, pp. 69–76; Lee et al., 2019, pp. 348–354; Ranoliya et al., 2017). In terms of mentioning the academic department, Hien et al. (2018, pp. 69–76) depicted an agent responding to students' questions regarding their learning performance. As a virtual assistant, the chatbot will offer institutional advice on enhancing its current services, coming up with fresh, creative ideas, and saving labor expenses. Another investigation looked at a conversational assistant that can assist students with administrative tasks like enrollment, training, and commitment (Elnozahy et al., 2019). Chatbot optimization for administrative and educational activities is one of the most current AI uses in education (Okonkwo & Ade-Ibijola, 2020). Of all educational fields, the one that receives the most attention is the possible impact of chatbots; according to Chen et al. (2020), the performance in multiple tasks, notably literacy work assessment and feedback, as well as evaluation. With these benefits chatbots brings, students may readily get crucial information about admittance requirements, scholarships, and tuition costs (Hwang et al., 2020).

How To Develop A Chatbot To Fit The Needs

Mechanism

A chatbot has two interaction styles: user-driven and chatbot-driven (Kuhail, Alturki, Alramlawi, and Alhejori, 2022), as well as two techniques for a discussion inside a user session of chatbots: task-oriented/ declarative and data-driven/conversational, or intent-based or flow-based. These techniques apply to both mechanisms; however, whether one should be employed depends on the domain and role of a chatbot. In other words, the developer's goal is the most crucial consideration.

On the one hand, flow-based chatbots require the user to follow a preset learning route determined by the chatbot. A notable example is Rodrigo et al. (2012) and Griol et al. (2014), who introduced a chatbot that asks students questions and presents them with alternatives. Other writers, such as Daud et al. (2020) took a slightly different strategy, guiding learners to choose the topic they wanted to learn. Succeeding that, the evaluation of specific issues is offered, with the user required to fill in values and the chatbot responding with comments. As the pupil progresses, the level of the examination grows increasingly complex. Winkler et al. (2020) offer a slightly different form of interaction, where chatbots ask students questions. If students respond incorrectly, they are told why and given a scaffolding question. The remaining articles (13 articles; 36.11%) feature intent-based chatbots powered by chatbots. The chatbot is supposed to respond to the user's words with a prewritten answer. Pattern matching, as detailed in Benotti et al. (2017); Clarizia et al. (2018), or simply depending on a specialized conversational tool such as Dialogflow (Mendez et al., 2020; Lee et al., 2020; Ondá et al., 2019), might be used.

On the other hand, chatbots participate in user-driven discussions in which the user controls the conversation, and the chatbot does not have a pre-programmed answer. For example, Cleverbot, a chatbot built to learn from previous human talks (Fryer et al., 2017), is used in foreign language instruction. User-driven chatbots are suitable for language learning because students benefit from unguided conversations. Other agents have taken a similar approach, allowing kids to freely speak a foreign language (Ruan et al., 2021). The chatbot evaluates the transcription quality and gives helpful criticism. Tegos (2020), on the other hand, used a somewhat different technique in which students discussed a single programming subject continuously. The chatbot interjects to pique students' interest or direct their attention to a fascinating, related concept.

In short, it is clear that in the present world, the use of chatbots is essential, not only because of their favorable characteristics but also because of their adaptability in many industries. However, because each industry demands distinct qualities, developers must adjust the use of chatbots to each scenario. This idea creates an additional issue regarding resources, time, budget, and personnel use. Consequently, the only approach to tackle some problems is to build a simple formula that will serve as a basis for future chatbot developers. As previously discussed, the technique provides a shortcut to reduce resources while reserving more area for customization and creativity. In terms of education, it is critical to consider technical maturity and integration with educational institutions while designing chatbot use cases to boost the chatbot's capabilities. International frameworks for 21st-century learning, in particular, propose that critical thinking, making judgments and decisions, clear communication, teamwork, and technology awareness will be essential competencies in the future (ISTE, 2017). Chatbots may assist learners in developing, improving, and reflecting on these abilities.

To begin, all researchers must agree on a complete understanding. It is now necessary to create some essential groundwork before creating a chatbot:

- What are the (pedagogical) aims of using a chatbot?
- What is the situation?
- Who are the chatbots targeting?
- What is the chatbot's job, and what are its responsibilities?
- What is the user's role?

- What are the technological constraints or requirements?
- What (sensitive) information is used?
- What are the time, human resources, and cost constraints?

Only when all of the questions mentioned earlier have been appropriately answered can all developers begin to dive into their tasks. Otherwise, other challenges will arise during the production process, such as personal or ethical concerns. There are several crucial factors for the chatbot to perform correctly:

- The capacity to collect and analyze large volumes of data from various sources in real time.
- Knows how to learn (has been pre-trained) and has been fed domain-specific information and rules for its unique use case
- From a linguistic standpoint, communicate grammatically correctly and meaningfully.

Considering all that has been said so far, it is determined that when it comes to establishing a chatbot in education, Satow (2019) defines the following development steps:

- Ideas for developing robots
- Real-life conversations and questions
- Bot script creation
- Bot training with intent definitions
- Bot skill enhancement
- The chatbot is being tested.
- Optimized for production use

Apart from that kind of contact and chatbot intelligence, the main issue is its integration or embedding from a technical perspective. Learning management systems are commonly used in educational institutions such as schools and colleges and educational organizations within companies. Therefore, it is crucial to specify whether chatbots can be integrated into current learning platforms or, if alternative channels are used, how learners can authenticate themselves to chatbots if required. This event is especially critical if the chatbot is to access not only generic information (factual, conceptual, procedural, or social) but also content-specific knowledge about the individual learner. This idea might include personal, performance-related, or behavioral data.

Despite all of the chatbots' benefits, users and developers fully know the agent's various flaws and limits. Depending on the chatbot's job, data storage, or database connection, it is critical to define the themes of data protection, data storage, data security, data integrity, and data deletion at an early stage. Chatbots using messaging programs or services are problematic from a privacy standpoint, according to Cahn (2017), because services such as Facebook Messenger do not provide end-to-end encryption by default and cannot guarantee user identity. Simultaneously, many chatbots and services contain and analyze sensitive data (personal data, images, audio, and video). Furthermore, there is a trend among institutions for in-house development and local data storage and processing.

Experts highlight the benefits of intelligent assistants or messaging apps, such as a familiar user interface, no installation, no charges, game integration, and media sharing (Smutny & Schreiberova, 2020). Another critical aspect of chatbot integrity is that ethical problems must be addressed. Aside from data security, there is a high need for explainable AI (XAI), which is especially significant in education (Gunning, 2017). Zanzotto (2019) advocates for responsible AI with a "human-in-the-loop" and a defined knowledge life cycle to avoid AI or chatbot bias. Meanwhile, practically all chatbots, up to date, are typically in forms of text-based because of modern contexts and trends. They are more likely to convey and solve problems through text-based versions. Nonverbal ones tend to concentrate on multidisciplinary fields such as education and healthcare, most notably utilizing an embodied agent to instruct autistic patients (Rafayet et al., 2020).

Implications

According to Adamopoulou and Moussiades (2020), chatbots can enhance customer service and reduce service costs. From a user's viewpoint, the most significant reasons to use chatbots are productivity, amusement, social elements, and novelty engagement. In addition, the advent of chatbots has significantly impacted human work, especially in education. Some examples are teaching assessments, reflections, language learning, inspiration, coaching, administration, or productivity help (Garcia Brustenga et al., 2018). So far, chatbots have focused on the help they can provide, ranging from broad to minimal, namely the learning process, administrative work, and, last but not least psychological difficulties.

Chatbots can be customized and personalized based on a given basic framework due to their self-learning (pre-training) nature and domain-specific information and rules for their unique use cases. Developers use cognitive computing for educational reasons, in which a cognitive assistant (e.g., a cognitive bot) combines several AI functions (Lytras et al., 2019). Most chatbots use a retrieval-based approach, where replies are created based on pre-trained criteria and matched using a machine learning classification task. On the contrary, while retrieval-based models offer precise and proper replies in case of a correct match, they cannot answer unobserved queries or intentions that do not have predetermined responses or actions (Winkler & Söllner, 2018).

Students collaborate with digital assistants in a current educational requirement, which will become standard in future professional activities. The authors of "Human+Machine." and "Reimagining Work in the Age of AI" contend that people need new abilities to collaborate with intelligent machines, as well as a better knowledge of the complementing human-machine relationship (Daugherty & Wilson, 2018): "Various AI applications require the development, training, and management of humans." They are allowing such systems to act as real collaborative partners. Machines in the missing middle, for their part, are assisting everyone to punch above their weight by giving them superhuman powers, such as the capacity to collect and analyze massive volumes of data from disparate sources in real-time. Human talents are being enhanced by machines" (p. 6). This idea leads to true personalization and the merging or self-storage of learning items and even learning routes (Hobert, 2019).

There are numerous creation techniques, with retrieval-based models distinct from generative models. The former is based on a list of predetermined replies, with an algorithm selecting the best-matching response, whereas the latter is dependent on the input. Chatbot input modality, specific speech over text input, is acceptable for our context and learning architecture. In order to determine the appropriate solutions, developers might use contextual information such as time, location, user information, and learning path data.

With this in mind, several educational institutions are incorporating chatbots into their systems. In general, a company called Engati has created a paradigm that other institutions may modify and utilize to establish their chatbots for personal use. For example, the University of Rochester sought to make obstetrician-gynecologist (OBGYN) and mental health information accessible to students and staff. Their Engati bot assists students and professors with physical and emotional wellness, including delivering guided meditations and workouts. They found the platform so easy to use that they were able to create an almost human-sounding bot in just 14 days. Podar Education Network, on the other hand, needs a method to grow its parent outreach. They needed to expedite their sales cycle, handle a flood of inquiries, and combine their engagement system with their existing marketing platform to store leads. Their Engati bot handles 79% of all inquiries, with only the most complicated ones routed to live chat agents. This assisted Podar in reducing resolution time by 89% and converting 31% of users into MQLs ("Education Chatbot: 10 Powerful Applications for 2022," n.d.).

Furthermore, The UK Cabinet wants to undertake a campaign to reach students, particularly those from underrepresented groups, and urge them to pursue STEM studies. It launched the Young Scientist Competition with the Ministry of Innovation, Business, and Sustainability. Consequently, they used a conversational model to build an AI-powered chatbot to reach out to students and spread the word about the campaign. The bot shares tales about former Young Scientists competition winners and even prompts current participants to write about prior winners' work on social media, bringing further attention to the initiative. The bot even assisted students in drafting social media postings and selecting appropriate hashtags. The UK Cabinet Office increased user engagement by 43.5% by implementing this chatbot.

Qassim University, located in Qassim, Saudi Arabia, was one of the earliest modern institutions. It attempted to engage and support students and prospects through social media and its website. The school desired to respond to inquiries about admissions, scholarships, student communities, faculties, and other topics as quickly as possible. Qassim University created a chatbot using Engati's no-code conversational modeler to speed up the resolution of these inquiries and handle as many of them as needed. The bot is now live on Twitter, Telegram, WhatsApp, and the university website, allowing the university to manage 30 times as many requests as before. They also used the live chat option included with Engati to provide additional help when needed. The bot resolves 90% of incoming requests without needing to escalate to an agent, and the university's response time has increased by 88%. AsasaraBot appeared in the Greek educational system as a supplement to offline instructors, delivering knowledge about the Minoan civilization and representing the figure of the Minoan serpent goddess. In Greece, a public Lyceum and two private language schools examined the associated chatbot-based teaching program in two foreign languages, French and English (Mageira et al., 2022).

Evaluation The Feasibility

There will be no successful outcome unless evidence of feasibility is shown. Hence, Hobert (2019) developed evaluation objectives and related them to the primary research techniques. This fact supports the goal of presenting a complete framework and providing a foundation for future research initiatives that evaluate the use of chatbots beyond specific evaluation criteria (Pinkwart & Konert, 2019).

The following are the seven features of evaluation objectives:

- Adoption and acceptance
- Success in education
- Motivation
- Usability
- Technical accuracy
- Additional psychological aspects
- Advantageous outcomes

Procedures have four characteristics:

- Wizard of Oz test
- Technical verification
- Experiment in the laboratory
- Experiment in the field

The following are five properties of measuring instruments:

- A quantitative survey is conducted following a laboratory or field investigation with users of a pedagogical conversational agent. (Post)
- Quantitative survey involving users of a pedagogical conversational agent before and after a laboratory or field investigation (Pre/Post)
- Qualitative interview research with pedagogical conversational agent users
- Discourse analysis of transcripts from learners' interactions with a pedagogical conversational agent
- Analysis of technical log files generated when using a pedagogical conversational agent

Those are the criteria inspired by Hobert (2019). Other publications and journals describe the assessment process, but this is by far the most extensive and exhaustive description, intending to measure the capacity to fulfill all needs in constructing a chatbot. Above all, a chatbot must provide proper replies, ease human work, and assist users in their intended purpose (Hobert, 2019).

CHALLENGES AND FUTURE DIRECTIONS

The preceding sections indicate a large body of research on educational chatbots regarding application areas, design concepts, interaction mechanisms, and evaluation methods. However, there are significant barriers to using chatbots in educational applications.

Data Efficiency

Chatbots, like other machine learning systems, are enabled by training datasets. Data-driven conversation systems, in particular, are more data-hungry than ever. Unfortunately, because data collection is time-consuming and expensive, there is little or no training data for all areas of education. In addition, the relevant educational data cannot be accessed due to legal restrictions on privacy protection.

One method for addressing the problem of insufficient data in training conversation systems is to use pre-trained large language models in zero-shot or few-shot learning scenarios (Kuhail, Alturki, Alramlawi, and Alhejori, 2022). These techniques allow dialogue systems to talk to humans without further training.

Despite their strength, such models are better suited for general chat-chit rather than task-oriented conversational systems. Specialized data is necessary to teach chatbots in diverse educational disciplines like medicine, science, and psychology. A massive source of relevant data was also needed to provide information for chatbots that went beyond common conversation utterances (Folstad et al., 2021).

In practice, businesses might use chatbots after training them with little data. The system improved by continuing to train the bots with incoming data in the scheme of active learning, continuous learning, or long-term learning (McTear, n.d.).

User Engagement

Avram Piltch described on the Tom's guide blog (Piltch, 2016) how end-users perceive chatbots as meaningless and dumb. The primary reasons for this conclusion are the lack of chatbots in comprehending the goal of end-users, the burden flow of discussion, and monotonous templated answers.

Educational chatbots, like regular chatbots, must reliably recognize the intent of each speech provided by instructors, students, or academic personnel. This performance is heavily reliant on the competence of the natural language understanding (NLU) module, which should be taught to recognize user utterances in the context of learning. For example, instead of clubs for amusement, a chatbot should refer to the phrase "club" of campus activities. The previously described issue should be solved by fine-tuning NLUs using appropriate data.

Another thing to think about is the design process. According to research (Verleger & Pembridge, 2018), the lack of participation of end-users, students, instructors, or educational officers in the design process may have decreased engagement and motivation over time. Hence, in the future, the design of a chatbot should be user-centered, including instructor approval, continuous feedback collection, and student knowledge evaluation.

Giving a chatbot personality can help consumers believe they are communicating in a human-like way of thinking. (Smestad & Volden, n.d.) Suggested that using a chatbot's personality to encourage a good user experience may have beneficial outcomes.

Finally, studying how responses are created and communicated in conversations is necessary. Knowledge, understanding, convergent thinking, assessment, and synthesis are all essential skills. The chatbot actively updates its language model with trendy phrases and new concepts to entice end users. A chatbot with an auto-generating module is more user-friendly than one with a template for each response.

Interdisciplinary Domains

Current research on educational chatbots focuses on several courses, including language, computer, engineering, health, medical, science, business, management, art, and design (Hwang & Chang, 2021). The domains mentioned earlier, however, do not give a comprehensive view of the educational landscapes. According to Anderson's book, Krathwohl's A taxonomy for learning, teaching, and evaluation, there are three learning domains: cognitive, psychomotor (skills), and emotional. According to Wollny et al. (2021), the majority of research involves the cognitive issue, which trains students in scientific and social elements; yet, only one study on writing skills (Lin & Chang, 2020) and one on communication abilities (Hwang & Chang, 2021) are included. A lesser number of persons are involved in the moving part. Meanwhile, territory institutions are focused mainly on research, with a constraint on other types of education like social, health care, cross-domains, etc. The image will be much more complete in the future by increasing the range of issues investigated by chatbots in education.

Localization

Shin, Al-Imamy & Hwang, (2022) discusses how cultural and social contexts affect user experience. The historical example is that the English use "football" whereas the Americans use "soccer." Integrating cultural and social context chatbots to adapt to people's learning is a promising direction.

Some nations, such as India, Malaysia, Singapore, and the United States, are multicultural and noted for their many dialects and slang. Hence, a multilingual chatbot is required in education to accommodate students with diverse mother tongues.

Development Framework

People working in education may not be experts in software development, and their IT infrastructure may range from small to large. In the future, a framework should help non-professional software engineers create a chatbot or a low-code system. A framework for educational development should enable several phases, including requirements, design, deployment, and assessment. The process should automatically go through all stages without human intervention for an extended period and process incoming data in the future. In the future, the rise of MLOPs in building machine learning systems will provide a fleshed-out system.

Embodied Agents:

According to Hobert & Meyer Von Wolff (2019), there are two pedagogical conversational agents: embodied and text. However, compared to textual agents, embodied agents have attracted less research attention because they involve multiple modeling, complex processes, and challenging integration.

Cassell (n.d.) was developed by Justine Cassell in 2000 and used in various fields ranging from health care to physics to education.

"An embodied chatbot has a physical body, typically in the shape of a human or a cartoon animal, which enables them to portray facial expressions and emotions" (Serenko, Bontis & Detlor, 2007). ECA is successful in educating students in settings to enhance peer engagement in learning ("RAPT | ArticuLab," n.d.) or to develop social skills in young learners (Mageira et al., 2022). As the presentation title suggests, several studies use Virtual Reality and Graphic Computing to improve the performance of embodied agents. For example, using Embodied Conversational Agents for Experiential Learning ("VR Meets AI Meets the Matrix: Using Embodied Conversational Agents for Experiential Learning," n.d).

REFERENCES

Adamopoulou, E., & Moussiades, L. (2020). Chatbots: History, technology, and applications. *Machine Learning with Applications*, 2(53), 100006. doi:10.1016/j.mlwa.2020.100006

Akcora, D. E., Belli, A., Berardi, M., Casola, S., Di Blas, N., Falletta, S., & Vannella, F. (2018, June). Conversational support for education. In *International conference on artificial intelligence in education* (pp. 14-19). Springer.

Alepis, E., & Virvou, M. (2011). Automatic generation of emotions in tutoring agents for affective e-learning in medical education. *Expert Systems with Applications*, 38(8), 9840–9847. doi:10.1016/j.eswa.2011.02.021

Alias, S., Sainin, M. S., Soo Fun, T., & Daut, N. (2019, November). Identification of Conversational Intent Pattern Using Pattern-Growth Technique for Academic Chatbot. In *International Conference on Multi-disciplinary Trends in Artificial Intelligence* (pp. 263-270). Springer. 10.1007/978-3-030-33709-4_24

Allison, D. (2012). Chatbors in the library: Is it time? *Library Hi Tech*, 30(1), 95–107. doi:10.1108/07378831211213238

Anderson, L., Krathwohl, D., Airasian, P., Cruikshank, K., Mayer, R., Pintrich, P., & Wittrock, M. (2001). *Assessing a revision Of Bloom's taxonomy of educational objectives.* Pearson. https://www.uky.edu/~rsand1/china2018/texts/Anderson-Krathwo hl%20-%20A%20taxonomy%20for%20learning%20teaching%20and%20as sessing.pdf

Ask Alice. (n.d.). *Homepage.* Ask Alice. http://www.alicebot.org/aiml.html

Benotti, L., Martnez, M. C., & Schapachnik, F. (2017). Atool for introducing computer science with automatic formative assessment. *IEEE Transactions on Learning Technologies, 11*(2), 179–192. doi:10.1109/TLT.2017.2682084

Bickmore, T. W., Mitchell, S. E., Jack, B. W., Paasche-Orlow, M. K., Pfeifer, L. M., & O'Donnell, J. (2010). Response to a relational agent by hospital patients with depressive symptoms. *Interacting with Computers, 22*(4), 289–298. doi:10.1016/j.intcom.2009.12.001 PMID:20628581

Bickmore, T. W., Schulman, D., & Sidner, C. (2013). Automated interventions for multiple health behaviors using conversational agents. *Patient Education and Counseling, 92*(2), 142–148. doi:10.1016/j.pec.2013.05.011 PMID:23763983

Cahn, J. (2017). *CHATBOT: Architecture.* Design, & Development.

Cassell, J. (n.d.). Embodied Conversational Agents Representation and Intelligence in User Interfaces. American Association for Artificial Intelligence. http://www.justinecassell.com/publications/AIMag22-04-007.PD F

Chang, M., & Hwang, J. (2019). Developing Chatbot with Deep Learning Techniques for Negotiation Course. *2019 8Th International Congress On Advanced Applied Informatics (IIAI-AAI).* IEEE. 10.1109/IIAI-AAI.2019.00220

Christensen, A. (2007). A Trend from Germany: Library Chatbots in Digital Reference. Tilburg university. https://www.tilburguniversity.nl/services/lis/ticer/07carte/publicat/07christensen

Ciupe, A., Mititica, D. F., Meza, S., & Orza, B. (2019, April). Learning Agile with Intelligent Conversational Agents. In *2019 IEEE Global Engineering Education Conference (EDUCON)* (pp. 1100-1107). IEEE. 10.1109/EDUCON.2019.8725192

Clarizia, F., Colace, F., Lombardi, M., Pascale, F., & Santaniello, D. (2018). Chatbot: An education support system for student. In *International symposium on cyberspace safety and security* (pp. 291–302). SCIRP.

Connaway, L. S., Dickey, T. J., & Radford, M. L. (2011). If it is too inconvenient I'm not going after it: Convenience as a critical factor in information-seeking behaviors. *Library & Information Science Research*, *33*(3), 179–190. doi:10.1016/j.lisr.2010.12.002

Crockett, K., Latham, A., & Whitton, N. (2017). On predicting learning styles in conversational intelligent tutoring systems using fuzzy decision trees. *International Journal of Human-Computer Studies*, *97*, 98–115. doi:10.1016/j.ijhcs.2016.08.005

Cunningham-Nelson, S., Boles, W., Trouton, L., & Margerison, E. (2019). A review of chatbots in education: practical steps forward. In *30th Annual Conference for the Australasian Association for Engineering Education (AAEE 2019): Educators Becoming Agents of Change: Innovate, Integrate, Motivate*, (pp. 299-306). Engineers Australia.

Daud, S. H. M., Teo, N. H. I., & Zain, N. H. M. (2020). Ejava chatbot for learning programming language: Apost-pandemic alternative virtual tutor. *International Journal (Toronto, Ont.)*, *8*(7), 3290–3298.

Daugherty, P. R., & Wilson, H. J. (2018). Human + machine: Reimagining work in the age of AI. *Harvard Business Review*.

Durall, E., & Kapros, E. (2020, July). Co-design for a competency self-assessment chatbot and survey in science education. In *International conference on human-computer interaction* (pp. 13-24). Springer. 10.1007/978-3-030-50506-6_2

Elnozahy, W. A., El Khayat, G. A., Cheniti-Belcadhi, L., & Said, B. (2019). Question Answering System to Support University Students' Orientation, Recruitment and Retention. *Procedia Computer Science*, *164*, 56–63. doi:10.1016/j.procs.2019.12.154

Fleming, M. (2018). Streamlining student course requests using chatbots. In *29th Australasian Association for Engineering Education Conference 2018 (AAEE 2018)*. Engineers Australia.

Følstad, A., Araujo, T., Law, E., Brandtzaeg, P., Papadopoulos, S., Reis, L., Baez, M., Laban, G., McAllister, P., Ischen, C., Wald, R., Catania, F., Meyer von Wolff, R., Hobert, S., & Luger, E. (2021). Future directions for chatbot research: An interdisciplinary research agenda. *Computing*, *103*(12), 2915–2942. doi:10.100700607-021-01016-7

Fryer, L. K., Ainley, M., Thompson, A., Gibson, A., & Sherlock, Z. (2017). Stimulating and sustaining interest in a language course: An experimental comparison of Chatbot and Human task partners. *Computers in Human Behavior*, *75*(17), 461–468. doi:10.1016/j.chb.2017.05.045

Galiamova, K., Pavlov, Y., Smirnova, E., Zakharov, M., & Zverev, A. (2018). Psychological adaptation mechanism of the higher education engineering students: artificial conversational entity usage for help. *Inted Proceedings*. Iated. 10.21125/inted.2018.0667

Garcia Brustenga, G., Fuertes Alpiste, M., & Molas Castells, N. (2018). *Briefing Paper: Chatbots in Education. Universitat Oberta de Catalunya*. UOC. doi:10.7238/elc.chatbots.2018

Graesser, A. C. (2016). Conversations with AutoTutor help students learn. *International Journal of Artificial Intelligence in Education, 26*(1), 124–132. doi:10.100740593-015-0086-4

Graves, S. J., & Desai, C. M. (2006). Instruction via chat reference: Does co-browse help? *RSR. Reference Services Review, 34*(3), 340–357. doi:10.1108/00907320610685300

Griol, D., Baena, I., Molina, J. M., & de Miguel, A. S. (2014). A multimodal conversational agent for personalized language learning. In *Ambient intelligence-software and applications* (pp. 13–21). Springer. doi:10.1007/978-3-319-07596-9_2

Gull, S., Qureshi, J., & Syed, N. (2019). An indelible link between learning and technology. *Journal of Asian and African Social Science and Humanities, 5*(2), 58–73.

Gunning, D. (2017). Explainable artificial intelligence (xai). Defense Advanced Research Projects Agency (DARPA). *Nd Web, 2*, 2.

Harley, J. M., Carter, C. K., Papaionnou, N., Bouchet, F., Landis, R. S., Azevedo, R., & Karabachian, L. (2016). Examining the predictive relationship between personality and emotion traits and students' agent-directed emotions: Towards emotionally-adaptive agent-based learning environments. *User Modeling and User-Adapted Interaction, 26*(2-3), 177–219. doi:10.100711257-016-9169-7

Harley, J. M., Carter, C. K., Papaionnou, N., Bouchet, F., Landis, R. S., Azevedo, R., & Karabachian, L. (2016). Examining the predictive relationship between personality and emotion traits and students' agent-directed emotions: towards emotionally-adaptive agent-based learning environments. *User Modeling and User-Adapted Interaction, 26*(2-3), 177-219. https://link.springer.com/article/10.1007/s11257-016-9169-7

Hien, H. T., Cuong, P. N., Nam, L. N. H., Nhung, H. L. T. K., & Thang, L. D. (2018, December). Intelligent assistants in higher-education environments: the FIT-EBot, a chatbot for administrative and learning support. In *Proceedings of the ninth international symposium on information and communication technology* (pp. 69-76). ACM. 10.1145/3287921.3287937

Hiremath, G., Hajare, A., Bhosale, P., Nanaware, R., & Wagh, K. S. (2018). Chatbot for education system. International Journal of Advance Research. *Ideas and Innovations in Technology*, 4(3), 37–43.

Hobert, S. (2019). How Are You, Chatbot? Evaluating Chatbots in Educational Settings – Results of a Literature Review. GI. doi:10.18420/DELFI2019_289

Hobert, S., & Meyer Von Wolff, R. (2019). Say Hello to Your New Automated Tutor -A Structured Literature Review on Pedagogical Conversational Agents. *Core*. https://core.ac.uk/download/pdf/301380749.pdf

Hwang, G.-J., & Chang, C.-Y. (2021). A review of opportunities and challenges of chatbots in education. *Interactive Learning Environments*, 1–14. doi:10.1080/104 94820.2021.1952615

ISTE. (2017). *ISTE standards for students*. ISTE. https://www.iste.org/standards/standards/for-students

Keierleber, M. (2022, April 13). Young and depressed? Try Woebot! The rise of mental health chatbots in the US. *The Guardian*. https://www.theguardian.com/us-news/2022/apr/13/chatbots-rob ot-therapists-youth-mental-health-crisis

Kuhail, M. A., Alturki, N., Alramlawi, S., & Alhejori, K. (2022). Interacting with educational chatbots: A systematic review. *Education and Information Technologies*, 1–46. doi:10.100710639-022-11177-3

Lam, C. S. N., Chan, L. K., & See, C. Y. H. (2018). Converse, connect and consolidate– The development of an artificial intelligence chatbot for health sciences education. In *Frontiers in medical and health sciences education conference*. Bau Institute of Medical and Health Sciences Education, The University of Hong Kong.

Lee, L.-K., Fung, Y.-C., Pun, Y.-W., Wong, K.-K., Yu, M. T.-Y., & Wu, N.-I. (2020). *Using a multiplatform chatbot as an onlinetutor in a university course. In 2020 international symposium on educational technology (ISET)*. IEEE.

Lin, M. P., & Chang, D. (2020). Enhancing Post-secondary Writers' Writing Skills with a Chatbot: A Mixed-Method Classroom Study. *Journal of Educational Technology & Society*, 23, 78–92.

Lin, Y. H., & Tsai, T. (2019, December). A conversational assistant on mobile devices for primitive learners of computer programming. In *2019 IEEE International Conference on Engineering, Technology and Education (TALE)* (pp. 1-4). IEEE. 10.1109/TALE48000.2019.9226015

Liu, Y., Muheidat, F., Papailler, K., & Prado, W. (n.d.). VR Meets AI Meets the Matrix: Using Embodied Conversational Agents for Experiential Learning. *Educause.* https://events.educause.edu/eli/annual-meeting/2022/agenda/vr-meets-ai-meets-the-matrix-using-embodied-conversational-agents-for-experiential-learning

Lytras, M., Visvizi, A., Damiani, E., & Mathkour, H. (2019). The cognitive computing turn in education Prospects and application. *Computers in Human Behavior*, *92*, 446–449. doi:10.1016/j.chb.2018.11.011

Mageira, K., Pittou, D., Papasalouros, A., Kotis, K., Zangogianni, P., & Daradoumis, A. (2022). Educational AI Chatbots for Content and Language Integrated Learning. *Applied Sciences (Basel, Switzerland)*, *12*(7), 3239. doi:10.3390/app12073239

Mckie, I. A. S., & Narayan, B. (2019). Enhancing the academic library experience with chatbots: An exploration of research and implications for practice. *Journal of the Australian Library and Information Association*, *68*(3), 268–277. doi:10.1080/24750158.2019.1611694

McNeal, M. L., & Newyear, D. (2013). Chapter 1: Introducing chatbots in libraries. Library Technolgy Reports, 49(8), 5-10.

McTear, M. (2021). *Conversational AI*. Morgan & Claypool.

Medeiros, R. P., Ramalho, G. L., & Falcão, T. P. (2018). A systematic literature review on teaching and learning introductory programming in higher education. *IEEE Transactions on Education*, *62*(2), 77–90. doi:10.1109/TE.2018.2864133

Mendez, S., Johanson, K., Martin Conley, V., Gosha, K., & Mack, A. (2020). Chatbots: Atoolto supplementthe future faculty mentoring of doctoral engineering students. *International Journal of Doctoral Studies*, *15*, 15. doi:10.28945/4579

Merchant, S. (2021, March 2). *The Best ChatBots For Behavioral Health.* AIM. https://www.aimblog.io/2021/03/02/these-chatbots-are-helping-with-mental-health-right-now/

Meyer von Wolff, R., & Hobert, S. (2019). Say Hello to Your New Automated Tutor – A Structured Literature Review on Pedagogical Conversational Agents, *Internationale Tagung Wirtschaftsinformatik*, *1*(14), 301-314. Tagungsband

Mikic-Fonte, F. A., Llamas-Nistal, M., & Caeiro-Rodríguez, M. (2018, October). Using a Chatterbot as a FAQ Assistant in a Course about Computers Architecture. In *2018 IEEE Frontiers in Education Conference (FIE)* (pp. 1-4). IEEE. 10.1109/FIE.2018.8659174

Molnár, G., & Szüts, Z. (2018, September). The role of chatbots in formal education. In *2018 IEEE 16th International Symposium on Intelligent Systems and Informatics (SISY)* (pp. 000197-000202). IEEE. 10.1109/SISY.2018.8524609

Murad, D. F., Irsan, M., Akhirianto, P. M., Fernando, E., Murad, S. A., & Wijaya, M. H. (2019, July). Learning Support System using Chatbot in" Kejar C Package" Homeschooling Program. In *2019 International Conference on Information and Communications Technology (ICOIACT)* (pp. 32-37). IEEE. 10.1109/ICOIACT46704.2019.8938479

Nardi, B. A., & O'Day, V. (1996). Intelligent agents: What we learned at the library. *Libri, 46*(2), 59–88. doi:10.1515/libr.1996.46.2.59

Ndukwe, I. G., Daniel, B. K., & Amadi, C. E. (2019, June). A machine learning grading system using chatbots. In *International conference on artificial intelligence in education* (pp. 365-368). Springer. 10.1007/978-3-030-23207-8_67

Nguyen, H. D., Pham, V. T., Tran, D. A., & Le, T. T. (2019, October). Intelligent tutoring chatbot for solving mathematical problems in High-school. In *2019 11th International Conference on Knowledge and Systems Engineering (KSE)* (pp. 1-6). IEEE. 10.1109/KSE.2019.8919396

Okonkwo, C. W., & Ade-Ibijola, A. (2020). Python-Bot: A Chatbot for Teaching Python Programming. *Engineering Letters, 29*(1).

Ondáš, S., Pleva, M., & Hládek, D. (2019). How chatbots can be involved in the education process. In *2019 17th international conference on emerging elearning technologies and applications (ICETA)* (pp. 575–580). IEEE. 10.1109/ICETA48886.2019.9040095

Oudeyer, P.-Y., Gottlieb, J., & Lopes, M. (2016). Intrinsic motivation, curiosity, and learning: Theory and applications in educational technologies. In B. S. S. Knecht (Ed.), Progress in Brain Research: Vol. 229. *MotivationTheory, Neurobiology and Applications* (pp. 257–284). Elsevier. doi:10.1016/bs.pbr.2016.05.005

Pham, X. L., Pham, T., Nguyen, Q. M., Nguyen, T. H., & Cao, T. T. H. (2018, November). Chatbot as an intelligent personal assistant for mobile language learning. In *Proceedings of the 2018 2nd International Conference on Education and E-Learning* (pp. 16-21). ACM. 10.1145/3291078.3291115

Piltch, A. (2016, April 18). Talk is CHEAP: Why Chatbots will always be a waste of time. *Tom's Guide.* https://www.tomsguide.com/us/chatbots-waste-our-time,news-22562.html

Pinkwart, N., & Konert, J. (2019). How Are You, Chatbot? Evaluating Chatbots in Educational Settings -Results of a Literature Review, 259. *GI.* doi:10.18420/delfi2019_289

Rafayet Ali, M., Sen, T., Kane, B., Bose, S., Carroll, T. M., Epstein, R. & Hoque, E. (2020). Novel Computational Linguistic Measures, Dialogue System, and the Development of SOPHIE: Standardized Online Patient for Healthcare Interaction Education. Cornell University.

Ranoliya, B. R., Raghuwanshi, N., & Singh, S. (2017, September). Chatbot for university related FAQs. In *2017 International Conference on Advances in Computing, Communications and Informatics (ICACCI)* (pp. 1525-1530). IEEE. 10.1109/ICACCI.2017.8126057

RAPT & ArticuLab. (n.d.). *Overview.* ArticuLab, CMU. http://articulab.hcii.cs.cmu.edu/projects/rapt/

Rodrigo, M. M. T., Baker, R. S., Agapito, J., Nabos, J., Repalam, M. C., Reyes, S. S., & San Pedro, M. O. C. (2012). The efects of an interactive software agent on student afective dynamics while using; an intelligent tutoring system. *IEEE Transactions on Affective Computing, 3*(2), 224–236. doi:10.1109/T AFFC.2011.41

Rooein, D. (2019, May). Data-driven edu chatbots. In *Companion Proceedings of The 2019 World Wide Web Conference* (pp. 46-49). ACM. 10.1145/3308560.3314191

Ruan, S., Jiang, L., Xu, Q., Liu, Z., Davis, G. M., Brunskill, E., & Landay, J. A. (2021). Englishbot: An ai-powered conversational system for second language learning. In *26th international conference on intelligent user interfaces* (pp. 434–444). ACM.

Rubin, V. L., Chen, Y., & Thorimbert, L. M. (2010). Artificially intelligent conversational agents in libraries. *Library Hi Tech, 28*(4), 496–522. doi:10.1108/07378831011096196

Sandu, N., & Gide, E. (2019, September). Adoption of AI-Chatbots to enhance student learning experience in higher education in India. In *2019 18th International Conference on Information Technology Based Higher Education and Training (ITHET)* (pp. 1-5). IEEE.

Satow, L. (2019). Lernen mit Chatbots und digitalin Assistenten. In A. Hohenstein & K. Wilbers (Eds.), *Handbuch E-Learning.* Wolters Kluwer.

Serenko, A., Bontis, N., & Detlor, B. (2007). End-user adoption of animated interface agentsin everyday work applications. Behaviour &Amp. *Información Tecnológica, 26*(2), 119–132. doi:10.1080/01449290500260538

Shin, D., Al-Imamy, S., & Hwang, Y. (2022). Cross-cultural differences in information processing of chatbot journalism: Chatbot news service as a cultural artifact. Cross Cultural &Amp. *Strategic Management, 29*(3), 618–638. doi:10.1108/CCSM-06-2020-0125

Sinha, S., Basak, S., Dey, Y., & Mondal, A. (2020). An educational Chatbot for answering queries. In *Emerging technology in modelling and graphics* (pp. 55–60). Springer. doi:10.1007/978-981-13-7403-6_7

Skjuve, M., Følstad, A., Fostervold, K. I., & Brandtzaeg, P. B. (2021). My chatbot companion-a study of human-chatbot relationships. *International Journal of Human-Computer Studies, 149*, 102601. doi:10.1016/j.ijhcs.2021.102601

Smestad, T., & Volden, F. (n.d.). Chatbot Personalities Matters Improving the user experience of chatbot interfaces. *Conversations 2018.* Springer. https://conversations2018.files.wordpress.com/2018/10/conversations_2018_paper_11_preprint1.pdf

Smith-Griffin, J. (2022, January 18). 3 ways chatbots can support mental health in schools. *eSchool News.* https://www.eschoolnews.com/2022/01/18/3-ways-chatbots-can-support-mental-health-in-schools/2/

Smutny, P., & Schreiberova, P. (2020). Chatbots for learning: A review of educational chatbots for the Facebook Messenger. *Computers & Education, 151*, 103862. doi:10.1016/j.compedu.2020.103862

Söllner, M., Bitzer, P., Janson, A., & Leimeister, J. M. (2017). Process is king: Evaluating the performance of technology-mediated learning in vocational software training. *Journal of Information Technology, 18*(2), 159.

Song, D., Oh, E. Y., & Rice, M. (2017, July). Interacting with a conversational agent system for educational purposes in online courses. In *2017 10th international conference on human system interactions (HSI)* (pp. 78-82). IEEE. 10.1109/HSI.2017.8005002

Sreelakshmi, A. S., Abhinaya, S. B., Nair, A., & Nirmala, S. J. (2019, November). A question answering and quiz generation chatbot for education. In *2019 Grace Hopper Celebration India (GHCI)* (pp. 1-6). IEEE.

Tegos, S., Psathas, G., Tsiatsos, T., Katsanos, C., Karakostas, A., Tsibanis, C., & Demetriadis, S. (2020). Enriching synchronous collaboration in online courses with confgurable conversational agents. In *International Conference on Intelligent Tutoring Systems* (pp. 284–294). Springer. 10.1007/978-3-030-49663-0_34

Troussas, C., Krouska, A., & Virvou, M. (2017, November). Integrating an adjusted conversational agent into a mobile-assisted language learning application. In *IEEE 29th International Conference on Tools with Artificial Intelligence (ICTAI)* (pp. 1153-1157). IEEE. 10.1109/ICTAI.2017.00176

UCI Libraries Reference Department. (2012, September 17). *Retrieved from Policies and procedures: Reference Statistics Category Definitions:* UCI. http://staff.lib.uci.edu/refstats-docs.php

Ureta, J., & Rivera, J. P. (2018). *Using chatbots to teach stem related research concepts t o high school students.* Research Gate.

van der Meij, H., van der Meij, J., & Harmsen, R. (2015). Animated pedagogical agents effects on enhancing student motivation and learning in a science inquiry learning environment. *Educational Technology Research and Development, 63*(3), 381–403. doi:10.100711423-015-9378-5

Verleger, M., & Pembridge, J. (2018). A Pilot Study Integrating an AI-driven Chatbot in an Introductory Programming Course. *2018 IEEE Frontiers In Education Conference (FIE).* IEEE. 10.1109/FIE.2018.8659282

Winkler, R., Hobert, S., Salovaara, A., & Söllner, M., & Leimeister, Jan Marco (2020). Sara, the lecturer: Improving learning in online education with a scafolding-based conversational agent. In *Proceedings of the 2020 CHI conference on human factors in computing systems* (pp. 1–14). ACM. 10.1145/3313831.3376781

Winkler, R., & Söllner, M. (2018). Unleashing the potential of chatbots in education: A state-of-the-art analysis. In *Academy of Management Annual Meeting (AOM).* AOM. 10.5465/AMBPP.2018.15903abstract

Wollny, S., Schneider, J., Di Mitri, D., Weidlich, J., Rittberger, M., & Drachsler, H. (2021). Are We There Yet? - A Systematic Literature Review on Chatbots in Education. *Frontiers in Artificial Intelligence, 4,* 654924. doi:10.3389/frai.2021.654924 PMID:34337392

Yang, S., & Evans, C. (2019, November). Opportunities and challenges in using AI chatbots in higher education. In *Proceedings of the 2019 3rd International Conference on Education and E-Learning* (pp. 79-83). 10.1145/3371647.3371659

Zanzotto, F. M. (2019). *Human-in-the-loop Artificial Intelligence.* ACM.

Chapter 7
Edubot:
A Framework for Chatbot in Education

Rawad Hammad
https://orcid.org/0000-0002-7900-8640
University of East London, UK

Mohammed Bhaja
University of Birmingham, UK

Jinal Patel
University of East London, UK

ABSTRACT

Recently, chatbots have been used in various domains including health care and entertainment. Despite the impact of using chatbots on student engagement, there is little investment in how to develop and use chatbots in education. Such use of advanced technologies supports student learning, both individually and collaboratively. The effective use of chatbots in education depends on different factors, including the learning process, teaching methods, communications, etc. In this paper, the authors focus on the systematic utilization of chatbots in education. A proof of concept has been developed and tested using two MSc module, i.e., cloud computing and software engineering. The authors have used AWS Services to build the backend of Chatbot and integrate it with Facebook Messenger to allow students to learn via an additional venue, i.e., social media. The use of EDUBOT proved that chatbot can improve student learning and engagement especially at the time of COVID-19 where higher education is moving towards online teaching. Extending EDUBOT framework will help to support students' admin and other queries.

DOI: 10.4018/978-1-6684-6234-8.ch007

INTRODUCTION

Education is a very important aspect of our daily life, with the aim of developing a community/person's character, abilities and social awareness. The central concern is to update the education system and make it interesting for the students to attracts them and keep them engaged all the time. The reception of innovation in the learning procedure causes people to improve their aptitudes, learn by their own time and spot. Additionally, in the ongoing time, the quantity of students per one class has increased, where a considerable part of them is not fully engaged or performing. Also, teaching at scales is getting more popularity in colleges or online such as massive open online courses (MOOCs) (Kuhail et al, 2022). However, such problems can be solved by intelligent learning tools such as chatbots or virtual assistants. A chatbot is an automated system designed to initiate a conversation with human users and other virtual agents. Chatbots provide a natural language interface to communicate with students through text or speech. Chatbots in education provide significant benefits to students but still in the early stage of in education.

Chatbots expand traditional learning and tutoring systems functionalities and outcomes. Traditional tutoring system are human-like interfaces between stakeholders in any learning scenario. Chatbot frameworks are computerised frameworks that provide prompt guidance to students (Bahja et al, 2019). Chatbot in education accompanies noteworthy positive results for study fulfilment (Kuhail et al, 2022). The utilisation of chatbot frameworks maintains additional channels for interaction with students, lecturers and teaching assistants (TAs). They also provide guidance to individuals to support learning goal achievements.

History of Chatbot

Chatbot applications in various domains have a long history returning in the time between 1964 - 1966 when the first chatbot Eliza made by Professor Joseph Weizenbaum in MIT Artificial Intelligence Lab (Zemcik, 2019). Eliza used to break down information sentences and make its reaction dependent on reassembly manages related with a deterioration of the information. Another well-known chatbot has been introduced by Kenneth Mark Colby at Stanford's Psychiatry Department in 1972 (Zemcik, 2019). The aim was to simulate the diseases and their spread processes. This technology was advanced then Eliza. In 1988 Jabberwacky has created another chatbot which has been designed to simulate a natural human conversation using a voice-operated system. In 1995, the Noble prize-winner Richard Wallace created A.L.I.C.E (Artificial Linguistic Internet Computer Entity), which uses heuristic pattern matching rules to human inputs. Furthermore, iPhone launched Siri in 2010, which is an intelligent personal assistant. Its discourse speech recognition engine was given by Nuance Communications and Siri utilizes progressed coordinating matching learning innovations to work. Google propelled its Google help in 2012, also Amazon launched Alexa in 2014. Cortana, virtual assistance created by Microsoft in 2015, which is a windows discourse stage including hardware and software components. It acts as a personal assistance recognizing Natural Language Processing (NLP) commands and interacts with users to respond to their queries and questions (Raj et al, 2019). More applications for voice based approaches, mainly depend on NLP, are getting more popularity due to the flexibility they provide, the easy way to interact with user and the effectiveness of handling users' requests. However, various technical issues exist but they are under continuous and rapid development which highlights the importance of this research.

Problem Statement

Students' engagement in education is a significant concern, which can be improved by Chatbots according to Georgescu (2018). It is challenging to maintain individual's attention for each and every student in traditional lectures, seminars or professional training. This is essential for learner's personal experience (Georgescu, 2018). As educational Chatbot has the capability to provide individualised and personalised teaching support to students, it can be a proper solution for student engagement (Hobert & Meyer, 2019). The continuously increasing number of contents published online amplified the difficulty of accessing information on time. However, the use of Artificial Intelligence (AI) as well as Machine Learning allow intelligent learning systems to be more effective (Hobert & Meyer, 2019). The presence of intelligent dialog-based systems such as Facebook Messenger bots rises the popularity of this kind of technology.

Research Questions

The recent development in information and communication technology has made AI more complex (Georgescu, 2018). The use of online learning dramatically increased at the time of COVID-19 crises. This research is an attempt to investigate the use of educational text-based or speech-based chatbots. Thus, the following research questions have been identified:

Research Question 1: What are the current chatbot-based innovations in learning processes?

Introducing Chatbots in different domains has led to various innovative use of technology. This research question will investigate the innovative use of chatbots in the currently existing learning and teaching environments. We will use a set of bibliographic databases including ACM, Springer, and IEEE to find related literature resources.

Research Question 2: Can the development and use of Educational Chatbots help to deliver effective and personalised learning to students? Providing one to one support for students is not possible in this era, but this problem can be solved, to some extent, by creating Chatbot. In this paper, we will create Educational Chatbot, henceforth EDUBOT, for providing one to one support to students.

To respond to the early-identified questions, we will explain the key concepts in traditional and modern educational systems and then move to the application of Chatbot in education. The rest of this paper is structure as follows. Section 2 summarises the key areas of research in chatbot and criticises related work. Section 3 demonstrates the research methodology used to carry out this research and how Design Science Research Methodology is used to create educational chatbots. Section 4 explains EDUBOT design and implementation, where various design artefacts have been presented to simplify the implementation of EDUBOT via a combination of: (i) Amazon Web Services (AWS) platform, i.e., Lambda and Lex, and (ii) Facebook Messenger console. Then, results and findings are discussed in Section 5, and finally conclusion is presented in Section 6.

LITERATURE REVIEW

A Chatbot provides its users with a natural language interface that can be adopted in many sectors such as education, commerce (Bahja, 2020). Recently, smart phone based Chatbots became popular, e.g., Apple Siri, Amazon Alexa, and Facebook messenger. The Facebook messenger has been used to send more than two billion business-related messages according to Facebook IQ Analysed Rising Topics and Trends in 2018. Since the online education system impacts student learning process and attention, technological tools have been used to support students in their learning process with creating online education environments. For instance, email, blogs, discussion boards, online whiteboards, chatrooms, social networking services, live presentation, which produce significant outcomes (Hammad et al, 2015). Such tools have been used widely in e-learning and their impact on learning and teaching process is documented (Molnár & Szüts, 2018). However, it should be noticed that without well-designed structures or content-related consideration, learning does not provide effective outcomes. Similarly, it is important to create systematic utilisation of Chatbot for learning, it could be difficult to make an effective learning structure for educational chatbots without knowing the underpinning technologies as explained in the following sub-sections.

Artificial Intelligence

The current advancements in technology pushed Artificial Intelligence (AI) into the focus of research and innovation (Hammad et al, 2015). The integration of AI in today's world makes our lives better but more complicated in many situations. There are two types of AI that might be relevant to the context of this research. These are: (i) weak AI and (ii) Artificial General Intelligence (AGI). Weak AI refers to computer program like playing a game or facial recognition. The program in weak AI techniques covers data mining and machine learning. However, programme belongs to AGI makes system which can solve problems like human does (Bahja, 2020). Most of the current innovation belong to weak AI and few can be considered as AGI. However, the effective integration of Artificial Intelligence in education requires the use of AGI.

Natural Language Processing (NLP) is the area of research and application that studies and examines how machines can interact with humans using natural language rather than formal commands (Molnár & Szüts, 2018). NLP computational techniques can be used to analyse large amount of natural language text for various reasons, which is central to Chatbots. In addition, NLP is useful in many applications such as multilingual, cross-language information retrieval, machine translations, speech recognition or text-based application.

Chatbot in Education

Chatbots have been utilised for a while in education. According to (Sandu & Gide, 2019), chatbots can be used for learning-focused purposes, e.g., teaching a concept, or for supportive administrative work that is necessary for education. Chatbots for administrative work are utilised in authoritative undertakings like understudy direction and assistance, e.g., admin supports. Chatbots with learning-focused purposes help students to learn and perform the required learning activities within their subjects/modules. Our research belongs to the second category, i.e., learning focused Chatbots. Besides this, there are exercises and practice Chatbots that present an improvement being referred to shape, to which the students give an answer that is surveyed by the Chatbot which at that point gives criticism (Sandu & Gide, 2019). For instance, the chatbot experiment conducted at Cardenal Herrera University shows few underpinning technologies and models of using chatbots in education (Sandu & Gide, 2019). During the previously-mentioned experiment, students used to type or say questions to the chatbot, which will give responses to students based on available data as well as techniques algorithms used by developers, e.g., Text Mining, NLP, etc. Later, students give feedback based on the responses provided by the Chatbot. They analysed the survey conducted and noticed that Chatbots

Table. 1. Comparing Traditional learning vs Educational-bot learning

Traditional Learning Environments	Modern Learning Environments, Chatbot-based
Mainly, driven by instructor	Students will be given more space to participate in their learning.
Depends on passive learning	Fuses both dynamic and active learning styles
Online platform are most likely repository areas	Online environments accommodate participatory learning approaches.
The learning condition is centred around educational programmes.	The learning environment is centred around student's profile, learning objectives, and needs.
The tutor is responsible for the student's excellence.	The student is exclusively liable for his/her greatness.

improved dialogic learning as it depends on informative conversations between the chatbot and the student.

Students' questions and responses were monitored for further analysis. On the one hand, it has been noticed that this chatbot was intelligent enough to analysis student's behaviours and give advice to them. Also, the results indicate that Chatbots are most likely used by students in resolving problems as it is easier than other forms, e.g., emails. On the other hand, results reveal that concerns such as getting incorrect advice and losing privacy remain central to considerable number of students. Table 1 highlights the differences between traditional learning environments and modern learning environments where chatbots and other AI-powered technologies are employed.

Other researchers such as Sjöström et al (2018) used design science research for designing Chatbots for higher education practices. They introduced a modular architecture for Chatbot and used Java programming to implement it. As shown in Figure 1, the core component of the proposed architecture is OrgBot which receives question form the user through UI and pass to AI as a services (AIaas). The OrgBot and AIaas is working with the basic chatbot principles. Results reveal that feedback from both students and lecturers was positive in general. Also, the Chatbot increased the communication between tutors and students and among students as well. hence, they conclude that chatbots increase the effectiveness of learning.

Another experiment conducted by Molnár and Szüts (2018) revealed the important role played by Chatbot in education. Students used Chatbot, i.e., NerdyBot, for various reasons such as getting information related to their studies, online tasks, assignments and other learning activities. They also used NerdyBot for sending reminders for exams, coursework and assignments. The chatbot performed better in supportive administrative tasks but showed some limitations when it comes to education-oriented tasks (the error rate was high than administrative). However, NerdyBot became smarter with more usage due to the application of AI algorithms.

Figure 1. An Architecture for Chatbots in Education (Sjöström et al., 2018)

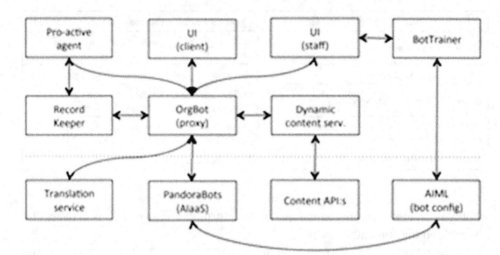

Additionally, the total number of users, length of conversations (i.e., time and number of questions) and response time and have increased.

Nonetheless, Chatbots in learning process is not utilised systematically according to various research publications and surveys, e.g., Winkler and Söllner (2018). Their study sample is quite sufficient as they reviewed 1405 titles and abstracts from education, management, information system and psychology. Therefore, they introduced an input-process-output framework with their literature review and highlight the research gap for Chatbot in education sector. However, unleashing the potential of chatbot in education only covers theoretical frameworks.

Other attempts to apply chatbots in education have been proposed, e.g., Hiremath et al (2018), where a simplified question answering method is employed. In this work, chatbot uses pattern-matching, data mining and natural language processing interface. The Chatbot matches input sentence from the user and reply based on the matched pattern in local, and potential global, databases. To conclude, Intelligent Chatbots can be used in learning process to improve the outcomes of the traditional learning. They can be used as well in different contexts such as web chatbots or mobile chatbots, but pedagogical conversation remains the key weakness in this context (Hobert et al, 2019).

Technology-Enhanced Learning

Technology-enhanced learning (TEL) is defined as a domain where the student's cooperation's with learning materials (readings, assignments, etc.), peers, as well as

Figure 2. Design Science Research Methodology (Geerts, 2011)

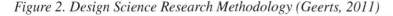

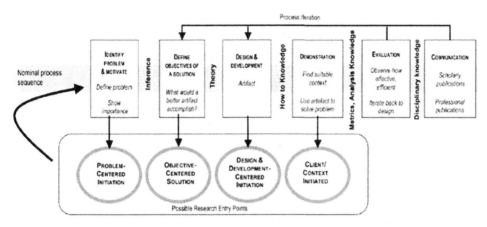

educators are interceded through cutting edge technology and data advances (Hobert et al, 2019). TEL developments such as developing adaptive learning systems have been in the focal point of research for more than four decades (Hammad, 2018). Chatbot-enhanced learning (CEL) can be considered as one of TEL sub-domains. The use of chatbots in education is simultaneous, self-guided, and focusses on individuals. A large number of TEL Chatbots are theoretical frameworks with some prototypes or initial implantations with limitations. From the previous studies, it is obvious that research gap exists in this area. We aim to focus on chatbot design and development in TEL domain to highlights its impact on student experience. In the next section, research methodology will be explained.

RESEARCH METHODOLOGY

In this section and as shown in Figure 2, we explained how design science research (DSR) methodology has been followed to design and develop our chatbot, i.e., EDUBOT. This is well aligned with software engineering processes since this research starts with finding and defining opportunities and issues in our research environment which will result in defining the research problem (Geerts, 2011). Further analysis for related work will be done in the second stage to define objectives and solutions for our research problem. The third stage refers to the design and development of our educational Chatbot, i.e., EDUBOT. A demonstration will be made in relation to two MSc modules, and then an evaluation stage has been carried out to assess the outcome of this research and disseminate it in proper research deliverables.

Design Science Research methodology allows improvements for developed artefacts via having more than one cycle to capture the feedback provided by the users of early versions of the produced artefacts (Venable, 2017). However, since this is a pilot project and still under an ongoing research and development, researchers did not implement more than two cycles. To make a swift start, the researchers pay extra attention to continuous improvements using agile approach based on feedback, discussions and focus group meetings with research colleagues, students, TAs and certain lecturers.

EDUBOT DESIGN AND IMPLEMENTATION

This section covers the design process of EDUBOT through the use of various design artefacts. This includes: (i) use case diagram and (ii) conversational flow. To increase the effectiveness of EDUBOT, a user-centric design and development approach has been followed. This has led to identifying a set of requirements, translated below in abstract considerations, related to EDUBOT design and development as shown below:

- The first concern is to think about all possible scenarios or tasks that can be done via EDUBOT and Collect all related questions in various forms that can be asked by students (Raj et al, 2019). Every activity or task done by EDUBOT is describe as an intent.
- Every question or intent can be represented in different forms, which depends on how the user expresses it while dealing with EDUBOT. Such as, "can you define to me what is cloud computing?" or "what is the definition of cloud computing please?" or "how cloud computing can be defined please?" A student may use any of these sentences for instructing our EDUBOT. All of these have the same intent or task, which is cloud computing definition, but different utterances or variances have been used (Molnár & Szüts, 2018).
- Write all probable logic to ensure that students are following our designed flow that we have built based on our throughs and close interaction with different type of stakeholders including students, lecturers, TAs and TEL experts. This has led to identifying potential user's intent. For our context, EDUBOT may ask the student about his/her modules or the topic he or she wants to inquire about (Raj et al, 2019).

EDUBOT Design

One critical part of designing educational bots in general and EDUNOT in specific, is to keep on track or building systematic educational flow which can help students to achieve their learning outcomes and keep them engaged most of the time. Conversational flow can be created by normal visualisation software as well as

Figure 3. Conversational Flow-chart for EDUBOT

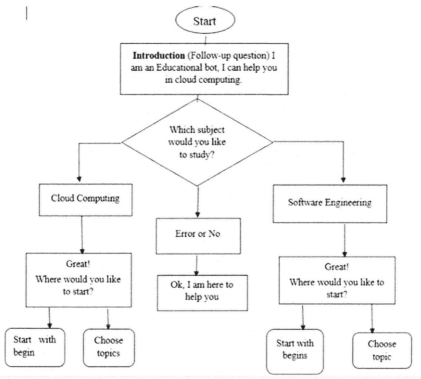

decision tree. Decision tree, as shown below in Figure 3, is simple to write but it is a powerful and efficient way to solve the problem. Visual representation is an easy and effective way to depict conversational flow, and it can be understood by developers, leaders, product managers to explain the expected behaviours form educational chatbots. In addition, we can make any changes on chatbots in an easier way since this flow decouple technical concerns from business concerns, education-oriented tasks (Raj et al, 2019). According to the workflow shown in Figure 3, student will be given an introductory greeting message as a starting point. Then he or she will be asked to select the subject to be taught, i.e., advanced software engineering or cloud computing. Then the student will be able to select the level of learning, i.e., beginner, intermediate or advance. As a result of that, EDUBOT will show the contents according to the conversation with the student.

Figure 4, as shown below, demonstrates the most common use cases of the EDUBOT. Use case diagram is used to depict the graphical representation of EDUBOT to indicates the key functionalities provided by the system and potential way of interaction with users. In EDUBOT, students can ask queries and receive

Figure 4. EDUBOT Use Case Diagram

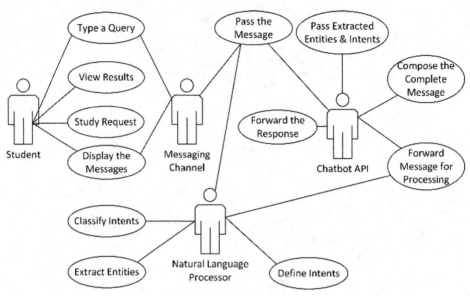

responses form EDUBOT. The Messaging Channel passes request to Chatbot-API which will be sent to Natural Language Processor where the particular intent will be invoked and analysed to send the appropriate response to the student.

Based on the analysis we performed, a decision has been made to utilise the existing technologies/platforms. Hence, both AWS platform (i.e., Amazon Lambda and Amazon Lex) and Facebook Messenger have been incorporated in the architectural design of EDUBOT as shown in Figure 5. According to the proposed architecture, students will access this service through Facebook Messenger which will work as interface for EDUBOT. It was possible to build the chatbot and get it integrated with online systems, such as content management systems, but to meet our initial requirements and our user-centric design and development approach, we decided to use one of the most common social media platforms which will also encourage students to adopt social learning processes when they learn and study. Social learning processes don't have to happen over social media, but students get encouraged by their presence on social media to talk to each other and collaborate in meaningful ways. Additionally, the role of Amazon platform here is more important as it represents the core of EDUBOT implementation. Amazon platforms offers an integrated set of tools to facilitate chatbot functionalities as will be explained below. So, Facebook Messenger will connect the user with Amazon API gateway, which will send all the requests to Amazon Lex. In such scenario, Amazon Lex will work as an intermediate component to get requests sent to Amazon Lambda, which invoke intents for fulfilling analysis and then send responses or particular information to the user. This framework can be used as a guidance to create any type of chatbots. The next section will highlight the key implementation concerns.

EDUBOT Implementation

AWS introduces a comprehensive approach to implement chatbots in agile way. It can be customised via programming using AWS Lex or API to fast track the development of chatbots for any generic domain. Hence, we will be utilising AWS platform and its associated components for developing EDUBOT. The provided tools (Amzon Lex and API) are available for everyone who has an Amazon account. AWS provides a year free account to test your model and make sure it works well according to your requirements. Once we have identified our requirements, the first and foremost step was to align what we need to do with the conversational flow appeared in Figure 3. Conversational stream implies what EDUBOT does and how it works, how its reactions rely upon input given by students. The second step was to create intents. The intents are the action or process which we need it to do by EDUBOT. There are many intents, for example, *welcome*, *startlearnning*, *cloudcomputing*, *softwareengineering*.

Our first intent is welcome, it gives a follow up message like: Hi, Hello or How may I help you. We utilised a group message response type or follow-up messages in it. It means the developer creates more than one message group for response and at run time. Lex selects random responses from each group, In the last, EDUBOT will inquire as to whether the student needs to learn or not through the response card. If the student says No, then EDUBOT will send a normal goodbye message. If the answer is Yes then EDUBOT will show a card for the choices available to students, i.e., in this case these choices are the subjects: (i) Advance Software Engineering and (ii) Cloud Computing. EDUBOT offers educational contents related to the previously mentioned subjects. Once the subject is selected by the students, EDUBOT will inquire about user learning level, which can be beginner, intermediate or advanced. Depending on the choice EDUBOT will provide appropriate data form the early-developed database. Amazon Lambda will provide the connectivity or the platform to build the code and to make EDUBOT more flexible. Various programming languages like Java Script, Python can be used in order to customise the developed Chatbot. In our scenario Java Script has been used for this purpose.

Amazon Lex provides build-in error handler, and also allows developer to create or customise them whenever needed. In case that error handlers are flagged, i.e., there is no match for the input, the error handler will trigger responses like "Sorry, can you repeat please" or "Sorry, I was unable to comprehend". Besides, if these messages continue for a number of time threshold can be identify by the developer

Figure 5. EDUBOT Architecture

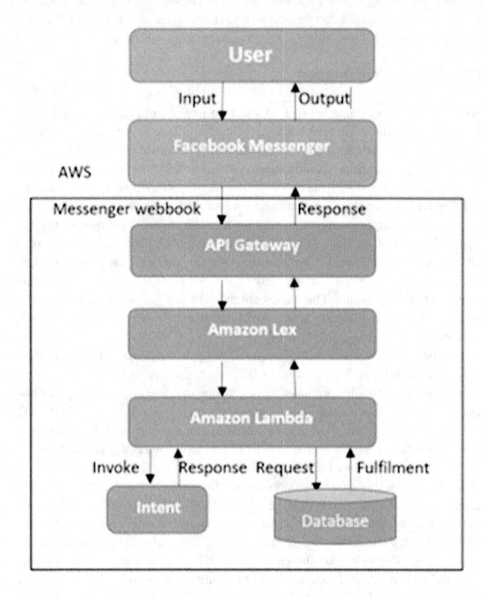

– EDUBOT will send a "Goodbye" message. The most convenient part of this platform is developer can create code and test it directly. Below, Figure 6, shows a sample code of start-learning lambda function.

Start-learning function has a *dialogAction* field which direct AWS Lex in the next course of action. It describes what to expect from the user after Amazon Lex returns a response to the client. The type field indicates other action, determines

Figure 6. AWS Lambda Code

```
index.js          x

1   exports.handler = (event,context,callback) => {
2       var choosessubjects =event.currentIntent.slots.choosessubjects;
3       var wheretostart =event.currentIntent.slots.wheretostart;
4       callback(null,{
5           "dialogAction":{
6               "type":"Delegate",
7               "fulfillmentState":"DelegateDialogActio",
8               "message":{
9                   "contentType":"plainText",
10                  "content":"you request for studying :" + choosessubjects + "form    " +    " + wheretostart
11              }
12          }
13      });
14
15  };
16
```

the value of *dialogAction*. Delegate shows the next action which is based on Lex configuration. If the response does not include any session attributes Amazon Lex retains the existing attributes. Message includes: (i) content type, e.g., plain text, and (ii) content which shows the users and the "+*intentname*", which will be interpreted during the run time.

RESULT AND DISCUSSION

Amazon Lex provides the following four ways to deploy chatbot: (i) Facebook, (ii) Kik, (iii) Slack, and (iv) Twilio SMS. There are four methods to integrate your bot with any application or website. We are using Facebook for deployment. In the AWS management console, Amazon Lex provides channels, in which we must fulfil required information such as channel name, channel description, etc. On that IAM (Identity Access Management) is automatically created by Amazon. Amazon Key Management Service (KMS) is also set by default as discussed previously. Alias is simply a pointer that can help to printout the least or available version of chatbot which can help to upgrade the chatbot and it helps to publish it. We must create alias before coming to channel section. Verify Token is an important and memorable part that is used in further implementation processes. To link both Amazon platform and Facebook Management Console, we can get page access key and app secret key form Facebook. We created a Facebook page named Educational Bot in which users click or hover the mouse on send message button for chatting with educational Bot (EDUBOT). Then conversation is shown in Facebook Messenger as appeared in Figure 7 below.

Figure 7. Deployment of EDUBOT with Facebook Messenger

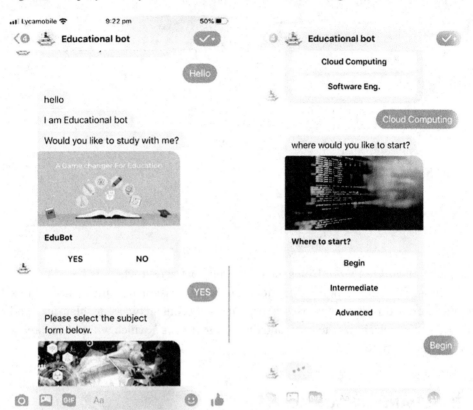

Amazon Lex provides publishing versions of the bot, intents, and slot types so that it can be controlled by implementing the client applications. A version is numbered for the developer's work which can publish for use in various parts of the workflow as well, such as development, beta development, and production. So, the final version, captured above, has been published after different consultations with students and other stakeholders.

Educational chatbots are becoming more popular and the main aim of this study is to make EDUBOT available to MSC in Computing students. We have tested the prototype with different students from the University of East London MSc in Computer Science and the results revealed that it was effective in responding to key students questions such as comparison between software as a service, platform as a service and infrastructure as a service. As discussed above, the experimented EDUBOT is used by different students from different backgrounds where English is not the first language, so some English language errors impacted its accuracy, however the majority of answers were appropriate. This assures that our framework and method is effective and can improve student's engagement with learning. Furthermore, it can be of great help for disabled students or those who cannot attend the classes for various reasons. Nevertheless, some limitations have been noticed such as less satisfactions when students cannot find appropriate answers. As a result of EDUBOT design and implementation, we can answer the early identified research questions as follows:

Research Question 1: What are the current chatbot-based innovations in learning processes?

Chatbots are innovatively used in education in different ways but mainly in the following forms: A question answering and quiz generation chatbot for education. This type of chatbots allow user to upload a file or any document and perform two functions on them. Answer extraction and question generating. The uploaded document is based on number of data cleaning and pre-processing step [20]. Moreover, the adoption of chatbot in higher education gained more popularity, for instance this includes CQU University, Sydney, Australia and many others. Also, a wide range of audience usually in involved in developing educational chatbots such as developers, project managers, researchers and educational experts, which provided a venue for a comprehensive discussion around educational technologies and how to improve learning and teaching. Finally, it has been found that a combination of advanced AI techniques such as Machine Learning and NLP have been used to empower chatbot technology for learning and teaching purposes (Sreelakshmi, 2019).

Research Question 2: Can the development and use of Educational Chatbots help to deliver effective and personalised learning to students?

Yes, we developed EDUBOT for education support for students using AWS platform. We cover small learning portion for explanation, which is cloud computing and software engineering. However, students were satisfied with our initial prototyping and wanted to see more functionalities provided in the future.

EDUBOT Limitations

EDUBOT was created for students to provide learning-oriented information about the early mentioned subjects, i.e., Cloud Computing and Software Engineering. It covers the basic questions asked by students while learning in a class. Yet, our first version from the above developed chatbot faces few limitations while giving responses to some of the questions such as:

First, common User Requests: EDUBOT should provide responses appropriately to the question identified as frequent or of particular impotence. But in some cases, EDUBOT cannot respond correctly due to question formatting. Researchers will work more on this to find out relevant NLP techniques to overcome this.

Second, deliver an effective conversation: the presented chatbot enhanced learning approach will be effective in particular subjects and in certain conditions. If users want to be self-learning, EDUBOT may provide all information related to specific topics. However, EDUBOT, similar to other chatbots, cannot function without having the appropriate access for the data. This is crucial for education as educational data/contents need to be revised and designed frequently.

CONCLUSION AND FUTURE WORK

This research highlights the importance of using Chatbots in different fields such as healthcare (Holmes et al, 2019) and (Xu, 2021), finance (Khan & Rabbani, 2020), to name but a few. Education is not exception in this regard. Hence, a framework for chatbot in education, i.e., EDUBOT, has been introduced and developed. Moreover, this research followed a user-centric design and development where frequent communications with stakeholders have been used to create the appropriate conversational flow. As mentioned earlier, EDUBOT has been tested using two MSc in Computing subjects, i.e., Cloud Computing and Software Engineering. A combination of technology has been used here. This includes AWS Lambda and Amazon Lex as well as Facebook Management Console. EDUBOT proved that chatbot can improve student engagement especially at the time of COVID-19 where no physical contact between learners and lecturers exists. Extending EDUBOT Framework to support student's admin, library and other capabilities and also integrating it with university systems remain for future work.

REFERENCES

Bahja, M., Hammad, R., & Butt, G. (2020). A user-centric framework for educational chatbots design and development. In *International Conference on Human-Computer Interaction*, (pp. 32-43). Springer. 10.1007/978-3-030-60117-1_3

Bahja, M., Hammad, R., & Hassouna, M. (2019). Talk2Learn: a framework for chatbot learning. In *the European Conference on Technology Enhanced Learning*, (pp. 582-586). Springer. 10.1007/978-3-030-29736-7_44

Geerts, G. L. (2011). A design science research methodology and its application to accounting information systems research. *International Journal of Accounting Information Systems*, *12*(2), 142–151. doi:10.1016/j.accinf.2011.02.004

Georgescu, A. A. (2018). Chatbots for education–trends, benefits and challenges. In *Conference proceedings of» eLearning and Software for Education «(eLSE)* (pp. 195-200). Carol I National Defence University Publishing House.

Hammad, R. (2018). *A hybrid e-learning framework: Process-based, semantically-enriched and service-oriented* [Doctoral dissertation, University of the West of England].

Hammad, R., Odeh, M., & Khan, Z. (2015). Towards a model-based approach to evaluate the effectiveness of e-learning. In *Proceeding of the 9th European Conference on IS Management and Evaluation ECIME* (pp. 111-119). Research Gate.

Hiremath, G., Hajare, A., Bhosale, P., Nanaware, R., & Wagh, K. S. (2018). Chatbot for education system. *International Journal of Advance Research. Ideas and Innovations in Technology, 4*(3), 37–43.

Hobert, S., & Meyer von Wolff, R. (2019). *Say hello to your new automated tutor–a structured literature review on pedagogical conversational agents.* CORE.

Holmes, S., Moorhead, A., Bond, R., Zheng, H., Coates, V., & McTear, M. (2019). Usability testing of a healthcare chatbot: Can we use conventional methods to assess conversational user interfaces? In *Proceedings of the 31st European Conference on Cognitive Ergonomics*, (pp. 207-214). ACM. 10.1145/3335082.3335094

Khan, S., & Rabbani, M. R. (2020). Chatbot as Islamic Finance Expert (CaIFE) When Finance Meets Artificial Intelligence. In *Proceedings of the 2020 4th International Symposium on Computer Science and Intelligent Control*, (pp. 1-5).

Kuhail, M. A., Al Katheeri, H., Negreiros, J., Seffah, A., & Alfandi, O. (2022). Engaging Students With a Chatbot-Based Academic Advising System. *International Journal of Human-Computer Interaction*, 1–27. doi:10.1080/10447318.2022.2074645

Kuhail, M. A., Alturki, N., Alramlawi, S., & Alhejori, K. (2022). Interacting with educational chatbots: A systematic review. *Education and Information Technologies.* doi:10.100710639-022-11177-3

Molnár, G., & Szüts, Z. (2018). The role of chatbots in formal education. In *2018 IEEE 16th International Symposium on Intelligent Systems and Informatics (SISY)*, (pp. 197-202). IEEE. 10.1109/SISY.2018.8524609

Raj, S., Raj, K., & Karkal. (2019). *Building chatbots with Python.* Apress, doi:10.1007/978-1-4842-4096-0

Sandu, N., & Gide, E. (2019). Adoption of AI-Chatbots to enhance student learning experience in higher education in India. In *2019 18th International Conference on Information Technology Based Higher Education and Training (ITHET)*, pp. 1-5. IEEE. 10.1109/ITHET46829.2019.8937382

Sjöström, J., Aghaee, N., Dahlin, M., & Ågerfalk, P. J. (2018). *Designing chatbots for higher education practice.* Research Gate.

Sreelakshmi, A. S., Abhinaya, S. B., Nair, A., & Nirmala, S. J. (2019). A question answering and quiz generation chatbot for education. In 2019 Grace Hopper Celebration India (GHCI) (pp. 1-6). IEEE. doi:10.1109/GHCI47972.2019.9071832

Venable, J. R., Pries-Heje, J., & Baskerville, R. L. (2017). *Choosing a design science research methodology.* AISEL.

Winkler, R., & Söllner, M. (2018). Unleashing the potential of chatbots in education: A state-of-the-art analysis. In *Academy of Management Annual Meeting (AOM).* AOM. 10.5465/AMBPP.2018.15903abstract

Xu, L., Sanders, L., Li, K., & Chow, J. C. (2021). Chatbot for health care and oncology applications using artificial intelligence and machine learning: Systematic review. *JMIR Cancer, 7*(4), e27850. doi:10.2196/27850 PMID:34847056

Zemcik, M. T. (2019). A brief history of chatbots. *DEStech Transactions on Computer Science and Engineering, 10.*

KEY TERMS AND DEFINITIONS

EDUBOT: A framework for an educational chatbot.

Amazon Web Services (AWS) platform: This is one of the world's most comprehensive and broadly adopted cloud computing platform, offering a wide range of featured services from data centres globally.

Lambda: Is a one of the AWS serverless compute service that runs developer's code in response to events and automatically manages the underlying compute resources for users.

Amazon Lex: Is an AWS service for building conversational interfaces for applications using voice and text. With Amazon Lex, the same conversational engine that powers Amazon Alexa is now available to developers to develop a sophisticated, natural language chatbots into their applications.

Amazon Key Management Service (KMS): Also known as AWS KMS, and allows developers to create, manage, and control cryptographic keys across their applications in addition to certain group of AWS services.

Facebook Messenger console: It facilitates the integration capability between AWS Amazon Lex and Facebook Messenger.

APPENDIX

Table 2.

#	Comment	Our reply
1	The title it's misleading. It is a complete product. Maybe "EDUBOT - A Prototype for Chatbot in Education"?	We thank the reviewer for his comment, however we believe the contribution her is the framework itself not the implementation. Hence, we would like to keep the same title, if possible.
2	I would recommend to split into smaller components. I suggested in the above question (front-end and back-end framework) The front end can focus on the framework of ChatBot functionality in terms of making it more engaging and usable for the students.	We thank the reviewer for his comment. We have expanded the design and implementation sections to address this point.
3	More research on chatbot usage for a domain specific should be done, maybe another domain like healthcare The back end can focus on the architecture of Chatbot.	We discussed few examples of chatbots in healthcare and finance.
4	Is interface with existing social media portal is better? and details of AWS services. A common model for education bot from the back end architecture	We expanded this section in the paper.
5	The organization of the chapter. First few paragraphs of Section 5 belong to Section 4 (the implementation) >> Missing diagrams.	Sorry for missing this diagram by mistake, it has been added now.
6	I recommend Section 4 - to follow any software development methodology eg: Agile Section 4 Chatbot Design and Implementation The core component is using AWS services, hence it is best to include glossary in the document. AWS has its own glossary which can be included in the document when it comes to explain the AWS components.	We expanded on this part of the paper. We also linked the software engineering methodology with the research method utilised in the research.
7	The paragraphs explain the interface, the objects and many aspect of the design. It is best to include diagrams for clear illustration, for example Data Flow Diagram (use one example of scenario); object sequence diagram (you have interface from Facebook to AWS Lex -Lambda)	More explanations have been added, also key terms and definition section has been added to the paper.

Chapter 8

KalaamBot and KalimaBot:
Applications of Chatbots in Learning Arabic as a Foreign Language

Elsayed Issa
https://orcid.org/0000-0003-2006-9008
University of Arizona, USA

Michael Hammond
University of Arizona, USA

ABSTRACT

Chatbot technology is a subfield of Artificial Intelligence (AI) that deals with text-based or speech-based conversational agents. In general terms, a chatbot enables a user to have a conversational interaction with a computer. Chatbots have applications in several fields including trade, tourism, customer care, health services, education, et cetera. This chapter describes two chatbot systems that we are developing for learning Arabic as a foreign language. KalaamBot is a speech-based chatbot that converses with learners and teaches them the language in a conversational setting. KalimaBot is a text-based personal vocabulary assistant that enables students to search for the meaning of words, synonyms, antonyms, and word usage in context. This chapter provides extensive discussion of the several challenges second language researchers and chatbot practitioners encounter when designing chatbots for language learning. Then, it concludes with recommendations and future research.

INTRODUCTION

Conversational AI is a subfield of artificial intelligence (AI) that deals with text-based

DOI: 10.4018/978-1-6684-6234-8.ch008

or speech-based conversational agents: chatbots. These agents automate intelligent conversations and verbal interactions between humans and machines. Scholars have referred to chatbots in a variety of ways, including machine conversation systems, virtual agents, dialogue systems, chatterbots (Abu Shawar & Atwell, 2007), conversational agents, and chatbots (Jurafsky & Martin, 2021). Chatbots have applications in trade, tourism, customer care, education, health services, automatic telephone answering systems, et cetera. They range from simple systems that extract responses from conversational datasets to more sophisticated systems that employ natural language processing (NLP) tools and deep learning techniques. Chatbot domains are classified as open or closed based on user input. Open-domain chatbots are trained on massive corpora of conversations. Consequently, the user can ask about anything without a clear goal (Shang et al., 2015). Closed-domain chatbots restrict user input and chatbot responses to a specific goal, such as booking a ticket, learning a language, et cetera.

This chapter focuses on incorporating recent advances in NLP, such as neural net transformers[1] (represented by the wav2vec 2.0 speech recognition system; Baevski et al., 2020), into the design of end-to-end language learning systems in order to leverage students' acquisition of both textual and oral language learning. It provides demos for two different chatbots in action and argues for ruled-based closed-domain architectures when using chatbots for second language learning. We argue that these architectures are suitable for second language learning with the aim of training learners on language tasks to achieve proficiency.

The rest of the chapter is organized as follows: *Chatbots' Architectures and Techniques* presents an overview of chatbots' architectures and techniques, and it discusses traditional, rule-based, and machine-learning chatbot design techniques. *Chatbots in language learning* provides an overview of recent advances and the use of chatbots in language learning. Both *KalaamBot* and *KalimaBot* sections overview the implementation and the design of the speech-based and text-based chatbots, respectively. The *Challenges and Future Directions* section overviews the technical and pedagogical challenges when designing chatbots for language learning. The chapter concludes with recommendations and future remarks.

CHATBOTS' ARCHITECTURES AND TECHNIQUES

Typically, the architecture of a chatbot involves three main components: Natural Language Understanding (NLU), Natural Language Generation (NLG), and a Dialogue Management Engine (DME). Some scholars consider the User Interface (UI) as a fourth component, while others do not. In speech-based architectures, two components are added: a text-to-speech engine (TTS) and a speech-to-text engine

(STT) (Kulkarni et al., 2019; McTear, 2020; Freed, 2021). Each of these components represents an active research domain that complicates the design of chatbots.

NLU is a branch of AI and NLP that enables computers to understand text or speech. NLU does not only enable computers to understand the meanings but also discern the speaker's intents. In addition, such a system can extract "entities," like things, people, or places. It involves two tasks: Intent Classification and Entity Recognition. Intent Classification helps the agent to understand the intent behind the user's utterance. In other words, the intent is what the end user intends a chatbot should do for them. The intent is mainly expressed through the verb in a sentence. Entity Recognition identifies the discrete pieces of information received from the user. Entities are typically expressed as nuns in a sentence. For example, consider the sentence: **Book flight tickets for me**. *Book* is an intent, while *flight* and *ticket* are entities. By identifying intents and entities, this component extracts the meaning from the user input using NLP and NLU.

The input is analyzed syntactically in the syntax-driven semantic analysis approach to determine different constituents. Then, semantic rules are used to extract the meaning from these constituents. An alternative approach uses semantic *grammar* to extract the meaning directly from the word sequence w. In semantic grammar, rules classify constituents based on their functions or meanings rather than their syntactic categories. A third approach is handcrafted syntactic grammars that can capture fine-grained distinctions in the input. However, these require separate rules for every possible input. Examples of state-of-the-art NLU platforms include Google's Dialog Flow (Google, n.d.) and Rasa NLU/Core (Bocklisch et al., 2017).

Several state-of-the-art machine learning-based dialogue systems do not use any of the previous approaches. Instead, they use machine learning methods to classify utterances and extract the user's intents and entities. Applications created with machine learning methods are generally domain-specific (McTear, 2020). Identifying the domain can reduce ambiguity in the interpretation of utterances. The dialogue management engine (DME) is the central component and the moderator between the NLU on one side and NLG on the other side. In other words, it accepts the input from the ASR/NLU components, interacts with external knowledge, and produces a message conveyed to the user by the TTS/NLG components.

Inside the DME, the mapping between the user input and the chatbot response is managed by two sub-components: the Dialogue Context Model and the Dialogue Decision Model. They make the necessary decisions to send the appropriate response to the user (Kulkarni et al., 2019). These decisions include several processes such as grounding, input modification, slot filling, context switching, et cetera (Kulkarni et al., 2019). Grounding, for example, is a process used when the user input and the chatbot response are mapped and based on common ground (Jurafsky & Martin, 2021), while slot filing is when the bot requests extra information from the user to

Figure 1. The architecture of a typical dialogue system: the typical components include Natural Language Understanding (NLU), Natural Language Generation (NLG), and Dialogue Manager (DME). In speech-based architecture, two components are added: text-to-speech and speech-to-text. Source: (McTear, 2020)

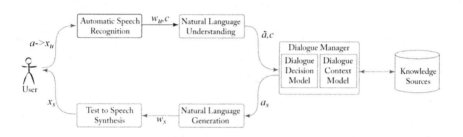

find an appropriate response. When the user wants to change the conversation, the DME's sub-components switch the context to satisfy the user's input.

Kulkarni et al. (2019) provide several types of DME. The most basic type is *Switch Statement*. It is a control structure with previously defined actions for each possible input. The user is always required to initiate the conversation. In addition, the scope of the conversation is limited to predefined actions and responses. Some dialogue engines use *finite ftate machines* to guide the user and agent involved in the conversation with limited inputs. The third type involves *machine learning approaches* where the dialogue engine uses user intents as input parameters to the machine learning algorithm and predicts what the agent should say. The only disadvantage of this approach is the need for improvement in the conversation in some cases. In general, the dialogue engine's task is to observe the user inputs and decide on actions to take. Therefore, *deep reinforcement learning* (Cuayáhuitl et al., 2015) is a suitable approach where the goal is to develop an agent that improves its performance based on interaction with the environment.

The NLG component is responsible for conveying the responses to the user in an understandable format. Most corpus-based chatbots produce their responses by retrieval methods (from a given corpus) or generation methods (using a language model or encoder-decoder) (see: Lokman & Ameedeen, 2018). Other methods of NLG include template-based or rule-based approaches, n-gram generation, neural network approaches, and sequence-to-sequence generation. Both neural network and sequence-to-sequence approaches provide state-of-the-art performance (Kulkarni et al., 2019). NLU involves content determination, document structuring, aggregation, lexical choice, referring expression generation, and realization (Kulkarni et al., 2019).

Rule-based chatbot architectures include early chatbot dialogue systems such as ELIZA (Weizenbaum, 1966), PARRY (Colby et al., 1971), and ALICE (Abu Shawar

& Atwell, 2003; Wallace, 2003). ELIZA is a Rogerian psychologist that encourages patients to talk by employing pattern/transform rules using regular expressions (i.e., a set of characters that specifies a search pattern in a text). It is a closed-domain system that uses users' input and a set of pattern/transform rules to reflect transformations of the patient's statements back at them. In 1971, PARRY used ELIZA's logic and was created to study schizophrenia. It was the first chatbot to pass the Turing Test (Turing, 1950) in 1972. ALICE (Artificial Linguistic Internet Computer Entity) chatbot system is an updated version of ELIZA's pattern/transform architecture. ALICE is the language used to store knowledge about conversations as patterns and templates in AIML (Artificial Intelligence Markup Language) files. AIML is derived from XML (Extensible Markup Language) and contains units called topics and categories (Abu Shawar & Atwell, 2007). Categories are the central units of knowledge in AIML where each category contains "a rule for matching an input and converting to an output, and consists of a pattern, which matches against the user input, and a template, which is used in generating the ALICE chatbot answer" (Abu Shawar & Atwell, 2007).

Specifically with respect to second language learning, the authors argue that ruled-based, closed-domain systems provide second language learners with "attested language use." This argument requires resources for authentic language, which, in turn, provides learners with more exposure to natural language. They enable learners to study the different linguistic patterns, sounds, and structures in an authentic, naturally occurring environment. In other words, the design of chatbots intended for second language learning should be guided by several criteria, such as authenticity, accessibility, ease of use, genres of language, and several additional pedagogical considerations. Chatbots that use authentic language (rather than generated language) are believed to enable second language learners to gain communicative competence by exposing them to natural language in the wild and how it is used and pronounced in the real world.

The knowledge source type in chatbots is determined by the type of dataset used. Hence, there are two types: retrieval-based and generative-based systems. Retrieval-based architectures involve predefined responses for the chatbot to select from to respond to an inquiry. In contrast, generative-based architectures use techniques to generate new responses via neural approaches (AlHumoud et al., 2018). Based on the tasks a conversational agent is required to perform, Jurafsky & Martin (2021) classify conversational agents into two main types: tasked-oriented dialogue agents and chatbots. While tasked-oriented dialogue agents converse with users to help them complete specific tasks such as making calls, finding restaurants, giving directions, et cetera, chatbots are systems for extended conversations. This entails that they are designed to mimic human-human interactions while conversing.

Like AlHumoud et al. (2018), Jurafsky & Martin (2021) classify chatbots into three architectures: rule-based systems, information retrieval systems, and encoder-decoder systems. They further introduce the frame-based architecture (GUS) used in most task-based systems. Although chatbots are the most straightforward dialogue systems because they carry on extended conversations mimicking unstructured human conversations, complexity of design and pedagogy arises when using them in learning a second language. Techniques to build these dialogue systems differ according to the architecture used. While pattern matching, Artificial Intelligence Markup Language (AIML), Ontology parsing, Markov Chain Model, and ChatScript are used in the design of retrieval-based systems, generative-based systems use neural and deep learning techniques (AlHumoud et al., 2018).

To conclude, chatbot design can involve three main architectures: traditional, machine-learning, and rule-based architectures. There is an overlap between the three architectures where machine learning, deep learning, and deep reinforcement learning can be part of the DME in the traditional architectures. Chatbot design is governed by several factors, such as the datasets used (rule-based versus corpus-based), user input (open domain versus closed domain), and knowledge source (retrieval-based versus generative-based). The latter is another classification some scholars use to refer to the datasets used.

CHATBOTS IN LANGUAGE LEARNING

Given ongoing advancements in language learning platforms, conversational AI, and machine learning applications, as well as the lack of attention paid to language practice, pronunciation, and oral interaction in the target language inside the classroom, chatbots seem like an excellent technology for second language learning. Several scholars agree that there is generally insufficient time for enough practice and feedback on language practice, speaking, and pronunciation in face-to-face language learning environments (Ehsani & Knodt, 1998; Hsu, 2016; Tsai, 2019; Timpe-Laughlin et al., 2020; among others). Hence, it is argued that chatbots are the perfect language-learning companions allowing learners to learn multiple languages simultaneously and at their own pace (Fryer et al., 2020).

Regarding language learning, chatbots have been used for language knowledge practice, learning language skills, role-playing, learning scenario representations, delivering well-targeted interventions, et cetera (Wollny et al., 2021; Huang et al., 2022). Here the authors summarize two of the most recent reviews of chatbot technology in education and language learning.

The first is Wollny et al. in 2021. Its authors identified 20 domains of chatbots in education after reviewing 74 relevant papers out of 2678 publications. These 20

Figure 2. A schematic diagram summarizing the techniques of chatbots discussed in this section.

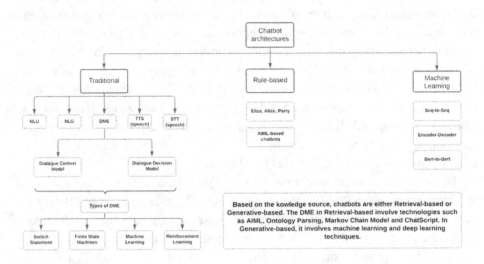

domains are broadly divided into three main categories based on their pedagogical roles: learning chatbots, assisting chatbots, and mentoring chatbots. Language learning belongs to the first category, and more than half of the research (53%) involves designing chatbots for language learning. Most chatbots are used for conversation practice or vocabulary testing. The authors identified 19 publications that use chatbots in the language learning domain. None of these studies, unfortunately, involved learning or teaching Arabic as a foreign language.

Huang et al. (2022) review the use of chatbots in language learning. The review authors identified 25 empirical studies that investigated the use of chatbots in language learning. Their results showed that the English language is the dominant language. Twenty studies included teaching English as a second/foreign language, one study involved teaching Chinese as a second language, one study involved teaching Irish as an endangered language, and three studies were conducted on teaching creative writing to native English speakers. Although none of the studies reported in these two reviews are conducted on Arabic, Fryer et al. (2020) review the Cleverbot and Mondly language-learning chatbots. The Mondly chatbot was developed as part of the Mondly language learning platform (Fryer et al., 2020). The chatbot includes Arabic as one of its 33 languages. It also uses Augmented Reality (AR) to make the learning experience closer to real-life interactions.

Despite the absence of research on Arabic chatbots for language learning, research on Arabic chatbot technology is active in several other domains. These include dialect chatbots (Ali & Habash, 2016; Al-Ghadhban & Al-Twairesh, 2020;

Al-Madi et al., 2021), Quranic chatbots (Abu Shawar & Atwell, 2004), web question-answering bots (Abu Shawar, 2011), tourism (AlHumoud et al., 2022), prophets' biography (Zubair Khan & Mahamat Yassin, 2021), helping children with Autism Spectrum Disorder (ASD) (Aljameel et al., 2017), and teaching essentials of Islam to children (Alobaidi et al., 2013). In the medical domain, Ollobot (Fadhil & Abu Ra'ed, 2019) and COVIBOT (Driss et al., 2022) were released to help with medical information. In the education domain, ArabChat (Hijjawi et al., 2014; Hijjawi et al., 2016) is a mobile-based chatbot used as an advisor for students at the Applied Science University in Amman, Jordan. Finally, IbnSina (Mavridis et al., 2011) and Hala (Makatchev et al., 2010) are two speech-based chatbots that converse about the public domain. Most of these chatbots follow a retrieval-based approach where AIML chatbot style and pattern matching are used.

Recently, several generative-based and deep-learning models have been used to design chatbots for Arabic. These are chatbots that handle the public domain and learn conversational patterns from data following deep learning approaches such as Sequence-to-Sequence, encoder-decoder models, and Bert-to-Bert models (Naous et al., 2020).

Guiding Principles for Designing Chatbots for Language Learning:

Except for Mondly's chatbot, there has not been any work on chatbots for Arabic language learning. This chapter presents two implemented chatbots that can be used in teaching Arabic as a foreign language. Several recent advances in speech recognition, speech synthesis, deep learning, and conversational AI are used to design end-to-end language learning systems to leverage students' acquisition of textual and oral language learning. However, the authors do not use all these advances because they commit to Mayers' principles for generative e-learning.

According to Clark and Mayer (2016) and Mayer (2017), the factors that enhance generative language learning in any e-learning platform (including chatbots) are personalization, voice, and embodiment, described respectively as follows:

1. Learners learn better when the vocabulary is presented in a conversational format instead of a formal style.
2. Learners learn better from a human voice than a machine-generated voice.
3. Learners learn better when an onscreen agent uses humanlike gestures and movement.

Following these principles, the authors argue for reusable rule-based chatbots for specific language tasks where vocabulary in context is maximized over vocabulary in isolation. STT is used to recognize learners' speech, while TTS is discarded. Pre-recorded native speakers' speech is used to meet the second requirement by Mayer instead of using TTS (i.e., generated speech).

KALAAMBOT

KalaamBot (*meaning*: speech-bot), a language learning conversational chatbot, is developed to train learners to practice conversations interactively. This conversational agent benefits language learners to gain a mastery of vocabulary and sentence structures. This chatbot's design involves using an automatic speech recognition component to deliver the speech to second language learners.

KalaamBot system is implemented using React, a Javascript framework for user interfaces, as the frontend and Python Flask as the backend. Figure 2 shows the chatbot's main interface, which serves as the primary learning window where all conversations occur. This main conversation window has two principal components. The first component triggers the chatbot to start the conversion by clicking the audio message. The chatbot will start a brief introduction, greet the user, and ask questions. The conversation bubbles between the learner and the chatbot in the figure represent the second component. These two components are schematically shown in figure 3. When the chatbot finishes the introduction and asks questions, the user replies by clicking on the *speak* button. Then, the chatbot listens and transcribes the response using the speech recognition component; then, the transcription is shown on the screen. Once the user's transcription is on the user dialogue bubble, the chatbot's dialogue bubble appears with the chatbot's new response. This response is also typed in the dialogue bubble and spoken by the chatbot. The user starts a new cycle by clicking on the *speak* button. The researchers designed this conversational cycle to focus the learner's attention on the chatbot's response and give them enough time to think about the appropriate response. The authors intend that this should reduce speaking anxiety when interacting with the chatbot. Moreover, this cycle gives the users a chance to wait, think, and rest before starting a new conversational cycle. This is also expected to maximize learning and allow learners to learn independently.

The design of the conversations and the conversational cycles follow scaffolding, a process by which language instructors build on learners' experiences and knowledge while learning or mastering new tasks. Among the most successful strategies in scaffolding is to give students the time to process new information, communicate new ideas, and tap into their knowledge. Conversational cycles help implement this scaffolding by giving learners the time to think and respond. According to table 1, the content of the conversation is a theme or a topic that mimics real conversations. The conversation has two roles. The first role is "the chatbot" that

Figure 3. The Interface of KalaamBot: a speech-based chatbot that teaches Arabic conversation

begins the conversational cycle with a question, and the second role is "the learner" who provides an answer. The conversation in table 1 also shows some scaffolding where the conversation moves from more accessible question/answer pairs to more difficult ones. The chatbot starts asking questions about the users themselves; then, it asks them about people around them to expand the conversation.

The authors use a Wav2vec 2.0 (Baevski et al., 2020) finetuned Arabic system[3] as the speech recognition component. The model is equipped with a separate language model to improve recognition accuracy. Since KalaamBot does not provide learners with feedback, the improved recognized speech by the language model will encourage learners to converse more with the chatbot rather than focusing on the errors they make. KalaamBot uses pre-recorded speech by an Arab native speaker

Figure 4. A schematic diagram of the conversation flow

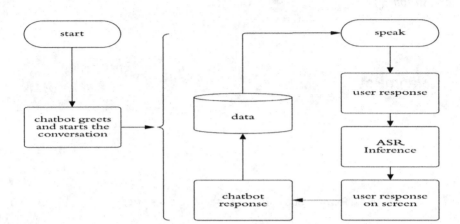

as the chatbot's responses to enhance the learning process with authentic language. The chatbot is reproducible, meaning that it can be used with any Arabic variety on condition that the relevant pre-recorded files and the relevant speech recognition component are used.

Future enhancements will include a *replay* button to replay the audio in both the user and the chatbot's bubbles. Also, a *translation* button can be added to the chatbot bubble to translate the sentences by the chatbot into English. In contrast, a *feedback* button can be added to the users' bubble to provide feedback on their pronunciation. Personification is important in chatbot technology; therefore, the researchers will consider giving the bot a persona and providing learners with more encouraging feedback. Other enhancements will include designing another component to switch the roles of both the chatbot and the user to guarantee that students can take turns and ask questions while conversing with the chatbot. In an empirical study to understand the effect of chatbot personality, Kuhail et al. (2022b) show evidence that chatbot personality positively impacts aspects of user behaviors such as engagement and the authenticity of the chatbot.

KALIMABOT

KalimaBot (*meaning*: word-bot) is a text-based personal vocabulary assistant. KalimaBot serves as a dictionary that contributes to acquiring Arabic words. It enables students to search for words' meanings, synonyms, antonyms, and usage in context. The chatbot can be part of a language teaching curriculum that integrates

Table 1. An example of a conversation. Scaffolding is shown by the complexity and the increasing number of words in the questions and their answers[2].

User		Chabot	
My name is …	… اسمي ismī …	What is your name?	ما اسمك؟ mā ismuk?
I study at the University of …	… أدرس في جامعة adrus fī jām'at …	Where do you study?	أين تدرس؟ ayna tadrus (masc.)?
No. I do not work.	لا، لا أعمل. lā lā a'mal	Do you work? where?	هل تعملين؟ وأين؟ hall ta'malīn? wa ayna?
I live in … city.	… أسكن في مدينة askun fī madīnat …	Where do you live?	أين تسكن؟ ayna taskun (masc.)
My father's name is …	… اسم والدي ism wālidī	What's your father's name?	ما اسم والدك؟ mā ism wāliduki (fem.)?
My Mother's name is …	… اسم والدتي ism wālidatī	What's your mother's name?	ما اسم والدتك؟ mā ism wālidutak (masc.)?
My father is … and he works at the University of …	والدي يعمل … في … جامعة wālidī ya'mal … fī jām'at …	What does your father do? where?	ماذا يعمل والدك؟ وأين؟ mādhā ya'mal wāliduki? wa ayna?
My Mother is … and she works at … hospital.	والدتي بعمل … في مستشفى … wālidatī ta'mal fī mustashfa ..	What does your mother do? where?	ماذا تعمل والدتك؟ وأين؟ mādhā ta'mal wālidutak? wa ayna?
My father and my mother live in … city. I do not live with them.	والدتي ووالدتي يسكنان في مدينة أنا لا أسكن معهم. … wālidī wa-wālidatī yaskunān fī madīnat .. ana lā askun m'ahum.	Where do your father and your mother live? Do you live with them?	أين يسكن والدك ووالدتك؟ وهل تسكن معهم؟ ayna yaskun wālidutak wa-wālidutak? wa-hall taskun m'ahum?

corpus-based teaching. Corpus-based teaching exploits the use of corpora (i.e., extensive collections of authentic language), including activities that ask students to mine these corpora and learn by discovery (see: Bernardini, 2000; Sinclair, 2004, among others). KalimaBot can serve as a vocabulary-learning companion that can be used as a corpus-based teaching tool to help students to find synonyms and antonyms when they attempt to write compositions and essays in Arabic[4].

The architecture of KalimaBot involves

1. the development of a specific dataset that the authors will release shortly,
2. training a seq-to-seq model to learn the mappings between the inputs and outputs designed for the chatbot,
3. an interface that helps learners retrieve the information they need.

Given Mayer's principles for generative e-learning and the necessary pedagogical considerations (i.e., the authenticity of the learning materials), the authors created a dataset specifically for this chatbot. The dataset consists of the following columns: word, category, gloss, synonym, antonym, and sentence.

Table 2. The data used in building KalimaBot

word	category	gloss	synonym	antonym	sentence
استيقظ istayqaẓ	فعل fiʻl	to wake up	صحا ṣaḥa	نام أو رقد nām aww raqad	استيقظ مبكرا دائماً 'astayqẓ mubakiran dā'man
في الصباح fī al-ṣabāḥ	جار ومجرور jār wa-majrūr	In the morning	صباحاً ṣabāḥan	في المساء أو مساءً fī al-masā' aww masā'an	في الصباح، أصحو مبكراً في الساعة السادسة. fī al-ṣabāḥ 'aṣḥu mubakiran fī al-sā'a al-sādisa

These data are processed and saved to a JSON (JavaScript Object Notation) file. The authors developed python code that iterates through the CSV dataset and stores it in the JSON file. The training data are as follows:

Figure 5. Training data for KalimaBot. Intents is a list of tags. Each tag represents a pattern (user input) and a response (a list of bots' responses).

```
{"intents": [
    {"tag": synonym_wakeup,
     "patterns": "مرادف استيقظ",
     "responses": ["صحا", "نهض"],
    },
}
```

The training data consist of a list of tags. Each tag represents the information in a cell in table 2, where the pattern represents the user input. In figure 4, the user input means a *synonym for wake up*. The bot's response should be a synonym of the two provided. This data is used to train a simple sequence-to-sequence model for classification where the input X is the patterns, and the labels y are the tags. The trained model is used for inference to search for any information about the Arabic

Figure 6. KalimaBot Interface: the left pane shows some instructions on how to search for words while the right pane shows the chatbot.

words. The chatbot takes the users' input and returns the appropriate response if it is the most probable one, with a percentage of more than 80%.

The authors hypothesize that presenting vocabulary learning with a chatbot will help eliminate redundancy which addresses Fryer et al.'s (2020) claim about the importance of chatbots in language learning. Therefore, we argue that KalimaBot can be used to enrich students' vocabulary when using it within a corpus-based or learning-by-discovery environment. To elaborate on this point, the authors provide a learning-by-discovery activity. In Arabic classes in the US, students learn how to write about their daily schedule, and instructors provide them with some supporting materials.

Figure 7 represents an activity worksheet provided by the instructor. After students learn to talk about their daily schedule, they are required to provide an essay in which they narrate their daily activities. This activity enables them to expand their vocabulary, learn different sentence structures and manipulate word order in Arabic. Students are supposed to find synonyms and examples for the underlined words in KalimaBot. In turn, they should produce different sentences for the first sentences in the table as follows: أصحو مبكراً في الساعة السادسة صباحاً (I wake up early in the morning at 6.00) or في الساعة السادسة صباحاً، أصحو مبكراً كل يوم (At 6.00 am, I wake up early every day). Students can provide various sentences using KalimaBot because they will learn different synonyms and sentence structures. In addition, the free word order that Arabic sentences follow will enable them to write more diverse sentences.

Figure 7. An example of vocabulary and sentence building using KalimaBot

Daily Schedule with KalimaBot

Complete the table below using KalimaBot as follows:
- Find synonyms or antonyms for the underlined words and rephrase the sentence.
- Find the use of the underlined words in context and compare the sentence/s you get with the ones provided here. This helps you rephrasing and creating new sentences.
- Provide a write-up of your new daily schedule.

Your Sentence	Example Sentence
	أستيقظ مبكراً في الصباح في الساعة السادسة.
	أنظف أسناني جيداً.
	أتناول الفطور مع أسرتي في الساعة السابعة والنصف.

Please note to change the word order and conjugate the verbs as necessary

Finally, this chatbot is a demo and needs several enhancements. A voice recognition component can be added to enable search by voice. Also, a powerful TTS component can be added to pronounce the searched words.

CHALLENGES AND FUTURE DIRECTIONS

The remainder of the discussion will focus on 1) how chatbots should be designed to make this valuable technology for language learning and 2) the pedagogical as well as technical challenges that face developers and educators.

To address the first point, the authors argue that educators should work hard to design the necessary datasets (i.e., intelligent dialogs) to enhance students' language proficiency. Brandtzaeg and Følstad (2018) argue that the design of intelligent dialogues in chatbots is problematic for developers regardless of the advancements in machine learning and artificial intelligence. Foreign language learners tend to make mistakes, especially in spelling. The chatbot might return irrelevant responses depending on the spelling mistakes. This suggests that intelligent dialogue systems are inevitable in the design of chatbots. Research has been found to use the CALL HOME conversational dataset, originally intended for speech recognition tasks, to design general-purpose chatbots (Ali & Habash, 2016). Other research generates dialogues from different sources such as blogs, plays, Twitter, Quora Arabic, and Movie subtitles (Boussakssou et al., 2022). Although these datasets represent authentic resources for language learning, they might be challenging to novice or intermediate language learners. Hence, the authors recommend that educators work towards creating authentic conversational datasets for learning Arabic as a foreign language. This aligns with Kuhail et al. (2022a) 's findings about the insufficiency and inadequacy of the datasets used to build chatbots. They claim that chatbots with limited datasets result in a frustrating experience for learners who struggle to learn because the chatbot cannot handle their inquiries.

Furthermore, the design of intelligent dialogs should carry the properties of human conversations. The authors recommend that efforts be directed toward designing conversations for second language learners so that these conversations can reflect the properties of actual human conversations. These properties include taking turns, speech acts, grounding, taking the initiative, inference, conversational implicature, asking for clarifications, et cetera. Second, the authors argue for rule-based reusable chatbot templates for language learning. KalaamBot is a rule-based reusable chatbot that converses with students in an authentic language learning environment. It adopts thematic learning by which it takes the role of chatting with students about specific themes. These themes can change, which entails the chatbot being re-used to teach other themes. Teachers can customize and control the conversations and the learning content to be delivered to their students using these rule-based reusable chatbots. These chatbots can help teachers commit to several pedagogical considerations and principles to achieve their learning goals. On the other hand, Generative-based large chatbots might cause what Fryer et al. (2020) call "extraneous processing." Therefore, small, customizable, and specifically intended chatbots for foreign language learning can reduce extraneous processing and support learners in managing the necessary processing of the language they acquire.

The second point represents the pedagogical considerations, principles, and challenges, as well as the technological challenges when designing chatbots. The technological challenges/limitations include UI design, frontend-backend design, and handling errors. In this work, the authors have combined Vanilla Javascript, HTML, CSS, and REACT framework in designing the frontend of these chatbots, which always represents a challenge for educators and developers. Connecting the backend, designed using Python's FLASK library, and the frontend represented another challenge for the researchers. Some recent frameworks, such as gradio (Abid et al., 2019) and streamlit and its streamlit implementation for chatbots (st-chat), provide easy-to-design interfaces for machine learning applications. However, they are intended for demoing machine learning applications. They might work for text-based chatbots as this tutorial by gradio shows.

Regarding language instruction, a custom UI might be the best solution to satisfy the necessity of a friendly interface for language learners. Other challenges pertain to enhancing the chatbot's three components: NLU, dialogue management system, and NLG. Each component represents a research area. Using neural automatic speech recognition such as wav2vec 2.0 (Baevski et al., 2020) has issues with longer inference time. The technological considerations in the design of both chatbots are 1) the chatbots can provide real-time interactions with students without delays, especially in the case of speech-based chatbots.

In the same vein, Kuhail et al. (2022a) discuss other challenges that pertain to ensuring software usability through User-Centered Design (UCD), which facilitates the active involvement of learners with the chatbot, losing interest over time, lack of feedback, and usability heuristics. The application of usability heuristics in the design of chatbots is becoming critical, primarily if chatbots are used for language learning. Kuhail et al. (2022c) summarize these usability heuristics and principles as follows: the system should provide feedback, the system should use a language familiar to the learner, users should have control when to start and when to end conversation, consistency, the chatbot should reduce learners' cognitive load, the efficiency of use, the interface should contain the essential elements, error prevention, error messages, and documentation for learners to understand the chatbot's functionality. These heuristics are essential when designing chatbots for foreign language learning and should be considered by L2 practitioners.

The pedagogical goals of the intended language activities using chatbots represent fundamental challenges for linguists and L2 practitioners. These language activities might include language knowledge practice, learning language skills, role-playing, learning scenario representations, delivering well-targeted interventions, et cetera (Huang et al., 2022). Chatbots should be designed following the intended pedagogical concerns to teach the language, which suggests using small carefully-designed systems. These systems might be rule-based rather than statistical/deep learning-trained chatbots. This imposes the following question: Do chatbots always follow the traditional architecture when used in education? By traditional architecture, the authors refer to the different architectures reviewed earlier in the second section of this article. The authors' position is that the design of chatbots for second language learning should only sometimes follow traditional architecture. For example, the TTS component is a component in speech-based chatbots. However, KalaamBot uses pre-recorded native speaker responses to provide learners with authentic language and avoid any problems in the generated speech. Moreover, the use of conversational cycles in the design of KalaamBot does not comply with the traditional architectures of chatbots. The authors find it helpful in helping students practice the language.

Using authentic language and simulating an authentic language environment is crucial to leverage students' linguistic proficiency. Ayedoun et al. (2015) show that students raised their self-confidence when interacting in a simulated authentic language environment. In the design of KalaamBot, the authors adopted thematic learning by which the chatbot takes the lead to chat with students about specific themes such as introductions, buying groceries, ordering food in a restaurant, booking a flight/train ticket, et cetera. This, in turn, can help students use the language they learned in this simulated environment in real-life contexts. The authors have found that there is an agreement that the learning experience in speech-based chatbots should immerse students in simulations of real scenarios as if they are physically interacting with real people (Ayedoun et al., 2015).

Pedagogies that promote students' critical thinking and cognitive outcomes are also considered. Chatbots should be designed with pedagogies that promote proactive behaviors toward learning a foreign language. In other words, they should enhance students' self-confidence and encourage them to participate proactively in classroom group discussions. The teachers can use them as complementary tools to enhance students' linguistic outcomes when instructors use them to enable students to expand their language beyond the class curriculum. Students' levels must be considered when designing the pedagogical goals and lesson plans. These should help move students from one level to another level. Several studies show chatbots' positive effect on students' performance (Goda et al., 2014; Kim, 2016). Kim (2016) indicated that students with medium and high language proficiency processed more interactions with a voice-based chatbot than students with low language proficiency. This claim suggests that medium- and high-level students benefit more from the voice-based chatbot than the low-level students who were burdened with a higher cognitive load to process the auditory information. In such a situation, using chatbots may be a barrier to students' language learning. A higher extraneous cognitive load could diminish students' learning outcomes (Fryer et al., 2020).

Motivation is another important consideration when using chatbots in language learning. Although several studies show that chatbots are engaging and enjoyable (Anderson et al., 2008; Fryer & Carpenter, 2006; Chiaráin & Chasaide, 2016; among others), others indicate that chatbots provide learning with short-term learning experiences (Fryer et al., 2017; Fryer et al., 2019). Both developers and educators should work together towards creating chatbots that support motivation and students' self-confidence.

One final important point is that chatbots should be assessed in a classroom setting to investigate their roles in fostering students' learning outcomes. These outcomes must be assessed to reflect the efficacy of the chatbot and the pedagogy employed. Future directions will include adding more enhancements to the two demos mentioned above and testing them in a classroom setting to investigate their effectiveness in the educational process.

CONCLUSION

This chapter presented two chatbots that can be used in learning Arabic as a foreign language. *KalaamBot* is a rule-based, speech-based chatbot that converses with learners to teach them conversations about different themes. *KalimaBot* is a text-based chatbot designed to train a neural network on a dataset created specifically for this chatbot. The chatbot can help learners to improve their learning of Arabic vocabulary by incorporating a learning-by-discovery approach. The implementation of chatbots for language learning is complicated due to 1) several technological challenges pertaining to the design of the UI and the appropriate architecture used in designing the chatbot, 2) the language pedagogy used by educators, 3) students' different levels, 4) the pedagogical goals that the chatbot should deliver, 5) the use of authentic language, and 6) the motivation affordances involved in the design. Software developers and educators should collaborate to provide more reliable chatbots for Arabic language learners. Educators and L2 practitioners should work on designing intelligent dialogues that can be used in Arabic chatbot technology.

REFERENCES:

Abid, A., Abdalla, A., Abid, A., Khan, D., Alfozan, A., & Zou, J. (2019). *Gradio: Hassle-free sharing and testing of ml models in the wild*. Cornell University.

Abu Shawar, B. (2011). A Chatbot as a natural web Interface to Arabic web QA. [iJET]. *International Journal of Emerging Technologies in Learning*, 6(1), 37–43. doi:10.3991/ijet.v6i1.1502

Abu Shawar, B., & Atwell, E. (2003). Accessing an information system by chatting. *In the International Conference on Application of Natural Language to Information Systems* (pp. 407-412). Springer.

Abu Shawar, B., & Atwell, E. (2007). Chatbots: are they really useful? In Ldv forum, 22(1), 29-49.

Abu Shawar, B., & Atwell, E. S. (2004). An Arabic chatbot giving answers from the Qur'an. In Proceedings of *TALN 04: XI Conférence sur le Traitement Automatique des Langues Naturelles [Conference on Natural Language Processing]*, *(Vol. 2, pp. 197-202). ATALA.

Al-Ghadhban, D., & Al-Twairesh, N. (2020). Nabiha: An Arabic dialect chatbot. *International Journal of Advanced Computer Science and Applications*, *11*(3). doi:10.14569/IJACSA.2020.0110357

Al-Madi, N. A., Maria, K. A., Al-Madi, M. A., Alia, M. A., & Maria, E. A. (2021). An intelligent Arabic chatbot system proposed framework. *In 2021 International Conference on Information Technology (ICIT)* (pp. 592-597). IEEE. 10.1109/ICIT52682.2021.9491699

AlHumoud, S., Al Wazrah, A., & Aldamegh, W. (2018). Arabic chatbots: a survey. *Int. J. Adv. Comp. Sci. Appl.*, 535-541.

AlHumoud, S., Diab, A., AlDukhai, D., AlShalhoub, A., AlAbdullatif, R., AlQahtany, D., & Bin-Aqeel, F. (2022). Rahhal: A Tourist Arabic Chatbot. *In 2022 2nd International Conference of Smart Systems and Emerging Technologies (SMARTTECH)* (pp. 66-73). IEEE.

Ali, D. A., & Habash, N. (2016). Botta: An Arabic dialect chatbot. *In Proceedings of COLING 2016, the 26th International Conference on Computational Linguistics: System Demonstrations* (pp. 208-212). NYU.

Aljameel, S. S., O'Shea, J. D., Crockett, K. A., Latham, A., & Kaleem, M. (2017). Development of an Arabic conversational intelligent tutoring system for education of children with ASD. In *2017 IEEE International Conference on Computational Intelligence and Virtual Environments for Measurement Systems and Applications (CIVEMSA)* (pp. 24-29). IEEE. 10.1109/CIVEMSA.2017.7995296

Alobaidi, O. G., Crockett, K. A., O'Shea, J. D., & Jarad, T. M. (2013). Abdullah: An intelligent Arabic conversational tutoring system for modern Islamic education. In *Proceedings of the World Congress on Engineering* (Vol. 2). IAENG.

Anderson, J. N., Davidson, N., Morton, H., & Jack, M. A. (2008). Language learning with interactive virtual agent scenarios and speech recognition: Lessons learned. *Computer Animation and Virtual Worlds*, *19*(5), 605–619. doi:10.1002/cav.265

Ayedoun, E., Hayashi, Y., & Seta, K. (2015). A conversational agent to encourage willingness to communicate in the context of English as a foreign language. *Procedia Computer Science*, *60*, 1433–1442. doi:10.1016/j.procs.2015.08.219

Baevski, A., Zhou, Y., Mohamed, A., & Auli, M. (2020). wav2vec 2.0: A framework for self-supervised learning of speech representations. *Advances in Neural Information Processing Systems*, *33*, 12449–12460.

Bernardini, S. (2000). *Competence, capacity, corpora: a study in corpus-aided language learning*. CLUEB.

Bocklisch, T., Faulkner, J., Pawlowski, N., & Nichol, A. (2017). *Rasa: Open-source language understanding and dialogue management*. Cornell University.

Boussakssou, M., Ezzikouri, H., & Erritali, M. (2022). Chatbot in Arabic language using seq to seq model. *Multimedia Tools and Applications*, *81*(2), 2859–2871. doi:10.100711042-021-11709-y

Brandtzaeg, P. B., & Følstad, A. (2018). Chatbots: changing user needs and motivations. *interactions*, *25*(5), 38-43.

Chiaráin, N. N., & Chasaide, A. N. (2016). Chatbot technology with synthetic voices in the acquisition of an endangered language: Motivation, development, and evaluation of a platform for Irish. *In Proceedings of the Tenth International Conference on Language Resources and Evaluation (LREC'16)* (pp. 3429-3435). ACLA.

Clark, R. C., & Mayer, R. E. (2016). *E-learning and the science of instruction: Proven guidelines for consumers and designers of multimedia learning.* John Wiley & sons. doi:10.1002/9781119239086

Colby, K. M., Weber, S., & Hilf, F. D. (1971). Artificial paranoia. *Artificial Intelligence*, *2*(1), 1–25. doi:10.1016/0004-3702(71)90002-6

Cuayáhuitl, H., Keizer, S., & Lemon, O. (2015). *Strategic dialogue management via deep reinforcement learning.* Cornell University.

Driss, M., Almomani, I., Alahmadi, L., Alhajjam, L., Alharbi, R., & Alanazi, S. (2022). *COVIBOT: A Smart Chatbot for Assistance and E-Awareness during COVID-19 Pandemic.* Cornell University., doi:10.1109/SMARTTECH54121.2022.00038

Ehsani, F., & Knodt, E. (1998). Speech technology in computer-aided lan- guage learning: Strengths and limitations of a new call paradigm. *Language Learning & Technology*, *2*(1), 54–73.

Fadhil, A., & Abu Ra'ed, A. (2019). Ollobot-Towards a text-based Arabic health conversational agent: Evaluation and results. *In Proceedings of the International Conference on Recent Advances in Natural Language Processing (RANLP 2019)* (pp. 295-303). ACL. 10.26615/978-954-452-056-4_034

Freed, A. (2021). *Conversational AI.* Manning Publications.

Fryer, L., & Carpenter, R. (2006). Bots as language learning tools. *Language Learning & Technology*, *10*(3), 8–14.

Fryer, L., Coniam, D., Carpenter, R., & Lăpuşneanu, D. (2020). Bots for language learning now: Current and future directions. *Language Learning & Technology*, *24*(2), 8–22.

Fryer, L. K., Ainley, M., Thompson, A., Gibson, A., & Sherlock, Z. (2017). Stimulating and sustaining interest in a language course: An experimental comparison of Chatbot and Human task partners. *Computers in Human Behavior*, *75*, 461–468. doi:10.1016/j.chb.2017.05.045

Fryer, L. K., Nakao, K., & Thompson, A. (2019). Chatbot learning partners: Connecting learning experiences, interest, and competence. *Computers in Human Behavior*, *93*, 279–289. doi:10.1016/j.chb.2018.12.023

Goda, Y., Yamada, M., Matsukawa, H., Hata, K., & Yasunami, S. (2014). Conversation with a chatbot before an online EFL group discussion and the effects on critical thinking. *Journal of Information Systems Education*, *13*(1), 1–7. doi:10.12937/ejsise.13.1

Google. (n.d.). *Dialogflow: natural language processing platform*. Google. https://cloud.google.com/dialogflow.

Hijjawi, M., Bandar, Z., & Crockett, K. (2016). The Enhanced Arabchat: An Arabic Conversational Agent. *International Journal of Advanced Computer Science and Applications*, *7*(2), 7. doi:10.14569/IJACSA.2016.070247

Hijjawi, M., Bandar, Z., Crockett, K., & Mclean, D. (2014). ArabChat: An arabic conversational agent. In *2014 6th International Conference on Computer Science and Information Technology (CSIT)* (pp. 227-237). IEEE.

Hsu, L. (2016). An empirical examination of efl learners' perceptual learning styles and acceptance of asr-based computer-assisted pronunciation training. *Computer Assisted Language Learning*, *29*(5), 881–900. doi:10.1080/09588221.2015.1069747

Huang, W., Hew, K. F., & Fryer, L. K. (2022). Chatbots for language learning are they really useful? a systematic review of chatbot-supported language learning. *Journal of Computer Assisted Learning*, *38*(1), 237–257. doi:10.1111/jcal.12610

Huang, W., Hew, K. F., & Fryer, L. K. (2022). Chatbots for language learning—Are they really useful? A systematic review of chatbot-supported language learning. *Journal of Computer Assisted Learning*, *38*(1), 237–257. doi:10.1111/jcal.12610

Jurafsky, D., & Martin, J. H. (2021). Speech and Language Processing. *Stanford Press*. https://web.stanford.edu/~jurafsky/slp3/

Kim, N. Y. (2016). Effects of voice chat on EFL learners' speaking ability according to proficiency levels. *Multimedia-Assisted Language Learning*, *19*(4), 63–88.

Kuhail, M. A., Al Katheeri, H., Negreiros, J., Seffah, A., & Alfandi, O. (2022c). Engaging Students With a Chatbot-Based Academic Advising System. *International Journal of Human-Computer Interaction*, 1–27. doi:10.1080/10447318.2022.2074645

Kuhail, M. A., Alturki, N., Alramlawi, S., & Alhejori, K. (2022a). Interacting with educational chatbots: A systematic review. *Education and Information Technologies*, 1–46. doi:10.100710639-022-11177-3

Kuhail, M. A., Thomas, J., Alramlawi, S., Shah, S. J. H., & Thornquist, E. (2022b). Interacting with a Chatbot-Based Advising System: Understanding the Effect of Chatbot Personality and User Gender on Behavior. In Informatics, 9(4), 81. MDPI.

Kulkarni, P., Mahabaleshwarkar, A., Kulkarni, M., Sirsikar, N., & Gadgil, K. (2019). Conversational ai: An overview of methodologies, applications & future scope. In *2019 5th International Conference on Computing, Communication, Control and Automation (ICCUBEA)*, (pp. 1–7). IEEE.

Lokman, A. S., & Ameedeen, M. A. (2018). Modern chatbot systems: A technical review. *In Proceedings of the future technologies conference* (pp. 1012-1023). Springer.

Makatchev, M., Fanaswala, I., Abdulsalam, A., Browning, B., Ghazzawi, W., Sakr, M., & Simmons, R. (2010). Dialogue patterns of an Arabic robot receptionist. In *2010 5th ACM/IEEE International Conference on Human-Robot Interaction (HRI)* (pp. 167-168). IEEE.

Mavridis, N., AlDhaheri, A., AlDhaheri, L., Khanii, M., & AlDarmaki, N. (2011). Transforming IbnSina into an advanced multilingual interactive android robot. In 2011 IEEE GCC Conference and Exhibition (GCC) (pp. 120-123). IEEE. doi:10.1109/IEEEGCC.2011.5752467

Mayer, R. E. (2017). Using multimedia for e-learning. *Journal of Computer Assisted Learning*, *33*(5), 403–423. doi:10.1111/jcal.12197

McTear, M. (2020). Conversational ai: Dialogue systems, conversational agents, and chatbots. *Synthesis Lectures on Human Language Technologies*, *13*(3), 1–251. doi:10.1007/978-3-031-02176-3

Naous, T., Hokayem, C., & Hajj, H. (2020). Empathy-driven Arabic conversational chatbot. *In Proceedings of the Fifth Arabic Natural Language Processing Workshop* (pp. 58-68). ACLA.

Shang, L., Lu, Z., & Li, H. (2015). *Neural responding machine for short-text conversation*. Cornell University., doi:10.3115/v1/P15-1152

Sinclair, J. (Ed.). (2004). *How to use corpora in language teaching*. John Benjamins. doi:10.1075cl.12

Timpe-Laughlin, V., Sydorenko, T., & Daurio, P. (2020). Using spoken dialogue technology for l2 speaking practice: What do teachers think? *Computer Assisted Language Learning*, 1–24.

Tsai, P. (2019). Beyond self-directed computer-assisted pronunciation learning: A qualitative investigation of a collaborative approach. *Computer Assisted Language Learning*, *32*(7), 713–744. doi:10.1080/09588221.2019.1614069

Turing, A. (1950). Computing machinery and intelligence. *Mind*, *59*(236), 433–460. doi:10.1093/mind/LIX.236.433

Wallace, R. (2003). *The elements of AIML style*, 139. Alice AI Foundation.

Weizenbaum, J. (1966). ELIZA—A computer program for the study of natural language communication between man and machine. *Communications of the ACM*, *9*(1), 36–45. doi:10.1145/365153.365168

Wollny, S., Schneider, J., Di Mitri, D., Weidlich, J., Rittberger, M., & Drachsler, H. (2021). Are we there yet? -A systematic literature review on chatbots in education. *Frontiers in artificial intelligence*, *4*.

Zaki, M. (2017). Corpus-based teaching in the Arabic classroom: Theoretical and practical perspectives. *International Journal of Applied Linguistics*, *27*(2), 514–541. doi:10.1111/ijal.12159

Zubair Khan, M., & Mahamat Yassin, S. (2021). *SeerahBot: An Arabic Chatbot About Prophet's Biography*. *International Journal of Innovative Research in Computer Science & Technology*. IJIRCST.

KEY TERMS AND DEFINITIONS

Automatic Speech Recognition (ASR): The ability to take speech as input and produce a transcript as an output. It is also known as speech-to-text (STT).

Conversational AI: The application of machine learning to develop text-based and speech-based chatbots to handle conversations the way humans do.

Language Proficiency: The ability to use a language as appropriate and accepted by native speakers of that language. This ability can be demonstrated in real-world scenarios.

Learning by Discovery: The students' ability to independently investigate problems and find answers themselves.

Reinforcement Learning: A branch of machine learning that trains agents (or bots) to choose the actions that maximize their rewards over time in a certain environment.

Sequence-to-Sequence: A model that takes a sequence of elements (i.e., words, sentences, letters, sounds, time series, et cetera.) and outputs another sequence of elements.

Thematic Learning: A teaching method that focuses on a specific theme which forms the core of a learning/teaching unit.

Transformers: Innovative neural architecture in natural language processing that tried to solve the problems of long sequences in sequence-to-sequence learning by using the attention mechanism.

Wav2vec 2.0: A transformer-based automatic speech recognition system with great abilities to learn from raw audio data. It is one of the state-of-the-art ASR engines.

ENDNOTES

[1]   All transformer models and their variants are provided on the Huggingface website (https://huggingface.co). Huggingface is a community that works towards democratizing NLP, and it has become the home for all machine learning tasks. Researchers can find demos, use cases, models, datasets, et cetera.

[2]   IJMES (International of Middle East Studies) transliteration system is used for the Arabic language throughout this article. See it here: https://www.cambridge.org/core/services/aop-file-manager/fil e/57d83390f6ea5a022234b400/TransChart.pdf

[3]   The model can be found on Huggingface: (jonatasgrosman/wav2vec2-large-xlsr-53-arabic), and the code to build a language model and run the model with it is found on Github: https://github.com/elsayed-issa/stt-toolkit

[4]   The Arabic language is under-resourced regarding corpora intended for language teaching (Zaki, 2017).

Section 3

Chatbots in Business: Overview and Challenges

Chapter 9

Chatbots for Business and Customer Support

Syed Jawad Hussain Shah
University of Missouri-Kansas City, USA

ABSTRACT

Artificial intelligence (AI)-driven chatbots have established themselves as standard front-line solutions for companies looking to update consumer experiences while maximizing client engagement. Chatbots have become a crucial component of a company's customer-centric operations because of their fast replies, round-the-clock assistance, and ability to comprehend user inquiries. This chapter will describe the function of chatbots as customer service representatives and some of the benefits they offer to organizations. There will also be a discussion of the present difficulties facing the industry in integrating these conversational bots.

INTRODUCTION

Artificial intelligence (AI) is becoming a part of our daily lives by creating intelligent applications, such as conversational agents. Conversational agents, called chatbots, can perform a wide range of jobs, from simple tasks to complex procedures, and can be personality imbued (Kuhail et al, 2022). Chatbots are the classic example of an AI system and are one of the simplest and most common forms of intelligent human-computer interaction (HCI) (Bansal, 2018). The advances in natural language processing (NLP) have enabled them to understand multiple human languages and converse intelligently with users through auditory or textual methods. Per one of the definitions, a chatbot is "a computer program that simulates human conversation through voice commands or text chats or both" (Frankenfield, 2022). Indeed, there

DOI: 10.4018/978-1-6684-6234-8.ch009

are several fields where virtual assistants are already in use. Users may access it using SMS text messages, cellphones, PCs, or other connected devices, and it just needs internet connectivity to function. The chatbot and user may converse in human language in what seems to be a standard conversation window. Users either type their query straight into the designated field or select certain buttons. It has been demonstrated that chatbots are a valuable and efficient way to inform customers.

Companies must be clear about the problems they encounter, how they plan to tackle them, and their goals while striving for gradual improvements considering current trends toward improving client touch points. For this purpose, several businesses are beginning to provide "chatbots" as a service to automate conversations with humans using computers for consumer interaction (Okuda & Shoda, 2018). In business, chatbots are widely used to speed up numerous processes, especially those involving personalization and customer support (Przegalinska, Ciechanowski, Stroz, Gloor, & Mazurek, 2019). Chatbots have developed into lucrative solutions for organizations due to their capacity for intelligent human interaction and simplicity of development and integration into current digital platforms. Chatbots are widely used nowadays for a range of online interactions between businesses and their clients in marketing and customer support. By giving clients high value, chatbots can enhance customer service, for instance, when searching for real-time information on the dependability and accessibility of goods and services. Customers' experience is flawless because of automatic responses to repetitive queries on frequent problems (Behera, Bala, & Ray, 2021).

CHATBOTS FOR BUSINESS

One of the main issues CEOs of contemporary businesses presently must cope with is digitalization. The word "digitalization" refers to the proliferation of digital technology across society as well as changes in individual communication styles and interpersonal interactions (Gimpel & Röglinger, 2015). The emergence of new digital technologies (such as social networks and cloud computing) has increased market transparency while reducing the knowledge asymmetry between sellers and consumers (Patil et al, 2017). As a result, building long-term client loyalty is crucial for businesses. The emergence of new technologies also had an impact on how individuals interact with businesses, and an increasing number of customers prefer to contact businesses through digital channels (such as online forms, social media, etc.) to express service requests or complete transactions, among other things. Businesses are now connecting with clients on digital platforms instead of conventional ones because of recent advancements in AI applications. The primary driver of this transformation is, among other things, the ease that technology offers to firms operating on the digital platform. The time it takes to convert a potential customer into a paying client has decreased with the development of e-commerce. The definition of e-commerce is that transactions can happen at any time and anywhere (Balasubrama et al., 2002). For these transactions to take place, regular one-on-one live client interactions are necessary to respond to marketing inquiries and provide additional services. Businesses and retail house use websites to help with marketing requirements and to compete with their rivals.

The company website is basically a virtual store or an online catalog of products that not only offers information about the products and online purchasing choices to clients but also includes marketing materials and promotions that draw them in the first place. Customers may visit a company website, examine the products, make their selections, search for any available coupons or discounts, and then complete an online purchase. According to one research (Pachamanova et al., 2020), an immediate response is now a crucial component of marketing management and must be backed up by operational strategies. However, it is neither operationally efficient nor cost-effective to provide human services around-the-clock for customers who communicate with brands primarily through online platforms. On the other hand, many businesses are using chatbots (powered by AI) as the most affordable solution for this issue. Chatbots must fulfill several criteria to be utilized with the intention of promoting businesses.

A growing number of firms are beginning to make use of chatbots' and conversational systems' capacity to conduct routine communication duties. Chatbots are a promising technology that may significantly automate customer interactions, build customer connections by providing round-the-clock customer support, and free up human resources for the primary company operations. However, businesses will only engage in the implementation of chatbots if the desired value propositions outweigh the associated costs (Barba-Sanchez et al, 2007). The next competitive advantage for many organizations is chatbots. Chatbots offer much value for the money spent on them due to the many advantages they offer. Small and medium-sized businesses (SMEs) are rapidly becoming interested in the use of chatbots to assist customer relationship management (CRM) operations in business-to-consumer (B2C) markets. SMEs are essential for countries' economic growth (Newby, Nguyen, & Waring, 2014). However, due to a lack of human resources, SMEs acquire and sell in small amounts, have restricted budgets, and have the same departments or people do several responsibilities. Maintaining tight ties with the clientele is essential for SMEs to keep a competitive edge. Due to this, SMEs have realized the significance of IT in strengthening customer interactions effectively and efficiently.

ADVANTAGES OF CHATBOTS FOR CUSTOMER SUPPORT

Numerous characteristics of chatbots make them appropriate tools for customer service and business assistance on online platforms. Chatbots help in reducing the operational cost of customer care initiatives. They might aid businesses in cost savings. This is because companies do not always need to hire fresh employees to manage customer service. The automation of customer care by chatbots is a vital advantage they provide to SMEs and startups as well as to enterprises in general. A high customer-to-staff ratio is typical of small firms and startups. They are unable to individually serve every consumer. Customer assistance systems for such small firms must be automated. The customer assistance portion may be automated using chatbots. These conversational agents can boost earnings by relieving resource pressure. Chatbots allow employees to focus on more difficult work by freeing them up from routinely occurring inquiries. FAQ chatbots may boost workplace efficiency, reduce staff expenses, and eventually boost revenue. For instance, Toshiba could cut the number of support calls by 30 to 50%, reducing the effort of the service staff. Similarly, chatbots can also improve response time for customer service queries because of automation. Businesses usually face revenue reduction due to slow and unreliable customer service. To increase their profit, they must improve the response time. People now anticipate speedier reaction times in the era of immediate communication. Businesses may make their consumers feel noticed by employing chatbots to automate answers, even if it's simply to promise to connect them with a human as quickly as feasible. People are considerably more likely to purchase from a company when they feel listened to and valued. Chatbots can converse with customers in their native tongue if they have been built to speak many languages. This will broaden the client base and facilitate user interaction with the brand. Additionally, their speech recognition feature might improve online security.

Due to the chatbot's availability 24 hours a day, users may submit service requests outside of regular office hours, which improves customer satisfaction. Chatbots' always-on capabilities are one of their most important features. If businesses have 24/7 assistance in place, their staff may enjoy valuable vacation time while their clients can get their problems handled on weekends and after business hours. Chatbots won't be abrupt or sarcastic with clients. They are really patient with inquiries that they have previously provided a million times. Human customer service representatives should be cheerful when chatting with clients. They do, however, have good and terrible days. Unfortunately, this may negatively affect how they interact with consumers and impair the customer experience. Conversely, chatbots are virtual robots and are emotionless. They are conditioned to obey commands and to abide by rules. No matter how unpleasant the consumer is, chatbots can always speak to them respectfully. Businesses may improve and increase customer satisfaction levels and may rely on chatbots to avoid mistakes that people could make. Additionally, they could enhance users' online buying experiences. For example, the Bank of America employs a chatbot to analyze consumer behavior and present personalized and adapted product proposals (Kusber, 2017). They can effectively engage with visitors via text or voice, welcome them to the website, guide them through the various products, respond to inquiries about the products, and assist with online transactions to buy the goods.

Chatbots also provide implementation benefits from a developmental standpoint in addition to benefits from the perspective of the consumer. This includes platform-independent implementations of many chatbots and making them instantly accessible to users without the need for installs. Further, it is very simple to integrate them with social networking platform messengers. Without leaving the messaging app, the chatbot resides in, which gives and ensures the user's identification, contacts with the chatbot are distributed over a user's social network, hence providing a chance for publicity. Additionally, a notification system re-engages dormant users, and payment services are incorporated into the message system and may be utilized safely and reliably. They also provide the ability of multiple interactions in parallel along with group conversations and contact sharing. Data needs are minimal, and lessons learned from using one instance can be easily applied to other. Developmental efforts can also benefit from communication dependability, quick and simple development cycles, a lack of version fragmentation, and less interface design work (Klopfenstein, Delpriori, Malatini, & Bogliolo, 2017).

EXAMPLES OF CHATBOTS FOR CUSTOMER SERVICE AND BUSINESS ASSISTANCE

To assist customer services in e-commerce sales and marketing, one of the studies suggests an intelligent knowledge-based conversational agent system architecture (Ngai, Lee, Luo, Chan, & Liang, 2021). A prominent manufacturer of women's intimate clothing has reported using a chatbot as part of a trial program for customer assistance. The suggested system integrates several cutting-edge technologies, including web crawling, NLP, knowledge bases, and AI. A prototype system is constructed in the context of this investigation. The examination of the system prototype produced positive findings that confirm the system's efficacy (Ngai et al, 2021).

In the banking sector, chatbots are used for sales and customer care. An AI-based corporate chatbot solution called FUJITSU Financial Services Solution Finplex Robot Agent Platform (FRAP) was created by Fujitsu (Okuda & Shoda, 2018). By allowing customers to communicate with a robot that has knowledge amassed through machine learning, FRAP provides autonomous robot assistance in financial product sales and customer service.

The way people approach customer service has changed due to social media. As they can quickly shoot off a Tweet or Facebook status rather than dial a 1-800 number or compose a thorough email, over half of American Internet users are turning to social media for assistance (Corporation, 2011). A new conversational system was developed through research to provide automated replies to user queries on social media (Xu, Liu, Guo, Sinha, & Akkiraju, 2017). The roughly 1 million Twitter discussions between users and representatives from more than 60 businesses served as the training data for this system, which incorporates deep learning techniques. The results of the test suggest that the system can empathize with users in emotional circumstances roughly as well as human agents can (Xu et al, 2017).

The creation and use of a customer care chatbot at the Venice Airport is the subject of another research (Carisi, Albarelli, & Luccio, 2019). The goal was to create a common core that could communicate around the clock using a variety of paradigms, from voice to touch displays, and user interfaces, including mobile phones, fixed installations, and roaming robots. By utilizing contemporary cloud-based services and creating a particularly constructed modular system capable of interacting with both online information providers and old data sources provided by the airport infrastructure, this objective has been accomplished (Carisi et al, 2019).

A different conversational agent developed as a customer support chatbot named SuperAgent makes use of extensive and freely accessible e-commerce data (Cui et al, 2017). In contrast to its competitors, SuperAgent uses user-generated material from e-commerce websites and data from in-page product descriptions to provide more practical and cost-effective answers to repetitive queries, freeing up human support workers to address issues of far greater value. The utility of SuperAgent in users' online purchasing experiences is demonstrated by its deployment as an add-on extension for popular web browsers (Cui et al, 2017).

Due to the vast range of services that chatbots may offer, research utilizing the Dialogflow bot architecture produced a conversational chatbot for the parking sector (Ayyagari & Mohaghegh, 2021). The built-in chatbot manages complex tasks, including distributing parking places, changing license plates, and terminating subscriptions. The key contribution of this work is the seamless interaction of the user's mobile application with the chatbot, which uses customized business logic to carry out dynamic actions. The outcomes showed that a chatbot is capable of handling sophisticated real-time inquiries and acting appropriately without the assistance of a person (Ayyagari & Mohaghegh, 2021).

Another study introduces Cardbot, a virtual assistant that blends chatbot and OCR technologies (Ko & Lin, 2018). CardBot's primary goal is to make managing business cards simple and straightforward for users while offering specialized assistance in the form of a virtual assistant.

CHALLENGES

Interpreting the messages and determining the user purpose while utilizing chatbots for customer assistance is one of the toughest challenges. As soon as a chatbot is created, adaptable algorithms for determining the message's purpose must be programmed. People express themselves in a multitude of ways, as opposed to computers that only know one way to convey anything. Some people use brief sentences. Some people compose lengthy pieces. Some people write in a colloquial, while others use bitter mistakes. Customers won't accept the response "Sorry, I can't tolerate it" and don't really care if what they are saying is unsuitable for the computer to grasp. The natural next step is to leverage the context gathered to your advantage after the chatbot can understand the user and provide suitable answers. Personalization is what it implies in terms of the user experience. The easiest method is to maintain user history. It must be savable and accessible to the bot in accordance. That certainly aids in keeping the consumer pleased and engaged throughout the process. The whole "you might also like" approach, which frequently confounds people, is made easier by personalization. The bot will be able to generate a more viable offer for the user based on past requests and trends across several users. However, finding the best strategies for user adaptation is the challenging part.

Understanding the limitations of Natural Language Processing (NLP) is another significant obstacle to designing and modifying chatbot behavior. In the manner individuals anticipate while conversing with another human, chatbots fall short of understanding actual context. Chatbots make assumptions based on keywords and avoid understanding context through inquiries, which leaves users, at best, perplexed and more frequently dissatisfied. Businesses need help to make chatbots adaptable to human answers and reactions, which may result in awkward consumer encounters and cost them a significant amount of money.

When it comes to protecting their personal information, customers are sensitive and vigilant. Therefore, it is essential that companies develop chatbots that can guarantee client data protection. Chatbots must gather pertinent facts and information and safely deliver it over the internet. Businesses must certainly ensure that it is safe to exchange information with chatbots if they plan to utilize them for customer care. This is because consumer data is delicate, easily exploited, or managed improperly, and can harm a company's reputation. With VoiceBots, businesses can create conversational AI platforms. The goal of these VoiceBots is to identify the feelings and emotions of consumers. The firm might suffer greatly if they misjudge human feelings and thoughts. It might be difficult to recognize the user's sentiment from their speech and reply appropriately.

REFERENCES

Ayyagari, A., & Mohaghegh, M. (2021, October). Dynamic Chatbot for Parking Service. In *2021 International Conference on Engineering and Emerging Technologies (ICEET)* (pp. 1-6). IEEE.

Balasubraman, S., Peterson, R. A., & Jarvenpaa, S. L. (2002). Exploring the implications of m-commerce for markets and marketing. *Journal of the Academy of Marketing Science*, *30*(4), 348–361. doi:10.1177/009207002236910

Bansal, H., & Khan, R. (2018). A review paper on human computer interaction. *International Journal of Advanced Research in Computer Science and Software Engineering*, *8*(4), 53–56. doi:10.23956/ijarcsse.v8i4.630

Barba-Sánchez, V., & Jimenez-Zarco, A. I. (2007). Drivers, Benefits and Challenges of ICT adoption by small and medium sized en-terprises (SMEs): A Literature Review. *Problems and Perspectives in Management*, (5, Iss. 1), 103–114.

Behera, R. K., Bala, P. K., & Ray, A. (2021). Cognitive Chatbot for personalised contextual customer service: Behind the scene and beyond the hype. *Information Systems Frontiers*, 1–21. doi:10.100710796-021-10168-y

Carisi, M., Albarelli, A., & Luccio, F. L. (2019, September). Design and implementation of an airport chatbot. In *Proceedings of the 5th EAI International Conference on Smart Objects and Technologies for Social Good* (pp. 49-54). ACM. 10.1145/3342428.3342664

Cui, L., Huang, S., Wei, F., Tan, C., Duan, C., & Zhou, M. (2017, July). Superagent: A customer service chatbot for e-commerce websites. In *Proceedings of ACL 2017, system demonstrations* (pp. 97-102). ACL. 10.18653/v1/P17-4017

Frankenfield, J. (2022) What is Chatbot? *Investopedia.* https://www.investopedia.com/terms/c/chatbot.asp

Gimpel, H., & Röglinger, M. (2015). *Digital transformation: changes and chances–insights based on an empirical study.* Semantic Scholar.

Klopfenstein, L. C., Delpriori, S., Malatini, S., & Bogliolo, A. (2017, June). The rise of bots: A survey of conversational interfaces, patterns, and paradigms. In *Proceedings of the 2017 conference on designing interactive systems* (pp. 555-565). ACM. 10.1145/3064663.3064672

Ko, M. C., & Lin, Z. H. (2018, March). CardBot: A chatbot for business card management. In *Proceedings of the 23rd International Conference on Intelligent User Interfaces Companion* (pp. 1-2). ACM. 10.1145/3180308.3180313

Kuhail, M. A., Thomas, J., Alramlawi, S., Shah, S. J. H., & Thornquist, E. (2022, October). Interacting with a Chatbot-Based Advising System: Understanding the Effect of Chatbot Personality and User Gender on Behavior. In Informatics, 9(4), 81. MDPI.

Kusber, R. (2017). Chatbots–conversational UX platforms. In *Innovationen und Innovationsmanagement in der Finanzbranche* (pp. 231–244). Springer Gabler. doi:10.1007/978-3-658-15648-0_11

Newby, M., Nguyen, T. H., & Waring, T. S. (2014). Understanding customer relationship management technology adoption in small and medium-sized enterprises: An empirical study in the USA. *Journal of Enterprise Information Management.* doi:10.1108/JEIM-11-2012-0078

Ngai, E. W., Lee, M. C., Luo, M., Chan, P. S., & Liang, T. (2021). An intelligent knowledge-based chatbot for customer service. *Electronic Commerce Research and Applications*, *50*, 101098. doi:10.1016/j.elerap.2021.101098

Nielsen Corporation. (2011) *State of the Media: Social Media Report Q3*. Nielsen. https://www.nielsen.com/insights/2011/social-mediareport-q3/, urldate = 2022-10-15

Okuda, T., & Shoda, S. (2018). AI-based chatbot service for financial industry. *Fujitsu Scientific and Technical Journal*, *54*(2), 4–8.

Pachamanova, D., Lo, V. S., & Gülpınar, N. (2020). Uncertainty representation and risk management for direct segmented marketing. *Journal of Marketing Management*, *36*(1-2), 149–175. doi:10.1080/0267257X.2019.1707265

Patil, A., Marimuthu, K., & Niranchana, R. (2017). Comparative study of cloud platforms to develop a Chatbot. *IACSIT International Journal of Engineering and Technology*, *6*(3), 57–61. doi:10.14419/ijet.v6i3.7628

Przegalinska, A., Ciechanowski, L., Stroz, A., Gloor, P., & Mazurek, G. (2019). In bot we trust: A new methodology of chatbot performance measures. *Business Horizons, 62*(6), 785–797. doi:10.1016/j.bushor.2019.08.005

Xu, A., Liu, Z., Guo, Y., Sinha, V., & Akkiraju, R. (2017, May). A new chatbot for customer service on social media. In *Proceedings of the 2017 CHI conference on human factors in computing systems* (pp. 3506-3510). ACM. 10.1145/3025453.3025496

Chapter 10
A Review on Chatbot Personality and Its Expected Effects on Users

Marta Ferreira
University of Porto, Portugal

Belem Barbosa
iD https://orcid.org/0000-0002-4057-360X
University of Porto, Portugal

ABSTRACT

The main objectives of this chapter are to provide an overview of chatbot personality dimensions and to analyze the expected impacts on user behavior. To accomplish these objectives, the chapter provides a detailed review of the main contributions in the literature regarding this topic. It highlights the chatbot personality characteristics that are expected to foster user satisfaction, trust, loyalty, and engagement. This information is useful for both practitioners and researchers, particularly related to customer service, as it provides clear guidance on what characteristics to incorporate in chatbots and on what factors need to be further studied in the future.

INTRODUCTION

In recent years, due to technological advances in machine learning, there has been a great development and growth in the use of artificial intelligence (Smestad & Volden, 2019). Artificial Intelligence (AI) can be defined as a "technological science that researches and develops theories, methods, technologies, and application systems

DOI: 10.4018/978-1-6684-6234-8.ch010

for simulating, extending, and expanding human intelligence" (Yang et al., 2021, p. 1). AI has been used to facilitate and improve customer relationships and service namely by the creation of chatbots.

A chatbot (short for "Chat Robot") consists of a "computer program that communicates with a human being through text or voice messaging in real-time, in a way that is very personalized" (Chandel et al., 2019, p. 1). This type of program uses AI algorithms and natural language processing technology to create an intelligent response, which is based on the programmers' human input. The goal is to create conversations that increasingly resemble human-to-human interaction so that it is virtually impossible to distinguish (Chandel et al., 2019).

The use of this technology grew abruptly from 2014 when a large investment was made in this area of virtual assistance, and several assistants were already being used for simple tasks (Grudin & Jacques, 2019). However, even in 2010, the emergence of Siri, Apple's voice chatbot, had already revolutionized the market with its possibility of interaction based on human language. The fact that large companies are starting to use AI has created a growing interest in the public (Rapp et al., 2021). Chandel et al. (2019) note that chatbots have been implemented in quite different business areas, but with a high incidence in consumer service centers, e-commerce platforms, healthcare areas, and messaging applications. According to Insider Intelligence (2021), retail turnover via chatbots will reach $142 billion in 2024, in contrast to $2.8 billion in 2019.

Given their wide applicability, virtual assistants can be created with different goals, defined by the organization they represent. Grudin and Jacques (2019) propose the categorization of chatbots into three groups – "virtual companions", which create relationships and maintain conversations on any topic (where the personality issue is most notorious), "intelligent assistants", which carry out conversational short stories on any topic, and "task-oriented chatbots", which are smaller in scope and deeper in knowledge, focusing on creating succinct conversations.

According to Følstad and Skjuve (2019), the greatest motivation for users to choose the chatbot is its ability to offer adequate assistance, help them, and present relevant information. Still, the performance of this type of program must be able to progressively approach the behavior of a human assistant. One relevant way to do it is to attribute personality to chatbots, aiming to create a strong image and identity and to influence users' satisfaction.

Personality can be defined as "the enduring set of traits and styles that he or she exhibits, which characteristics represent (a) dispositions (i.e., natural tendencies or personal inclinations) of this person, and (b) ways in which this person differs from the "standard normal person" in his or her society" (Bergner, 2020, p. 4). In the past, personalities have been attributed for instance to brands. In this regard, brand personality is described as "the set of human characteristics associated with a brand"

(Aaker, 2021, p. 1). Smestad and Volden (2019) state that the fact that a chatbot has a specific personality has a significant positive impact on the user experience, although it depends on the context, the performance of the chatbot, and the characteristics of the user himself. Xiao et al. (2020) highlight some characteristics of the robot that can contribute positively to user engagement: paraphrasing the user's idea (as confirmation of understanding), verbalizing emotions and empathy, encouraging conversation, and responding in a summarized way. Thus, it is expected that the chatbot personality and related emotions impact on user engagement.

The main objectives of this chapter are to provide an overview of chatbot personality dimensions and to analyze the expected impacts on user behavior. To accomplish these objectives, the chapter provides a detailed review of the main contributions in the literature regarding this topic.

BACKGROUND

The literature often refers to a chatbot as an agent or virtual assistant, which can be defined as "a specific type of social robot designed to interact and talk with people" (Westerman et al., 2019, p. 3). Chatbots offer several advantages for the user. Tasks such as scheduling appointments, offering suggestions for online purchases, booking services, customer support, quickly accessing online content, placing and tracking orders, getting answers to certain questions, making complaints, or even getting medical advice (Brandtzaeg & Følstad, 2017; Peng & Ma, 2019) can be quickly fulfilled by a virtual agent. In certain cases, for simple and straightforward questions, the performance of a chatbot can surpass that of a human assistant (Følstad & Skjuve, 2019), and the understanding and use of natural language leads to appropriate and useful responses in a short time (Jain et al., 2018).

Currently, the use of Artificial Intelligence is gaining ground in the area of customer service (Svenningsson & Faraon, 2019) and a large part of computer-mediated communication takes place through the use of chatbots (Beattie et al., 2020). Often, users recognize chatbots as non-human due to their quick responses, the lack of personalization, and the repetition of responses (Følstad & Skjuve, 2019). However, Araujo (2018) notes that users tend to respond socially to a computer, even when they are aware that they are talking to a machine.

Mou and Xu (2017) suggest that one possible solution to improve users' experience is the inclusion of different personality types in machines and applications, based on the user's needs and social responses. This personality attribution is a form of anthropomorphization of a chatbot, which consists of the attribution of "human characteristics, motivations, beliefs, and feelings to non-human entities" (Smestad & Volden, 2019, p. 3). Personality can be defined as "a stable set of traits that determines the agent's interaction style, describes its character, and allows the end-user to understand its general behavior" (Angeli et al., 2001, p. 5). The presence of human attributes leads to the conscious and unconscious feeling of being talking to a person, rather than a machine (Araujo, 2018). Shi et al. (2020) note that the chatbot's humanity (e.g., identity, personality) tends to lead to better results in conversation, perception of competence, trust, sincerity, and friendliness. Dryer (1999) provides an example of the preference for interacting with cooperative, extroverted, calm, organized, and curious virtual agents, in comparison with those who present characteristics such as competitiveness, introversion, restlessness, ambiguity, or closed mind.

Personality Dimensions

Personality characteristics can be defined as "aspects of an individual's cognition, affect, or behavior that tends to be stable over time and consistent across relevant situations" (Soto et al., 2015, p. 1). The Big Five model, which identifies five personality dimensions, is the most referred to in the literature on chatbot personality. This model offers a "hierarchical organization of personality traits in terms of five basic dimensions: Extraversion, Agreeableness, Conscientiousness, Neuroticism, and Openness to Experience" (McCrae & John, 1992, p. 1). The dimensions of the model are explored below.

Agreeableness

Agreeableness is the tendency to show compassion, tolerance, kindness, and cooperation towards others (Shumanov & Johnson, 2021) and is usually related to the more "human" side of the personality (McCrae & John, 1992). It can be defined as "the extent to which one behaves prosocially towards another and maintains pleasant and harmonious interpersonal relationships" (Soto et al., 2015, p. 1). This dimension is essentially manifested through compassion (McCrae & John, 1992; Soto et al., 2015), empathy (McCrae & John, 1992), trust (Soto et al., 2015), and cooperation (Dryer, 1999). A personality with a high level of agreement generally displays characteristics such as friendliness, femininity, amiability, care, and sensitivity (McCrae & John, 1992). The willingness to help, and the ability to forgive and respect are also associated with this personality dimension (Soto et al., 2015). Mou and Xu (2017) highlight two common behaviors that enhance agreement – believing that others have good intentions and calming people down. On the other hand, when the level of agreement is low, this is evidenced by the presence of aggression, criticism, rancor, and paranoia (McCrae & John, 1992; Soto et al., 2015).

Conscientiousness

Consciousness is "an individual's ability to organize things, complete tasks, and work towards long-term goals" (Soto et al., 2015, p. 1) and is evidenced mainly by the organization, discipline, and consistency of one's actions. Organization is the most mentioned feature in the literature in relation to consciousness (Dryer, 1999; McCrae & Costa, 1985; McCrae & John, 1992; Shumanov & Johnson, 2021; Soto et al., 2015). McCrae and John (1992) suggest that a more conscientious individual tends to be more prudent, regulated, controlled, leader, restrained, and judgmental. Smestad and Volden (2019) define the most conscientious personality as consistent, faithful, and perceptive. Knowledge and intelligence are also associated with this dimension of personality (McCrae & Costa, 1985).

When there is a high level of consciousness in a personality, there is a preference for order, structure, rules, and productivity. On the other hand, when this level is low, the behavior becomes more impulsive and distracted (Soto et al., 2015).

Extraversion

Extraversion refers to the ability to socialize, being self-confident, outgoing, influential, exposed, and dominant (McCrae & John, 1992). Mou and Xu (2017) summarize this dimension as the ability to manage social situations and captivate people. The characteristics associated with this personality variable are sociability, assertiveness, and energy (Soto et al., 2015), as well as friendliness, fun, and confidence (Smestad & Volden, 2019). Extraverted personalities exhibit behaviors such as being gregarious and expressive, enjoying socializing and meeting new people, being less inhibited, speaking positively and more self-centered (Shumanov & Johnson, 2021), communicating a lot, leading, expressing positive emotions (Shumanov & Johnson, 2021). As a rule, an individual with a high level of extraversion uses more words, less complex, and emotional and social language (Shumanov & Johnson, 2021).

On the other hand, personalities with a low level of extraversion – introverts – tend to demonstrate less sociable behaviors, such as wanting to be alone, avoiding interactions with groups, performing activities that do not involve other people, being more analytical, using more precise language (Shumanov & Johnson, 2021), being uncomfortable in social situations and not being expressive (Soto et al., 2015).

Personality, which can also be attributed to virtual assistants, can present different levels of extroversion. Chatbots with a high level of extraversion communicate assertively, while those more introverted tend to focus on objectivity and efficiency (Shumanov & Johnson, 2021).

Neuroticism

Neuroticism refers to someone's sensitivity to the environment in which they find themselves, and how this affects their emotions, such as nervousness, anxiety, and insecurity (Shumanov & Johnson, 2021) and "represents individual differences in the tendency to suffer, and in the cognitive and behavioral form that follows this trend" (McCrae & John, 1992, p. 21). Soto et al. (2015) define it as "the extent to which someone is prone to experience negative emotions and moods" (Soto et al., 2015, p. 2) and refer that the socially desirable pole of this dimension is emotional stability. A personality with a high level of neuroticism shows characteristics such as stress reactions and extremism (McCrae & John, 1992), anxiety, hostility, depression, discomfort, impulsiveness, and vulnerability (Dryer, 1999; McCrae & Costa, 1985; Soto et al., 2015). Mou and Xu (2017) highlight two behaviors closely associated with neuroticism – easy annoyance and self-discomfort.

A low level of neuroticism leads to adaptability, well-being, objectivity (McCrae & John, 1992), calmness, emotional control, and optimism (Soto et al., 2015). Soto et al. (2015) also mention that this dimension leads to an increased risk of conflict and experiencing intense negative emotions.

As such, this is a personality trait that should be avoided in any service encounters, namely by chatbots.

Openness

Openness to experience, often referred to as 'openness', is the "depth and dimension of an individual's intellectual, artistic and experiential life" (Soto et al., 2015, p. 2) and is associated with the need for variety and experience, in terms of ideas, fantasies, feelings, sensations, and values (McCrae & John, 1992). Soto et al. (2015) highlight the aesthetic sense, imagination, and intellectual curiosity. Smestad and Volden (2019) describe an open personality as insightful, original, smart, and adventurous.

Vivid imagination and a taste for listening to new ideas are two behaviors closely associated with openness (Mou & Xu, 2017). On the other hand, a reduced level of openness is manifested through a narrow range of interests and a preference for familiarity and routine (Soto et al., 2015).

Personality Traits and Corresponding Characteristics

McCrae and John (1992) associate each of the five personality dimensions with personality characteristics, as presented in Table 1.

Table 1. Personality characteristics of a chatbot that contribute to user's trust

Personality trait	Personality characteristics
Agreeableness	Grateful, Forgiving, Generous, Pleasant, Empathetic, Trustworthy, Uncritical, Direct, Altruistic, Modest, Tender, Observant
Conscientiousness	Efficient, organized, planner, faithful, responsible, thorough, productive, ethical, ambitious, disciplined
Extroversion	Active, assertive, energetic, enthusiastic, sociable, talkative, fun, humorous, expressive, warm, positive
Neuroticism	Anxious, critical, tense, unstable, worried, vulnerable, hostile, impulsive
Openness	Artistic, curious, imaginative, original, interested in many areas, introspective, intellectual

This classification will be adopted in the next sections to code the personality characteristics pointed out by the literature on chatbots.

EXPECTED EFFECTS OF CHATBOT PERSONALITY ON USERS

According to the literature, there are several positive effects expected from the chatbot personality on the users of chatbot-based services. They are analyzed in detail in the following sections.

User Trust

Several authors argue that the attribution of personality to the virtual assistant tends to lead to better results regarding user trust (e.g., Shi et al., 2020; Svenningsson & Faraon, 2019).

Trust can be broadly defined as the "firm belief in the reliability, truth, or ability of someone or something" (Przegalinska et al., 2019, p. 4). Rapp et al. (2021) argue that chatbots that appear more human foster the desire to resolve misunderstandings, trust, tolerance, a sense of co-presence, and closeness. This aspect of trust is widely explored in medical data collection services, for example, where the user has to trust the agent. The feeling that the chatbot is a social partner is important for the interaction with the company and a significant factor in this dimension (Araujo, 2018).

According to Smestad and Volden (2019), through personality, it is possible to control how the user perceives the attributes of the chatbot and how different levels of humanization influence expectations and trust. Przegalinska et al. (2019) mention that there must be a sense of security in the interaction and that trust is the main point of it.

Table 2. Personality characteristics of a chatbot that contribute to user's trust

Personality trait	Personality characteristics	Authors
Agreeableness	Benevolent	(Zhou et al., 2019)
Agreeableness	Cooperative	(Zhou et al., 2019)
Agreeableness	Empathetic	(Zhou et al., 2019)
Agreeableness	Integrity	(Chung et al., 2020; Zhou et al., 2019)
Agreeableness	Sympathetic	(Følstad et al., 2018)
Agreeableness	Tolerant	(Zhou et al., 2019)
Conscientiousness	Assertive	(Rapp et al., 2021; Zhou et al., 2019)
Conscientiousness	Competent	(Yen & Chiang, 2021; Zhou et al., 2019)
Conscientiousness	Intelligent	(Følstad et al., 2018; Svenningsson & Faraon, 2019)
Conscientiousness	Professional	(Følstad et al., 2018)
Conscientiousness	Reliable	(Følstad et al., 2018; Przegalinska et al., 2019; Zhou et al., 2019)
Conscientiousness	Serious	(Zhou et al., 2019)
Conscientiousness	Transparent	(Følstad et al., 2018; Rapp et al., 2021; Svenningsson & Faraon, 2019)
Extroversion	Interactive	(Go & Sundar, 2019)
Extroversion	Social	(Araujo, 2018; Go & Sundar, 2019; Rapp et al., 2021; Svenningsson & Faraon, 2019; Yen & Chiang, 2021)
Openness	Open	(Følstad et al., 2018)

Trust in the virtual agent depends, in part, on the agent's personality. Factors that can contribute to this trust include small talk, transparency, the ability to react and respond to cues of emotional or social behavior (Svenningsson & Pharaoh, 2019), and the truthfulness of the information presented by Chung et al. (2020). Rapp et al. (2021) report that, depending on the context and the user, an assertive, transparent personality that interacts socially is beneficial. Zhou et al. (2019) highlight as relevant factors the demonstration of empathy, cooperation, security, tolerance, assertiveness, seriousness, benevolence, integrity, and competence. Yen and Chiang (2021), in turn, mention credibility, competence, social presence, and also the relevance of the information presented. Følstad et al. (2018) refer to understanding, the ability to interpret and advise, professionalism, openness, honesty, and the guarantee of security and privacy.

Table 2 summarizes the personality characteristics that, according to several authors, positively impact the trust of the chatbot user.

Table 3. Personality characteristics of a chatbot that contribute to brand image

Personality trait	Personality characteristics	Authors
Agreeableness	Coherent	(Smestad & Volden, 2019)
Conscientiousness	Competent	(Zarouali et al., 2018)
Conscientiousness	Helpful	(Zarouali et al., 2018)
Conscientiousness	Suitable	(Smestad & Volden, 2019)
Extroversion	Fun	(Zarouali et al., 2018)
Extroversion	Interactive	(Go & Sundar, 2019)
Extroversion	Social	(Araujo, 2018; Go & Sundar, 2019)

Based on the contributions in the literature, the two personality traits that are more frequently associated with user trust are conscientiousness and agreeableness. Indeed, trust is based on the perception of reliability of the service provider and will also be improved in the case this provider is cooperative and benevolent. Hence, these two personality traits should be attributed to the chatbot in service contexts (e.g., health) in which trust is fundamental.

Brand Image

Currently, most virtual assistants work as extensions of the services provided by one brand, and therefore it is important to assign a personality that fits the target audience and the brand that is being represented. Hence, it is necessary to guarantee consistency between chatbot personality and the brand's mission, objectives, and values, as well as with the needs identified by customers and with the function performed (Smestad & Volden, 2019).

Brand image is how "consumers perceive and remember a brand" (Gómez-Rico et al., 2022, p. 4), and the feeling that the chatbot is a social partner is important for the interaction and perception that the user has of the company or brand that owns it. A virtual agent with human attributes contributes to the conscious and unconscious sensation of talking to a person and, therefore, to the creation of an emotional connection with the company (Araujo, 2018). A company can convey its brand personality through the use of a chatbot – customizing services increases user affinity for the brand.

Table 3 presents the personality characteristics of a chatbot that, according to several authors, positively impact on brand image.

Clearly, the list of personality characteristics that may benefit brand image is short and diversified. Apparently, several personality traits seem adequate to improve brand image and, as noted by Jain et al. (2018), the context should be carefully considered to identify the best personality trait for the chatbot. One could add that the chatbot personality should be consistent with the brand personality – and these three personality traits are adequate for different brands. Additionally, other traits (i.e., openness) have not been approached by extant literature and may also contribute to brand image – particularly for a brand with that type of personality.

User Engagement

Engagement is addressed several times in the literature related to chatbots. Shumanov and Johnson (2021) defined it as the average duration of an interaction between the virtual assistant and the user.

Chatbot personality has a big impact on interaction (Jain et al., 2018), as it creates involvement and encourages entertainment (Svenningsson & Faraon, 2019). Also, chatbot personality is expected to significantly improve dialogue and prevent communication failures (Rapp et al., 2021). In fact, the main task should never be neglected, because if the response obtained is not quick and useful, most users leave the conversation in a short time (Akhtar et al., 2019) independently of the personality of the chatbot. Jain et al. (2018) stress that understanding negative phrases and admitting faults, in addition to recovering and retaining the context of the conversation and asking intelligent questions, are key factors for user engagement.

The literature also mentions many other characteristics that, when identified in the chatbot, positively impact on user engagement. Chung et al. (2020) explain that users respond positively to the service if it is pleasant, fun, and relaxing, and Shumanov and Johnson (2021) emphasize the importance of extroversion. Xiao et al. (2020) focus on the importance of the ability to pay attention to the user, also highlighted by Rapp et al. (2021). Pérez-Marín and Pascual-Nieto (2013) stress empathy and affectivity. Zhou et al. (2019) report that a warm and lively personality promotes user relaxation and authenticity, while a serious and assertive personality increases respect and cooperation.

The personalization of the virtual agent's conversation and expression are also referred to in the literature. The use of emojis can be beneficial for engagement (Beattie et al., 2020; Rapp et al., 2021) and the use of the first person singular as well (Nazareno et al., 2021).

Dryer (1999) also adds that cooperative, extroverted, calm, organized, and curious virtual assistants are more appreciated. However, the user identifies more with the chatbot if it has some weakness, given the association of perfection with something non-human, although this cannot correspond to a very evident negative personality characteristic.

Table 4. Personality characteristics of a chatbot that contribute to user engagement

Personality trait	Personality characteristics	Authors
Agreeableness	Affectionate	(Pérez-Marín & Pascual-Nieto, 2013; Zhou et al., 2019)
Agreeableness	Calm	(Dryer, 1999)
Agreeableness	Comprehensive	(Ashktorab et al., 2019)
Agreeableness	Cooperative	(Dryer, 1999)
Agreeableness	Empathetic	(Perez-Marín & Pascual-Nieto, 2013)
Agreeableness	Nice	(Chung et al., 2020)
Agreeableness	Polite	(Ashktorab et al., 2019)
Agreeableness	Simple	(Ashktorab et al., 2019)
Agreeableness	Sincere	(Jain et al., 2018)
Conscientiousness	Competent	(Akhtar et al., 2019; Ashktorab et al., 2019; Beattie et al., 2020; Rapp et al., 2021)
Conscientiousness	Consistent	(Dryer, 1999)
Conscientiousness	Intelligent	(Jain et al., 2018; Rapp et al., 2021; Xiao et al., 2020)
Conscientiousness	Organized	(Dryer, 1999)
Conscientiousness	Suitable	(Jain et al., 2018)
Extroversion	Expressive	(Beattie et al., 2020; Dryer, 1999; Jain et al., 2018; Nazareno et al., 2021; Rapp et al., 2021)
Extroversion	Extroverted	(Dryer, 1999; Shumanov & Johnson, 2021)
Extroversion	Fun	(Chung et al., 2020; Zhou et al., 2019)
Extroversion	Humorous	(Jain et al., 2018; Pérez-Marín & Pascual-Nieto, 2013)
Extroversion	Interactive	(Jain et al., 2018)
Openness	Curious	(Dryer, 1999)
Openness	Imperfect	(Dryer, 1999)

Finally, Jain et al. (2018) conclude that the personality of the virtual agent must be distinct and appropriate to the context, for greater involvement – a chatbot that presents news must be more professional, for example, while one that is intended to make purchases can use an informal language. In addition, the proximity to the user (such as the reference to his name), the attention given to the user, and humor create engagement.

In summary, Table 4 lists the personality characteristics that, according to several authors, positively impact chatbot user engagement.

Agreeableness stands out as the personality trait mostly associated with chatbot user engagement. Still, it should be noted that, except for neuroticism, all personality traits seem able to foster engagement, reinforcing the idea that chatbot personality improves user experience.

User Satisfaction

Satisfaction occurs when the user's perception of the virtual agent equals or exceeds her expectations. Naturally, realistic expectations generally generate greater satisfaction (Rapp et al., 2021). Chatbot satisfaction is one great challenge since the feedback obtained from chatbot users is often negative (Akhtar et al., 2019).

Satisfaction with the performance of the chatbot depends, firstly, on the fulfillment of its primary function. However, it is also favored by a personality suited to the context of the task (Brandtzaeg & Følstad, 2017; Jain et al., 2018), with a general preference for including socialization and entertainment factors (Brandtzaeg & Følstad, 2017). Overall, successful chatbot interaction culminates in satisfying interactions and responses (Dryer, 1999; Peng & Ma, 2019). As such, chatbot personality offers a great potential to improve users' satisfaction. Indeed, users tend to prefer a strong and consistent personality, marked by social and engaging behavior, to the detriment of an exclusive orientation towards providing information and a neutral personality (Følstad & Skjuve, 2019). Consequently, Jain et al. (2018) argue that, in order to increase user satisfaction, the chatbot should be able to explain its functions, engage in casual conversations, personalize the interaction, respond using humor, and be polite.

Despite this evidence, the context of the chatbot should be carefully considered. As stressed by Rapp et al. (2021), chatbot personality should be adequate to the context – in the health sector, empathy proves to be very impactful, while in the entertainment sector, pleasure and fun gain more relevance. Additionally, humor may or may not be relevant, depending on the performance context (Nazareno et al., 2021).

The perception of expression (through the use of emojis, for example) and competence are also key factors for satisfaction (Beattie et al., 2020). Several authors reinforce the importance of competence, referring that the promptness of the correct answer and the understanding of the user (needs, preferences, and behaviors) lead to an increase in user satisfaction (Akhtar et al., 2019; Ashktorab et al., 2019; Brandtzaeg & Følstad, 2017; Chung et al., 2020; Jain et al., 2018; Peng & Ma, 2019). The simplicity and interactivity of the answers are also relevant factors for satisfaction, making them easier to understand (Følstad & Skjuve, 2019; Go & Sundar, 2019).

Good communication leads to greater satisfaction (Chung et al., 2020) and, as a general rule, there is a preference for longer conversations, often denoting a more pleasant interaction. Ashktorab et al. (2019) also refer to proactivity, in addition to initiative, as personality characteristics with a positive impact, which are revealed through the presentation of options and explanations when it presents a failure, in addition to recognizing it naturally, for example.

There are also other characteristics mentioned in the literature that lead to increased user satisfaction with a virtual assistant. Ashktorab et al. (2019) refer to the importance of chatbot simplicity and adaptability. Følstad & Skjuve (2019) advocate friendly and polite interaction and Dryer (1999) points to cooperation, extroversion, calmness, organization, and curiosity as factors with a positive impact. Conversely, competitiveness, introversion, restlessness, laziness, and closed-mindedness can negatively impact satisfaction (Dryer, 1999). According to Smestad and Volden (2019), a concordant personality is more likely to positively influence user satisfaction than a conscientious personality. Finally, Xiao et al. (2020) identify several characteristics of chatbots that ultimately will foster user satisfaction, including the ability to pay attention to the user, the verbalization of emotions and empathy, the encouragement of conversation, and the synthesis of the conversation.

Hence, the literature provides a long list of suggestions regarding the characteristics of a chatbot that may foster users' satisfaction. Those characteristics are summarized in Table 5.

Given the challenge to satisfy chatbot users, it is interesting to note that satisfaction is one of the most discussed consequences of chatbot personality. Moreover, all personality traits, except neuroticism, may contribute to user satisfaction. Overall, these findings confirm the relevance of attributing a personality to chatbots in order to improve user satisfaction.

User Loyalty

Loyalty can be defined as a customer's consistent preference to buy/use the same product or service in the future (Oliver, 1999). Loyalty is also an aspect studied by extant literature regarding chatbots. In fact, the humanization of chatbots enables the creation and improvement of relationships with users (Araujo, 2018; Rapp et al., 2021), and can create a sense of partnership if the personality of the former is suited to the context of action (Dryer, 1999). If the user sees the chatbot as a conversation partner, it is important to design it with characteristics that make it more socially attractive and, as such, lead to repeated interactions (Beattie et al., 2020).

Dryer (1999) argues that, in general, a person is more likely to create a good relationship with a chatbot that has personality characteristics related to cooperation, socialization, calmness, organization, and curiosity. In contrast, some characteristics seem inadequate to create chatbot loyalty, including competition, introversion, anxiety, ambiguity, and closed-mindedness. Rapp et al. (2021) highlight empathy as a key feature for establishing a user-chatbot relationship. Zhou et al. (2019) argue

Table 5. Personality characteristics of a chatbot that contribute to user satisfaction

Personality trait	Personality characteristics	Authors
Agreeableness	Calm	(Dryer, 1999)
Agreeableness	Concurring	(Smestad & Volden, 2019)
Agreeableness	Cooperative	(Dryer, 1999)
Agreeableness	Empathetic	(Nazareno et al., 2021; Rapp et al., 2021; Xiao et al., 2020)
Agreeableness	Friendly	(Følstad & Skjuve, 2019; Nazareno et al., 2021; Xiao et al., 2020)
Agreeableness	Polite	(Cervone et al., 2018; Følstad & Skjuve, 2019; Jain et al., 2018; Nazareno et al., 2021; Rapp et al., 2021)
Agreeableness	Simple	(Ashktorab et al., 2019; Følstad & Skjuve, 2019)
Agreeableness	Sincere	(Jain et al., 2018)
Conscientiousness	Competent	(Akhtar et al., 2019; Ashktorab et al., 2019; Beattie et al., 2020; Brandtzaeg & Følstad, 2017; Chung et al., 2020; Jain et al., 2018; Peng & Ma, 2019)
Conscientiousness	Conscious	(Rapp et al., 2021)
Conscientiousness	Consistent	(Dryer, 1999; Zhou et al., 2019)
Conscientiousness	Intelligent	(Akhtar et al., 2019; Ashktorab et al., 2019; Nazareno et al., 2021)
Conscientiousness	Organized	(Dryer, 1999)
Conscientiousness	Suitable	(Jain et al., 2018; Zhou et al., 2019)
Extroversion	Engaging	(Følstad & Skjuve, 2019; Przegalinska et al., 2019)
Extroversion	Expressive	(Beattie et al., 2020; Zhou et al., 2019)
Extroversion	Extroverted	(Dryer, 1999)
Extroversion	Fun	(Brandtzaeg & Følstad, 2017; Chung et al., 2020; Rapp et al., 2021)
Extroversion	Humorous	(Jain et al., 2018; Rapp et al., 2021)
Extroversion	Identifiable	(Go & Sundar, 2019)
Extroversion	Interactive	(Chung et al., 2020; Følstad & Skjuve, 2019; Go & Sundar, 2019; Jain et al., 2018; Rapp et al., 2021; Xiao et al., 2020)
Extroversion	Social	(Brandtzaeg & Følstad, 2017; Chung et al., 2020; Følstad & Skjuve, 2019; Go & Sundar, 2019)
Openness	Adaptable	(Ashktorab et al., 2019)
Openness	Curious	(Dryer, 1999)
Openness	Original	(Rapp et al., 2021)
Openness	Proactive	(Ashktorab et al., 2019; Cervone et al., 2018)

Table 6. Personality characteristics of a chatbot that contribute to user loyalty

Personality trait	Personality characteristics	Authors
Agreeableness	Affectionate	(Zhou et al., 2019)
Agreeableness	Calm	(Chung et al., 2020; Dryer, 1999)
Agreeableness	Comprehensive	(Følstad et al., 2018)
Agreeableness	Cooperative	(Dryer, 1999)
Agreeableness	Empathetic	(Rapp et al., 2021)
Agreeableness	Helpful	(Zarouali et al., 2018)
Conscientiousness	Competent	(Brandtzaeg & Følstad, 2017; Chung et al., 2020; Følstad et al., 2018; Zarouali et al., 2018)
Conscientiousness	Consistent	(Dryer, 1999; Pérez-Marín & Pascual-Nieto, 2013)
Conscientiousness	Constant	(Perez-Marín & Pascual-Nieto, 2013)
Conscientiousness	Organized	(Dryer, 1999)
Conscientiousness	Reliable	(Skjuve et al., 2021; Yen & Chiang, 2021)
Conscientiousness	Suitable	(Dryer, 1999)
Extroversion	Engaging	(Skjuve et al., 2021)
Extroversion	Expressive	(Beattie et al., 2020)
Extroversion	Extroverted	(Shumanov & Johnson, 2021)
Extroversion	Fun	(Zarouali et al., 2018; Zhou et al., 2019)
Extroversion	Interactive	(Jain et al., 2018)
Extroversion	Social	(Beattie et al., 2020; Dryer, 1999)
Openness	Curious	(Dryer, 1999; Zhou et al., 2019)

that a warm and lively personality, in addition to interest in the user, increases the effectiveness of creating a relationship. Additionally. Chung et al. (2020) note that a good relationship is developed when the virtual agent pays attention to the questions asked and solves them correctly, calmly, on time, and completely.

Zarouali et al. (2018) add to the perceived usefulness and help, the user's pleasure, entertainment, and knowledge positively impact the intention to use and recommend the virtual agent. Beattie et al. (2020) add that the use of emojis can contribute to increasing the social attraction of the assistant and, as such, create an emotional relationship more easily.

Hence, several personality characteristics are pointed out by the literature as effectively fostering loyalty regarding chatbot usage. These characteristics are summarized in Table 6.

Ultimately, the sustainability of chatbot services will depend on users' willingness to continue to use them, and for that reason, it is important to analyze the ability of chatbot personality to foster user loyalty. Conscientiousness and agreeableness seem the most relevant personality traits to foster loyalty. Still, the literature points out potential positive impacts of all personality traits, except neuroticism.

RECOMMENDATIONS FOR MANAGERS

The literature provides important insight into the possible consequences of chatbot personality, especially for customer service and relationship management. Overall, four personality traits (agreeableness, conscientiousness, extroversion, and openness) are shown as relevant features of the chatbot to improve satisfaction, loyalty, brand image, engagement, and user trust. However, some of these traits seem more effective for certain management objectives.

Conscientiousness and agreeableness stand out as the most studied personality traits, and the ones that apparently have further relevant outcomes, as they emerge as essential to building satisfaction and loyalty to chatbot usage. Still, extroversion seems also particularly relevant for building engagement and fostering satisfaction. Moreover, Conscientiousness stands out for building user trust, although agreeableness is also frequently mentioned regarding its ability to make users more confident and perceive the chatbot as a safe and reliable service.

Finally, and as alerted by Jain et al. (2018), it is essential to consider the context in which the chatbot operates. This obviously has to do with the activity sector (e.g., health or fashion) and the service provided (e.g., booking a hotel or getting suggestions for a cosmetic), and the user profile (e.g., tech enthusiast or uncomfortable user), but also with the brand itself, its positioning, and the overall business strategy. In this regard, it is interesting to note that any of the four mentioned personality traits seem to contribute to brand image, but the personalities of the chatbot and the brand need to be compatible. Aligned with this, extroversion is also a relevant personality trait for chatbots. In adequate contexts, this personality trait is effective to build engagement, satisfaction, and loyalty, as it tends to make the interaction with the chatbot more pleasant and fun. It is also mentioned as a possible feature for chatbots to increase trust and reinforce brand image.

Overall, personality traits make chatbots less dull, and it is highly recommended that companies operating with chatbots try to improve their personalities – aligned with the characteristics of the brand, the users, and the service provided, to mention but a few aspects of the context. The potential of personality to overcome the general dissatisfaction associated with chatbot usage should not be neglected by managers.

FUTURE RESEARCH DIRECTIONS

This chapter demonstrates the relevance of chatbot personality for managers and brands, as well as the rich literature available on the topic. However, it also evidences some research gaps that need to be addressed.

This review shows that four personality traits (agreeableness, conscientiousness, extroversion, and openness) are generally associated with positive outcomes in terms of consumer behavior, namely: trust, brand image, chatbot engagement, satisfaction, and loyalty. Still, two traits (agreeableness and conscientiousness) are the most studied so far, and more research is needed to both explore the impacts of less studied traits (e.g., openness) and to compare the impacts of alternative traits.

Additionally, other aspects of consumer behavior need to be approached by future research, particularly buying intention and buying behavior.

Furthermore, considering that the efficacy of chatbot personality is context-dependent, more applied research is needed to provide insights into relevant contexts such as different sectors of activity (e.g., education, health, counseling, tourism, personal care), critical types of services (e.g., complaints, churn request, customer recovery), high and low involvement products and services (e.g., luxury products, fast fashion), and the different profiles of users (e.g., age, education, cultural background, tech savviness).

In this regard, it is recommended that future research adopt methods that enable the comparison of results such as multiple case studies, experimental design, longitudinal studies, and meta-analyses. Still, the focus should be on users' perspectives, so that the impacts on consumer behavior can be properly evaluated. The mechanisms leading to consumer behavior are beyond the scope of this chapter and should be considered by future research. Also, there are several economic fields that require the use of chatbots, namely to solve customer service challenges and problems. Hence, future research should address specific sectors and customer service activities and challenges when studying chatbot personality. Sectors such as healthcare, traveling, and entertainment are some of the examples of the domains that are particularly relevant to apply the contributions of this chapter.

CONCLUSION

This chapter provides a review of the effects of chatbot personally on their users, from a consumer behavior perspective. Based on the contributions in the literature, it was possible to demonstrate that chatbot personality is a relevant tool to foster positive consumer behaviors, namely regarding trust, engagement, satisfaction, loyalty, and brand image.

To this end, the article provides detailed information on the personality traits and the corresponding personality characteristics that are expected to affect users' behaviors. This information is useful for both practitioners and researchers, as it provides clear guidance on what characteristics to incorporate in chatbots and on what factors need to be further studied in the future.

REFERENCES

Aaker, J. L. (2021). Dimensions of brand personality. *JMR, Journal of Marketing Research*, *34*(3), 347–356. doi:10.1177/002224379703400304

Akhtar, M., Neidhardt, J., & Werthner, H. (2019). The potential of chatbots: Analysis of chatbot conversations. *2019 IEEE 21st Conference on Business Informatics (CBI)*, (pp. 397–404). IEEE. 10.1109/CBI.2019.00052

Angeli, A. D., Johnson, G. I., & Coventry, L. (2001). The unfriendly user: Exploring social reactions to chatterbots. *Proceedings of the International Conference on Affective Human Factors Design*, (pp. 467-474). Abertay University.

Araujo, T. (2018). Living up to the chatbot hype: The influence of anthropomorphic design cues and communicative agency framing on conversational agent and company perceptions. *Computers in Human Behavior*, *85*, 183–189. doi:10.1016/j.chb.2018.03.051

Ashktorab, Z., Jain, M., Liao, Q. V., & Weisz, J. D. (2019). Resilient chatbots: Repair strategy preferences for conversational breakdowns. *Proceedings of the 2019 CHI Conference on Human Factors in Computing Systems*, (pp. 1–12). ACM. 10.1145/3290605.3300484

Beattie, A., Edwards, A. P., & Edwards, C. (2020). A bot and a smile: Interpersonal impressions of chatbots and humans using emoji in computer-mediated communication. *Communication Studies*, *71*(3), 409–427. doi:10.1080/10510974.2020.1725082

Bergner, R. M. (2020). What is personality? Two myths and a definition. *New Ideas in Psychology*, *57*, 100759. doi:10.1016/j.newideapsych.2019.100759

Brandtzaeg, P. B., & Følstad, A. (2017). Why people use chatbots. In I. Kompatsiaris, J. Cave, A. Satsiou, G. Carle, A. Passani, E. Kontopoulos, S. Diplaris, & D. McMillan (Eds.), *Internet Science* (Vol. 10673, pp. 377–392). Springer International Publishing. doi:10.1007/978-3-319-70284-1_30

Cervone, A., Gambi, E., Tortoreto, G., Stepanov, E. A., & Riccardi, G. (2018). Automatically predicting user ratings for conversational systems. In E. Cabrio, A. Mazzei, & F. Tamburini (Eds.), *Proceedings of the Fifth Italian Conference on Computational Linguistics CLiC-it 2018* (pp. 99–104). Accademia University Press. 10.4000/books.aaccademia.3151

Chandel, S., Yuying, Y., Yujie, G., Razaque, A., & Yang, G. (2019). Chatbot: Efficient and utility-based platform. In K. Arai, S. Kapoor, & R. Bhatia (Eds.), *Intelligent Computing* (Vol. 858, pp. 109–122). Springer International Publishing., doi:10.1007/978-3-030-01174-1_9

Chung, M., Ko, E., Joung, H., & Kim, S. J. (2020). Chatbot e-service and customer satisfaction regarding luxury brands. *Journal of Business Research, 117*, 587–595. doi:10.1016/j.jbusres.2018.10.004

Dryer, D. C. (1999). Getting personal with computers: How to design personalities for agents. *Applied Artificial Intelligence, 13*(3), 273–295. doi:10.1080/088395199117423

Følstad, A., Nordheim, C. B., & Bjørkli, C. A. (2018). What makes users trust a chatbot for customer service? An exploratory interview study. In S. S. Bodrunova (Ed.), *Internet Science* (Vol. 11193, pp. 194–208). Springer International Publishing. doi:10.1007/978-3-030-01437-7_16

Følstad, A., & Skjuve, M. (2019). Chatbots for customer service: User experience and motivation. *Proceedings of the 1st International Conference on Conversational User Interfaces - CUI '19*, (pp. 1–9). ACM. 10.1145/3342775.3342784

Go, E., & Sundar, S. S. (2019). Humanizing chatbots: The effects of visual, identity and conversational cues on humanness perceptions. *Computers in Human Behavior, 97*, 304–316. doi:10.1016/j.chb.2019.01.020

Gómez-Rico, M., Molina-Collado, A., Santos-Vijande, M. L., Molina-Collado, M. V., & Imhoff, B. (2022). The role of novel instruments of brand communication and brand image in building consumers' brand preference and intention to visit wineries. *Current Psychology (New Brunswick, N.J.)*. doi:10.100712144-021-02656-w PMID:35035183

Grudin, J., & Jacques, R. (2019). Chatbots, humbots, and the quest for artificial general intelligence. *Proceedings of the 2019 CHI Conference on Human Factors in Computing Systems*, (pp. 1–11). ACM. 10.1145/3290605.3300439

Insider Intelligence. (2022). Chatbot market in 2021: Stats, trends, and companies in the growing AI chatbot industry. *Business Insider*. https://www.businessinsider.com/chatbot-market-stats-trends

Jain, M., Kumar, P., Kota, R., & Patel, S. N. (2018). Evaluating and informing the design of chatbots. *Proceedings of the 2018 Designing Interactive Systems Conference*, (pp. 895–906). ACM. 10.1145/3196709.3196735

McCrae, R. R., & Costa, P. T. (1985). Updating Norman's «adequacy taxonomy»: Intelligence and personality dimensions in natural language and in questionnaires. *Journal of Personality and Social Psychology*, *49*(3), 710–721. doi:10.1037/0022-3514.49.3.710 PMID:4045699

McCrae, R. R., & John, O. P. (1992). An introduction to the five-factor model and its applications. *Journal of Personality*, *60*(2), 175–215. doi:10.1111/j.1467-6494.1992.tb00970.x PMID:1635039

Mou, Y., & Xu, K. (2017). The media inequality: Comparing the initial human-human and human-AI social interactions. *Computers in Human Behavior*, *72*, 432–440. doi:10.1016/j.chb.2017.02.067

Nazareno, D., de Melo, A., & Monteiro, I. T. (2021). Communication and personality: How COVID-19 government chatbots express themselves. *Proceedings of the XX Brazilian Symposium on Human Factors in Computing Systems*, (pp. 1–10). ACM. 10.1145/3472301.3484362

Peng, Z., & Ma, X. (2019). A survey on construction and enhancement methods in service chatbots design. *CCF Transactions on Pervasive Computing and Interaction*, *1*(3), 204–223. doi:10.100742486-019-00012-3

Pérez-Marín, D., & Pascual-Nieto, I. (2013). An exploratory study on how children interact with pedagogic conversational agents. *Behaviour & Information Technology*, *32*(9), 955–964. doi:10.1080/0144929X.2012.687774

Przegalinska, A., Ciechanowski, L., Stroz, A., Gloor, P., & Mazurek, G. (2019). In bot we trust: A new methodology of chatbot performance measures. *Business Horizons*, *62*(6), 785–797. doi:10.1016/j.bushor.2019.08.005

Rapp, A., Curti, L., & Boldi, A. (2021). The human side of human-chatbot interaction: A systematic literature review of ten years of research on text-based chatbots. *International Journal of Human-Computer Studies*, *151*, 102630. doi:10.1016/j.ijhcs.2021.102630

Shi, W., Wang, X., Oh, Y. J., Zhang, J., Sahay, S., & Yu, Z. (2020). Effects of persuasive dialogues: Testing bot identities and inquiry strategies. *Proceedings of the 2020 CHI Conference on Human Factors in Computing Systems*, (pp. 1–13). ACM. 10.1145/3313831.3376843

Shumanov, M., & Johnson, L. (2021). Making conversations with chatbots more personalized. *Computers in Human Behavior*, *117*, 106627. doi:10.1016/j.chb.2020.106627

Skjuve, M., Følstad, A., Fostervold, K. I., & Brandtzaeg, P. B. (2021). My chatbot companion: A study of human-chatbot relationships. *International Journal of Human-Computer Studies*, *149*, 102601. doi:10.1016/j.ijhcs.2021.102601

Smestad, T. L., & Volden, F. (2019). Chatbot personalities matters: Improving the user experience of chatbot interfaces. In S. S. Bodrunova, O. Koltsova, A. Følstad, H. Halpin, P. Kolozaridi, L. Yuldashev, A. Smoliarova, & H. Niedermayer (Eds.), *Internet Science* (Vol. 11551, pp. 170–181). Springer International Publishing. doi:10.1007/978-3-030-17705-8_15

Soto, C. J., Kronauer, A., & Liang, J. K. (2015). Five-factor model of personality. In S. K. Whitbourne (Ed.), *The Encyclopedia of Adulthood and Aging* (pp. 1–5). John Wiley & Sons, Inc. doi:10.1002/9781118521373.wbeaa014

Svenningsson, N., & Faraon, M. (2019). Artificial intelligence in conversational agents: A study of factors related to perceived humanness in chatbots. *Proceedings of the 2019 2nd Artificial Intelligence and Cloud Computing Conference*, (pp. 151–161). ACM. 10.1145/3375959.3375973

Westerman, D., Cross, A. C., & Lindmark, P. G. (2019). I believe in a thing called bot: Perceptions of the humanness of chatbots. *Communication Studies*, *70*(3), 295–312. doi:10.1080/10510974.2018.1557233

Xiao, Z., Zhou, M. X., Chen, W., Yang, H., & Chi, C. (2020). If I hear you correctly: Building and evaluating interview chatbots with active listening skills. *Proceedings of the 2020 CHI Conference on Human Factors in Computing Systems*, (pp. 1–14). ACM. 10.1145/3313831.3376131

Yang, X., Li, H., Ni, L., & Li, T. (2021). Application of artificial intelligence in precision marketing. *Journal of Organizational and End User Computing*, *33*(4), 209–219. doi:10.4018/JOEUC.20210701.oa10

Yen, C., & Chiang, M.-C. (2021). Trust me, if you can: A study on the factors that influence consumers' purchase intention triggered by chatbots based on brain image evidence and self-reported assessments. *Behaviour & Information Technology*, *40*(11), 1177–1194. doi:10.1080/0144929X.2020.1743362

Zarouali, B., Van den Broeck, E., Walrave, M., & Poels, K. (2018). Predicting consumer responses to a chatbot on Facebook. *Cyberpsychology, Behavior, and Social Networking*, *21*(8), 491–497. doi:10.1089/cyber.2017.0518 PMID:30036074

Zhou, M. X., Mark, G., Li, J., & Yang, H. (2019). Trusting virtual agents: The effect of personality. *ACM Transactions on Interactive Intelligent Systems*, *9*(2–3), 1–36. doi:10.1145/3232077

KEY TERMS AND DEFINITIONS

Anthropomorphization: The attribution of human characteristics to objects (e.g., robots), namely human form or personality.

Big Five: A set of main personality traits that comprise: agreeableness, conscientiousness, extroversion, neuroticism, and openness.

Chatbot: Computer program that is able to make conversations with humans in the context of a certain service.

Consumer Behavior: Often associated with marketing, consumer behavior focuses on studying individuals' characteristics as consumers and their decisions regarding the choice, purchase, consumption and use of products and services.

Loyalty: Customer or user predisposition to continuing doing business with a certain seller or service provider.

Personality: A set of traits that define one's behavior, namely the way we communicate and interact with others.

Virtual Assistant: Computer program that performs some tasks and support services to customers, similar to the ones that are usually offered by human assistants.

Section 4
Chatbot Algorithms and Privacy Concerns

Chapter 11
Recent Advances in Chatbot Algorithms, Techniques, and Technologies:
Designing Chatbots

Guendalina Caldarini
ⓘD https://orcid.org/0000-0001-5317-0845
University of Sunderland, UK

Sardar Jaf
University of Sunderland, UK

ABSTRACT

Intelligent conversational computer systems, known as chatbots, have always been at the forefront of artificial intelligence. They are made to sound like humans in order for machines to communicate with humans. Because of the rising benefits of chatbots, numerous sectors have adopted them to give virtual support to clients. They are also used as companions and virtual assistants. Natural language processing and deep learning are two artificial intelligence disciplines that are used in chatbots. This chapter will examine current advancements in chatbot algorithms, approaches, and technologies that use artificial intelligence and/or natural language processing.

INTRODUCTION

Chatbots are intelligent conversational computer programs that simulate human dialogue (Sojasingarayar, 2020; Bala et al., 2017; Jia, 2003). A chatbot processes

DOI: 10.4018/978-1-6684-6234-8.ch011

user input and provides a response (Ayanouz et al., 2020; Kumar & Ali, 2008). Chatbots often use natural language (text or speech) as input, to provide the most appropriate output to the user input sentence. Chatbots have been at the forefront of many major AI (artificial intelligence) revolutions since their inception: human-computer interaction, knowledge engineering, expert systems, natural language processing, natural language understanding, deep learning, and many others (Yu et al., 2020). Several factors contributed to their prevalent growth in recent years, such as the commoditization of technology; increased computer power; and the sharing of open-source tools and frameworks. Moreover, recent advances in artificial intelligence and natural language processing methods made chatbots easy to construct, more versatile in terms of applicability and maintainability, and increasingly capable of mimicking human communication. However, there are still many challenges to be addressed.

This chapter aims to offer readers a detailed overview of the background of chatbots, recent advances in chatbots algorithms and technologies, evaluation tools and metrics, and some future research ideas.

BACKGROUND

Despite the popularity of chatbots, creating chatbots that deliver satisfactory responses to the requirements of specific users remains an arduous task. For example, a chatbot must understand any user's speech or text as an input request and respond appropriately (e.g., on the same topic, make sense), helpfully (e.g., contains useful and concrete information), and even be tone-aware (e.g., conveys feelings like empathy and passion) (Xu et al., 2017; Hu et al., 2018).

A common way to design chatbots is the rule-based method (Young et al., 2013; Mesnil et al., 2015). It defines the structure of a dialogue state as a series of slots to be filled throughout a discussion. The chatbot responses depend on certain hand-crafted rules.

However, one of the main limitations of rule-based chatbots is that they are domain dependent. Each set of rules developed applies only to a limited number of cases and a limited field.

The alternative approach to rule-based chatbot design is data-driven techniques, also known as Machine Learning techniques. This design approach may handle more diverse user inquiries than rule-based chatbots (Song et al., 2018). The main types of data-driven chatbots are Information retrieval-based and Generative chatbots. Information retrieval-based chatbots may retrieve an existing response to users' queries from a pre-compiled dataset. Generative chatbots build a new response word by word depending on the input sequence provided by the user (Yan et al.,

2016; Serban et al., 2016). One of the main strengths of information retrieval-based chatbots is they can provide the user with highly accurate responses. But they are restricted by the size of the corpus because they cannot develop new responses. Generation-based chatbots may be able to solve this problem. But they are prone to providing grammatically incorrect or useless replies (Song et al., 2018).

This chapter will focus on providing an overview of chatbot implementation methods. This will include recent technologies, algorithms, techniques, and evaluation methods. A distinction will be drawn between two approaches to chatbot design: Rule-based chatbots and Machine Learning (ML) based chatbots. Within ML-based chatbots, a further distinction will be drawn between Information-Retrieval chatbots and Generative Chatbots. A distinct section will be dedicated to transformers and transformer-based chatbots, as these are the most recent algorithms applied to the problem of Dialogue Modelling. The last section of this chapter will explore evaluation techniques and differentiate between automatic evaluation metrics and human evaluation metrics and techniques.

The methodology for including recent chatbot techniques has focused on different transformers algorithms and their direct predecessors, recurrent neural networks, since these are at present not only the most recent algorithm used for dialogue modelling but also widely used in industry and research at large, in a variety of different applications.

Rule-Based Chatbots

Although rule-based models are typically simpler to build and deploy, their capabilities are constrained since they have trouble responding to complicated questions. Rule-based chatbots respond to users' questions by searching for patterns that match the users' query; as a result, they are prone to give incorrect replies if they encounter a sentence that does not fit any established pattern. Additionally, manually encoding pattern-matching rules may be time-consuming and complicated. The following subsection will cover a few Rule-Based chatbots.

ELIZA

ELIZA is a conversational agent developed at MIT in 1966 and is regarded as the first chatbot implementation in history. ELIZA has been designed to function like a Rogerian psychotherapist, which means that it seeks to advance dialogue by rephrasing and restating what the other person has just stated. ELIZA may communicate with a user through text. For this purpose, it is not necessary for the chatbot to fully comprehend the user's input into the conversation; rather, it searches for an appropriate transformation rule to reformulate the input and provide an output, i.e., a response to the user. To accomplish this task, it uses a script made of a series of "direct match" pattern matching rules. Nonetheless, even though ELIZA's scope of knowledge remains limited, and pattern-matching rules are not flexible to be adopted in new domains, the first users that interacted with ELIZA were reportedly quick to humanize her and enjoyed talking with her (Shum et al., 2018; Weizenbaum, 1966; Zemčík, 2019).

PARRY

PARRY is the first chatbot ever to undergo a version of the Turing Test. PARRY was created in 1972, and it was supposed to simulate the speech of a paranoid schizophrenic patient. Like ELIZA, PARRY also used a set of rules for pattern matching to interpret human input. However, PARRY had a more effective regulating structure and a mental model that could imitate emotions. Psychiatrists were given transcripts of chats with PARRY along with transcripts of interactions with real paranoid schizophrenic patients; yet only 52% (Colby et al., 1972) of the time psychiatrists were able to identify who had generated the transcript.

Artificial Linguistic Internet Computer Entity [A.L.I.C.E.]

A.L.I.C.E. is a chatbot built on the artificial intelligence mark-up language (AIML), which is an extension of XML, an interesting development in chatbot technologies. A.L.I.C.E. was created specifically so that dialogue pattern knowledge could be added to its software and expand its knowledge base. The Graphmaster, part of the A.L.I.C.E. knowledge base, is a node-and-edge network that functions like a file system with folders and subfolders. After receiving input, the computer repeatedly searches through each word in the phrase to locate the closest and longest match using a system of folders and subfolders. Since its knowledge base could be quickly expanded by the inclusion of new data items in AIML, A.L.I.C.E. marked a substantial advancement over earlier pattern-matching systems. However, it was still dependent on pattern-matching rules and consequently not easily scalable to new domains.

ChatScript

The scripting language ChatScript was created to receive user text input and provide a text response. Not merely for creating chatbots, ChatScript is a method for manipulating natural language. Starting with the input words, ChatScript changes them using replacements files. It includes databases for texting, common spelling errors, contractions, abbreviations, noise, and interjections that are mapped to speech acts. All of these are live data, which means that they are loaded at startup rather than being saved in the dictionary.

ChatScript was AIML's successor and served as the foundation for other Loebner Prize-winning chatbots. This new technology's major goal was to match user text inputs to topics, with each subject having a unique set of rules that would be used to produce an output. Since ChatScript began to reorient the attention toward semantic analysis and comprehension, a new era in the technological development of chatbots has begun. (AbuShawar and Atwell, 2015; Cahn, 2017; Shum et al., 2018; Wilcox, 2014; Zemčík, 2019).

ARTIFICIAL INTELLIGENCE CHATBOTS

Contrary to rule-based models, ML models are built using machine learning algorithms to learn from a library of recorded human interactions. The algorithms are initially applied to samples of data (known as training data) to learn patterns, features, and various information. This is known as the training phase in AI chatbot design. This phase produces a machine learning model (i.e., 'oracle') that can produce responses in communicating with humans. This type of chatbot may be more adaptable and independent from domain-specific expertise thanks to the usage of Machine Learning techniques, which eliminates the need to manually create and implement new pattern-matching rules. AI-based chatbots include two types: information retrieval-based models and generative models.

Information-Retrieval Chatbots

Information retrieval-based (IR) models are created such that the algorithm can successfully retrieve the required information from a given dataset based on the user's input. Typically, a Shallow Learning algorithm[1] is employed. The chatbot evaluates the user inquiry and chooses one of the replies from its collection of potential responses depending on this input. Information retrieval-based models have a pre-defined set of answers (knowledge base). A database of question-answer pairs often serves as the knowledge foundation for these types of models. This database is used to create a chat index, which lists all potential responses according to the message that provoked them. An information retrieval approach like those used for online searches is used to match the user's input to comparable ones in the chat index when the user presents the chatbot with an input. Thus, the response sent to the user is the answer coupled with the chosen query from those listed in the chat index (Shum et al., 2018). The key benefit of this approach is that it guarantees the replies' quality because they are not produced mechanically. With the rise of Web

2.0 and the availability of more textual material on social media platforms, forums, and chats, these models have become increasingly popular (Yan et al., 2016).

One of the biggest drawbacks of IR chatbots is it can be expensive, time-consuming, and laborious to create the prerequisite knowledge base. Furthermore, matching a user's input to the right answer could be time inefficient due to processing/searching a large amount of data available, which also means a larger training set and knowledge base. A significant amount of time and resources must be used to train the system to choose one of the available correct answers (Yan et al., 2016). Finally, information retrieval systems are less ideal to be utilized as the underlying algorithm for conversational agents, the so-called social chatbots, because they do not develop replies but rather retrieve them from a pre-defined set in their knowledge base. Information Retrieval models are less suited to personality development, which is a crucial quality for this type of chatbot (Shum et al., 2018).

The development of novel information retrieval algorithms has recently, however, made some headway. It is important to note that machine learning techniques are now utilized as the foundation for these kinds of models.

For more semantically distant phrases, innovative approaches to describe local textual co-occurrence and map hierarchical information across domains have been proposed (Lu and Li, 2013). This approach was built on the premise that the more frequently two phrases occur together across fields, the more closely they are connected. A strong co-occurrence within a specific area might therefore influence the information retrieval process. The two phases that formed this approach were obtaining hierarchical architecture and subject modelling for parallel text. Finding significant word co-occurrence patterns is the first stage. The second stage seeks to model the co-occurrences across topic architectures. This neural network, which drives this machine learning method, is used to build this type of architecture. This model's use of word co-occurrences to identify context is hence an intriguing advance in chatbot design. The method provided by Yan et al., is a fascinating breakthrough that examines past turns in the discussion to gather additional contextual information and enhance the output's quality and accuracy (2016). In this approach, a Deep Neural Network rates not only the question/answer pairs that correspond with the most recent user's input but also those question/answer pairs that match with rephrased versions of past conversation turns, enhancing the information retrieval process. The rating lists for the various reformulations are then combined. By doing so, contextual data from the user's prior inquiries may be utilized, and these bits of data can be used to extract a better response from the knowledge base (Yan et al., 2016).

Generative Models

As their name implies, generative-based models create new replies word by word based on the user's input. Thus, these models may generate whole new sentences in response to user requests. But they must be trained to understand grammar and sentence structure, thus their results may not always be of high quality or consistency (Shang et al., 2015; Sojasingarayar, 2020; Sordoni et al., 2015; Sutskever et al., 2015; Vinyals and Le, 2015). Typically, generative models are trained on a sizable dataset of real-world conversational terms. By providing it with training data the model learns vocabulary, grammar, and sentence structure. The overarching goal is for the algorithm's ability to provide a suitable and linguistically sound answer based on the input text. This strategy often relies on a Deep Learning algorithm, which is made up of an encoder-decoder neural network model with long short-term memory mechanisms. The aim is to offset the vanishing gradient[2] phenomenon inherent in basic recurrent neural networks (Vinyals and Le, 2015).

Sequence-to-Sequence models are now the de facto norm for chatbot modelling among AI models. Although they were first developed to address issues with machine translation, the basic ideas appear to work well for natural language generation (NLG) as well. Two recurrent neural networks (RNN), an encoder and a decoder make up these models. The chatbot user's input sentence is passed to the encoder, which processes it one word at a time in a particular hidden state of the RNN. The context vector, which is the state that conveys the sequence's goal, is the final state. The Decoder creates a new sequence (or phrase) one word at a time using the context vector as its input. This model's overarching goal is to learn to provide the most probable response given the conversational context, which in this case is made up of the input sentence or the preceding turn in the discussion. The model is provided with the response—or output sentence—during the learning phase so that it can gain knowledge through backpropagation (part of a learning technique in deep learning). Two alternative methods may be applied for the inference phase: beam search and greedy search methods with the beam search method, the output sentence is chosen depending on which contender has the best likelihood of being true. With the greedy search method, the model predicts the conversation's next phrase using the expected output token as an input (Vinyals and Le, 2015). There are certainly some intriguing benefits to this concept. It is an end-to-end solution that can be trained using various datasets, and hence on many domains, rather than requiring domain-specific expertise. Even though the model may produce useful results without domain-specific information, it can still be modified to operate with different algorithms if additional research on domain-specific knowledge is required. Thus, it is a straightforward yet broadly generic and versatile model that may be used for many NLP (Natural Language Processing) tasks (Vinyals and Le, 2015; Shum et al., 2018). For these reasons, the Sequence-to-Sequence paradigm appears to have recently taken over as the preferred option in the NLP and conversation-generating industries. However, the main limitation of this approach is that the longer the phrase, the more information is lost in the process since the whole amount of information in the input sentence must be captured in the context vector, which has a fixed length. Therefore, Sequence to Sequence models struggle to reply to lengthy statements and they tend to provide ambiguous replies. Additionally, these models concentrate on a single response when generating an answer, which results in a lack of coherence in the conversational turns (Sojasingarayar, 2020; Jurafsky, 2020; Strigér, 2016).

TRANSFORMER CHATBOTS

An area of study within artificial intelligence and machine learning that is expanding quickly is attention-based and transformer language models. Transformers have helped to progress the field of Natural Language Processing (NLP) since their method of reading is more in line with human behavior than traditional sequential procedures. Since artificial intelligence (AI) solutions are becoming increasingly popular among those who lack specialized technical expertise in the field, models have an increasing need for robustness, explainability (which is the need to understand the way model parameters generate responses), and accessibility as more sectors turn to AI solutions (Bird et al., 2021). The Transformer based model is a fairly novel idea in the field of deep learning (Vaswani et al., 2017). While NLP is currently the focus of Transformers, innovative image processing utilizing similar networks has recently been investigated (Qi et al., 2020). The theory underlying the investigation of transformers in natural language processing (NLP) is their more natural approach to sentences than other deep learning approaches, such as sequence-to-sequence. This is comparable to the human propensity to fully "listen" to a statement or sequence before reacting appropriately in conversations, translations, or other tasks of a similar kind.

The foundation for sequence transduction activities is the sequence-to-sequence encoder-decoder architecture. It advises encoding the entire sequence at once and utilizing that encoding as the background for creating the target sequence or the decoded sequence.

Before Transformers made them outdated, RNNs in their different forms (such as LSTMs and GRUs) were the de facto architecture for all NLP applications. In the traditional sequence-to-sequence paradigm, separate RNNs are used for the encoder and decoder. The hidden state of the RNN at the encoder network is the encoded sequence. Traditional sequence-to-sequence models create the target sequence using this encoded sequence and (often) word-level generative modelling. The well-known attention technique was added as a final layer to "pay attention" to keywords in the sequence that significantly contribute to the production of the target sequence since word-level encoding makes it difficult for the encoder to keep context for longer sequences. Each word in the input sequence is given attention based on how it affects the creation of the target sequence.

These models presented two drawbacks, though:

1. **Long-Range Dependencies**: Dealing with long-range dependencies between words that were placed far apart in a lengthy phrase proved difficult (Figure 1).

Figure 1. Figure 1 represents a Recurrent Neural Network. Each word of the input sentence X is represented by a green box. Each word of the output sentence is represented by an orange box. The grey box represents the activation function at timestep zero. Blue cells represent the hidden states of the Neural Network. As the graph shows, the RNN must compute the calculations at timestep one before it is possible to move to the following timestep. For a more detailed representation, see (CS 230 - Recurrent Neural Networks Cheatsheet)

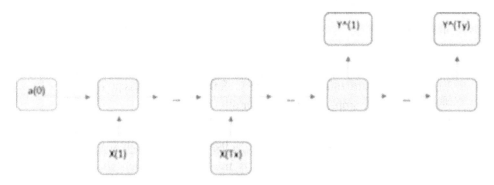

2. **Sequential Computation**: They handle the input sequence sequentially, processing each word one at a time, hence they cannot compute for time-step t until they have computed for time-step t — 1. Training and inference take longer as a result (Refer to Figure 1).

The above two drawbacks are addressed by the Transformer architecture. It completely abandoned RNNs in favor of relying only on the advantages of Attention. They perform a parallel processing operation on each word in the sequence, accelerating computing.

Figure 2. Using computational efficiency criteria, RNN, Convolutional Neural Network (CNN), and Self-Attention models are compared (Vaswani et al., 2017)

Layer Type	Complexity per Layer	Sequential Operations	Maximum Path Length
Self-Attention	$O(n^2 \cdot d)$	$O(1)$	$O(1)$
Recurrent	$O(n \cdot d^2)$	$O(n)$	$O(n)$
Convolutional	$O(k \cdot n \cdot d^2)$	$O(1)$	$O(log_k(n))$
Self-Attention (restricted)	$O(r \cdot n \cdot d)$	$O(1)$	$O(n/r)$

Instead of suffering from the vanishing gradient problem present in Recurrent Neural Networks, (Schmidhuber 1992), transformer-based models pay attention to tokens in a learned order and as a result enable more parallelization while improving upon many NLP problems. New benchmarks and standards have been established since the application of Transformers to a variety of fields (Vaswani et al., 2017).

In the original Transformer article (Vaswani et al., 2017), several parameters for the capable models were compared, as presented in Figure 2:

Here, n is the sequence length (often in the range of 40–70), k is the convolution kernel size, and r is the attention window size for restricted self-attention. D (or d_model) is the representation dimension or embedding dimension of a word (typically in the range 128–512).

From the table presented above, the following points may be deduced:

- **Lower Computational Complexity**: Self-attention has a lower per-layer computational complexity than other attention does.
- **Parallelization**: Except for RNNs, all other methods allow parallelization when it comes to sequential processes, hence their complexity is $O(1)$.
- **Path Length**: The fourth statistic is maximum path length, which on the surface refers to the difficulties of attention to distant words or long-term dependencies. Self-attention models attend all the words at the same step; hence their complexity is O, but convolutional models employ hierarchical representations, which makes their complexity $n*log(n)(1)$.

The Transformer utilizes a self-attention mechanism, which makes parallelization easy by calculating attention weights using all the words in the input sequence at once. Additionally, because the Transformer's per-layer operations include words in the same sequence, the complexity is less than $O(n2d)$. As a result, the transformer is shown to be both a computationally efficient model and effective (because it makes use of attention).

Due to these factors, such methods are quickly creating State-of-the-Art results for various NLP issues (Tenney et al., 2019). The following are examples of text data processing techniques that have benefitted from the application of Transformers: generation (Devlin and Chang 2018; Radford et al., 2019), question answering (Shao et al., 2019; Lukovnikov et al., 2019), sentiment analysis (Naseem et al., 2020; Shangipour ataei et al., 2020), paraphrasing (Chada 2020; Lewis et al., 2020), translation (Zhang et al., 2018; Wang et al., 2019b; Gangi et al., 2019), and classification (Sun et al., 2019).

The basic structure of the Transformer consists of a stack of encoder and decoder layers. To prevent misunderstanding, each layer will be referred to as either an encoder or a decoder, and a stack of encoder layers or decoder layers will be referred to as either an encoder stack or a decoder stack.

For each of their inputs, the Encoder stack, and the Decoder stack each have an associated Embedding layer. An output layer is present at the end to produce the finished product. The Encoders are all exact replicas of one another. In a similar vein, every decoder is the same.

The crucial Self-attention layer, which calculates the relationships between the words in the sequence, is included in the encoder along with a Feed-forward layer. The Self-attention layer, Feed-forward layer, and a second Encoder-Decoder attention layer are all included in the Decoder.

There is a unique set of weights for each encoder and decoder.

All Transformer designs are defined by a reusable module called The Encoder. Along with the two levels mentioned above, it also features two LayerNorm layers and Residual skip connections all around both layers.

Transformer architecture comes in a variety of forms. Some Transformer topologies solely rely on the encoder and lack any sort of decoder.

At the very core of the Transformer's innovation lies the computation of scaled dot product attention units, according to Vaswani et al., (2017). Each word in the input word vector has its weights determined (document or sentence). The attention unit's output is an embedding for each relevant token combination in the input sequence. The following formula [Equation 1] is used to determine the query Wq, key Wk and value Wv weights:

$$Attention\left(Q,K,V\right) = soft\max\left(\frac{QK^{T}}{\sqrt{d_k}}\right)V$$

The values are generated by matching the query against the keys, which are vector representations of the input sequence. A query is an object inside the sequence.

Unsupervised models pay attention to themselves since they acquire Q, K, and V from the same source.

K and V are derived from the source, whereas Q is derived from the goal for tasks like classification and translation. For instance, Q may be a class that the text is assigned to, such as "positive" and "neutral" for sentiment analysis and the classification model's prediction.

For supervised English-Spanish machine translation, values K and V might be taken from the English phrase "Hello, how are you?" while Q could be derived from the phrase "Hola, cómo estas?"

The Multi-headed Attention theory is used to guide all of the State-of-the-Art models benchmarked in these trials. This is just a wider network of interconnected attention units created by concatenating many attention heads together:

As opposed to a machine learning model, humans can compare one word in a phrase to other words in the same sentence; to produce human-like text, engineers and researchers must produce a means for the model to acquire this understanding. This is where the self-attention notion comes into play. It is crucial to remember that humans do not read in a token-sequential fashion like traditional RNN models as in the case of the Long Short-Term Memory (LSTM) network (Hochreiter and Schmidhuber 1997). Several pieces of research in the field (Shagass et al., 1976; Kruger and Steyn 2014; Wang et al., 2019a) demonstrate that reading right-to-left (or left-to-right) is not the only option. However, it may be noticed that attention-based models are more like human reading comprehension than sequential models like the LSTM. Of course, a person does not follow the previously mentioned equations.

However, training powerful Transformers still requires significant computational resources and a large amount of data. For this reason, research centers from large organizations like Google, Microsoft, OpenAI and HuggingFace train exceptionally large transformers models that can even reach hundreds of billions of parameters and then share these foundational models with the community, which can easily fine-tune them with fewer data and computational power.

This trend seems to apply to the application of Transformer models for dialogue modelling. Several works of literature have already investigated the possibility of fine-tuning foundational transformer models on dialogue modelling tasks.

Yu et al., (2020) developed a financial service chatbot based on BERT. The chatbot is closed domain and trained on the task of intent classification to correctly identify the intent of a question and provide a relevant answer among a specific set of possibilities. The authors also provided a novel discussion about uncertainty measures for BERT. Bathija et al., (2020) propose a chatbot for interactive learning. Questions to the user are generated through extractive summarization of content. This allows users to obtain important sentences out of a document or set of documents. The summarization is performed using BERT. Bird et al., (2021) propose augmenting conversational data through paraphrasing with the T5 model and then using augmented data to finetune several other transformers for dialogue generation. A novel approach has been developed by Google. Their neural conversational model, Meena, has 2.6 billion parameters. Meena has one Evolved Transformer encoder block and thirteen Evolved Transformer decoder blocks. For Meena to grasp what was said in the discussion, the encoder processes the conversation context. The answer is subsequently created by the decoder using that data. We found that the key to better conversational quality was a more potent decoder by tweaking the hyper-parameters (Adiwardana et al., 2020).

Transformer-XL and Reformer

Since then, several other Transformer iterations have been released, including the Reformer and the Transformer XL. Each iteration of the transformer has been created to address certain difficulties associated with the work at hand. Transformers may be tweaked and adjusted to carry out conversation modelling activities even though they were first developed to address Machine Translation problems.

The Reformer, a more effective variation of the Transformer, was introduced by Kitaev et. al (2020), using two strategies to raise the efficiency of the Transformer. First, the complexity is increased from $O(L2)$ to $O(LlogL)$, where L is the length of the sequence, by replacing dot-product attention with one that makes use of locality-sensitive hashing. Second, instead of using traditional residuals, reversible residual layers are used to store activation just once during training as opposed to N times, where N is the number of layers. The Reformer is hence much quicker on longer sequences and significantly more memory efficient.

The Transformer-XL is an improved version of the Transformer (Dai et. al, 2019). By utilizing sentence-level recurrence, this model can overcome the Transformer's fixed-length context restrictions. Transformers can learn longer-term dependencies, but in the context of language modelling, they are limited by fixed-length context. Dai et. al (2019) describe the Transformer-XL as a novel neural design that allows learning reliance to extend beyond a certain length without compromising temporal coherence. It includes a mechanism for segment-level recurrence and a special method of positional encoding. This approach seeks to both capture long-term reliance and address the context fragmentation problem. Even though this method has not yet been used for dialogue modelling, it may be claimed that, when the proper and essential modifications are made, it may help to resolve some of the problems that the existing dialogue models have, particularly context comprehension.

EVALUATION

In the deep learning domain, assessing the quality of text produced by Natural Language Generation (NLG) models remains a challenging task. Among the available evaluation metrics, a distinction can be drawn between human evaluation and automated evaluation. Although human-based measures are thought to be a better indicator of the text's quality, they are expensive; time-consuming; prone to bias; difficult to compare to one another; and not readily scalable. Due to these factors, the search for a useful automated evaluation metric is ongoing.

In general, human evaluation, where human annotators evaluate the generated texts' quality, continues to be the gold-standard way for evaluating such documents. A few typical types of viewpoints that can be used for this examination are described below, as presented by Yuan et al., (2021):

1. **Informativeness (INFO): The degree to which the derived hypothesis adequately expresses the original text's main points.**
2. **Relevance (REL)**: The degree to which the produced hypothesis is congruent with the original text (Grusky et al., 2018).
3. **Fluency (FLU)**: Whether the content is easily readable and free of formatting issues, capitalization mistakes, and evident grammatical flaws (such as gaps and missing parts) (Fabbri et al., 2021).
4. **Coherence (COH)**: The text's ability to develop a cohesive body of information on a topic from sentence to sentence (Dang, 2005).
5. **Factuality**: Whether the derived hypothesis merely includes claims implied by the source text (Kryscinski et al., 2020).
6. **Semantic Content**: The number of semantic content units from reference texts that the developed hypothesis covers (Nenkova & Passonneau, 2004).
7. **Adequacy (ADE)**: Whether the output accurately captures the meaning of the input sentence without adding any unnecessary information or distorting the meaning in any way (Koehn, 2007). A limited fraction of these viewpoints was intended to be covered by many existing assessment criteria. For instance, ROUGE (Lin & Hovy, 2003) was created to match the semantic coverage measure, whereas BLEU (Papineni et al., 2002) tries to capture the adequacy and fluency of translations.

Some metrics, especially those that are trainable, can evaluate many angles, although they often need to maximize correlation with each sort of judgment independently (Denkowski & Lavie, 2010; Yuan et al., 2021)

According to Sai et al., (2020), humans are frequently expected to consider a wider range of factors when assessing conversation systems. The following is an example of a comprehensive list of criteria used by See et al., (2019), along with the questions that were given to the human assessors following those criteria:

- **Logic**: Does the bot occasionally say things that do not make sense?
- **Engagingness**: Is talking to the conversation agent fun?
- **Interactivity**: Did you find talking to the bot engaging?
- **Inquisitiveness**: Is the bot sufficiently inquisitive?
- **Listening**: Can you tell if the robot is listening to you?
- **Refraining**: Does the bot keep repeating itself? (Between utterances or inside them)
- **Humanness**: Are you speaking to a living person or a robot?

In many cases, while analyzing dialogues, the evaluators are only asked to score the overall quality of the response or, more precisely, to determine if the response was relevant (Lowe et al., 2018; Tao et al., 2018; Ghazarian et al., 2020). Additional restrictions are considered for task-oriented conversations, such as giving the right information or service, directing the discussion toward a specific end goal, etc. Additional limitations like persona adherence (Zhang et al., 2018), emotion-consistency (Ghandeharioun et al., 2019), etc. are also being employed in open-domain discussion contexts to push the boundaries of what is possible (Sai et al., 2020).

It is therefore clear why it is hard to define an automated measure to evaluate dialogue models. Many measures currently in use in academia and business were first created to assess machine translation models and were based on String Matching. Researchers have attempted to create new metrics that might more accurately assess many tasks, including Data to Text (D2T) production, dialogue modelling, summarization, and more. This has been made possible by the rise of Large Language Models (LLMs) and the commoditization of Deep Learning.

Considering this, it is possible to distinguish between four separate categories of automated evaluation metrics: string matching, word embeddings, language models, and discriminators.

Metrics Based on String Matching

The very first metrics to be established presupposed the existence of a reference standard phrase and were created for tasks like machine translation. The output sentence is then put up against the reference sentence to evaluate. Different metrics, including BLEU, ROUGE, TER, METEOR, and others, take into consideration the number of times the same word appears in both phrases, the number of modifications required to duplicate the reference sentence beginning from the output, the accuracy, or the recall. These metrics have been in use for many years because they are simple to use with many available libraries, cost-effective to compute, and they have been used in numerous studies, where they have been the norm for comparison. They are, however, insufficient to assess "open-ended" tasks like NLG since they do not account for semantic correspondences or word order and are therefore inadequate to fully evaluate the complexity of dialogue modelling.

It is important to note that one of these measures has been created to partially take synonyms and semantic similarity into consideration. TERp aligns the output using a reference sentence through stemming and synonymy. Additionally, it considers potential phrase substitutions using probabilistic phrasal substitution computations, which consider potential paraphrases of the reference text (Snover et al., 2009).

Metrics Based on Word Embedding

Researchers began creating metrics based on word embeddings that may better account for semantic correspondences to solve the shortcomings of String-Matching measures. The score is determined by computing the cosine similarity between the output sentence and the reference sentence after transforming the phrases into a vector format. Even if two sentences use synonyms or have different word ordering, they will be closer in the representation space because the vector representation created after word embeddings is somewhat of an abstraction of the sentence's semantic content. Therefore, compared to earlier String-Matching techniques, these measures show an improvement. Researchers have begun using Bert-based metrics in place of the original Word2Vec technique since they are more dynamically able to capture semantic similarity and contextual information. These systems have been used to create metrics like Bertscore (Zhang et al., 2020) and BLEURT (Sellam et al., 2020). By applying token-level matching functions in distributed representation space, Bertscore executes unsupervised matching with the goal of "measuring the semantic equivalence between the reference and hypothesis" (Yuan et al., 2021). Contrarily, BLEURT uses supervised learning to develop a parametrized regression layer that forecasts human judgments (Sellam et al., 2020).

Bartscore is a notable measure that differs from the others. The evaluation task is presented by Bartscore as a text creation task using a pre-trained model (namely BART). The ease with which a hypothesis may be produced from an input sentence would then be used to determine its quality. As a result, Bartscore may be adjusted to evaluate activities, such as summarizing and paraphrasing. It has also been adjusted for data-to-text generation (Yuan et al., 2021).

All these measures, meanwhile, are still required for a reference phrase, which is not always accessible for NLG activities. This requirement may be too constricting for more flexible generation tasks, such as dialogue modelling.

Metrics Based on Language Models

Another metric for measuring language production is perplexity (PPL). By computing the joint probability of the sentences in the test set, it functions at the language model level. The likelihood of the phrase appearing increases with lower PPL scores. Since it provides a gauge of the language model's modelling capabilities, this metric is frequently employed in research. PPL is still not acceptable, though, because it does not consider other elements of generation quality, such as relevance to context, subject, and task.

Perplexity may be used to gauge how effectively a model has learnt the distribution of the text it was trained on if it is compared against the training text (Perplexity - a Hugging Face Space by evaluate-metric; Perplexity of fixed-length models).

Discriminators

Discriminators have been developed to be a functional solution to NLG evaluation challenges. By training a discriminator to identify if a text has been machine or human-generated, it is possible to account for language fluency and context at the same time. Previous work in the area has been developed by Kannan and Vinyals (2017) and by Liu and Yao (2021). Liu and Yao (2021), specifically, use a discriminator not only to determine if a sentence has been written by a human or by a machine but also to compare the performances of two models.

The work of Kannan and Vinyals (2017) specifically investigates using an adversarial evaluation method for dialogue models. The authors stipulate that the level of easiness in distinguishing a model's output from a human output represents a good measure of a model's quality. The authors' work is based on previous successful research in generative adversarial networks (GANs). The goal of the study is to understand if adversarial networks are a viable evaluation metric for dialogue generation. The Smart Reply system includes a fully trained production-scale conversation model. This generator is kept fixed for the initial exploration. A second RNN called the "discriminator" is then trained to predict, given an input, whether the output was produced by the generator or a human (Kannan and Vinyals 2017).

Discriminators have the advantage of working without the need for a reference sentence, which allows them to correctly score different outputs without bias. In a conversational model, there might be several possible valid answers to a query, especially in the case of open-ended questions, and penalizing one of them because it differs from one or more references skews the evaluation of the model. At the same time, discriminators do not penalize synonymy or changes in word order within the same semantic space. Moreover, they have the advantage of being an objective evaluation metric, which makes them more convenient than human evaluation not only because they are less costly and time-consuming, but also because they are unbiased Liu and Yao (2021).

Evaluation Metric Based on Task Modeling

Another way to distinguish between automated evaluation metrics is based on the approach they adopt to model the evaluation task.

Unsupervised matching is the first category. Unsupervised matching metrics, like BERTScore (Zhang et al., 2020); MoverScore (Zhao et al., 2019); discrete string spaces like ROUGE (Lin, 2004); BLEU (Papineni et al., 2002); or CHRF (Popović, 2015), use token-level matching functions to measure the semantic equivalence between the reference and hypothesis. To our knowledge, previous research has not attested to the capability of unsupervised matching methods in this regard; the authors further explore this in their experiments. Similar matching functions can be used to assess the quality beyond semantic equivalence (e.g., factuality, a relationship between source text and hypothesis), but to our knowledge, prior research has not attested to this capability.

Supervised regression falls within the second group. To successfully anticipate human judgements, regression-based models include a parameterized regression layer that is learnt under supervision. Examples include the more recent measures COMET (Rei et al., 2020), BLEURT (Sellam et al., 2020), and S 3 (Peyrard et al., 2017), as well as more established measurements like VRM (Hirao et al., 2007).

The third category is supervised ranking. The basic goal of learning a scoring function that gives better hypotheses a higher score than inferior ones is to learn how to rank hypotheses, which is another way to think of evaluation. Examples include COMET (Rei et al., 2020) and BEER (Stanojević & Sima'an, 2014), where BEER combines many simple features in a tunable linear model of Machine Translation (MT) evaluation metrics and COMET concentrates on the machine translation task and relies on human judgments to tune parameters in ranking or regression layers.

Text generation is another way of modelling the evaluation task. Yuan et al., (2021), define text evaluation as a text generation task using language models that have already been trained. The fundamental tenet is that a strong hypothesis may be produced quickly based on a source or reference material, or the other way around. With PRISM (Thompson & Post, 2020) being a significant exception, this has not been examined as thoroughly in earlier studies. PRISM formulates assessment as a paraphrasing problem, which restricts its applicability in scenarios like factuality evaluation in text summarizing that uses source documents and produced summaries as input but in separate semantic spaces. While BARTSCORE is built on open-sourced pre-trained seq2seq models, PRISM developed a model from scratch using parallel data. Prompt-based learning, which has not been studied in PRISM, is supported by BARTSCORE (Yuan et al., 2021).

Finally, automated Turing Test models include all discriminators trained to distinguish between human and machine dialogue generation, such as those designed by Kannan and Vinyals (2017) and by Liu and Yao (2021). As explained above, discriminators use GAN to model the evaluation task as an automated Turing test, aimed at distinguishing between human-generated and chatbot-generated sentences.

FUTURE RESEARCH DIRECTIONS

Given the present state of research in natural language processing, future approaches in dialogue modelling and chatbot designing will include transfer learning and fine-tuning large language models. Another research direction should investigate designing an automated evaluation system that considers all aspects of dialogue evaluation factors.

Another significant issue that is currently the object of research and will be in the future, is how to make large language models, like transformers, broad and flexible enough to be utilized in different production environments without excessive computational power or latency. To address some of the current issues, such as the absence of contextual information in conversation modelling, better modelling of dialogue activities is also required.

CONCLUSION

This chapter explored recent advances in chatbot algorithms and technologies, from the first rule-based algorithms to the state-of-the-art models currently used on a variety of Natural Language Processing tasks. In conclusion, the field of dialogue modelling and chatbot designing is still evolving and ever-changing. The wide range of fields of application makes this task particularly arduous to accomplish since the text generated must be specific and coherent with the user input, yet the answer generation task must remain flexible at the same time.

ACKNOWLEDGMENT

This research received no specific grant from any funding agency in the public, commercial, or not-for-profit sectors.

REFERENCES

AbuShawar, B., & Atwell, E. (2015). ALICE Chatbot: Trials and Outputs. *Computación y Sistemas*, *19*(4). doi:10.13053/cys-19-4-2326

Adiwardana, D., Luong, M.-T., So, D. R., Hall, J., Fiedel, N., Thoppilan, R., Yang, Z., Kulshreshtha, A., Nemade, G., Lu, Y., & Le, Q. V. (2020). Towards a Human-like Open-Domain Chatbot. https://arxiv.org/abs/2001.09977

Ayanouz, S., Abdelhakim, B. A., & Benhmed, M. (2020). A Smart Chatbot Architecture based NLP and Machine Learning for Health Care Assistance. *Proceedings of the 3rd International Conference on Networking, Information Systems & Security*, (pp. 1–6). ACM. 10.1145/3386723.3387897

Bala, K., Kumar, M., Hulawale, S., & Pandita, S. (2017). Chat-Bot For College Management System Using A.I. [IRJET]. *International Research Journal of Engineering and Technology*, *04*(11), 4.

Bathija, R., Agarwal, P., Somanna, R., & Pallavi, G. B. (2020). Guided Interactive Learning through Chatbot using Bi-directional Encoder Representations from Transformers (BERT). *2020 2ⁿᵈ International Conference on Innovative Mechanisms for Industry Applications (ICIMIA)*, (pp. 82–87). IEEE. 10.1109/ICIMIA48430.2020.9074905

Bird, J. J., Ekárt, A., & Faria, D. R. (2021). Chatbot Interaction with Artificial Intelligence: Human data augmentation with T5 and language transformer ensemble for text classification. *Journal of Ambient Intelligence and Humanized Computing*. doi:10.100712652-021-03439-8

Cahn, J. (2017). *CHATBOT: Architecture, Design, & Development*. University of Pennsylvania.

Chada, R. (2020). Simultaneous paraphrasing and translation by fine-tuning Transformer models. *Proceedings of the Fourth Workshop on Neural Generation and Translation*, (pp. 198–203). ACL. 10.18653/v1/2020.ngt-1.23

Colby, K. M., Hilf, F. D., Weber, S., & Kraemer, H. C. (1972). Turing-like indistinguishability tests for the validation of a computer simulation of paranoid processes. *Artificial Intelligence*, *3*, 199–221. doi:10.1016/0004-3702(72)90049-5

CS 230—Recurrent Neural Networks Cheatsheet. (n.d.). Shervine Amidi. https://stanford.edu/~shervine/teaching/cs-230/cheatsheet-recurrent-neural-networks

Dai, Z., Yang, Z., Yang, Y., Carbonell, J., Le, Q. V., & Salakhutdinov, R. (2019). Transformer-XL: Attentive Language Models Beyond a Fixed-Length Context https://arxiv.org/abs/1901.02860 doi:10.18653/v1/P19-1285

Dang, H. T. (2005). *Information Access Division National Institute of Standards and Technology Gaithersburg, MD, 20899*, 12.

Denkowski, M., & Lavie, A. (2010). Extending the METEOR Machine Translation Evaluation Metric to the Phrase Level. Human Language Technologies: The *2010 Annual Conference of the North American Chapter of the Association for Computational Linguistics,* (pp. 250–253). ACL. https://aclanthology.org/N10-1031

Devlin, J., Chang, M.-W., Lee, K., & Toutanova, K. (2019). BERT: Pre-training of Deep Bidirectional Transformers for Language Understanding. https://arxiv.org/abs/1810.04805

Fabbri, A. R., Kryściński, W., McCann, B., Xiong, C., Socher, R., & Radev, D. (2021). SummEval: Re-evaluating Summarization Evaluation. *Transactions of the Association for Computational Linguistics*, 9, 391–409. doi:10.1162/tacl_a_00373

Gangi, M. A. D., Negri, M., & Turchi, M. (2019). Adapting Transformer to End-to-End Spoken Language Translation. *Interspeech, 1133–1137*, 1133–1137. doi:10.21437/Interspeech.2019-3045

Ghandeharioun, A., Shen, J. H., Jaques, N., Ferguson, C., Jones, N., Lapedriza, A., & Picard, R. (2019). Approximating Interactive Human Evaluation with Self-Play for Open-Domain Dialog Systems. *Advances in Neural Information Processing Systems, 32*. https://proceedings.neurips.cc/paper/2019/hash/fc9812127bf09c7bd29ad6723c683fb5-Abstract.html

Ghazarian, S., Weischedel, R., Galstyan, A., & Peng, N. (2020). Predictive Engagement: An Efficient Metric for Automatic Evaluation of Open-Domain Dialogue Systems. *Proceedings of the AAAI Conference on Artificial Intelligence, 34*(05), 7789–7796. doi:10.1609/aaai.v34i05.6283

Grudin, J., & Jacques, R. (2019). Chatbots, Humbots, and the Quest for Artificial General Intelligence. *Proceedings of the 2019 CHI Conference on Human Factors in Computing Systems,* (pp. 1–11). ACM. 10.1145/3290605.3300439

Grusky, M., Naaman, M., & Artzi, Y. (2018). Newsroom: A Dataset of 1.3 Million Summaries with Diverse Extractive Strategies. *Proceedings of the 2018 Conference of the North American Chapter of the Association for Computational Linguistics: Human Language Technologies,* (pp. 708–719). ACL. 10.18653/v1/N18-1065

Hirao, T., Okumura, M., Yasuda, N., & Isozaki, H. (2007). Supervised automatic evaluation for summarization with voted regression model. *Information Processing & Management*, *43*(6), 1521–1535. doi:10.1016/j.ipm.2007.01.012

Hochreiter, S., & Schmidhuber, J. (1997). Long Short-term Memory. *Neural Computation*, *9*(8), 1735–1780. doi:10.1162/neco.1997.9.8.1735 PMID:9377276

Hu, T., Xu, A., Liu, Z., You, Q., Guo, Y., Sinha, V., Luo, J., & Akkiraju, R. (2018). Touch Your Heart: A Tone-aware Chatbot for Customer Care on Social Media. *Proceedings of the 2018 CHI Conference on Human Factors in Computing Systems*, (pp. 1–12). ACM. 10.1145/3173574.3173989

Jia, J. (2003). *The Study of the Application of a Keywords-based Chatbot System on the Teaching of Foreign Languages*. Cornell University.

Jurafsky, D., & Martin, J. (2020). *Speech and Language Processing: An Introduction to Natural Language Processing* (Vol. 2). Computational Linguistics, and Speech Recognition.

Kannan, A., & Vinyals, O. (2017). Adversarial Evaluation of Dialogue Models. https://arxiv.org/abs/1701.08198

Kitaev, N., Kaiser, Ł., & Levskaya, A. (2020). Reformer: The Efficient Transformer. https://arxiv.org/abs/2001.04451

Koehn, P., Hoang, H., Birch, A., Callison-Burch, C., Federico, M., Bertoldi, N., Cowan, B., Shen, W., Moran, C., Zens, R., Dyer, C., Bojar, O., Constantin, A., & Herbst, E. (2007). Moses: Open Source Toolkit for Statistical Machine Translation. *Proceedings of the 45th Annual Meeting of the Association for Computational Linguistics Companion*, (pp. 177–180). ACL. https://aclanthology.org/P07-2045

Kruger, J.-L., & Steyn, F. (2013). Subtitles and Eye Tracking: Reading and Performance. *Reading Research Quarterly*, *49*(1), 105–120. doi:10.1002/rrq.59

Kryscinski, W., McCann, B., Xiong, C., & Socher, R. (2020). Evaluating the Factual Consistency of Abstractive Text Summarization. *Proceedings of the 2020 Conference on Empirical Methods in Natural Language Processing (EMNLP)*, (pp. 9332–9346). ACL. 10.18653/v1/2020.emnlp-main.750

Kumar, R., & Ali, M. (2008). *A Review on Chatbot Design and Implementation Techniques*. Research Gate.

Lewis, M., Liu, Y., Goyal, N., Ghazvininejad, M., Mohamed, A., Levy, O., Stoyanov, V., & Zettlemoyer, L. (2020). BART: Denoising Sequence-to-Sequence Pre-training for Natural Language Generation, Translation, and Comprehension. *Proceedings of the 58th Annual Meeting of the Association for Computational Linguistics*, (pp. 7871–7880). ACL. 10.18653/v1/2020.acl-main.703

Li, T. J.-J., Azaria, A., & Myers, B. A. (2017). SUGILITE: Creating Multimodal Smartphone Automation by Demonstration. *Proceedings of the 2017 CHI Conference on Human Factors in Computing Systems*, (pp. 6038–6049). ACM. 10.1145/3025453.3025483

Lin, C.-Y., & Hovy, E. (2003). Automatic Evaluation of Summaries Using N-gram Co-occurrence Statistics. *Proceedings of the 2003 Human Language Technology Conference of the North American Chapter of the Association for Computational Linguistics*, (pp. 150–157). ACL. https://aclanthology.org/N03-1020

Liu, Q., Liu, W., Yao, J., Liu, Y., & Pan, M. (2021). An Improved Method of Reservoir Facies Modeling Based on Generative Adversarial Networks. *Energies*, *14*(13), 3873. doi:10.3390/en14133873

Lowe, R., Noseworthy, M., Serban, I. V., Angelard-Gontier, N., Bengio, Y., & Pineau, J. (2018). Towards an Automatic Turing Test: Learning to Evaluate Dialogue Responses. https://arxiv.org/abs/1708.07149

Lu, Z., & Li, H. (2013). A Deep Architecture for Matching Short Texts. *Advances in Neural Information Processing Systems, 26*. https://papers.nips.cc/paper/2013/hash/8a0e1141fd37fa5b98d5b b769ba1a7cc-Abstract.html

Lukovnikov, D., Fischer, A., & Lehmann, J. (2019). Pretrained Transformers for Simple Question Answering over Knowledge Graphs. In C. Ghidini, O. Hartig, M. Maleshkova, V. Svátek, I. Cruz, A. Hogan, J. Song, M. Lefrançois, & F. Gandon (eds.), The Semantic Web – ISWC 2019, (pp. 470–486). Springer International Publishing. doi:10.1007/978-3-030-30793-6_27

Mesnil, G., Dauphin, Y., Yao, K., Bengio, Y., Deng, L., Hakkani-Tur, D., He, X., Heck, L., Tur, G., Yu, D., & Zweig, G. (2015). Using recurrent neural networks for slot filling in spoken language understanding. *IEEE/ACM Transactions on Audio, Speech, and Language Processing*, *23*(3), 530–539. doi:10.1109/TASLP.2014.2383614

Naseem, U., Razzak, I., Musial, K., & Imran, M. (2020). Transformer-based Deep Intelligent Contextual Embedding for Twitter sentiment analysis. *Future Generation Computer Systems*, *113*, 58–69. doi:10.1016/j.future.2020.06.050

Nenkova, A., & Passonneau, R. (2004). Evaluating Content Selection in Summarization: The Pyramid Method. *Proceedings of the Human Language Technology Conference of the North American Chapter of the Association for Computational Linguistics*. (pp. 145–152). ACL. https://aclanthology.org/N04-1019

Papineni, K., Roukos, S., Ward, T., & Zhu, W.-J. (2002). Bleu: A Method for Automatic Evaluation of Machine Translation. *Proceedings of the 40th Annual Meeting of the Association for Computational Linguistics*, (pp. 311–318). ACM. 10.3115/1073083.1073135

Peyrard, M., Botschen, T., & Gurevych, I. (2017). Learning to Score System Summaries for Better Content Selection Evaluation. *Proceedings of the Workshop on New Frontiers in Summarization*, (pp. 74–84). ACL. 10.18653/v1/W17-4510

Popović, M. (2015). chrF: Character n-gram F-score for automatic MT evaluation. *Proceedings of the Tenth Workshop on Statistical Machine Translation*, (pp. 392–395). ACL. 10.18653/v1/W15-3049

Radford, A., Wu, J., Child, R., Luan, D., Amodei, D., & Sutskever, I. (2019). *Language Models are Unsupervised Multitask Learners*. Semantic Scholar.

Rei, R., Stewart, C., Farinha, A. C., & Lavie, A. (2020). COMET: A Neural Framework for MT Evaluation. *Proceedings of the 2020 Conference on Empirical Methods in Natural Language Processing (EMNLP)*, (pp. 2685–2702). ACL. 10.18653/v1/2020. emnlp-main.213

Sai, A. B., Mohankumar, A. K., Arora, S., & Khapra, M. M. (2020). Improving Dialog Evaluation with a Multi-reference Adversarial Dataset and Large Scale Pretraining. *Transactions of the Association for Computational Linguistics*, 8, 810–827. doi:10.1162/tacl_a_00347

Schmidhuber, J. (1992). Learning to Control Fast-Weight Memories: An Alternative to Dynamic Recurrent Networks. *Neural Computation*, 4(1), 131–139. doi:10.1162/neco.1992.4.1.131

See, A., Pappu, A., Saxena, R., Yerukola, A., & Manning, C. D. (2019). Do Massively Pretrained Language Models Make Better Storytellers? https://arxiv.org/abs/1909.10705 doi:10.18653/v1/K19-1079

Sellam, T., Das, D., & Parikh, A. P. (2020). BLEURT: Learning Robust Metrics for Text Generation. https://arxiv.org/abs/2004.04696 doi:10.18653/v1/2020.acl-main.704

Serban, I. V., Sankar, C., Germain, M., Zhang, S., Lin, Z., Subramanian, S., Kim, T., Pieper, M., Chandar, S., Ke, N. R., Rajeshwar, S., de Brebisson, A., Sotelo, J. M. R., Suhubdy, D., Michalski, V., Nguyen, A., Pineau, J., & Bengio, Y. (2017). A Deep Reinforcement Learning Chatbot. https://arxiv.org/abs/1709.02349

Serban, I. V., Sordoni, A., Bengio, Y., Courville, A., & Pineau, J. (2016). Building end-to-end dialogue systems using generative hierarchical neural network models. *Proceedings of the Thirtieth AAAI Conference on Artificial Intelligence*, (pp. 3776–3783). AAAI. 10.1609/aaai.v30i1.9883

Shagass, C., Roemer, R. A., & Amadeo, M. (1976). Eye-Tracking Performance and Engagement of Attention. *Archives of General Psychiatry*, *33*(1), 121–125. doi:10.1001/archpsyc.1976.01770010077015 PMID:1247358

Shang, L., Lu, Z., & Li, H. (2015). Neural Responding Machine for Short-Text Conversation. https://arxiv.org/abs/1503.02364 doi:10.3115/v1/P15-1152

Shangipour Ataei, T., Javdan, S., & Minaei-Bidgoli, B. (2020). Applying Transformers and Aspect-based Sentiment Analysis approaches on Sarcasm Detection. *Proceedings of the Second Workshop on Figurative Language Processing*, (pp. 67–71). ACL. doi:10.18653/v1/2020.figlang-1.9

Shao, T., Guo, Y., Chen, H., & Hao, Z. (2019). Transformer-Based Neural Network for Answer Selection in Question Answering. *IEEE Access: Practical Innovations, Open Solutions*, *7*, 26146–26156. doi:10.1109/ACCESS.2019.2900753

Shum, H., He, X., & Li, D. (2018). From Eliza to XiaoIce: Challenges and opportunities with social chatbots. *Frontiers of Information Technology & Electronic Engineering*, *19*(1), 10–26. doi:10.1631/FITEE.1700826

Snover, M. G., Madnani, N., Dorr, B., & Schwartz, R. (2009). TER-Plus: Paraphrase, semantic, and alignment enhancements to Translation Edit Rate. *Machine Translation*, *23*(2–3), 117–127. doi:10.100710590-009-9062-9

Sojasingarayar, A. (2020). *Seq2Seq AI Chatbot with Attention Mechanism*. Academia. https://www.academia.edu/43262982/Seq2Seq_AI_Chatbot_with_Attention_Mechanism

Song, Y., Li, C.-T., Nie, J.-Y., Zhang, M., Zhao, D., & Yan, R. (2018). An Ensemble of Retrieval-Based and Generation-Based Human-Computer Conversation Systems. *Proceedings of the Twenty-Seventh International Joint Conference on Artificial Intelligence*, (pp. 4382–4388). IJCAI. 10.24963/ijcai.2018/609

Sordoni, A., Galley, M., Auli, M., Brockett, C., Ji, Y., Mitchell, M., Nie, J.-Y., Gao, J., & Dolan, B. (2015). A Neural Network Approach to Context-Sensitive Generation of Conversational Responses. https://arxiv.org/abs/1506.06714 doi:10.3115/v1/N15-1020

Stanojević, M., & Sima'an, K. (2014). BEER: BEtter Evaluation as Ranking. *Proceedings of the Ninth Workshop on Statistical Machine Translation*, (pp. 414–419). ACL. 10.3115/v1/W14-3354

Strigér, A. (2017). *End-to-End Trainable Chatbot for Restaurant Recommendations*. KTH. https://www.diva-portal.org/smash/get/diva2:1139496/FULLTEXT01.pdf

Sun, C., Baradel, F., Murphy, K., & Schmid, C. (2019). Learning Video Representations using Contrastive Bidirectional Transformer. https://arxiv.org/abs/1906.05743

Tao, C., Mou, L., Zhao, D., & Yan, R. (2017). RUBER: An Unsupervised Method for Automatic Evaluation of Open-Domain Dialog Systems. *Proceedings of the AAAI Conference on Artificial Intelligence*, 32. AAAI. 10.1609/aaai.v32i1.11321

Tenney, I., Das, D., & Pavlick, E. (2019). BERT Rediscovers the Classical NLP Pipeline. https://arxiv.org/abs/1905.05950 doi:10.18653/v1/P19-1452

Thompson, B., & Post, M. (2020). Paraphrase Generation as Zero-Shot Multilingual Translation: Disentangling Semantic Similarity from Lexical and Syntactic Diversity https://arxiv.org/abs/2008.04935

Vaswani, A., Shazeer, N., Parmar, N., Uszkoreit, J., Jones, L., Gomez, A. N., Kaiser, L., & Polosukhin, I. (2017). Attention Is All You Need. https://arxiv.org/abs/1706.03762

Vinyals, O., & Le, Q. (2015). A Neural Conversational Model. https://arxiv.org/abs/1506.05869

Wang, H., Tan, M., Yu, M., Chang, S., Wang, D., Xu, K., Guo, X., & Potdar, S. (2019). Extracting Multiple-Relations in One-Pass with Pre-Trained Transformers. https://arxiv.org/abs/1902.01030 doi:10.18653/v1/P19-1132

Wang, Q., Li, B., Xiao, T., Zhu, J., Li, C., Wong, D. F., & Chao, L. S. (2019). Learning Deep Transformer Models for Machine Translation. https://arxiv.org/abs/1906.01787 doi:10.18653/v1/P19-1176

Weizenbaum, J. (1966). ELIZA— a computer program for the study of natural language communication between man and machine. *Communications of the ACM, 9*(1), 36–45. doi:10.1145/365153.365168

Wilcox, B. (2014). Winning the Loebner's. https://www. gamasutra.com/blogs/BruceWilcox/20141020/228091/ Winning_the_Loebners.php

Xu, A., Liu, Z., Guo, Y., Sinha, V., & Akkiraju, R. (2017). A New Chatbot for Customer Service on Social Media. *Proceedings of the 2017 CHI Conference on Human Factors in Computing Systems*, 3506–3510. 10.1145/3025453.3025496

Yan, J. N., Gu, Z., Lin, H., & Rzeszotarski, J. M. (2020). Silva: Interactively Assessing Machine Learning Fairness Using Causality. *Proceedings of the 2020 CHI Conference on Human Factors in Computing Systems*, (pp. 1–13). ACM. 10.1145/3313831.3376447

Yan, Z., Duan, N., Bao, J., Chen, P., Zhou, M., Li, Z., & Zhou, J. (2016). DocChat: An Information Retrieval Approach for Chatbot Engines Using Unstructured Documents. *Proceedings of the 54th Annual Meeting of the Association for Computational Linguistics* (Volume 1, pp. 516–525). ACL. 10.18653/v1/P16-1049

Young, S., Gašić, M., Thomson, B., & Williams, J. D. (2013). POMDP-Based Statistical Spoken Dialog Systems: A Review. *Proceedings of the IEEE, 101*(5), 1160–1179. doi:10.1109/JPROC.2012.2225812

Yu, S., Chen, Y., & Zaidi, H. (2020). A Financial Service Chatbot based on Deep Bidirectional Transformers. https://arxiv.org/abs/2003.04987

Yuan, W., Neubig, G., & Liu, P. (2021). BARTSCORE: Evaluating Generated Text as Text Generation. Cornell University.

Zemčík, T. (2019). A Brief History of Chatbots. *DEStech Transactions on Computer Science and Engineering*. doi:10.12783/dtcse/aicae2019/31439

Zhang, T., Kishore, V., Wu, F., Weinberger, K. Q., & Artzi, Y. (2020). BERTScore: Evaluating Text Generation with BERT. https://arxiv.org/abs/1904.09675

Zhang, Z., Li, J., Zhu, P., Zhao, H., & Liu, G. (2018). Modelling Multi-turn Conversation with Deep Utterance Aggregation. https://arxiv.org/abs/1806.09102

Zhao, W., Peyrard, M., Liu, F., Gao, Y., Meyer, C. M., & Eger, S. (2019). MoverScore: Text Generation Evaluating with Contextualized Embeddings and Earth Mover Distance. https://arxiv.org/abs/1909.02622 doi:10.18653/v1/D19-1053

KEY TERMS AND DEFINITIONS

Chatbot: A computer program or software application created to mimic communication with human users, particularly online, through text or voice.

Dialogue Modeling: An abstract representation of how a user interacts with an interactive computer system. The notations used in user interface management systems are based on dialogue models (UIMS).

Human-Computer Interaction (HCI): An interdisciplinary branch of research devoted to the design of computer technology and the interaction between people (the users) and computers.

Information Retrieval (IR): The process of locating information system resources that are pertinent to a particular information demand from a collection of those resources in computing and information science. Searches may use full-text indexing or another type of content-based indexing.

Natural Language Processing (NLP): The analysis and synthesis of natural language and speech using computational methods. Building machines that comprehend and react to text or voice data—and answer with text or speech of their own—much like humans do is the goal of natural language processing.

Recurrent Neural Network (RNN): A subset of artificial neural networks where the connections between the nodes can cycle, allowing the output from one node to influence the input to another node. It can display temporal dynamic behavior because of this. RNNs, which are derived from feedforward neural networks, may process input sequences of different lengths by using their internal state (memory).

Transformer: A deep learning model that uses the self-attention process and weights the importance of each component of the input data differently.

ENDNOTES

[1] The difference between Shallow Learning and Deep Learning consists of the depth of the neural network used to carry out the Machine Learning task. Deep Learning is a subclass of machine learning algorithms with a higher degree of complexity, due to the multiple hidden layers used in the neural network. Deep neural nets can automatically execute feature extraction due to their sophisticated architecture. In contrast, this activity is completed outside of the algorithmic stage in conventional machine learning or shallow learning. The primary benefit of deep learning is the ability to train algorithms on unstructured data with limitless access to information.

[2] Vanishing gradients are a common issue in RNNs that makes learning from lengthy data sequences difficult. Parameter updates in an RNN are done

with the help of the gradient. When the gradient gets smaller and smaller, the parameter updates become unimportant, which implies no meaningful learning is done. More information on the matter can be found in Hochreiter, S. (1998). The Vanishing Gradient Problem During Learning Recurrent Neural Nets and Problem Solutions. International Journal of Uncertainty, Fuzziness and Knowledge-Based Systems, 06(02), 107–116. https://doi.org/10.1142/S0218488598000094

Chapter 12

Conversational AI Chatbots in Digital Engagement:
Privacy and Security Concerns

Uma S.

Hindusthan College of Engineering and Technology, Coimbatore, India

ABSTRACT

Digital transformation and globalisation have taken the online business to the next frontier, embracing the customer engagements with conversational artificial intelligence or chatbots. Chatbots are deployed across several industries ranging from e-commerce to healthcare. While the advantages of using chatbots are enormous, chatbots also introduce certain pitfalls. A lack of diversity among creators may result in biased responses from the chatbot. Though chatbots are widely used, not all of their security issues are satisfactorily resolved. It causes significant security issues and risks, which needs immediate attention. Many chatbots are built on top of social/ messaging platforms, which has its own set of terms and conditions governing data collection and usage. This work gives a detailed analysis of security considerations in the context of communication with bots. This chapter has the potential to spark a debate and draw attention to the issues surrounding data storage and usage of chatbots to protect users.

INTRODUCTION

Face-to-face human interactions are becoming less common, and communication through technology is gaining prominence. Chatbots are machines that replicate interactive human interaction utilizing artificial intelligence (AI), pre-calculated user

DOI: 10.4018/978-1-6684-6234-8.ch012

words, and audio and written signals. Chatbots can process user input and produce outputs. A chatbot usually accepts natural language text as input and produces the most relevant output to the user's input. A chatbot can also be defined as "an online human-computer dialogue system using natural language" (Andrej Godina, 2018). Chatbots constitute an automated dialogue system that can attend to thousands of potential users simultaneously. An artificial messenger, or "bot," allows customers to communicate with a service provider (e.g., a bank, online shopping catalog, or public utility). Chatbots are also often integrated into operating systems as intelligent virtual assistants. Customer support and marketing systems rely on chatbots in social networking hubs and instant messaging (IM) applications.

Artificial intelligence (AI)-based chatbots like Google's LaMDA, Open AI's GPT-3, Meta's BlenderBot, Amazon's Alexa, and Apple's Siri have been trained on billions of documents, giving the concept of "massive data" (O'Leary, 2022). These systems use documents that people create themselves to record the words and connections between words they use when speaking. These chatbot technologies are increasingly becoming part of our daily lives. As a result, businesses are now implementing chatbots into their networks, offering consumers a more efficient and user-friendly experience across many platforms. Retail and e-commerce, learning management systems (LMS), travel and hospitality, sales, marketing, customer relationship management (CRM), banking, financial services, insurance, healthcare, media, and entertainment are some of the other applications of chatbots.

Artificial intelligence is already enabling chatbots in the commercial sector to interact with customers on a far more personal level than the conventional, automated "Press one for admin" phone reply. Voice is becoming more essential in chatbot technology (Andrej Godina, 2018). For example, today's chatbot technology can also answer more complex inquiries orally; Amazon's Alexa, for instance, is a popular AI assistant that works with Amazon's home hub. The reality is that it's often difficult to tell whether the conversation is with a real person or a chatbot.

The advent of chatbots has changed the way people think and live. They are always available and ready to provide service assistance as well as carry out other tasks whenever and wherever people need them. In addition to communication tools, chatbot technology comes with significant IT-related benefits, but it can also entail risks for the organizations using it. There are several security threats associated with the use of chatbots. The existing chatbot solutions are not completely secure, and the organizations using chatbots may get exposed to cyberattacks. Cyberattacks are increasing in number, but detecting and analyzing such attacks requires a lot of knowledge and tools. Information security incidents require experts who can investigate security incidents and have a broad knowledge base. Using a reliable security tool on the Internet is crucial for using these virtual assistants. Such vulnerabilities provide hackers with direct access to an organization's applications, databases, and networks. Hence, there is an increasing concern over chatbot security as the popularity of chatbots increases (What Are the Privacy and Security Issues Associated with Chatbots? n.d.)? Organizations and individuals need to educate themselves and be aware of the dangers of using chatbots. They must think about crucial issues like sharing and preserving the information, as well as, most critically, who can access it.

CHATBOT BACKGROUND

Conversational AI and chatbots with AI power have practically infinite possibilities. For small firms, chatbots that support cloud-based operations have proven successful. When more companies use the cloud, their ability to manage customer interactions, data management, and internal communication will dramatically increase, and they won't have to be concerned about security risks or additional infrastructure costs (Vaish, 2022). Maintaining client loyalty and shaping brand views depend heavily on the customer service and support role. For businesses, providing a satisfying client experience is now a mandate, not a free-form pastime.

A chatbot also known as a chatterbot or chatter robot is a computer program that attempts to simulate a human-like conversation using a text or voice message. A user can ask a chatbot a set of questions. The chatbot will respond in a human-like way. It understands the natural language conversation a user inputs, in the request of a certain task, and the chatbot can perform that task. Additionally, they can distinguish between the uniqueness of words, including emoticons. In 1966, ELIZA, the first chatbot ever designed, was created. In the past, creating a bot required specialized equipment and in-depth programming experience.

Even though a chatbot appears to be a social media messaging app, it has a layer of application code, a database, and Application Programming Interfaces working in the background (Akma et al., 2018). User interfaces provide an easy way to communicate with users. While chatbots are simple to use, they are complex to implement. Chatbots usually have logs of conversations, which are used by developers to understand user requests. Chatbot conversation is then improved using the logs.

Chatbots are of two types: rule-based chatbots and machine-language (ML)-based or AI chatbots. A rule-based chatbot is an application that uses established rules, such as pattern recognition or certain words or phrases. A rule-based chatbot will be able to answer only specific commands and represent a fixed smartness level. If it cannot recognize the command, it will not be able to respond properly. Once the rules are created, the bot immediately comprehends any language that the engine supports. These rules have the advantage of being more dependable and enabling developers to construct and delete rules with assurance for managing novel scenarios and bug fixes (Ong et al., 2021). While chatbots based on machine learning (ML) are less reliable, rule-based chatbot systems do not learn through user interaction but can guarantee a positive user experience (Ong et al., 2021).

On the other hand, the AI-based chatbot uses artificial intelligence to understand commands and natural language. Since machine learning is the ability of a computer to learn based on experience without explicitly being programmed, AI-based chatbots will be able to respond to commands/queries.

Applications for chatbots powered by machine learning (ML) get better over time as more data is collected and learned from. However, machine language-based approaches are more challenging to correct when anything goes wrong. To reduce the cost of development, machine language-based approaches must amass a large number of character sequences until the Chatbot application has observed and learned enough to abstract from the original training sentences (Ong et al., 2021).

In both cases, chatbots should be able to recognize similar queries and respond with the same output. Usually, chatbots are trained with thousands of logs from human conversations for better performance and intelligence.

Evolution of Chatbots

The 1950 article "Computer Machinery and Intelligence" by Alan Turing, usually recognized as the pioneer of computer science, laid the groundwork for the intelligence of computer programs. He posed the question, "Can Machines think?," in his essay and described the "Turing Test," which determines if a computer program can compel human-like behavior in a textual real-time dialogue (Turing, 1950). Elizabot (Shah et al., 2016), one of the earliest well-known chatbots, was developed in a lab at the Massachusetts Institute of Technology (MIT) in 1966 to imitate a human-machine natural language conversation. To provide appropriate responses, ELIZA would find keywords and patterns that fit those keywords depending on several pre-programmed criteria based on the user-provided input sentences.

Racter (short for raconteur, a storyteller), a program created by William Chamberlain and Thomas Etter under the Inrac Corporation, was another intriguing chatbot in 1983 (Racter, 1984). This artificial intelligence simulator, which was originally developed for Amiga, Apple II, and Macintosh platforms, successfully generates English prose at random.

Dr. Sabaitso, a milestone in chatbot history was created in 1992 by Creative Labs, a technology corporation with headquarters in Singapore. An artificial intelligence (AI) speech synthesis algorithm was doing the impersonation. The company sold sound cards together with the program that was supplied. They intended to demonstrate the digital voices that their sound cards might generate (Chatbot Architecture, n.d.).

Natural language processing is used by the open-source Artificial Linguistic Internet Computer Entity (ALICE) chatbot application, which was first introduced in 1995. ALICE uses pattern matching to generate responses and outputs to knowledge bases through eXtensible Markup Language (XML). Artificial Intelligence Markup Language (AIML), is an XML extension that was used to construct these documents. The use of ALICE is still widespread today (Ilamathi et al., 2020).

Jabberwacky, which was published in 1982, was one of the first attempts to create artificial intelligence for communication with humans. The system was created for use with only text (Sree et al., 2019).

Watson, IBM's most famous chatbot created in 2006, revives the data in Question Answer format. The system incorporates cutting-edge technologies for autonomous reasoning, knowledge base representation, natural language processing, and machine learning (IBM Research Editorial Staff, 2011).

Virtual assistants have been more popular since Apple introduced Siri in 2010. Apple introduced Siri which uses automatic speech recognition (ASP), natural language processing (NLP), and Question Answer matching to transform spoken input into written text.

The first personal assistant made available globally was Siri. Google released Google Now in 2012, following Apple's lead. In 2014, both CORTANA from Microsoft and Alexa from Amazon was released (Chatbot Architecture, n.d.). The Microsoft version of an intelligent assistant, CORTANA, uses the Bing search engine to send reminders and provide information. CORTANA is accessible in a variety of languages and can understand natural voice commands.

Google created "Google Now" for the Google search Mobile app in 2012. It uses a natural language user interface to respond to inquiries, offer advice, and carry out tasks by sending requests to several online services.

AIML was used in 2012 to create Mitsuku, the most well-liked single chatbot. Heuristic patterns and NLP are also used in Mitsuku. When the bot is unable to find a good match, Mitsuku can hold for a protracted conversation before abruptly switching to the default category (Nirala et al., 2022). Additionally, it offers the ability to use specific items as arguments. Mitsuku alias Kuki won the Loebner Prize Turing Test five times, an annual AI contest to determine the world's most human-like chatbot. It is an altered version of Alan Turing's original Turing Test, which he developed in 1950 to judge how well a machine could imitate human speech in a conversation.

The digital assistant Alexa was developed by Amazon Lab 126 in 2015. Real-time home automation, playing, streaming, and voice commands are the various features of Alexa (Trivialworks Solutions Pvt Ltd., 2018).

"Chatbots respond to users' messages by selecting the relevant expression from pre-programmed schemas. In emerging bots, the selection is done with adaptive

Figure 1. Chatbot System

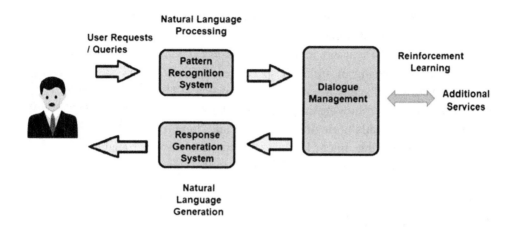

machine learning algorithms," according to literature (Neff & Nagy, 2016). Functional chatbots are commonplace in 2018.

Sophia, from Saudi Arabia a chatbot that hides behind the interface of a humanoid woman robot with sophisticated facial expressions, is an intriguing development in the field of chatbots. It became the first robot with citizenship in October 2016 (Peterson, 2017).

Facebook made chatbots available on its Messenger platform in 2016. As a result, significant growth in automated communication platforms started booming. In 2018, LiveChat introduced Chatbot, a framework that enables users to create chatbots without writing any code. Currently, over 300,000 bots are active on Messenger.

Basic Components of a Chatbot

An overview of the chatbot's overall architectural design is provided in this section, along with a brief discussion of the key elements of each component. A standard chatbot architecture is made up of the following five basic components (Adamopoulou & Moussiades, 2020), as shown in figure 1.

- User Interface component
- Natural Language Understanding (NLU) component
- Dialogue Management (DM) component
- Backend component and
- Response Generation (RG) Component

User Interface

Users may converse and interact with a chatbot using messenger services like Facebook Messenger, Cortana, or Slack thanks to the user interface. A user's request initiates a chatbot's operation. The user's input for speech-based conversational agents is first converted into text using an automatic speech recognition (ASR) system. A speech-based conversational agent also has a text-to-speech (TTS) system that transforms text back into speech following the generation of a text answer (Firdaus et al., 2020).

Text analysis entails normalizing the text and doing phonetic (pronunciation) and prosodic (phrasing, pitch, loudness, tempo, and rhythm) analyses, whereas waveform synthesis entails choosing the pre-recorded speech that best fits the query (McTear et al., 2016).

Natural Language Understanding

The NLU component is utilized by the system after it has received the user's request to extract data from the input and create a representation of its meaning that may be used later in the process. Dialogue act categorization, intent classification, and slot filling are the three tasks that NLU typically works with.

- *Dialogue Act Classification*

It is the process of identifying the purpose of a user's input, or more accurately, assigning a dialogue act type to a user's utterance. The phrase may be categorized as a remark, a question, an offer, or another kind of dialogue act. Understanding the dialogue act being carried out can help the system better understand the user's request and choose the right course of action (Tur & Deng, 2011).

- *Intent Classification*

The user's main objective is identified by the intent classification process. Most intents depend on a specific domain. A request could pertain to ordering food, making hotel reservations, getting the weather, etc. Similar to how an agent within the food ordering domain can have the purpose to place, inquire about, or change an order, an agent within the hotel reservations domain can have the intent to book, cancel, or change a reservation (McTear et al., 2016).

- *Slot Filling*

The final phase in NLU is slot filling. The agent gathers additional information that, along with the dialogue act and the intent, enables it to completely comprehend the user's request (McTear et al., 2016).

Dialogue Management

It handles data from the other components and is in charge of managing the chatbot's behaviors as well as controlling and changing the context of talks (McTear et al., 2016).

Backend

Chatbots forward messages to the Dialogue Management Component and Response Generation Component after retrieving the data from the Backend that is required to complete the necessary tasks (Adamopoulou & Moussiades, 2020).

Response Generation

The dialogue system will then decide the response's content and the most effective manner to present it after the required data has been retrieved. The Response Generation component is responsible for producing responses that are easy for the user to understand (McTear et al., 2016).

Well-KnownChatbots

More than 300000 active chatbots are in use in Facebook Messenger itself (Bleu, 2021). Chatbots are used for several applications such as e-commerce education, content delivery, ordering food, booking flights, companionship, health care, transportation, etc., The world's most popular list of chatbots is listed in Table 1 (Kim, 2020). Some of the Innovative Chatbots considered top 10 are listed in Table 2 (Kim, 2020). A list of the 10 Best AI Chatbots in 2022 used in India is given in Table 3.

Types Of Chatbot Technologies

Several different types of chatbots are used in practice depending on the requirements of the specific application (Engati, n.d.). A brief explanation of the various chatbots is listed below (Figure 2).

- Menu/Button based chatbots
- Linguistic Based (Rule-based chatbots)

Table 1. World's Popular Chatbots

Company Name	About the Chatbot
Fandango	The ticketing company Fandango, which sells movie tickets, utilizes a Facebook Messenger chatbot to assist consumers in learning what movies are playing, learning when and where they're playing, and ultimately asking them if they want to buy tickets, which directs them to the Fandango website.
Sephora	The personal care and beauty retailer Sephora utilizes a chatbot on Facebook Messenger to let users do a variety of tasks.
Wall Street Journal	The Wall Street Journal, an international daily newspaper with a focus on American business, employs a chatbot to share news and podcasts with users. The user can choose from several news themes, such as "Latest News" or "Today's Market," and the bot will then connect to numerous recent articles that are relevant to that topic.
National Geographic	With Pop Geo, a game of global trivia, National Geographic engages users with their Facebook Messenger chatbot originally and enjoyably. Users can alter the chatbot game to reflect popular themes like space that interest people.
James Patterson's "The Chef" Short Story	A classic game of trivia can be modified by the user, or the user can utterly shock everyone with something that has never been attempted before. James Patterson, a best-selling author, went with the latter option when he released a thriller short story via a chilling chatbot.
AccuWeather	The Facebook Messenger chatbot for AccuWeather connects users with an AI meteorologist. Dawn not only provides meteorological information for whatever place the user chooses but also warns users of any severe weather alerts so they can be safe.
TGIFridays	TGI Fridays, an organization sought to enter the market for order-ahead bot business. With their Facebook Messenger App, users may place, orders, find the nearest locations, or book reservations. It's a simple method for office workers to order lunch, cater a meeting, or reserve an after-work meal.
Western Union	The financial services provider Western Union entered the chatbot market by making it simpler for their customers to send money. Users may send money or track transfers with the help of their Facebook Messenger chatbot by just clicking a button. Customers no longer need to log in or go through pages on Western Union's website, making it a clever use-case for the company. Wherever they need to go can easily be reached, and they can accomplish it immediately.
Summit Academy OIC	More students were enrolled at Summit Academy OIC thanks to their well-liked chatbots. A 30% increase in potential pupils was the result of their marketing.
Mobile Monkey	A well-known chatbot has been employed by MobileMonkey to increase reach and reduce lead acquisition costs.
Stanford's Quizbot	QuizBot from Stanford University showcases the possibilities of intelligent robots in the future. A bot created by Stanford researchers that aids in the study of factual material outperform other study techniques like flashcards. Compared to students that utilized a flashcard app, QuizBot users got almost 20% more correct answers. This well-known chatbot uses conversation to teach users scientific, English, and safety language and is intended for self-paced learning.

Source: (Kim, 2020)

- Keyword recognition-based chatbots

Table 2. Top 10 Innovative Chatbots on the Web

Chatbot Name	Purpose	Key Features
Endurance	A Companion for Dementia Patients	Since many Alzheimer's patients experience short-term memory loss this chatbot is designed to recognize variations in conversational branches that may signal difficulty with instant remembering. Additionally, because the chatbot is a cloud-based solution, medical professionals and family members can examine communication logs extracted from the bot to spot probable memory loss and other communication difficulties that could indicate a worsening of the patient's health.
Casper	Helping Insomniacs Get through the Night	Insomnobot 3000 is a conversational agent designed to help people suffering from sleeping disorders such as insomnia.
Disney	Solving Crimes with Fictional Characters	Disney recently used a chatbot that featured a character from the 2016 animated family criminal caper Zootopia to captivate younger audiences. Disney invited moviegoers to solve crimes alongside Lieutenant Judy Hopps, the movie's tenacious, long-eared lead. By interacting with the bot, which investigated potential lines of inquiry based on user input, kids could assist Lt. Hopps in investigating mysteries similar to those in the film. The chatbot will respond to user recommendations for Lt. Hopps' investigations. Users can investigate mysteries like those depicted in the movie by interacting with a bot that explores avenues of inquiry based on their inputs.
Marvel	Guarding the Galaxy with Comic-Book Crossovers	Although the bots can follow several predefined conversational paths depending on the user's input, the app's main objective is to sell comic books and movie tickets.
UNICEF	Helping Marginalized Communities Be Heard	UNICEF, a global organization that advocates for children, is utilizing chatbots to assist individuals in underdeveloped countries in speaking out about the most pressing needs in their communities. This is not a chatty bot; instead, U-Report concentrates on obtaining extensive data through surveys. Users (known as "U-Reporters") can react to prepared polls that U-Report frequently distributes on a variety of pressing social concerns. Then, UNICEF bases prospective policy suggestions on this feedback.
MedWhat	Making Medical Diagnoses Faster	This chatbot is a talking, intelligent version of WebMD that promises to make medical diagnosis quicker, simpler, and more transparent for both patients and doctors. A complex machine learning algorithm powers MedWhat, which provides users with progressively accurate answers depending on behaviors it "learns" from interacting with people.
Roof Ai	Generating and Assigning Leads Automatically	Roof Ai is a chatbot that assists real estate marketing in automating lead assignments and social media interaction. The bot uses Facebook to find possible leads, then almost immediately answers in a helpful, polite, and conversational tone that closely matches that of a human person. Before automatically allocating a lead to a sales agent, Roof AI asks potential leads for extra information based on user input.
NBC	Helping Newshounds Navigate the Headlines	The NBC Politics Bot was introduced by NBC on Facebook Messenger just before the 2016 U.S. presidential election. Users can interact with the conversational agent through Facebook to find breaking news stories that would appeal to the network's various audience segments.
Unilever	Raising Awareness with Brand Mascots	A London-based agency called Ubisend, which specializes in creating custom chatbot applications for brands, transformed a televised advertising campaign into a fully interactive chatbot for PG Tips' parent company, Unilever, which also happens to own an alarming number of the most well-known household brands.
ALICE	The Bot That Launched a Thousand… Other Bots	Dr. Richard Wallace, invented ALICE, in 1995, during the early Internet gloomy days. ALICE is an acronym for Artificial Linguistic Internet Computer Entity that seems like it may have come from an episode of The X-Files. Despite being created and introduced more than 20 years ago, ALICE is one of the very first bots to go online. Without Dr. Wallace's groundbreaking work, none of the chatbots of today would exist.

Source: (Shewan, 2022)

Table 3. 10 Best AI Chatbots in India (Updated 2022)

Chatbot Name	Introduced By	Key Features	Milestones
JioMart Whatsapp Chatbot	JioMart	• Improved user experience throughout their shopping journey • Maximized use of the JioMart WhatsApp chatbot	• First-ever WhatsApp commerce solution in India! • Delivering services to more than 10 million customers each month and maximizing conversion rates. • In just three months, JioMart was able to improve average customer spending by 20%, while also seeing a 582% rise in orders and a roughly 733% increase in revenue due to the chat-based solution.
24/7 WhatsApp Chatbot	Disney + Hotstar	• 24x7 WhatsApp chatbot • provides strong, consistent experiences for customers	• While handling more than 5000 monthly interactions, the WhatsApp chatbot assists in providing support for more than 500,000 users. • The first response time has decreased by 99.72% (from three hours to 30 seconds), while the resolution time has decreased by 97%. (12 hours to 30 minutes).
Railway Food Order & Delivery	Zoop India	• WhatsApp chatbot • Food orders are delivered straight to their seats. • Automatic identification of the passenger's seat/berth using the Passenger Name Record Number. • Provision for checking the delivery status of the food ordered	• Key contributor for eCatering on trains. • Planning to serve 20 thousand meals daily and cover all reserved trains. • Plans to expand to cover 250 stations in FY 2021-22, serving 20 thousand meals daily and covering all reserved trains.
Kaya Virtual Assistant	Kotak Life Insurance	• Customer engagement • Digital Transformation • Enhancing user experience	• 88 percent of common user queries are handled, and the platform's discovery and user engagement are both improved. • By saving 8000 hours of agent work and generating 700,000 monthly discussions, Kaya has assisted KLI in achieving a CSAT score of 82%.
Omnichannel Support	Starhub	A significant telco in Singapore, Starhub, uses an AI chatbot with more than 3000 different intents and more than 50 pre-built routes.	• A noticeably faster first response time for inquiries about account balance, billing, new offers, and other topics. • Starhub's Net Promoter Score (NPS) increased overall by 125% as a result of the intelligent virtual assistant's (IVA) 80% accuracy rate. Additionally, it drove operational efficiency and enhanced customer experience by cutting customer "support wait times by almost half."
Dr		• With regards to COVID-related information, finding the closest centre, tracking reports, etc., Dr. Lal PathLabs' intelligent chatbot can assist its users. • Furthermore, it provides information on the costs and a range of testing.	• Today, an increasing number of people prefer to receive their medical care virtually rather than in person.
Borosil Virtual Assistant	Borosil	• Borosil has incorporated an intelligent virtual assistant to help its visitors get what they're looking for in the fewest possible steps, saving them the trouble of having to navigate through numerous websites. • Additionally, the assistant assists with warranty registration and after-sale assistance.	• Assists clients with questions and requests like tracking order progress, delivery status, and payment updates. • The bot can assist clients in completing their purchases by guiding them through the purchasing process.
EVA	HDFC	It takes a lot of effort to navigate a banking website with its abundance of options. Getting even the smallest amount of information seems like a huge undertaking that will take too much time. With the introduction of EVA(Electronic Virtual Assistant), HDFC has liberated clients from this aimless searching, numerous clicks, and hours-long phone wait times.	• (Electronic Virtual Assistant), is India's first and largest AI-powered banking chatbot. • EVA is available around-the-clock to assist clients in learning more about their accounts, cards, or any other service they have signed up for or are curious about. • It also helps in logging complaints. • It can be found on Amazon Echo and Google Assistant gadgets.
Tally's Intelligent Virtual Assistant	Tally	A B2B company must offer a consistent and individualized customer experience to its clients. This is what Tally's Intelligent Virtual Assistant is designed to accomplish.	• Engages with visitors as soon as they arrive, responds to common questions and Invites them to schedule a demo with the sales staff. • To increase user involvement, it also advertises new product releases, feature upgrades, intriguing news, and notifications.
MyGov Corona Helpdesk WhatsApp Chatbot	Government of India	The goal of MyGov Corona Helpdesk, the official chatbot of the Indian government, was to make it easier for individuals to find accurate and dependable information on the coronavirus.	• This WhatsApp chatbot responds to COVID-19 questions, offers advice, suggests safety precautions, and shares the most recent Ministry of Health updates and recommendations. • To broaden its appeal, the WhatsApp chatbot was also made available in Hindi. • The chatbot was enhanced to allow millions of Indians to book vaccination slots and download their immunization certificates as the nationwide vaccination blitz got underway.

Source: (Chaturvedi, 2022)

- Machine Learning chatbots
- The hybrid model
- Voice bots

Menu/Button-Based Chatbots

The most basic type of chatbot implemented in the market is the menu/button-based chatbot. It is designed in the form of decision tree hierarchies with buttons. The users have to make several selections to dig deep to get the required answer. The advantage of this kind of chatbot is that they are sufficient for answering FAQs that make up 80% of support queries (Engati, n.d.). Yet, in advanced scenarios with too many variables or when too much knowledge is required to answer the query, these chatbots cannot answer the queries with confidence. A limitation of such chatbots is they are too slow in getting the user to their desired results.

Linguistic Based

Linguistic chatbots are also known as Rule-based chatbots. It is better than machine learning chatbots in terms of fine-tuned control and flexibility. If the kind of questions/queries the customers will raise is known already, this type of chatbot will be the best option to design. The automation of conversations in these chatbots is created using if, then logic (Engati, n.d.). Words and their order of occurrence and synonyms in the user's query are used to assess the conditions to answer. If the conditions match the predefined conditions, the users will be able to get specific help in a short duration of time.

Occasionally, if the chatbot is unable to understand the conditions given by the user, it will take time to compute the permutations and combinations of variables. Since these chatbots also demand more specific and rigid queries, to get the specific answer, it takes more time to develop linguistic chatbots.

Keyword Recognition-Based Chatbots

These chatbots listen to what the user types and respond correctly, unlike menu-based chatbots. Customizable keywords and Natural Language processing are used in these chatbots to provide the correct response to the user.

In case, similar questions of the same sort have to be answered several times, and when there are keyword redundancies between several related questions these chatbots start to slip.

A combination of keyword recognition-based and menu/button-based chatbots hybrid chatbots are popular. The users are given the choice of either asking the questions directly or using the chatbot's menu buttons in case the keyword recognition functionality is not getting good results or the user requires some guidance to find the answer.

Machine Learning Chatbots

These are chatbots that use machine learning and artificial intelligence and perform far better than the above-mentioned chatbots (Engati, n.d.). These chatbots learn from their experience with the customers/users and improve their performance with time. Context-aware chatbots are smart enough and improve themselves based on customer queries and also provide customized solutions.

Figure 2. Types of Chatbot Technologies

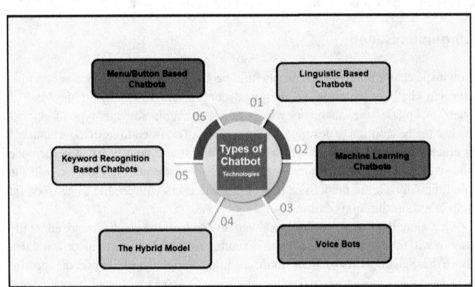

The Hybrid Model

Machine learning and chatbots need large volumes of data to provide the best performance. Since business organizations could not provide the same, the hybrid chatbots model which provides the best of both the rule-based chatbots and machine learning models is always opted for (Engati, n.d.).

Voice Bots

Voice-based chatbots are used with virtual assistants like Apple's Siri, to Amazon's Alexa due to the convenience it provides. Since it is always easy to speak out rather than type, voice bots are usually preferred in business applications.

In selecting the specific type of chatbot for the business application, it is important to understand the several use cases from the point of users (Engati, n.d.). In addition, the type of user interface that will provide the best solutions for all categories of users which will convert the users to customers, drive sales and improve the overall consumer experience are the deciding factors.

Power of Chatbots

Customer engagement is an essential activity to promote business growth. Chatbots are the most advanced and promising customer engagement tools that streamline the interaction between users and services in enhancing customer experience. With only a few banks like Master Card, Bank of America, JP Morgan Chase, Capital One, and American Express using chatbots to support their services, by 2022, cost savings of over $8 billion is expected in the banking industry. The cost of service is experienced between $0.5 and $0.7 per interaction using chatbots (Singh Gill, 2022).

Based on original research conducted by DigitasLBi and Harris Poll, more than one in three Americans would consider buying a bot. It is estimated that consumers spend $55.80 on average per purchase (Singh Gill, 2022).

Significant and expensive call centres can be replaced with chatbots and can also provide 24/7 customer support. Unlike human beings, machines don't get weary. Hence there is no possibility of spiking at customers halfway through a support call, thus, eliminating the tendency for human error. Juniper Networks claims that these technologies will streamline customer support and save businesses and consumers over 2.5 billion customer service hours by 2023(Jay Selig, 2022). It has also been estimated that e-commerce sales from chatbot interactions will total $112 billion by 2023 (Jay Selig, 2022).

According to the statistics mentioned by Jay Selig (Jay Selig, 2022),

- the growth of chatbots as a brand communication channel has seen a growth of 92%.
- sixty-seven percent of global consumers use chatbots.
- approximately 75-90% of healthcare and banking queries will be handled by chatbots in 2022.
- customer support costs are expected to save businesses to the extent of 30%.

Chatbots or digital service tools are expected to provide the following benefits (Jay Selig, 2022):

- Sixty-Eight percent of customers cite 24-hour support.
- Sixty-Four percent of customers cite quick answers to simple questions.
- Fifty-one percent of customers cite instant responses.

Chatbot Advantages

Using a chatbot for business is rapidly enticing more organizations and has become a common practice not only to improve global business but also to enhance marketing, sales, and customer service operations. The presence of a chatbot on a website demonstrates to site visitors that a company is serious about embracing new technologies to provide the best service possible to its clients(What Are the Benefits of Chatbots? 2021 Chatbot Guide, n.d.). Users are switching from complicated websites and apps with hierarchical menus to a command-line interface that is more user-friendly and customizable thanks to chatbots. With a limited budget, the chatbot is a better option than Google Adwords because it is simpler to set up, requires minimal upkeep, and enables the testing of various marketing messages for a lower cost than any other channel. There isn't a market that this kind of advertising and marketing wouldn't succeed. Also, the chatbot industry is anticipated to reach $9.4 billion in 2024 at a compound annual growth rate (CAGR) of 29.7%, up from $2.6 billion in 2019 (Top 10 Benefits of Using AI Chatbots in Your Business, n.d.).

Any communication from a branded company to customers should be timely and effective, whether it's for sales, support, or marketing. To ensure customer satisfaction and retention, high levels of service must be provided. Using AI chatbots to provide personalized customer service can be professional, consistent, branded, and automated (Perera et al., 2019). Approximately 44% of US consumers prefer chatbots to humans for customer support, according to an online survey (Bafna, 2021). Though AI chatbots aren't intended to replace human agents entirely, they perform tasks that are difficult for humans to accomplish alone. Their popularity is not limited to industry-agnostic brands, but also extends to marketing, sales, lead generation, and customer support within companies. The advantages of using a chatbot in business have the following benefits.

Improved Interpersonal Communications

Chatbots are effective in enhancing corporate communications and business operations. For instance, chatbot software could be deployed for messenger during the onboarding process. Instead of rushing to several departments to have their questions answered, recruits can ask the AI chatbot to answer all of their questions (*11 Chatbot Software Advantages for Business*, n.d.). Chatbots assist customers with finding out about a company's services, checking product availability, finding store locations, making reservations or bookings, assessing customer satisfaction, and much more. The engagement rates of Facebook messenger chatbots are 10 to 80 times better than email marketing compared with an organic post on a news feed which has only 1 percent of visibility (Voroneckis, 2019). Hence, it is evident that messenger chatbots are an effective means of getting leads. Using conversational AI helps in answering customers' questions, reduces confusion on what to buy, eliminates navigation issues on the business website, and makes the shopping process more transparent, including registration, payment, checkout, and delivery. As a result, the organization's brand's value and perception will be strengthened (Bafna, 2021).

Reach Out To New Clients

A business can reach out to new clients by being active on particular message chatbots, such as Facebook Messenger. Otherwise, it's not possible that these clients would call or email the business organization(*11 Chatbot Software Advantages for Business*, n.d.).

Constant Accessibility

Whether day or night, chatbots can be used to answer client concerns! They don't require sleep! Human customer support would need to rotate teams, which would be more challenging to manage, making it much more difficult to do. This implies that chatbots can respond to consumer questions anytime they arise, which promotes greater customer loyalty. Customers may switch to another firm that offers superior customer service if businesses don't resolve consumer issues as soon as possible.

Round-the-clock availability of services using chatbots helps customers more than businesses. It also helps businesses whether they be local or global. As a result, customers will be able to get their queries answered instantly, which will not only satisfy them to a great extent but it will also be easy to advance them along the sales funnel.

It will be easier for the customers to reach a representative within their working hours without having to wait. This will lead to a higher level of trust and satisfaction which in turn will increase overall sales and is advantageous to the company (*11 Chatbot Software Advantages for Business*, n.d.).

Reliable Responses

With customer service executives and agents, the responses could differ from one another which will irritate any customer to some extent. However, if chatbots are used to address the majority of the client's frequent questions, it will produce a consistent response. This will assist in regaining the confidence of the clients in the business (*11 Chatbot Software Advantages for Business*, n.d.).

Multilingual

With AI-powered chatbots, customers will receive personalized, contextual, value-driven support. Support operations can be expanded to new markets and target audiences can receive personalized experiences (Bafna, 2021). They can understand and answer in any language. Although this benefit would appear to be for consumers as well, it can also be advantageous for enterprises. If the chatbot can answer people's questions from throughout the nation in different languages, it will help the business grow and expand its multilingual customer database (*11 Chatbot Software Advantages for Business*, n.d.).

Cost Reductions

While the cost of adopting an efficient AI-powered chatbot can be high, it can be a worthwhile investment for the company. When compared to the conventional customer service approach, which involves expenses for infrastructure, personnel pay, and training, it is more affordable. With conversational messaging, customer satisfaction can be improved by offering prompt, real-time support. Though introducing chatbot software could incur a cost initially, in the long term, it will appear to be far less expensive than hiring a group of customer service executives. The cost of chatbot software will be significantly outweighed by the cost of their salaries, infrastructure, training, and other variables (*11 Chatbot Software Advantages for Business*, n.d.). Personal touch to conversations, real-time responses, and one-to-one responses are considered the best tips to boost customer engagement using chatbots (Patel, 2019).

Higher Engagement and Increased Sales

Real-time chatbot communication is possible with users of an organization's website and followers on social media. This stands out in sharp contrast to other brand content that is typically only passively accessed. Such interaction can help visitors stay on the website longer, increase sales, and boost SEO. Social media engagement can improve sales by up to 40% (Voroneckis, 2019). Because of their adaptable design, chatbots may be easily integrated with various channels to increase engagement. For example, a chatbot can be programmed to interact with humanlike natural sound and humor which in turn will make customers put in their comfort zone and makes the conversations more pleasant.

Chatbots help in getting the actual information about the customers. A straightforward illustration of this would be a discussion with a client who has made an online reservation. The customer can be directed to an online checkout page by the bot, who can then clinch the deal with the pleased customer. The customer engagement rate with chatbots is more than eighty percent when compared with email marketing which is just a three percent open rate (Voroneckis, 2019). Customer engagement is crucial to running a successful business. Constellation Research found that businesses that increased engagement could achieve 22% more by cross-selling, increased order sizes from 5% to 8%, and sales revenue by 51% from 13% (What Are the Benefits of Chatbots? 2021 Chatbot Guide, n.d.).

Based on a customer's interests and needs, chatbots powered by AI can recommend products and introduce them to new goods and services. According to several business organizations, chatbots are considered a painless platform to increase their sales by giving algorithm-driven recommendations for clients. Additionally, surveys show that chatbots can boost sales by an average of 67 percent by accelerating the conversion process and providing quick responses with little wait time (Bafna, 2021). Also, it can respond quickly and continuously to customer inquiries (*11 Chatbot Software Advantages for Business*, n.d.).

Recognize Clients Better

Rarely do customers have the opportunity to speak with a company and share their problems. Using chatbots, the clients will have the option to communicate with the company whenever the need arises. Additionally, it might assist in identifying the biggest problems the customers have and enhance the general caliber of the company's offerings (*11 Chatbot Software Advantages for Business*, n.d.).

Smart Decisions

AI chatbots and CRMs can help an organization understand customer behavior, helping it improve products and services. Moreover, they can help determine how customers behave and track purchasing patterns. They can also help to optimize low-conversion pages. Furthermore, because conversations are recorded, they can be measured and the performance of the chatbot can be adjusted.

Fast Responses

Customer service representatives can serve only one customer at a time. During peak hours, a big line of customers has to be dealt with. Other clients must wait in the interim, since agents can only handle a few people concurrently, even with a centralized dashboard. However, chatbot software can listen to numerous consumers at once if it is designed and chosen for that option. Hence, customers have to wait less and be satisfied because they will get answers to their issues right away. Chatbots also improve the average response time. Keeping the customers happy with the products and services is beneficial for business (*11 Chatbot Software Advantages for Business*, n.d.).

Data Collection and Chat Logs

Data collection from customers with chatbots can be quite effective. They can interact with the customers and collect data about them, including names and email addresses. Integrating the chatbot with Customer Relationship Management (CRM) will make it simple to get these facts. Additionally, chatbots can be used to get information from clients about their preferences and then tailor services to better meet their demands. Any conversation a business has with a consumer needs to be documented. For instance, some chatbots can record interactions and provide clients with a copy of the recorded dialogue. This can be used as a reference at any time in the future (*11 Chatbot Software Advantages for Business*, n.d.).

Scalability

Scaling and optimizing the support channels may be a priority for an organization if the business has to grow and reach more potential customers. The platform can help the organization handle the increased influx of customer questions without having to alter the support operations or invest in a lot of capital. With a well-built chatbot, an organization can engage thousands of people at once and answer their questions, offering special coupons or limited-time promotions (Voroneckis, 2019).

Managing Possibilities

Customer service is constant and friendly, eliminating the irritation caused by cold calls from the customer. Hence, pushing notifications about new products and services can be done easily with chatbots. Utilizing established technology on social media platforms, companies can offer products and services directly to customers. The chatbot can do a variety of small, but extremely important things like scheduling appointments, checking emails, pulling data, and most importantly, providing conversational updates to family, friends, and customers. The entire digital life of the organization will be integrated into one place, where all of the organization's activities can be accessed and handled automatically within a short period.

Infinite Persistence

Both customers and customer service agents can become impatient at times. But, a chatbot is not susceptible to human-related failures, such as losing patience or getting frustrated at repeated questions. Under such circumstances, chatbots excel above human agents. Since it is a machine, the customer service chatbot has little risk of losing its cool. Additionally, it encourages calm behavior and expedites the delivery of the desired solution. Since a satisfied client base is advantageous to businesses chatbots are more suitable (*11 Chatbot Software Advantages for Business*, n.d.).

Employee Experience Transformation

According to a report by Deloitte, the organizations that invested most heavily in employee experience were listed 28 times more in Fast Company's list of the most innovative companies. Investments in enriching the employee experience increase Customer service, Innovation, Employer attractiveness, Admiration and respect, and brand value (Todd, 2022). Chatbots are used to transform the experience of the experienced employee across the organization.

With the introduction and the evolution of AI, natural language can be used to get a better understanding of how operations are carried out in an enterprise. Chatbots provide better employee engagement and provide the knowledge of doing operational tasks at ease which will enable the employees to contribute towards larger business values for an organization.

Chatbots are used in standard messaging channels for sending notifications or for top-down communication from the top management to the organization as a whole for direct dissemination of information.

It is used to get correct data insights from the customers without any bias as compared to humans meant for similar services. Chatbots used for such services are called business intelligence chatbots. The productivity of an organization can be further improved by using chatbots as personal assistants.

Chatbot Applications

Chatbot use is becoming more popular across many industries, including banking, healthcare, e-commerce, and education (Balatamoghna & Nagajayanthi 2022).

Chatbots are being used more frequently to assist patients with their inquiries as a result of COVID-19. To track the number of persons who contracted the COVID-19 virus, and respond to frequently asked questions, and other tasks, Laranjo et al. (2018) developed the COVID-19 chatbot, Chasey (El Hefny et al., 2021).

Medbot was developed by Bharti et al. utilizing artificial intelligence to assist patients by offering healthcare recommendations, treatment sessions, and other services (Bharti et al., 2020). Chatbots assist with medical treatment, offer suggestions relating to healthcare, and give patients healthcare information tailored to their requirements (Adamopoulou & Moussiades, 2020). Users must register and submit certain personal information, including some delicate healthcare information, to use the existing health chatbots (Wang & Siau, 2018). However, the rising popularity of chatbots is raising questions about privacy and security. Because the data is so sensitive, there is a greater privacy risk because users are ignorant of how chatbots use or disclose it.

Women will be able to report incidences of sexual harassment and gender-based violence thanks to an app and chatbot developed by the Ministry of Women's Affairs Secretary of State Hou Samith, MPA - Racha, Cambodia. It is intended that this will make it easier to track instances of these detrimental events, particularly among vulnerable women and girls, including those who work in factories (Kimmarita, 2022).

The app will make it simpler to tell victims of violence about the resources available to them and to report and refer violent situations to the appropriate authorities. The victim's confidentiality and privacy will be protected by the app.

Robot therapy has come as the use of mental health chatbots for therapy is on the rise. Although it's controversial, this might function best in a hybrid strategy where AI can automatically decide when to switch the conversation to human contact for the best of both worlds (Team, 2022).

Complex businesses with distributed or decentralized processes need distinct solutions sent across a variety of channels, according to complex Omni channel synthesis enabled by Artificial Intelligence. Compared to generic or cookie-cutter chatbot responses, this offers a far more personalized response. With voice and chat data bundled together in a seamless, coordinated manner, chatbots are increasingly being utilized to meet individuals where they are searching for information – Short Message Service (SMS), Whatsapp, call centres, etc.

As immersive learning is getting more popular, advanced Virtual Assistants and VR/AR headset technology can be useful tools for onboarding and welcoming new employees to a firm. Training can be designed to efficiently focus on the development of important skills to swiftly bring individuals up to speed with a tailored approach (Team, 2022).

By giving the chat system a name (such as Siri or Alexa), users experience an emotional connection (both consciously and subconsciously), as if they are talking to a reliable friend without the pressure of a personal relationship. Customer and employee retention rates spike with continued use resulting in satisfying results (Team, 2022).

Total Experience Automation (TX) is defined as the sum of the user, staff, and customer experiences. To provide the best service possible from a TX viewpoint, businesses need a complex, dynamic system that will optimize operations across the board, support the company's whole ecosystem, and flawlessly integrate with all the moving elements (Team, 2022).

The use of chatbots is rapidly growing across the economy, particularly in industries like insurance where customer satisfaction has a direct impact on the bottom line. Because the use of chatbots as a brand communication channel has nearly doubled since 2019, two-thirds of all customers globally have encountered at least one chatbot in the most recent years (Negosanti, 2022).

Building a Chatbot

There are several means by which a chatbot could be built. Nowadays, coding is not essential for building chatbots. A framework called Dialogflow, which is owned by Google, enables programmers to create human-computer interfaces that can support Natural Language Processing (NLP). Dialogflow has a prebuilt agent, Small Talk, coding is faster, it can be used on 20+ platforms from Google to Twitter, it supports all kinds of devices from wearables, to phones to devices and it is used in 14+ languages around the world (Ahmed Rebai, 2018). In essence, it enables developers to create Digital Programs that communicate with consumers in natural languages. So much so that the developer may claim that Dialogflow makes Conversational User Experience Platforms (CUXP) possible. Dialogflow is capable of analyzing a variety of consumer inputs, including text and audio inputs (such as a phone or voice recording). Additionally, it has the option of responding to clients through text or artificial speech. Dialogflow gives developers the option to "one-click integrate" with the majority of the widely used messaging services, including Facebook, Twitter, Instagram, and others.

The general steps in building a chatbot involve the following activities (Tettelin, 2022).

i.   Defining the scope
ii. Defining the use cases
iii. Selection of Technology
iv. Understanding the Users
v.   Defining the personality of the chatbot
vi. Mapping the flow of the chatbot

vii. Defining the edge cases
viii. Error management
ix. Testing
x. Optimising

CHALLENGES IN USING CHATBOTS

The technology behind chatbots is quite delicate. Since chatbots are prone to flaws, a hacker may use them to disseminate hate speech, incite violence, use racist or other inappropriate language, and utterly ruin a company's reputation as well as that of the entire community. Because of this, chatbot security and privacy are of vital importance while creating them. In addition, scientific literature reveals several challenges in using chatbots irrespective of the numerous benefits it provides.

Difficulty in Designing Chatbots

Natural Language Processing, is incredibly essential for customer service applications in chatbots. But designing chatbots capable of natural conversations indistinguishable from humans is difficult. Natural language processing is a component of machine learning used to communicate with users via text and respond to their questions. However, this necessitates intricate programming, which is challenging for businesses. Building chatbots from scratch is more difficult, which is why numerous web platforms make it easier for organizations to construct and operate chatbots (What Are the Advantages and Disadvantages of Chatbots in Business? 2020).

Data Protection

The data collected from the customers should be kept secure. Secure data transmission is required from the chatbot to the CRM (Barker, 2020). Only pertinent data from the customers should be acquired, and it must be maintained securely.

Inability To Understand Emotions

Since chatbots are composed of codes, it is challenging for them to understand the user's emotions. They might not be able to tell whether the person they are conversing with is joyful, anxious, or unhappy as a result (Barker, 2020). This could make the chatbot seem emotionally indifferent, which could be bad for a brand's reputation.

Limited Response

Companies need to have human customer service agents who can handle these issues because automated systems cannot handle complex problems or provide answers to questions that are not in the script. The market is currently seeing an increase in the sophistication of chatbots, therefore this is gradually changing.

Maintenance

Chatbots need ongoing maintenance. Businesses can't merely build a chatbot and hope that it will always appropriately respond to client questions. The company's products evolve, and as time goes on, so do increasingly sophisticated natural language processing (NLP) capabilities. To ensure that the chatbot has the most recent information, all of these modifications must be programmed into it. Additionally, chatbots must be routinely examined to identify the most often asked queries by users and change their responses for upcoming users.

New Challenges And Emerging Technology

Given that chatbot technology is still in its early stages, organizations might not be aware of how to address the difficulties that they face. While AI-enabled bots can adapt their behavior based on each interaction, this process can be quite costly for organizations if the first few interactions result in uninterested and uncooperative customers (Brush & Scardina, n.d.).

Various Message Formats

Different message styles may cause intentions to become unclear. Long and short utterances, numerous brief entries, and conversation bubbles with substantial content must all be handled by chatbots. Different varieties of speech patterns can be difficult for chatbots to comprehend these variations. For instance, the user might utilize slang, acronyms, or misspell words. Unfortunately, NLP's limitations prevent it from properly addressing this problem (Brush & Scardina, n.d.).

Predictably Varying Human Emotions, Moods, And Behavior

People are unpredictable, and emotions and moods regularly influence user behavior, therefore users may quickly change their ideas (Brush & Scardina, n.d.). They might want to ask for advice before giving a command. This irrationality and spontaneity must be accommodated by chatbots, as well as understood.

User Satisfaction

The best experiences are always sought after by users. They keep hoping that the chatbot will get better. To give users the idea that they are speaking with informed, dependable sources, companies that utilize chatbots must constantly update and improve them (Brush & Scardina, n.d.).

SECURITY AND PRIVACY RISKS IN CHATBOTS

The online industry is becoming more and more dependent on chatbot services that give clients information in real time. With an easy-to-use interface, chatbots respond to questions regarding the goods and services they are built for and respond engagingly. Although it satisfies the functional requirements, because it has access to enormous amounts of data and personal information, it is nonetheless susceptible to harmful actions (Bozic & Wotawa, 2018). Customer security and privacy may be compromised by chatbots with AI characteristics. Security has emerged as a critical problem that chatbots must take into consideration. Threats and vulnerabilities are the two basic types of security problems that chatbots face.

Threats

Security threats are defined as the potential for an organization's systems to be compromised. A threat is a one-time event such as malware or a DDoS attack. The system can be locked out and held for ransom as a result of targeted attacks aimed at a business (Andrej Godina, 2018). It is also possible for hackers to threaten to expose (supposedly) secure customer data. Spoofing, Tampering, Information Disclosure, Repudiation, Elevation of Privileges, and Denial of Service are the common security threats identified in computers. But protection against each type of threat is required and is ensured with availability, authorization, authenticity, integrity, confidentiality, and non-repudiation properties of the system to name a few (Ucedavélez & Morana, 2015).

Vulnerabilities

Vulnerabilities in systems allow attackers to cross privilege boundaries (i.e., take unauthorized actions) within a computer system. It is a crack in the target system that allows cybercriminals to gain access. Weak coding, outdated hardware drivers, an ineffective firewall, etc. make a system vulnerable (Firch, 2019). System vulnerabilities are mostly caused by human error. Despite this, chatbot security specialists are constantly updating the technology's defenses, ensuring any cracks are closed immediately (Andrej Godina, 2018).

Many chatbots are using cloud computing services since threats and vulnerabilities are well handled in these environments. So companies that don't use cloud services have to carefully deal with these issues since, the lack of a robust security and privacy framework in chatbots can result in the following issues (Shanbhag, 2020):

- Data breaches and loss of sensitive personal data
- Increased Mean Time To Detect and Respond (MTTD & R)
- Reduced consumer trust
- Compliance and regulatory violations
- Heavy fines and penalties

SECURITY AND PRIVACY IN CHATBOTS: A GLOBAL CONCERN

Meta, owned by Facebook, reveals that in Latin America 58% of people say they receive and send messages from the brands they consume (Cartagena, 2022). Also, two out of three people worldwide indicate that they have chatted with brands or businesses. With chatbots, businesses can save up to 30% on customer support costs, speed up response times, and answer up to 80% of routine questions (Ayat Shukairy, 2018). The technology behind Meta also makes use of recent improvements in AI that have led to significantly more linguistically skilled computer systems. It is possible to train artificial neural networks on huge amounts of data scraped from the internet to create algorithms that can summarise or generate text and conduct conversations more comprehensively and coherently than prewritten responses from traditional chatbots.

In contrast to earlier iterations of the chatbot, Meta's BlenderBot 3 can browse the internet and converse with people about almost anything (Tung, 2022). It can accomplish all of that by drawing on the features offered by earlier iterations of the BlenderBot, including personality, empathy, knowledge, and the capacity for long-term memory about discussions it has had (Silva, 2022).

A Google employee went so far as to claim that one of these AI chatbots, named LaMDA, is sentient after having a lengthy conversation with it. Despite their intelligence, most other AI language programs cannot learn new information because they are trained on a predetermined set of data, such as LaMDA and GPT-3 (Knight, 2022).

Using chatbots provides the following benefits.

- Enables seamless live communication

- Saves time and money
- Provides customer service 24x7
- Reduces person-to-person communications
- Avoids tedious time-consuming tasks
- Enables a smooth customer journey
- Reduces employee and consumer stress
- Eliminates interactive voice response systems
- Humanizes the brand
- Increases the possibility of more targeted marketing
- Aids in business growth and
- Provides prospects for advancement through machine learning and artificial intelligence.

In healthcare, it will have serious implications like poor guidance, incorrect diagnoses and failure to access timely interventions may lead to serious consequences. Information privacy is another serious consideration since natural language processing (NLP) powered virtual assistants are more sophisticated and more natural all the time, which means the patients will not be able to distinguish between a physician and a bot. It is crucial to protect user privacy and security while collecting sensitive client data, particularly in sectors like retail, consumer packaged goods, banking, healthcare, travel, etc.

While customized or personalized marketing is crucial for customer engagement, a lack of a strong privacy and security framework could result in sensitive personal data loss and data breaches, longer mean time to detect and respond (MTTD & R), decreased consumer trust, compliance, and regulatory violations, and harsh fines and penalties (Shanbhag, 2020). For example, Delta Airlines recently sued their chatbot technology provider for millions of dollars following a 2017 data breach. A total of 825,000 customers' credit card details and other personal information were exposed, according to the airline (Shanbhag, 2020). Hackers who gained access to the vendor's systems and modified the source code grabbed data about Delta Airlines customers from the chatbot on the airline's website (Shanbhag, 2020). As the global average cost of a data breach has grown to $3.92 million and chatbots have become a must-have tool in customer service operations, organizations must ensure that there is a standard security procedure and protocol in place while building and deploying chatbots (Shanbhag, 2020).

Privacy and security mechanisms for protecting the sensitive information acquired should be taken care of once the business/system requirements are identified and formalized for building the chatbot. The following security and privacy aspects have to be discussed in collaboration with the data protection officer.

- Data residency
- Data retention
- Data encryption
- Personally identifiable information handling
- Local regulations such as general data protection regulation (GDPR) requirements, the German Bundesdatenschutzgesetz (BDSG), a federal data protection act, etc.,

Thus, end-to-end encryption, compliance with the data acquired, and intent-level privacy features are achieved.

Public relations risk assessment, user consent and legal analysis, and accessibility review are other modules that need attention while building a chatbot that will overcome privacy and security breaches.

Understanding the underlying problems requires identifying and defining the crucial steps in the methodology used to develop chatbots that are pertinent to security. There are a variety of causes contributing to the increase in security threats and vulnerabilities. All of them have been thoroughly investigated, and security techniques that may be used to mitigate security holes have been presented. Modern chatbots are no longer dependent on rule-based models, but rather on natural language processing and machine learning approaches that are more up-to-date. Techniques like these learn from a conversation, which may contain sensitive information about the learner.

BEST PRACTICES IN DESIGNING A CHATBOT

With the advent of new technologies and business tools, security concerns are becoming increasingly important. In addition to providing businesses with better approaches to improving communication, bots enable organizations to discover new ways to communicate innovatively with their clients. Using chatbots for customer service will revolutionize the way companies deal with their customers. Chatbots are designed to provide customer service and ensure safety. However, there is still a great deal of speculation surrounding bot security despite all the advances they promise. The importance of bot security is growing substantially as the business framework becomes more connected than ever.

Chatbots are vulnerable to attacks by hackers that can access private and confidential information on the organization's website. Chatbots should be subjected to the same security precautions as websites. It will be more difficult for cybercriminals to prey on a website and its visitors if the security of the site is increased to several layers. To prevent hackers from stealing chatbot data, ThwateSSL certificates should be used(Learner, 2022).

A chatbot is secure when it has a conversational UI controlled by a Dialog Management System, and its intent classifier is authorized and logged securely. With GDPR and various regulatory issues around the corner, cybersecurity is presently the main concern of each organization. Questions such as how secure bots are, how data will be stored, how the information will be protected, which channels will have access to it, and so on are of main concern. Therefore, bot security is crucial in today's world. Enterprises can deploy bots in their business processes with the help of the following best practices.

Two-Factor Authentication

Two-factor authentication (2FA), also known as two-way confirmation, is a tried-and-true security measure that asks users to validate their identities through two distinct channels before accessing the chatbot. Due to the safety and security of confirming user credentials, it is employed as a powerful tool in the majority of digital services (Mathenge, 2022). By asking users to verify their identity with a verification code given to their phone or email before accessing their account, it offers an extra degree of protection (Learner, 2022). Additionally, it aids in the authorization process by allowing access to the appropriate individual and guaranteeing that data is not handled improperly or violated.

The user is authorised and given access to the bot after entering the code. Due to its thorough testing, 2FA is a very viable kind of assurance for ensuring chatbot security and safety. Many businesses, notably financial and banking ones where security is a core requirement, use bilateral verification (Dialani, 2020).

Time-Based Authentication

Better security levels may be ensured by time-based authentication. Only for the duration of the practice are validated tokens accessible. The bot immediately terminates access when the token expires (Mathenge, 2022). Before ending sessions, users are periodically asked if they are still active. The counter can stop hackers from trying to access a secure account repeatedly (Press, 2022). A hacker's repeated attempts to figure out how to access a secure account can be stopped by a "ticking clock" for the proper confirmation input (Dialani, 2020).

Web Application Firewall (WAF)

A WAF shields websites from dangerous requests and malicious traffic. Consequently, a WAF could aid in preventing dangerous bots from introducing malicious code into the iframe of a chatbot(SiteLock, 2019).

User IDs and Passwords

The chatbot might only be accessible to registered users rather than being open to everyone. Criminals aim for simple targets. A would-be cybercriminal could be deterred by taking just one more step, such as registering with a website. Verifying the user's identity is the next piece of advice for protecting chatbot data privacy. There are several ways to do that, like demanding a login, utilizing two-factor authentication, or confirming an email address or phone number. Checking if a website visitor has legitimate credentials, such as a login and password, is the goal of user authorization or authentication.

End-to-End Encryption

As cybercriminals improve their technology and intelligence, it's always feared that data during transit can be spoofed or tampered with. Encryption is important in the cyber world, and chatbot designers are undoubtedly implementing this method to ensure their chatbot's security is up to date. For businesses using chatbots, VPNs with encrypting internet traffic and messages are recommended (James, 2021). Additionally, a VPN can protect chatbots from threats and vulnerabilities. Encrypting the entire channel is essential to ensure the security of the entire conversation. Information sent can only be viewed by the sender and recipient (Press, 2022). Data cannot be extracted by hackers, regardless of whether they have access to the servers where it is stored. The data is only accessible to the two users at each end of the tunnel since public key encryption dominates. It's just random noise to everyone else. The decryption keys (Press, 2022) are needed for understanding the information. Since one of those keys is on the user's side, it is impossible to get it.

Recently, social media platforms have integrated their messaging channels with end-to-end encryption to protect themselves from digital threats (Mathenge, 2022).

Biometric Authentication

Biometrics such as iris scans and fingerprinting can be used for authentication instead of user ids and passwords (Dialani, 2020). Because iris and retinal scans have no physical contact with the user's body or device, iris and retinal scans are becoming more popular and safer than fingerprints (Mathenge, 2022). It protects chatbot data from unauthorized access. Chatbot data is only accessible to authorized users. There are a variety of authentication methods, such as fingerprints, iris recognition, or even voice prints.

Biometric verification ensures chatbot security. It is not unexpected that such developments are becoming more and more popular because they guarantee the security of portable electronics. Due to its effectiveness in ensuring personal device security, the iris is gaining popularity and can scan distinctive fingerprints. Thanks to developments in biometrics, iris scans, and distinctive fingerprints are becoming increasingly common and substantially more reliable.

Authentication Timeouts

The usage of authentication timeouts in chatbots enforces the requirement to produce fresh tokens after a brief interval. A temporal limit is imposed by this security procedure on how long an authenticated user may remain "logged in." Websites that deal with financial transactions, like banks, display this functionality. 2-Factor authentication is used to validate the user to secure Chatbot. Another technique to guarantee chatbot security is to use authentication timeouts. Since the token can be used for a predetermined amount of time, banks employ this method more frequently.

A pop-up window either prompts the user to log back in or asks if they are still active, or it simply notifies them that their time has run out. This can limit the amount of time a cybercriminal has to try to guess their way into a guarded account.

Self Destructing Messages

Self-destructing messages are useful for enhancing the security of the chatbot and the discussions. The messages and any sensitive information are permanently deleted after the chatbot's chat session is over or after a certain period. The privacy and security of users are safeguarded, and data breaches are avoided, by erasing all messages after a certain amount of time. By General Data Protection Regulation (GDPR), acquired data should not be kept for longer than necessary (Learner, 2022). The Chatbot should be hosted on a secure server to maintain its security. User data will be kept private and the Chatbot will be protected from hackers thanks to a secure server.

Using Digital Security Protocols

As their names imply, many levels of encryption and security principles are added by digital security protocols including Transport Layer Security (TLS), Hypertext

Transfer Protocol Secure (HTTPS), Secure Socket Layer (SSL), and others. These protocols also operate across various platforms (Mathenge, 2022). A top-notch security technology called Secure Sockets Layer can be used to create an encrypted relationship between a server and a client (Learner, 2022). An SSL certificate protects and maintains the privacy of data. Because it helps safeguard user data, including passwords, credit card numbers, and personal information, SSL is crucial for chatbots.

1. To encrypt all communications between the chatbot and its users, it is essential to get the Thawte SSL. This certificate guarantees data security and protects it from being intercepted by unauthorized parties.
2. To prevent unwanted access to the chatbot's server, it is essential to install a firewall. It will aid in preventing hackers from accessing the chatbot's data.

The certificates are available in various formats, each with unique characteristics and advantages. Domain Validation, Organization Validation, or Extended Validation certificates can all be chosen based on the user's requirements. All of these certificates have a warranty to cover damages if something goes wrong and use 256-bit encryption to safeguard user data.

There shouldn't be any problems as long as the IT security teams ensure that information is transferred through HTTP through scrambled connections secured by TLS or SSL (Press, 2022). By doing so, it is possible to securely lock down any potential indirect access to the business system (Dialani, 2020).

These security protocols work together on platforms that already have internal security measures, and there is more than one layer of encryption and protection to protect users from the start. These security protocols make use of encryption and cryptography. It is necessary to decrypt the data using a specific method, mathematical formula, logical key, or a combination of these (Dialani, 2020).

Check the Website for Vulnerabilities

To protect data, any chatbot engaging with website visitors needs to be adequately secured. Any website with a chatbot should have its security constantly checked for errors. Vulnerability screening is required to protect personal and company data. To make sure that the website has not been hacked and infected with malware or viruses, individuals check their website for one of these most popular reasons.

Regulatory Concerns

A domain-specific accreditation is also essential when working in privacy-sensitive sectors like industrial chatbots, in addition to government regulations. While accreditation is a common industry practice, it does not guarantee an organization's security. Compliance is a way to ensure domain-specific security. Two kinds of compliances namely common and industry-specific are in practice.

Under "common" compliance, Industry agnostic compliances apply based on demographic factors. International Organization for Standardization/International Electrotechnical Commission(ISO/IEC 27002), National Institute of Standards and Technology(NIST), and General Data Protection Regulation(GDPR) are some examples of common compliances.

Similarly, Industry-specific compliances apply based on industry and demography. Health Insurance Portability and Accountability Act (HIPPA), Payment Card Industry Data Security Standard (PCI-DSS), and Family Educational Rights and Privacy Act (FERPA) are some of the compliances meant for healthcare, payment cards, and education respectively (Saxena, 2019).

According to the demographics of various industries, there are other Non-Tech accreditations required. When developing a chatbot solution, it's good to keep these three points in mind. An authentication mechanism is in place for all users. The organization must know who is inside the system.

Organizations should have an authorization system that gives only the minimum permissions a person needs to perform their duties. It should also have a monitoring system that logs all activities occurring in its system, monitoring who is doing it, and ensuring they are authorized. It is essential to follow these measures to ensure the robust security of the chatbot system.

Exclusive Chatbot Account

Instead of using pre-existing customer credentials, it is wise to create unique bot accounts with comparable access levels across all applications. Only some accounts must be accessed by separate accounts, and they must be used for automated business processes. It increases the efficiency of the system and also provides clarity and transparency (Dialani, 2020). The key advantage is that it safeguards sensitive corporate information (Press, 2022).

Technology Stack

The chatbot has three basic functional units namely the Client Platforms, Natural Language Understanding (NLU), and backend infrastructure (Saxena, 2019). Ensuring the security of each of these functional units is essential. Checking answers to these questions before beta testing will confirm the security of the chatbot implementation.

1. Given that the client program is executed on the client's computer, can they reverse it? If so, would doing so reveal any vulnerabilities, such as a hardcoded password or access tokens, an insecure API, or server access? (Saxena, 2019)
2. Can other apps access or read sensitive data such as personally identifiable information (PII) of the app stored in local storage without decryption?
3. Since the client program is executed on the client's computer, and a user is limited to a maximum of 15 spins, can they reverse it?
4. Does the intent classifier distinguish between the intentions of normal users and premium users?

If a user can use the bot without logging in, is there any intent

1. In a chatbot that will not respond to questions and instead prompt him to log in?
2. Are the conversations recorded? Is the owner of the logs removed or encrypted the PII so that no one from the internal team can view them?
3. Is it certain that the backend development and infrastructure deployment follow optimal security standards under the chatbot security specification?

Educating Digital Security

Despite a growing awareness of the importance of digital security, people remain the system's most vulnerable link (Press, 2022). As long as user error exists, chatbot security will remain a major concern despite using advanced technologies (Mathenge, 2022). Educating the employees is necessary to ensure that digital advancements, such as bots, are used safely (Dialani, 2020).

Including developers and, IT specialists in bot development are as essential as educating employees to utilize the system safely to counteract the threats. Furthermore, it gives confidence to the team to engage with the system in a safe manner (Dialani, 2020).

Safe Chat Bot Management

To increase security, bot administration and client onboarding are crucial (Press, 2022). The design should have a platform that is capable of controlling integrated user access, approving bot development, delegating users to bots, etc. (Dialani, 2020). Observation and control can be centralized by a dashboard that shows all bots, users, tasks, patterns, handoffs, etc. (Press, 2022). A mechanism for keeping track of the activity of the bot in various log files, and creating custom logs to provide even more traceability is essential while using chatbots. Additionally, custom logging can help create log files that are easier to read for business users (Dialani, 2020).

FUTURE PROSPECTS

Artificial intelligence is impacting how marketing campaigns are managed and how companies communicate with their customers. With the advent of AI, the field of digital marketing has seen considerable upheaval. It assists businesses in developing effective digital strategies, optimizing marketing initiatives, and increasing return on investment. AI affects many facets of life with the aid of smart devices, chatbots, and self-driving automobiles. To provide a customized customer experience, these are intended to ascertain the preferences and interests of the client. Data entry, screening leads from a marketing campaign, and responding to commonly asked inquiries from clients are all examples of mundane and repetitive work that AI and chatbots may quickly complete.

Chatbots may offer expertise through automated processes, which is a very effective technique to increase the clientele. With the use of chatbots, targeted and predictive content, content creation, and image recognition technologies, AI can improve the customer experience.

Best Trends according to a global report by Vantage Market Research, the size of the global healthcare chatbots market is expected to surpass USD 431.47 million by 2028 at a CAGR of 15.20% over the projected period (V. M. Research, 2022).

According to Gartner research, the chatbot market will reach $8.8 billion in revenue by 2026. Between 2021 and 2023, a 320% increase in global voice assistant transaction values is anticipated, per research from Yellow.ai and C-Zentrix (Team, 2022).

Over the next few years, it is projected that the global conversational AI market would grow significantly as a result of the increasing demand for chatbots and AI-based virtual assistants among various companies. It is predicted that the chatbot sub-segment would expand at a rapid rate by 2028. Regionally, it is anticipated that the Asia-Pacific market would have profitable expansion throughout the analysis period (Dive, 2022b).

According to a report by Fortune Business Insight, the global chatbot market size is projected to increase astonishingly between 2020 and 2027, with a CAGR of 22.5%. Additionally, the market has a 2019 value of USD 396.2 million and is anticipated to have a 2027 value of USD 1,953.3 million (Insights, 2021).

According to a research analysis by Research Dive, the global chatbot market is anticipated to grow with a 28.7% CAGR and surpass $19,570 million in the 2020 to 2027 timeframe (Dive, 2022a).

Straits Research estimates USD 526 million as the global market value for chatbots in 2021. By 2030, it is anticipated to reach USD 3,619 million, expanding at a CAGR of 23.9%. (2022–2030). The market's largest share will go to North America, which will expand at a CAGR of 25.2% by 2030 (Research, 2022).

The global no-code AI platform market is predicted to expand at a CAGR of 28.1% from 2022 to 2032, as per Future Market Insights. The market is anticipated to be valued at US$ 3,231.8 Mn in 2022 and US$ 38,518.0 Mn by the end of 2032 (Newswire, 2022).

In addition to the e-commerce market, the chatbot application has become more popular in the online gaming sector. With more consumers investing time and money in online gaming, chatbots' true potential is being gradually unlocked by gaming companies. These chatbots offer additional assistance channels while observing gamers' propensity to communicate through messaging apps such as WhatsApp, Line, Discord, etc.,

In the online gaming sector, chatbots are the most effective method for improving relationships with players. Chatbots assist the online gaming business in saving millions of dollars in costs by improving the consumer experience, lowering cart abandonment issues, and automating operations. As more gaming firms investigate and incorporate chatbot solutions into their operations, the industry anticipates that chatbot adoption will skyrocket in the coming days.

CONCLUSION

In customer service technology and artificial intelligence, chatbots are an exciting and innovative development that could revolutionize the way businesses interact with their customers. With this technology, the customer service provider has taken a giant step forward, as it offers a more personalized experience, a quicker response, and a user-friendly portal that makes use of already-familiar technology. As digital technology has become more prevalent in the digital age, online communication safety has become increasingly important. The role of bots in facilitating communication is crucial. Nevertheless, personal information must be protected and kept private. Keeping customer information safe is important for business owners. Ensure that the bots are safe to use. Data and information protection security measures should be taken and they should be easy to interact with.

Building confidence is crucial for a successful online company. Customers can give their personal information because they believe it is secure. By utilizing safe and reliable bots, businesses can guarantee that they provide the greatest customer service possible to their clients. Multi-layer, robust, and comprehensive security is essential. Businesses can give a truly 21st-century storefront to a tech-savvy client base that now demands chat-based interactions across a wide range of platforms thanks to chatbot security. A chatbot is a secure program that, if the right security precautions are taken, may significantly enhance customer satisfaction, enable businesses to reduce expenses, and offer a tremendous chance to automate high-volume client inquiries. Competitive firms intentionally differentiate themselves from the competition while interacting with customers. Chatbots are the new multi-talented individuals in this regard. According to research studies conducted by many organizations, AI-powered chatbots are considered a powerful technology that will provide value to businesses and strengthen the global economy.

REFERENCES

Adamopoulou, E., & Moussiades, L. (2020). Chatbots: History, technology, and applications. *Machine Learning with Applications, 2,* 100006. Sciencedirect. doi:10.1016/j.mlwa.2020.100006

Ahmed, R. (2018, November 15). *Dialogflow*. Slideshare. https://www.slideshare. net/Ahmedrebai2/dialogflow-123084875

Akma, N., Hafiz, M., Zainal, A., Fairuz, M., & Adnan, Z. (2018). Review of Chatbots Design Techniques. *International Journal of Computers and Applications, 181*(8), 7–10. https://doi.org/10.5120/ijca2018917606

Bafna, S. (2021, October 8). *8 Benefits of Using AI Chatbots for Your Business and Customers – Customer Service Blog from HappyFox*. Customer Service Blog from HappyFox - Improve Customer Service & Experience. https://blog.happyfox.com/8-benefits-of-using-ai-chatbots-fo r-your-business-and-customers/

Balatamoghna, B., & Nagajayanthi, B. (2022). Enhancement of Productivity Using Chatbots. In *Futuristic Communication and Network Technologies* (pp. 885–892). Springer.

Barker, S. (2020, June 16). *Pros and Cons of AI Chatbots: All You Must Know*. MoEngage Blog. https://www.moengage.com/blog/pros-and-cons-of-ai-chatbots/

Bharti, U., Bajaj, D., Batra, H., Lalit, S., Lalit, S., & Gangwani, A. (2020, June 1). *Medbot: Conversational Artificial Intelligence Powered Chatbot for Delivering Tele-Health after COVID-19*. IEEE Xplore. doi:10.1109/ICCES48766.2020.9137944

Bleu, N. (2021, October 5). *29 Top Chatbot Statistics For 2022: Usage, Demographics, Trends*. ADA.

Bleu, N. (2023). 29 Top Chatbox Statistics for 2023. *Blogging Wizard.* https://bloggingwizard.com/chatbot-statistics/#:~:text=23%25 %20of%20customer%20service%20companies

Bozic, J., & Wotawa, F. (2018). Security Testing for Chatbots. *Testing Software and Systems*, 33–38. doi:10.1007/978-3-319-99927-2_3

Brush, K., & Scardina, J. (n.d.). What is a Chatbot and Why is it Important? *Tech Target.* https://www.techtarget.com/searchcustomerexperience/definiti on/chatbot

Cartagena, S. (2022, May 2). Chatbots, their positive impact and how to take advantage of the customer experience. *Entrepreneur.* https://www.entrepreneur. com/article/426555

Chatbot Software Advantages for Business. (n.d.). Botup. https://botup.com/chatbot-software-advantages

Chaturvedi, S. (2022, September 30). *10 Best Chatbots In India.* Haptik. Www. haptik.ai. https://www.haptik.ai/blog/10-best-ai-chatbots-in-india

Dialani, P. (2020, August 8). *You are being redirected...* Www.analyticsinsight. net. https://www.analyticsinsight.net/top-8-best-practices-to-ens ure-bot-security/

Dive, R. (2022a, May 9). Global Conversational AI Market Expected to Rise at a CAGR of 21.4% and Surpass $13,291.3 Million during the Forecast Period from 2021 to 2028. *GlobeNewswire News Room.* https://www.globenewswire.com/en/news-release/2022/05/09/243 8721/0/en/Global-Conversational-AI-Market-Expected-to-Rise-a t-a-CAGR-of-21-4-and-Surpass-13-291-3-Million-during-the-For ecast-Period-from-2021-to-2028-224-Pages-Research-Dive.html

Dive, R. (2022b, May 18). Global Chatbot Market Expected to Grow with 28.7% CAGR and Exceed $19,570 Million in the 2020 to 2027 Timeframe. *GlobeNewswire News Room.* https://www.globenewswire.com/news-release/2022/05/18/244612 8/0/en/Global-Chatbot-Market-Expected-to-Grow-with-28-7-CAGR -and-Exceed-19-570-Million-in-the-2020-to-2027-Timeframe-241 -Pages-Reveals-by-Research-Dive.html

Editorial Team. (2022, August 20). 7 Ways Chatbots Improve Life. *InsideBIGDATA.* https://insidebigdata.com/2022/08/20/7-ways-chatbots-improve -life/

El Hefny, W., El Bolock, A., Herbert, C., & Abdennadher, S. (2021). Chase Away the Virus: A Character-Based Chatbot for COVID-19. *2021 IEEE 9th International Conference on Serious Games and Applications for Health(SeGAH)*. IEEE. https://doi.org/10.1109/segah52098.2021.9551895

Engati. (n.d.). *Chatbot Architecture*. Engati. https://www.engati.com/glossary/chatbot-architecture

Engati. (n.d.). *Types of chatbots*. Engati. https://www.engati.com/blog/types-of-chatbots-and-their-appl ications

Firch, J. (2019, June 17). *What Are The Common Types Of Network Vulnerabilities?* PurpleSec. https://purplesec.us/common-network-vulnerabilities/

Firdaus, M., Golchha, H., Ekbal, A., & Bhattacharyya, P. (2020). A Deep Multi-task Model for Dialogue Act Classification, Intent Detection and Slot Filling. *Cognitive Computation*. doi:10.1007/s12559-020-09718-4

Godina, A. (2018, January 17). *Chatbot Security - A Guide For Businesses*. Inform Comms. https://www.inform-comms.com/chatbot-security-what-you-need-to-know/

IBM Research Editorial Staff. (2011, February 3). Knowing what it knows: selected nuances of Watson's strategy. IBM *Research Blog*. https://www.ibm.com/blogs/research/2011/02/knowing-what-it-k nows-selected-nuances-of-watsons-strategy/

Ilamathi, K., & Banu, R. A., & Divya Priya, B. (2020). Integration of Intelligent Conversational Software or Chat-Bot. In *International Journal of Innovative Research in Science, Engineering and Technology*. http://www.ijirset.com/upload/2020/may/15_Integration_NC.PDF

Insights, F. B. (2021, December 2). Global Chatbot Market: Presence of Large Companies in North America to Facilitate Growth, while Generating USD 1,953.3 Million by 2027, reports Fortune Business InsightsTM. *GlobeNewswire News Room*. https://www.globenewswire.com/news-release/2021/12/02/234474 3/0/en/Global-Chatbot-Market-Presence-of-Large-Companies-in-North-America-to-Facilitate-Growth-while-Generating-USD-1-95 3-3-Million-by-2027-reports-Fortune-Business-Insights.html

James, R. (2021, February 11). Are Chatbots Vulnerable? Best Practices to Ensure Chatbots Security. *Medium*. https://chatbotslife.com/are-chatbots-vulnerable-best-practi ces-to-ensure-chatbots-security-d301b9f6ce17

Kim, L. (2020, March 11). The Big List of the World's Most Popular Chatbots. *MobileMonkey*. https://mobilemonkey.com/blog/popular-chatbots

Kimmarita, L. (2022, August 24). Ministry to launch app, chatbot to help counter gender violence. *The Phnom Penh Post*. Www.phnompenhpost. com. https://www.phnompenhpost.com/national/ministry-launch-app-c hatbot-help-counter-gender-violence

Knight, W. (2022, August 5). We Interviewed Meta's New AI Chatbot About ... Itself. *Wired*. https://www.wired.com/story/blenderbot3-ai-chatbot-meta-inte rview/

Laranjo, L., Dunn, A. G., Tong, H. L., Kocaballi, A. B., Chen, J., Bashir, R., Surian, D., Gallego, B., Magrabi, F., Lau, A. Y. S., & Coiera, E. (2018). Conversational agents in healthcare: A systematic review. *Journal of the American Medical Informatics Association: JAMIA*, 25(9), 1248–1258. https://doi.org/10.1093/jamia/ocy072

Learner, D. S. (2022, July 25). 7 Actionable Tips for Chatbot Security. *Data Science Learner*. https://www.datasciencelearner.com/actionable-tips-for-chatb ot-security/

Mathenge, R. (2022, June 29). Chatbot security measures you need to consider. *PrivacySavvy*. https://privacysavvy.com/security/business/chatbot-security/

McTear, M., Callejas, Z., & Griol, D. (2016). *The Conversational Interface*. Springer International Publishing. doi:10.1007/978-3-319-32967-3

Neff, G., & Nagy, P. (2016). Automation, Algorithms, and Politics| Talking to Bots: Symbiotic Agency and the Case of Tay. *International Journal of Communication*, 10(0), 17. https://ijoc.org/index.php/ijoc/article/view/6277/1804

Negosanti, P. (2022, August 24). *Chatbots are revolutionizing the insurance industry*. PropertyCasualty360. https:// www.propertycasualty360.com/2022/08/24/how-chatbots-are-revolutionizing-the-insurance-industry/?slreturn=2022072 5025922

Global Newswire. (2022, August 19). No-Code AI Platform Market to Surpass US$ 38,518.0 Mn by 2032 with Increasing Need to Build Chatbots. *Benzinga*. https://www.benzinga.com/pressreleases/22/08/g28564148/no-co de-ai-platform-market-to-surpass-us-38-518-0-mn-by-2032-with -increasing-need-to-build-chatbot

Nirala, K. K., Singh, N. K., & Purani, V. S. (2022). A survey on providing customer and public administration based services using AI: chatbot. *Multimedia Tools and Applications*. doi:10.1007/s11042-021-11458-y

O'Leary, D. E. (2022). Massive data language models and conversational artificial intelligence: Emerging issues. *Intelligent Systems in Accounting, Finance & Management*, 29(3), 182–198. https://doi.org/10.1002/isaf.1522

Ong, R. J., Raof, R. A. A., Sudin, S., & Choong, K. Y. (2021). A Review of Chatbot development for Dynamic Web-based Knowledge Management System (KMS) in Small Scale Agriculture. *Journal of Physics: Conference Series*, 1755(1), 012051. https://doi.org/10.1088/1742-6596/1755/1/012051

Patel, S. (2019, August 21). 9 Excellent Benefits of Using Chatbots in Your Business. *REVE Chat*. https://www.revechat.com/blog/chatbot-business-benefits/

Perera, V. H., Senarathne, A. N., & Rupasinghe, L. (2019). Intelligent SOC Chatbot for Security Operation Center. *2019 International Conference on Advancements in Computing (ICAC)*. doi:10.1109/icac49085.2019.9103388

Peterson, B. (2017, October 29). I met Sophia, the word's first robot citizen, and the way she said goodbye nearly broke my heart. *Business Insider*. https://www.businessinsider.in/tech/i-met-sophia-the-words-first-robot-citizen-and-the-way-she-said-goodbye-nearly-broke-my-heart/articleshow/61322091.cms

Press, G. (2022, April 24). *Practices that ensure the safety of chat bots*. WhatsApp Chatbot. https://wa-chatbot.com/practices-ensure-safety-chat-bots-your-company/

Racter,(1984). *The Policeman's Beard Is Half Constructed: Computer Prose and Poetry*. New York, Warner Books.

Straits Research. (2022, June 29). Chatbot Market Growth is projected to reach USD 3.62 Billion by 2030, growing at a CAGR of 23.9%: Straits Research. *GlobeNewswire News Room*. https://www.globenewswire.com/news-release/2022/06/29/2471371/0/en/Chatbot-Market-Growth-is-projected-to-reach-USD-3-62-Billion-by-2030-growing-at-a-CAGR-of-23-9-Straits-Research.html

Vantage Research Market. (2022, March 17). Top Trends Driving the Global Healthcare Chatbots Market | Size Will Cross USD 431.47 Million by 2028. *GlobeNewswire News Room.* https://www.globenewswire.com/en/news-release/2022/03/17/240 4993/0/en/Top-Trends-Driving-the-Global-Healthcare-Chatbots-Market-Size-Will-Cross-USD-431-47-Million-by-2028-Global-Rep ort-by-Vantage-Market-Research.html

Saxena, A. R. (2019, July 31). *Chatbot Security Framework: Everything you need to know about Chatbot security.* Medium. https:// medium.com/@secxena/chatbot-security-framework-every thing-you-need-to-know-about-chatbot-security-243468f977b6

Selig, J. (2022, March 24). Chatbot: What is a Chatbot? Why are Chatbots Important? *Expert.ai.* https://www.expert.ai/blog/chatbot/

Shah, H., Warwick, K., Vallverdú, J., & Wu, D. (2016). Can machines talk? Comparison of Eliza with modern dialogue systems. *Computers in Human Behavior, 58,* 278–295. https://doi.org/10.1016/j.chb.2016.01.004

Shanbhag, A. (2020, September 28). Privacy And Security Considerations For Consumer-facing Chatbots. *BotCore.* https://botcore.ai/blog/chatbot-privacy-security/

Shewan, D. (2022, April 22). 10 of the Most Innovative Chatbots on the Web. *WordStream.* https://www.wordstream.com/blog/ws/chatbots

Shukairy, A. (2018, May 9). Chatbots In Customer Service – Statistics and Trends [Infographic]. *The Invesp Blog: Conversion Rate Optimization Blog.* https://www.invespcro.com/blog/chatbots-customer-service/

Silva, C. (2022, August 8). It Took Just One Weekend For Meta's New AI Chatbot To Become Racist. *Mashable India.* https://in.mashable.com/apps-and-software/36425/it-took-just -one-weekend-for-metas-new-ai-chatbot-to-become-racist

Singh Gill, N. (2022, March 16). What are Chatbots and Why are they Important*?* *Xenonstack.* Www.xenonstack.com. https://www.xenonstack.com/insights/chatbots-applications

SiteLock. (2019). Chatbot Security Risks: What you need to know before starting an online chat – The SiteLock Blog. *Sitelock.* https://www.sitelock.com/blog/ chatbot-security-risks/

Sree, V. K. C, K., G, S., & Rohan, R. (2019). Various Real Time Chat Bots and Their Applications in Human Life. *International Journal of Recent Technology and Engineering, 8*(4), 3461–3467. doi:10.35940/ijrte.d6902.118419

Tettelin, T. (2022, June 24). How to build a chatbot in just 10 steps. *Medium*. https://tesstettelin.medium.com/how-to-build-a-chatbot-in-ju st-10-steps-a9f74e12c601

Todd, S. (2022). The Employee Experience Advantage – Jacob Morgan. *Open Sourced Workplace*. https://opensourcedworkplace.com/news/the-employee-experienc e-advantage-jacob-morgan

Top 10 Benefits of Using AI Chatbots in your Business. (n.d.). AgreeYa Solutions. https://agreeya.com/whitepaper/top-10-benefits-of-using-ai-c hatbots-in-your-business/

Trivialworks Solutions Pvt Ltd. (2018). Trivialworks.com. https://trivialworks.com/ amazon-alexa/

Tung, L. (2022, August 8). Meta warns its new chatbot may forget that it's a bot. *ZDNET*. https://www.zdnet.com/article/meta-warns-its-new-chatbot-may -not-tell-you-the-truth/

Tur, G., & Deng, L. (2011). Intent Determination and Spoken Utterance Classification. *Spoken Language Understanding*, 93–118. doi:10.1002/9781119992691.ch4

Turing, A. M. (1950). Computing Machinery and Intelligence. *Mind, LIX*(236), 433–460. https://doi.org/10.1093/mind/lix.236.433

Ucedavélez, T., & Morana, M. M. (2015). *Risk Centric Threat Modeling Process for Attack Simulation and Threat Analysis. Hoboken*. John Wiley & Sons, Inc.

Vaish, A. (2022, August 23). AI: How the Rise Of Chatbot Is Powering a Futuristic Present? *Entrepreneur*. https://www.entrepreneur.com/article/433939

Voroneckis, R. (2019, January 30). Main benefits of using a Chatbot for your business. *Medium*. https://towardsdatascience.com/main-benefits-of-using-a-chat bot-for-your-business-b4ad00f02fb

Wang, W., & Siau, K. (2018). Living with Artificial Intelligence–Developing a Theory on Trust in Health Chatbots. In *Proceedings of the Sixteenth Annual Pre-ICIS Workshop on HCI Research in MIS* (pp. 1-5). Association for Information Systems.

What are the Advantages and Disadvantages of Chatbots in Business? (2020, April 20). GeeksforGeeks. https://www.geeksforgeeks.org/what-are-the-advantages-and-di sadvantages-of-chatbots-in-business/

What Are The Benefits of Chatbots? 2021 Chatbot Guide. (n.d.). Whisbi. Retrieved August 27, 2022, from https://www.whisbi.com/guides/chatbot/benefits/#:~:text=They %20Improve%20Customer%20Experience&text=Conversational%20sal es%20and%20marketing%20help

What are the privacy and security issues associated with chatbots? (n.d.). Tutorialspoint. Www.tutorialspoint.com. https:// www.tutorialspoint.com/what-are-the-privacy-and-secu rity-issues-associated-with-chatbots

Compilation of References

Aaker, J. L. (2021). Dimensions of brand personality. *JMR, Journal of Marketing Research, 34*(3), 347–356. doi:10.1177/002224379703400304

Abbasi, S., & Kazi, H. (2014). Measuring effectiveness of learning chatbot systems on student's learning outcome and memory retention. *Asian Journal of Applied Science and Engineering, 3*(7), 57–66. doi:10.15590/ajase/2014/v3i7/53576

Abdelhamid, S., & Katz, A. (2020). Using chatbots as smart teaching assistants for first-year engineering students. In *Conference on First-Year Engineering Experience*. Washington DC, USA.

Abdul-Kader, S. A., & John, W. C. (2015). Survey on chatbot design techniques in speech conversation systems. *International Journal of Advanced Computer Science and Applications, 6*(7).

Abid, A., Abdalla, A., Abid, A., Khan, D., Alfozan, A., & Zou, J. (2019). *Gradio: Hassle-free sharing and testing of ml models in the wild*. Cornell University.

Abran, A., Khelifi, A., Suryn, W., & Seffah, A. (2003). Consolidating the ISO usability models. In *Proceedings of 11th International Software Quality Management Conference*, (pp. 23-25). Semantic Scholar.

Abu Shawar, B., & Atwell, E. (2003). Accessing an information system by chatting. *In the International Conference on Application of Natural Language to Information Systems* (pp. 407-412). Springer.

Abu Shawar, B., & Atwell, E. (2007). Chatbots: are they really useful? In Ldv forum, 22(1), 29-49.

Abu Shawar, B., & Atwell, E. S. (2004). An Arabic chatbot giving answers from the Qur'an. In Proceedings of *TALN 04: XI Conférence sur le Traitement Automatique des Langues Naturelles [Conference on Natural Language Processing]*, (Vol. 2, pp. 197-202). ATALA.

Abu Shawar, B. (2011). A Chatbot as a natural web Interface to Arabic web QA. [iJET]. *International Journal of Emerging Technologies in Learning, 6*(1), 37–43. doi:10.3991/ijet.v6i1.1502

Abu Shawar, B., & Atwell, E. (2007). Chatbots: Are they Really Useful? *Journal for Language Technology and Computational Linguistics, 22*(1), 29–49. https://jlcl.org/article/view/88

Abu Shawar, B., & Atwell, E. (2015). Alice chatbot: Trials and outputs. *Computación y Sistemas*, *19*(4), 625–632.

AbuShawar, B., & Atwell, E. (2015). ALICE Chatbot: Trials and Outputs. *Computación y Sistemas*, *19*(4). doi:10.13053/cys-19-4-2326

Adamopoulou, E., & Moussiades, L. (2020). Chatbots: History, technology, and applications. *Machine Learning with Applications*, *2*(53), 100006. doi:10.1016/j.mlwa.2020.100006

Adams Becker, S., Cummins, M., Davis, A., Freeman, A., Hall Giesinger, C., & Ananthanarayanan, V. (2017). *NMC Horizon Report: 2017 Higher Education Edition*. The New Media Consortium.

Adiwardana, D., Luong, M.-T., So, D. R., Hall, J., Fiedel, N., Thoppilan, R., Yang, Z., Kulshreshtha, A., Nemade, G., Lu, Y., & Le, Q. V. (2020). Towards a Human-like Open-Domain Chatbot. https://arxiv.org/abs/2001.09977

Agarwal, R., & Mani, W. (2020). Review of state-of-the-art design techniques for chatbots. *SN Computer Science*, *1*(5), 1–12. doi:10.100742979-020-00255-3

Agus Santoso, H., Anisa Sri Winarsih, N., & Mulyanto, E. Wilujeng sarSaswati, G., Enggar Sukmana, S., & Rustad, S. (2018). Dinus Intelligent Assistance (DINA) Chatbot for University Admission Services. *2018 International Seminar On Application For Technology Of Information And Communication*. IEEE. 10.1109/ISEMANTIC.2018.8549797

Ahmed, R. (2018, November 15). *Dialogflow*. Slideshare. https://www.slideshare.net/Ahmedrebai2/dialogflow-123084875

Akcora, D. E., Belli, A., Berardi, M., Casola, S., Di Blas, N., Falletta, S., & Vannella, F. (2018, June). Conversational support for education. In *International conference on artificial intelligence in education* (pp. 14-19). Springer.

Akhtar, M., Neidhardt, J., & Werthner, H. (2019). The potential of chatbots: Analysis of chatbot conversations. *2019 IEEE 21st Conference on Business Informatics (CBI)*, (pp. 397–404). IEEE. 10.1109/CBI.2019.00052

Akma, N., Hafiz, M., Zainal, A., Fairuz, M., & Adnan, Z. (2018). Review of Chatbots Design Techniques. *International Journal of Computers and Applications*, *181*(8), 7–10. https://doi.org/10.5120/ijca2018917606

Alepis, E., & Virvou, M. (2011). Automatic generation of emotions in tutoring agents for affective e-learning in medical education. *Expert Systems with Applications*, *38*(8), 9840–9847. doi:10.1016/j.eswa.2011.02.021

Al-Ghadhban, D., & Al-Twairesh, N. (2020). Nabiha: An Arabic dialect chatbot. *International Journal of Advanced Computer Science and Applications*, *11*(3). doi:10.14569/IJACSA.2020.0110357

AlHumoud, S., Al Wazrah, A., & Aldamegh, W. (2018). Arabic chatbots: a survey. *Int. J. Adv. Comp. Sci. Appl.*, 535-541.

AlHumoud, S., Diab, A., AlDukhai, D., AlShalhoub, A., AlAbdullatif, R., AlQahtany, D., & Bin-Aqeel, F. (2022). Rahhal: A Tourist Arabic Chatbot. *In 2022 2nd International Conference of Smart Systems and Emerging Technologies (SMARTTECH)* (pp. 66-73). IEEE.

Ali, D. A., & Habash, N. (2016). Botta: An Arabic dialect chatbot. *In Proceedings of COLING 2016, the 26th International Conference on Computational Linguistics: System Demonstrations* (pp. 208-212). NYU.

Alias, S., Sainin, M. S., Soo Fun, T., & Daut, N. (2019, November). Identification of Conversational Intent Pattern Using Pattern-Growth Technique for Academic Chatbot. In *International Conference on Multi-disciplinary Trends in Artificial Intelligence* (pp. 263-270). Springer. 10.1007/978-3-030-33709-4_24

Aljameel, S. S., O'Shea, J. D., Crockett, K. A., Latham, A., & Kaleem, M. (2017). Development of an Arabic conversational intelligent tutoring system for education of children with ASD. In *2017 IEEE International Conference on Computational Intelligence and Virtual Environments for Measurement Systems and Applications (CIVEMSA)* (pp. 24-29). IEEE. 10.1109/CIVEMSA.2017.7995296

Allison, D. (2012). Chatbors in the library: Is it time? *Library Hi Tech, 30*(1), 95–107. doi:10.1108/07378831211213238

Al-Madi, N. A., Maria, K. A., Al-Madi, M. A., Alia, M. A., & Maria, E. A. (2021). An intelligent Arabic chatbot system proposed framework. *In 2021 International Conference on Information Technology (ICIT)* (pp. 592-597). IEEE. 10.1109/ICIT52682.2021.9491699

Almurayh, A. (2021). The Challenges of Using Arabic Chatbot in Saudi Universities. *International Journal of Computational Science, 48*(1), 1–12.

Alobaidi, O. G., Crockett, K. A., O'Shea, J. D., & Jarad, T. M. (2013). Abdullah: An intelligent Arabic conversational tutoring system for modern Islamic education. In *Proceedings of the World Congress on Engineering (Vol. 2)*. Academic Press.

Alobaidi, O. G., Crockett, K. A., O'Shea, J. D., & Jarad, T. M. (2013). Abdullah: An intelligent Arabic conversational tutoring system for modern Islamic education. In *Proceedings of the World Congress on Engineering* (Vol. 2). IAENG.

Altman, I., & Taylor, D. A. (1973). Social penetration: The development of interpersonal relationships. Holt, Rinehart & Winston.

Anderson, L., Krathwohl, D., Airasian, P., Cruikshank, K., Mayer, R., Pintrich, P., & Wittrock, M. (2001). *Assessing a revision Of Bloom's taxonomy of educational objectives*. Pearson. https://www.uky.edu/~rsand1/china2018/texts/Anderson-Krathwohl%20-%20A%20taxonomy%20for%20learning%20teaching%20and%20assessing.pdf

Anderson, J. N., Davidson, N., Morton, H., & Jack, M. A. (2008). Language learning with interactive virtual agent scenarios and speech recognition: Lessons learned. *Computer Animation and Virtual Worlds, 19*(5), 605–619. doi:10.1002/cav.265

Angeli, A. D., Johnson, G. I., & Coventry, L. (2001). The unfriendly user: Exploring social reactions to chatterbots. *Proceedings of the International Conference on Affective Human Factors Design*, (pp. 467-474). Abertay University.

Araujo, T. (2018). Living up to the chatbot hype: The influence of anthropomorphic design cues and communicative agency framing on conversational agent and company perceptions. *Computers in Human Behavior*, *85*, 183–189. doi:10.1016/j.chb.2018.03.051

Asbjorn, F., Petter, B. B., Tom, F., Ese, L. L., Manfred, T., & Ewa, A. L. (2018). Sig:Chatbots for social good. In *Extended Abstracts of the 2018 CHI Conference on Human Factors in Computing Systems*. ACM.

Ashktorab, Z., Jain, M., Liao, Q. V., & Weisz, J. D. (2019). Resilient chatbots: Repair strategy preferences for conversational breakdowns. *Proceedings of the 2019 CHI Conference on Human Factors in Computing Systems*, (pp. 1–12). ACM. 10.1145/3290605.3300484

Ask Alice. (n.d.). *Homepage*. Ask Alice. http://www.alicebot.org/aiml.html

Athota, L., Shukla, V. K., Pandey, N., & Rana, A. (2020). Chatbot for healthcare system using artificial intelligence. In *Proceedings of the 8th International Conference on Reliability, Infocom Technologies and Optimization (Trends and Future Directions)*, (pp. 619-622). IEEE. 10.1109/ICRITO48877.2020.9197833

Auccahuasi, W., Santiago, G. B., Núñez, E. O., & Sernaque, F. (2019) Interactive online tool as an instrument for learning mathematics through programming techniques, aimed at high school students. In *ICIT 2018: 6th International Conference on Information Technology: IoT and Smart City*, New York, NY, USA.

Ayanouz, S., Abdelhakim, B. A., & Benhmed, M. (2020). A Smart Chatbot Architecture based NLP and Machine Learning for Health Care Assistance. *Proceedings of the 3rd International Conference on Networking, Information Systems & Security*, (pp. 1–6). ACM. 10.1145/3386723.3387897

Ayedoun, E., Hayashi, Y., & Seta, K. (2015). A conversational agent to encourage willingness to communicate in the context of English as a foreign language. *Procedia Computer Science*, *60*, 1433–1442. doi:10.1016/j.procs.2015.08.219

Ayyagari, A., & Mohaghegh, M. (2021, October). Dynamic Chatbot for Parking Service. In *2021 International Conference on Engineering and Emerging Technologies (ICEET)* (pp. 1-6). IEEE.

Baevski, A., Zhou, Y., Mohamed, A., & Auli, M. (2020). wav2vec 2.0: A framework for self-supervised learning of speech representations. *Advances in Neural Information Processing Systems*, *33*, 12449–12460.

Bafna, S. (2021, October 8). *8 Benefits of Using AI Chatbots for Your Business and Customers – Customer Service Blog from HappyFox*. Customer Service Blog from HappyFox - Improve Customer Service & Experience. https://blog.happyfox.com/8-benefits-of-using-ai-chatbots-for-your-business-and-customers/

Bahja, M., Hammad, R., & Hassouna, M. (2019). Talk2Learn: a framework for chatbot learning. In *the European Conference on Technology Enhanced Learning*, (pp. 582-586). Springer. 10.1007/978-3-030-29736-7_44

Bahja, M., Hammad, R., & Butt, G. (2020). A User-Centric Framework for Educational Chatbots Design and Development. In C. Stephanidis, M. Kurosu, H. Degen, & L. Reinerman-Jones (Eds.), Lecture Notes in Computer Science (vol. 12424). *HCI International 2020 - Late Breaking Papers: Multimodality and Intelligence. HCII 2020.* Springer. doi:10.1007/978-3-030-60117-1_3

Bahja, M., Hammad, R., & Hassouna, M. (2019). Talk2Learn: a framework for chatbot learning. In *European Conference on Technology Enhanced Learning* (pp. 582-586). Springer.

Bala, K., Kumar, M., Hulawale, S., & Pandita, S. (2017). Chat-Bot For College Management System Using A.I. [IRJET]. *International Research Journal of Engineering and Technology, 04*(11), 4.

Balasubraman, S., Peterson, R. A., & Jarvenpaa, S. L. (2002). Exploring the implications of m-commerce for markets and marketing. *Journal of the Academy of Marketing Science, 30*(4), 348–361. doi:10.1177/009207002236910

Balatamoghna, B., & Nagajayanthi, B. (2022). Enhancement of Productivity Using Chatbots. In *Futuristic Communication and Network Technologies* (pp. 885–892). Springer.

Bansal, H., & Khan, R. (2018). A review paper on human computer interaction. *International Journal of Advanced Research in Computer Science and Software Engineering, 8*(4), 53–56. doi:10.23956/ijarcsse.v8i4.630

Barba-Sánchez, V., & Jimenez-Zarco, A. I. (2007). Drivers, Benefits and Challenges of ICT adoption by small and medium sized en-terprises (SMEs): A Literature Review. *Problems and Perspectives in Management*, (5, Iss. 1), 103–114.

Barker, S. (2020, June 16). *Pros and Cons of AI Chatbots: All You Must Know*. MoEngage Blog. https://www.moengage.com/blog/pros-and-cons-of-ai-chatbots/

Bathija, R., Agarwal, P., Somanna, R., & Pallavi, G. B. (2020). Guided Interactive Learning through Chatbot using Bi-directional Encoder Representations from Transformers (BERT). *2020 2nd International Conference on Innovative Mechanisms for Industry Applications (ICIMIA)*, (pp. 82–87). IEEE. 10.1109/ICIMIA48430.2020.9074905

Beattie, A., Edwards, A. P., & Edwards, C. (2020). A bot and a smile: Interpersonal impressions of chatbots and humans using emoji in computer-mediated communication. *Communication Studies, 71*(3), 409–427. doi:10.1080/10510974.2020.1725082

Behera, R. K., Bala, P. K., & Ray, A. (2021). Cognitive Chatbot for personalised contextual customer service: Behind the scene and beyond the hype. *Information Systems Frontiers*, 1–21. doi:10.100710796-021-10168-y

Benke, I., Knierim, M. T., & Maedche, A. (2020). Chatbot-based Emotion Management for Distributed Teams: A Participatory Design Study, p. 30. Association for Computing Machinery. doi:10.1145/3415189

Benotti, L., Martínez, M., & Schapachnik, F. (2014). Engaging high school students using chatbots. Proceedings Of The *2014 Conference On Innovation &Amp; Technology In Computer Science Education.* ACM. 10.1145/2591708.2591728

Benotti, L., Martinez, M. C., & Schapachnik, F. (2017). A tool for introducing computer science with automatic formative assessment. *IEEE Transactions on Learning Technologies, 11*(2), 179–192. doi:10.1109/TLT.2017.2682084

Bergner, R. M. (2020). What is personality? Two myths and a definition. *New Ideas in Psychology, 57*, 100759. doi:10.1016/j.newideapsych.2019.100759

Bernardini, S. (2000). *Competence, capacity, corpora: a study in corpus-aided language learning.* CLUEB.

Bevan, N. (2016). New ISO standards for usability, usability reports and usability measures. *In International conference on human-computer interaction*, 268-278.

Bharti, U., Bajaj, D., Batra, H., Lalit, S., Lalit, S., & Gangwani, A. (2020, June 1). *Medbot: Conversational Artificial Intelligence Powered Chatbot for Delivering Tele-Health after COVID-19.* IEEE Xplore. doi:10.1109/ICCES48766.2020.9137944

Bhatia, A., & Pinto, A. (2021). Automated construction of knowledge-bases for safety critical applications: Challenges and opportunities. In *Proceedings of the AAAI 2021 Spring Symposium on Combining Machine Learning and Knowledge Engineering.* Stanford University.

Bibault, J., Chaix, B., Guillemassé, A., Cousin, S., Escande, A., Perrin, M., Pienkowski, A., Delamon, G., Nectoux, P., & Brouard, B. (2019). A Chatbot Versus Physicians to Provide Information for Patients With Breast Cancer: Blind, Randomized Controlled Noninferiority Trial. *Journal of Medical Internet Research, 21*(11), e15787. doi:10.2196/15787 PMID:31774408

Bickmore, T. W., Mitchell, S. E., Jack, B. W., Paasche-Orlow, M. K., Pfeifer, L. M., & O'Donnell, J. (2010). Response to a relational agent by hospital patients with depressive symptoms. *Interacting with Computers, 22*(4), 289–298. doi:10.1016/j.intcom.2009.12.001 PMID:20628581

Bickmore, T. W., Schulman, D., & Sidner, C. (2013). Automated interventions for multiple health behaviors using conversational agents. *Patient Education and Counseling, 92*(2), 142–148. doi:10.1016/j.pec.2013.05.011 PMID:23763983

Bird, J. J., Ekárt, A., & Faria, D. R. (2021). Chatbot Interaction with Artificial Intelligence: Human data augmentation with T5 and language transformer ensemble for text classification. *Journal of Ambient Intelligence and Humanized Computing.* doi:10.100712652-021-03439-8

Bleu, N. (2021, October 5). *29 Top Chatbot Statistics For 2022: Usage, Demographics, Trends.* ADA.

Bleu, N. (2023). 29 Top Chatbox Statistics for 2023. *Blogging Wizard.* https://bloggingwizard.com/chatbot-statistics/#:~:text=23%25%20of%20customer%20service%20companies

Bocklisch, T., Faulkner, J., Pawlowski, N., & Nichol, A. (2017). *Rasa: Open-source language understanding and dialogue management.* Cornell University.

Bos, J., Bohlin, P., Larsson, S., Lewin, I., Matheson, C, & Milward, D. (1999). Survey of existing interactive systems. Technical Report, Task Oriented Instructional Dialogue. *Gothenburg University.*

Boussakssou, M., Ezzikouri, H., & Erritali, M. (2022). Chatbot in Arabic language using seq to seq model. *Multimedia Tools and Applications, 81*(2), 2859–2871. doi:10.100711042-021-11709-y

Bozic, J., & Wotawa, F. (2018). Security Testing for Chatbots. *Testing Software and Systems*, 33–38. doi:10.1007/978-3-319-99927-2_3

Bradeško, L., & Mladenić, D. (2012). A survey of chatbot systemsthrough a loebner prize competition. *Proceedings of Slovenian language technologies society eighth conference of language technologies*, (pp. 34–37). Semantic Scholar.

Brandtzaeg, P. B., & Følstad, A. (2018). Chatbots: changing user needs and motivations. *interactions, 25*(5), 38-43.

Brandtzaeg, P. B., & Følstad, A. (2017). Why people use chatbots. In I. Kompatsiaris, J. Cave, A. Satsiou, G. Carle, A. Passani, E. Kontopoulos, S. Diplaris, & D. McMillan (Eds.), *Internet Science* (Vol. 10673, pp. 377–392). Springer International Publishing. doi:10.1007/978-3-319-70284-1_30

Brave, S., Nass, C., & Hutchinson, K. (2005). Computers that care: Investigating the effects of orientation of emotion exhibited by an embodied computer agent. *International Journal of Human-Computer Studies, 62*(2), 161–178. doi:10.1016/j.ijhcs.2004.11.002

Brooke, J. (1996). SUS-A quick and dirty usability scale. *Usability evaluation in industry, 194*(189), 4-7.

Brooks, D. C., & Pomerantz, J. (2017). ECAR Study of Undergraduate Students and Information Technology, Research Report. ECAR.

Brown, T. B., Mann, B., Ryder, N., Subbiah, M., Kaplan, J., Dhariwal, P., Neelakantan, A., Shyam, P., Sastry, G., Askell, A., Agarwal, S., Herbert-Voss, A., Krueger, G., Henighan, T., Child, R., Ramesh, A., Ziegler, D. M., Wu, J., Winter, C., & Amodei, D. (2020). Language models are few-shot learners. In *Proceedings of the 34th International Conference on Neural Information Processing Systems*, (pp: 1877–1901). Curran Associates Inc.

Brush, K., & Scardina, J. (n.d.). What is a Chatbot and Why is it Important? *Tech Target.* https://www.techtarget.com/searchcustomerexperience/definition/chatbot

Cahn, J. (2017). *CHATBOT: Architecture, design, & development.* University of Pennsylvania School of Engineering and Applied Science Department of Computer and Information Science.

Cahn, J. (2017). *CHATBOT: Architecture, Design, & Development.* University of Pennsylvania.

Cahn, J. (2017). *CHATBOT: Architecture*. Design, & Development.

Cai, W., Grossman, J., Lin, Z., Sheng, H., Wei, J., Williams, J., & Goel, S. (2021). Bandit algorithms to personalize educational chatbots. *Machine Learning*, *110*(9), 2389–2418. doi:10.100710994-021-05983-y

Caldarini, G., Jaf, S., & McGarry, K. (2022). A literature survey of recent advances in chatbots. *Information (Basel)*, *13*(1), 41. doi:10.3390/info13010041

Carisi, M., Albarelli, A., & Luccio, F. L. (2019, September). Design and implementation of an airport chatbot. In *Proceedings of the 5th EAI International Conference on Smart Objects and Technologies for Social Good* (pp. 49-54). ACM. 10.1145/3342428.3342664

Carlander-Reuterfelt, D., Carrera, A., Iglesias, C. A., Araque, O., Sanchez Rada, J. F. S., & Munoz, S. (2020). JAICOB: A data science chatbot. *IEEE Access: Practical Innovations, Open Solutions*, *8*, 180671–180680. doi:10.1109/ACCESS.2020.3024795

Cartagena, S. (2022, May 2). Chatbots, their positive impact and how to take advantage of the customer experience. *Entrepreneur*. https://www.entrepreneur.com/article/426555

Cassell, J. (n.d.). Embodied Conversational Agents Representation and Intelligence in User Interfaces. American Association for Artificial Intelligence. http://www.justinecassell.com/publications/AIMag22-04-007.PDF

Cebrián, J., Martínez-Jiménez, R., Rodriguez, N., & D'Haro, L. F. (2021). Considerations on creating conversational agents for multiple environments and users. *AI Magazine*, *42*(2), 71–86. doi:10.1609/aimag.v42i2.7484

Cervone, A., Gambi, E., Tortoreto, G., Stepanov, E. A., & Riccardi, G. (2018). Automatically predicting user ratings for conversational systems. In E. Cabrio, A. Mazzei, & F. Tamburini (Eds.), *Proceedings of the Fifth Italian Conference on Computational Linguistics CLiC-it 2018* (pp. 99–104). Accademia University Press. 10.4000/books.aaccademia.3151

Chada, R. (2020). Simultaneous paraphrasing and translation by fine-tuning Transformer models. *Proceedings of the Fourth Workshop on Neural Generation and Translation*, (pp. 198–203). ACL. 10.18653/v1/2020.ngt-1.23

Chandel, S., Yuying, Y., Yujie, G., Razaque, A., & Yang, G. (2019). Chatbot: Efficient and utility-based platform. In K. Arai, S. Kapoor, & R. Bhatia (Eds.), *Intelligent Computing* (Vol. 858, pp. 109–122). Springer International Publishing., doi:10.1007/978-3-030-01174-1_9

Chang, M., & Hwang, J. (2019). Developing Chatbot with Deep Learning Techniques for Negotiation Course. *2019 8Th International Congress On Advanced Applied Informatics (IIAI-AAI)*. IEEE. 10.1109/IIAI-AAI.2019.00220

Chang, C.-Y., Kuo, S.-Y., & Hwang, G.-H. (2022). Chatbot-facilitated Nursing Education: Incorporating a Knowledge-Based Chatbot System into a Nursing Training Program. *Journal of Educational Technology & Society*, *25*(1), 15–27.

Chatbotguide. (2022). Burberry. *Chatbotguide.* https://www.chatbotguide.org/burberry-bot [Accessed: 26 April 2022].

Chatfuel. (2022). How to Build Smarter Bots With AI. *Chatfuel.* https://chatfuel.com/blog/posts/build-ai-chatbots

Chaturvedi, S. (2022, September 30). *10 Best Chatbots In India.* Haptik. Www.haptik.ai. https://www.haptik.ai/blog/10-best-ai-chatbots-in-india

Cheng, X., Zhang, X., Yang, B., & Fu, Y. (2022). An investigation on trust in AI-enabled collaboration: Application of AI-Driven chatbot in accommodation-based sharing economy. *Electronic Commerce Research and Applications, 54,* 101164. doi:10.1016/j.elerap.2022.101164 PMID:35968256

Chen, H., Liu, X., Yin, D., & Tang, J. (2017). A survey on dialogue systems: Recent advances and new frontiers. *Acm Sigkdd Explorations Newsletter, 19*(2), 25–35. doi:10.1145/3166054.3166058

Chen, J. A., Tutwiler, M. S., Metcalf, S. J., Kamarainen, A., Grotzer, T., & Dede, C. (2016). A multi-user virtual environment to support students'self-efficacy and interest in science: A latent growth model analysis. *Learning and Instruction, 41,* 11–22. doi:10.1016/j.learninstruc.2015.09.007

Chen, Y., & Kuo, C. (2021). *Applying the Smartphone-Based Chatbot in Clinical Nursing Education.* Nurse Educator, Publish Ahead of Print., doi:10.1097/NNE.0000000000001131

Chiaráin, N. N., & Chasaide, A. N. (2016). Chatbot technology with synthetic voices in the acquisition of an endangered language: Motivation, development, and evaluation of a platform for Irish. *In Proceedings of the Tenth International Conference on Language Resources and Evaluation (LREC'16)* (pp. 3429-3435). ACLA.

Christensen, A. (2007). A Trend from Germany: Library Chatbots in Digital Reference. Tilburg university. https://www.tilburguniversity.nl/services/lis/ticer/07carte/publicat/07christensen

Chun Ho, C., Lee, H. L., Lo, W. K., & Lui, K. F. A. (2018). Developing a chatbot for college student program advisement. In *2018 IEEE International Symposium on Educational Technology,* (pp: 62-56). IEEE.

Chung, M., Ko, E., Joung, H., & Kim, S. J. (2020). Chatbot e-service and customer satisfaction regarding luxury brands. *Journal of Business Research, 117,* 587–595. doi:10.1016/j.jbusres.2018.10.004

Ciupe, A., Mititica, D. F., Meza, S., & Orza, B. (2019, April). Learning Agile with Intelligent Conversational Agents. In *2019 IEEE Global Engineering Education Conference (EDUCON)* (pp. 1100-1107). IEEE. 10.1109/EDUCON.2019.8725192

Clarizia, F., Colace, F., Lombardi, M., Pascale, F., & Santaniello, D. (2018). Chatbot: An education support system for student. In *International symposium on cyberspace safety and security* (pp. 291–302). SCIRP.

Clark, R. C., & Mayer, R. E. (2016). *E-learning and the science of instruction: Proven guidelines for consumers and designers of multimedia learning.* John Wiley & sons. doi:10.1002/9781119239086

Colace, F., De Santo, M., Lombardi, M., Pascale, F., & Pietrosanto, A. (2018). Chatbot for e-learning: A case of study. *International Journal of Mechanical Engineering and Robotics Research, 7*(5), 528–533. doi:10.18178/ijmerr.7.5.528-533

Colby, K. M., Hilf, F. D., Weber, S., & Kraemer, H. C. (1972). Turing-like indistinguishability tests for the validation of a computer simulation of paranoid processes. *Artificial Intelligence, 3,* 199–221. doi:10.1016/0004-3702(72)90049-5

Colby, K. M., Weber, S., & Hilf, F. D. (1971). Artificial paranoia. *Artificial Intelligence, 2*(1), 1–25. doi:10.1016/0004-3702(71)90002-6

Coniam, D. (2014). The linguistic accuracy of chatbots: Usability from an ESL perspective. *Text & Talk, 34*(5), 545–567. doi:10.1515/text-2014-0018

Connaway, L. S., Dickey, T. J., & Radford, M. L. (2011). If it is too inconvenient I'm not going after it: Convenience as a critical factor in information-seeking behaviors. *Library & Information Science Research, 33*(3), 179–190. doi:10.1016/j.lisr.2010.12.002

Crisseyb, R., Brechemiera, D., Balardya, L., & Nourhashemi, F. (2019). A smartphone chatbot application to optimize monitoring of older patients with cancer. *International Journal of Medical Informatics, 128,* 18–23. doi:10.1016/j.ijmedinf.2019.05.013 PMID:31160007

Crockett, K., Latham, A., & Whitton, N. (2017). On predicting learning styles in conversational intelligent tutoring systems using fuzzy decision trees. *International Journal of Human-Computer Studies, 97,* 98–115. doi:10.1016/j.ijhcs.2016.08.005

CS 230—Recurrent Neural Networks Cheatsheet. (n.d.). Shervine Amidi. https://stanford.edu/~shervine/teaching/cs-230/cheatsheet-recurrent-neural-networks

Cuayáhuitl, H., Keizer, S., & Lemon, O. (2015). *Strategic dialogue management via deep reinforcement learning.* Cornell University.

Cui, L., Huang, S., Wei, F., Tan, C., Duan, C., & Zhou, M. (2017, July). Superagent: A customer service chatbot for e-commerce websites. In *Proceedings of ACL 2017, system demonstrations* (pp. 97-102). ACL. 10.18653/v1/P17-4017

Cunningham-Nelson, S., Boles, W., Trouton, L., & Margerison, E. (2019). A review of chatbots in education: practical steps forward. In *30th Annual Conference for the Australasian Association for Engineering Education (AAEE 2019): Educators Becoming Agents of Change: Innovate, Integrate, Motivate,* (pp. 299-306). Engineers Australia.

Cunningham-Nelson, Sam, Boles, Wageeh, Trouton, Luke, & Margerison, E. (2019). A review of chatbots in education: Practical steps forward. In *30th Annual Conference for the Australasian Association for Engineering Education: Educators Becoming Agents of Change: Innovate, Integrate, Motivate. Engineers Australia, Australia,* (pp. 299-306). AAEE.

Cunningham-Nelson, S., Boles, W., Trouton, L., & Margerison, E. (2019). A review of chatbots in education: Practical steps forward. In *Proceedings of the 30th Annual Conference for the Australasian Association for Engineering Education: Educators Becoming Agents of Change: Innovate, Integrate, Motivate*, (pp: 299-306). AAEE.

Dahiya, M. (2017). A tool of conversation: Chatbot. *International Journal on Computer Science and Engineering*, *5*(5), 158–161.

Dai, Z., Yang, Z., Yang, Y., Carbonell, J., Le, Q. V., & Salakhutdinov, R. (2019). Transformer-XL: Attentive Language Models Beyond a Fixed-Length Context https://arxiv.org/abs/1901.02860 doi:10.18653/v1/P19-1285

Danescu-Niculescu-Mizil, C., & Lee, L. (2011). Chameleons in imagined conversations: A new approach to understanding coordination of linguistic style in dialogs. In *Proceedings of the 2nd Workshop on Cognitive Modeling and Computational Linguistics*. ACL.

Dang, H. T. (2005). *Information Access Division National Institute of Standards and Technology Gaithersburg, MD, 20899*, 12.

Daud, S. H. M., Teo, N. H. I., & Zain, N. H. M. (2020). Ejava chatbot for learning programming language: Apost-pandemic alternative virtual tutor. *International Journal (Toronto, Ont.)*, *8*(7), 3290–3298.

Daugherty, P. R., & Wilson, H. J. (2018). Human + machine: Reimagining work in the age of AI. *Harvard Business Review*.

Davis, F. D. (1989). Perceived usefulness, perceived ease of use, and user acceptance of information technology. *Management Information Systems Quarterly*, *13*(3), 319–340. doi:10.2307/249008

Debnath, B., & Agarwal, A. (2020). A framework to implement AI-integrated chatbot in educational institutes. *Journal of Student Research Fourth Middle East College Student Research Conference*.

Denkowski, M., & Lavie, A. (2010). Extending the METEOR Machine Translation Evaluation Metric to the Phrase Level. Human Language Technologies: The *2010 Annual Conference of the North American Chapter of the Association for Computational Linguistics*, (pp. 250–253). ACL. https://aclanthology.org/N10-1031

Desurvire, H., Caplan, M. & Toth, A. J. (2004). Using heuristics to evaluate the playability of games. *CHI '04*.

Deveci Topal, A., Dilek Eren, C., & Kolburan Geçer, A. (2021). Chatbot application in a 5th grade science course. *Education and Information Technologies*, *26*(5), 6241–6265. doi:10.100710639-021-10627-8 PMID:34177344

Devlin, J., Chang, M.-W., Lee, K., & Toutanova, K. (2019). BERT: Pre-training of Deep Bidirectional Transformers for Language Understanding. https://arxiv.org/abs/1810.04805

Dharmapuri, C. M., Agarwal, A., Anwer, F., & Mahor, J. (2022). AI Chatbot: Application in psychiatric treatment and suicide prevention. *International Mobile and Embedded Technology Conference*. IEEE. 10.1109/MECON53876.2022.9752126

Dharwadkar, R., & Deshpande, N. A. (2018). A medical ChatBot. *International Journal of Computer Trends and Technology*, *60*(1), 41–45. doi:10.14445/22312803/IJCTT-V60P106

Dialani, P. (2020, August 8). *You are being redirected...* Www.analyticsinsight. net. https://www.analyticsinsight.net/top-8-best-practices-to-ens ure-bot-security/

Dive, R. (2022a, May 9). Global Conversational AI Market Expected to Rise at a CAGR of 21.4% and Surpass $13,291.3 Million during the Forecast Period from 2021 to 2028. *GlobeNewswire News Room*. https://www.globenewswire.com/en/news-release/2022/05/09/243 8721/0/en/Global-Conversational-AI-Market-Expected-to-Rise-a t-a-CAGR-of-21-4-and-Surpass-13-291-3-Million-during-the-For ecast-Period-from-2021-to-2028-224-Pages-Research-Dive.html

Dive, R. (2022b, May 18). Global Chatbot Market Expected to Grow with 28.7% CAGR and Exceed $19,570 Million in the 2020 to 2027 Timeframe. *GlobeNewswire News Room*. https://www.globenewswire.com/news-release/2022/05/18/244612 8/0/en/Global-Chatbot-Market-Expected-to-Grow-with-28-7-CAGR -and-Exceed-19-570-Million-in-the-2020-to-2027-Timeframe-241 -Pages-Reveals-by-Research-Dive.html

Driss, M., Almomani, I., Alahmadi, L., Alhajjam, L., Alharbi, R., & Alanazi, S. (2022). *COVIBOT: A Smart Chatbot for Assistance and E-Awareness during COVID-19 Pandemic*. Cornell University., doi:10.1109/SMARTTECH54121.2022.00038

Dryer, D. C. (1999). Getting personal with computers: How to design personalities for agents. *Applied Artificial Intelligence*, *13*(3), 273–295. doi:10.1080/088395199117423

Durall, E., & Kapros, E. (2020). Co-design for a competency self-assessment chatbot and survey in science education. In P. Zaphiris & A. Ioannou (Eds.), Lecture Notes in Computer Science: Vol. 12206. *Learning and Collaboration Technologies. Human and Technology Ecosystems* (pp. 13–24). Springer. doi:10.1007/978-3-030-50506-6_2

Dutsinma, F. L. I., Pal, D., Funilkul, S. & H. Chan, J. (2022). A Systematic Review of Voice Assistant Usability: An ISO 9241–11 Approach. *SN Computer Science 3*(4), 1-23.

Duval, E., & Verbert, K. (2012). Learning analytics. *Eleed, 8*(1).

Editorial Team. (2022, August 20). 7 Ways Chatbots Improve Life. *InsideBIGDATA*. https://insidebigdata.com/2022/08/20/7-ways-chatbots-improve -life/

Edwards, A., & Westgate, D. (1994). *Investigating Classroom Talk*. Falmer Press.

Ehsani, F., & Knodt, E. (1998). Speech technology in computer-aided lan- guage learning: Strengths and limitations of a new call paradigm. *Language Learning & Technology*, *2*(1), 54–73.

El Hefny, W., El Bolock, A., Herbert, C., & Abdennadher, S. (2021). Chase Away the Virus: A Character-Based Chatbot for COVID-19. *2021 IEEE 9th International Conference on Serious Games and Applications for Health(SeGAH)*. IEEE. https://doi.org/10.1109/segah52098.2021.9551895

El Hefny, W., Mansy, Y., Abdallah, M., & Abdennadher, S. (2021). Jooka: A Bilingual Chatbot for University Admission. In Á. Rocha, H. Adeli, G. Dzemyda, F. Moreira, & A. M. Ramalho Correia (Eds.), *Trends and Applications in Information Systems and Technologies. WorldCIST 2021. Advances in Intelligent Systems and Computing* (vol. 1367). Springer. doi:10.1007/978-3-030-72660-7_64

Elnozahy, W. A., El Khayat, G. A., Cheniti-Belcadhi, L., & Said, B. (2019). Question Answering System to Support University Students' Orientation, Recruitment and Retention. *Procedia Computer Science*, *164*, 56–63. doi:10.1016/j.procs.2019.12.154

Engati. (n.d.). *Chatbot Architecture*. Engati. https://www.engati.com/glossary/chatbot-architecture

Engati. (n.d.). *Types of chatbots*. Engati. https://www.engati.com/blog/types-of-chatbots-and-their-appl ications

Eren, B. A. (2021). Determinants of customer satisfaction in chatbot use: Evidence from a banking application in Turkey. *International Journal of Bank Marketing*, *39*(2), 294–311. doi:10.1108/IJBM-02-2020-0056

Essel, H. B., Vlachopoulos, D., Tachie-Menson, A., Johnson, E. E., & Baah, P. K. (2022). The impact of a virtual teaching assistant (chatbot) on students' learning in Ghanaian higher education. *International Journal of Educational Technology in Higher Education*, *19*(1), 57. doi:10.118641239-022-00362-6

Fabbri, A. R., Kryściński, W., McCann, B., Xiong, C., Socher, R., & Radev, D. (2021). SummEval: Re-evaluating Summarization Evaluation. *Transactions of the Association for Computational Linguistics*, *9*, 391–409. doi:10.1162/tacl_a_00373

Fadhil, A., & Schiavo, G. (2019). *Designing for Health Chatbots*. Cornell University. https://arxiv.org/abs/1902.09022

Fadhil, A. (2018). *Can a chatbot determine my diet? Addressing challenges of chatbot application for meal recommendation*. Cornell University.

Fadhil, A., & Abu Ra'ed, A. (2019). Ollobot-Towards a text-based Arabic health conversational agent: Evaluation and results. *In Proceedings of the International Conference on Recent Advances in Natural Language Processing (RANLP 2019)* (pp. 295-303). ACL. 10.26615/978-954-452-056-4_034

Fadhil, A., & Gabrielli, S. (2017). Addressing challenges in promoting healthy lifestyles: The AI-chatbot approach. In *Proceedings of the 11th EAI International Conference on Pervasive Computing Technologies for Healthcare*, (pp: 261–265). ACM. 10.1145/3154862.3154914

Feine, J., Gnewuch, U., Morana, S., & Maedche, A. (2019). A taxonomy of social cues for conversational agents. *International Journal of Human-Computer Studies*, *132*, 138–161. doi:10.1016/j.ijhcs.2019.07.009

Feng, D., Shaw, E., Kim, J., & Hovy, E. (2006). An intelligent discussion-bot for answering student queries in threaded discussions. *Proceedings of the 11th International Conference on Intelligent User Interfaces*.

Firch, J. (2019, June 17). *What Are The Common Types Of Network Vulnerabilities?* PurpleSec. https://purplesec.us/common-network-vulnerabilities/

Firdaus, M., Golchha, H., Ekbal, A., & Bhattacharyya, P. (2020). A Deep Multi-task Model for Dialogue Act Classification, Intent Detection and Slot Filling. *Cognitive Computation*. doi:10.1007/s12559-020-09718-4

Fleming, M. (2018). Streamlining student course requests using chatbots. In *29th Australasian Association for Engineering Education Conference 2018 (AAEE 2018)*. Engineers Australia.

Følstad, A., Araujo, T., Law, E., Brandtzaeg, P., Papadopoulos, S., Reis, I., Baez, M., Laban, G., McAllister, P., Ischen, C., Wald, R., Catania, F., Meyer von Wolff, R., Hobert, S., & Luger, E. (2021). Future directions for chatbot research: An interdisciplinary research agenda. *Computing*, *103*(12), 2915–2942. doi:10.100700607-021-01016-7

Følstad, A., Nordheim, C. B., & Bjørkli, C. A. (2018). What makes users trust a chatbot for customer service? An exploratory interview study. In S. S. Bodrunova (Ed.), *Internet Science* (Vol. 11193, pp. 194–208). Springer International Publishing. doi:10.1007/978-3-030-01437-7_16

Følstad, A., & Skjuve, M. (2019). Chatbots for customer service: User experience and motivation. *Proceedings of the 1st International Conference on Conversational User Interfaces - CUI '19*, (pp. 1–9). ACM. 10.1145/3342775.3342784

Frankenfield, J. (2022) What is Chatbot? *Investopedia.* https://www.investopedia.com/terms/c/chatbot.asp

Freed, A. (2021). *Conversational AI*. Manning Publications.

Fryer, L. K., Ainley, M., Thompson, A., Gibson, A., & Sherlock, Z. (2017). Stimulating and sustaining interest in a language course: An experimental comparison of Chatbot and Human task partners.*Computers inHuman Behavior, 75*, 461–468.

Fryer, L. K., Ainley, M., Thompson, A., Gibson, A., & Sherlock, Z. (2017). Stimulating and sustaining interest in a language course: An experimental comparison of Chatbot and Human task partners. *Computers in Human Behavior*, *75*(17), 461–468. doi:10.1016/j.chb.2017.05.045

Fryer, L. K., & Carpenter, R. (2006). Bots as language learning tools. *Language Learning & Technology*, *10*(3), 8–14.

Fryer, L. K., Coniam, D., & Carpenter, R., & Lapuș neanu, D. (2020). Bots for language learning now: Current and future directions. *Language Learning & Technology*, *24*(2), 8–22.

Fryer, L. K., Nakao, K., & Thompson, A. (2019). Chatbot learning partners: Connecting learning experiences, interest and competence. *Computers in Human Behavior*, *93*, 279–289. doi:10.1016/j.chb.2018.12.023

Galiamova, K., Pavlov, Y., Smirnova, E., Zakharov, M., & Zverev, A. (2018). Psychological adaptation mechanism of the higher education engineering students: artificial conversational entity usage for help. *Inted Proceedings*. Iated. 10.21125/inted.2018.0667

Gallacher, A., Thompson, A., & Howarth, M. (2018). "My robot is an idiot!"–Students' perceptions of AI in the L2 classroom. In P. Taalas, J.Jalkanen, L. Bradley, & S. Thouësny (Eds.), Future-Proof CALL: LanguageLearning as Exploration and Encounters: Short Papers from EUROCALL(pp. 70–76). Research-publishing.

Gangi, M. A. D., Negri, M., & Turchi, M. (2019). Adapting Transformer to End-to-End Spoken Language Translation. *Interspeech*, *1133–1137*, 1133–1137. doi:10.21437/Interspeech.2019-3045

Garcia Brustenga, G., Fuertes Alpiste, M., & Molas Castells, N. (2018). *Briefing Paper: Chatbots in Education. Universitat Oberta de Catalunya.* UOC. doi:10.7238/elc.chatbots.2018

Gbenga, L. O., Oluwafunto, O. T., & Oluwatobi, A. H. (2020). An Improved Rapid Response Model for University Admission Enquiry System Using Chatbot. *International Journal of Computer*, *38*(1), 121–131.

Geerts, G. L. (2011). A design science research methodology and its application to accounting information systems research. *International Journal of Accounting Information Systems*, *12*(2), 142–151. doi:10.1016/j.accinf.2011.02.004

Georgescu, A. A. (2018). Chatbots for education–trends, benefits and challenges. In *Conference proceedings of» eLearning and Software for Education «(eLSE)* (pp. 195-200). Carol I National Defence University Publishing House.

Ghandeharioun, A., Shen, J. H., Jaques, N., Ferguson, C., Jones, N., Lapedriza, A., & Picard, R. (2019). Approximating Interactive Human Evaluation with Self-Play for Open-Domain Dialog Systems. *Advances in Neural Information Processing Systems, 32.* https://proceedings.neurips.cc/paper/2019/hash/fc9812127bf09c7bd29ad6723c683fb5-Abstract.html

Ghandeharioun, A., Shen, J. H., Jaques, N., Ferguson, C., Jones, N., Lapedriza, A., & Picard, R. (2019). *Approximating interactive human evaluation with self-play for open-domain dialog systems.* In *33rd Conference on Neural Information Processing Systems*, Vancouver, Canada.

Ghazarian, S., Weischedel, R., Galstyan, A., & Peng, N. (2020). Predictive Engagement: An Efficient Metric for Automatic Evaluation of Open-Domain Dialogue Systems. *Proceedings of the AAAI Conference on Artificial Intelligence*, *34*(05), 7789–7796. doi:10.1609/aaai.v34i05.6283

Gimpel, H., & Röglinger, M. (2015). *Digital transformation: changes and chances–insights based on an empirical study.* Semantic Scholar.

Global Newswire. (2022, August 19). No-Code AI Platform Market to Surpass US$ 38,518.0 Mn by 2032 with Increasing Need to Build Chatbots. *Benzinga.* https://www.benzinga.com/pressreleases/22/08/g28564148/no-co de-ai-platform-market-to-surpass-us-38-518-0-mn-by-2032-with -increasing-need-to-build-chatbot

Gnewuch, U., Morana, S. & Maedche, A. (2017). *Towards Designing Cooperative and Social Conversational Agents for Customer Service.* AIS eLibrary (AISeL).

Goda, Y., Yamada, M., Matsukawa, H., Hata, K., & Yasunami, S. (2014). Conversation with a chatbot before an online EFL group discussionand the effects on critical thinking. *Journal of Information Systems Education*, *13*(1), 1–7. doi:10.12937/ejsise.13.1

Godfrey, J., Holliman, E., & McDaniel, J. (1992). SWITCHBOARD: Telephone speech corpus for research and development. In *Proceedings of the 1992 IEEE International Conference on Acoustics, Speech, and Signal Processing,* (pp. 517-520). IEEE. 10.1109/ICASSP.1992.225858

Godina, A. (2018, January 17). *Chatbot Security - A Guide For Businesses.* Inform Comms. https://www.inform-comms.com/chatbot-security-what-you-need-to-know/

Go, E., & Sundar, S. S. (2019). Humanizing chatbots: The effects of visual, identity and conversational cues on humanness perceptions. *Computers in Human Behavior*, *97*, 304–316. doi:10.1016/j.chb.2019.01.020

Goh, O. S., Ardil, C., Wong, W., & Fung, C. C. (2007). A black-box approach for response quality evaluation of conversational agent systems. *International Journal of Computational Intelligence*, *3*(3), 195–203.

Gómez-Rico, M., Molina-Collado, A., Santos-Vijande, M. L., Molina-Collado, M. V., & Imhoff, B. (2022). The role of novel instruments of brand communication and brand image in building consumers' brand preference and intention to visit wineries. *Current Psychology (New Brunswick, N.J.).* doi:10.100712144-021-02656-w PMID:35035183

Gonda, D. E., Luo, J., Wong, Y., & Lei, C. (2019). Evaluation of developing educational chatbots based on the seven principles for good teaching. In *Proceedings of the 2018 IEEE International Conference on Teaching, Assessment, and Learning for Engineering,* (pp: 446-453). IEEE.

Google. (n.d.). *Dialogflow: natural language processing platform.* Google. https://cloud.google.com/dialogflow.

Graesser, A. C. (2016). Conversations with AutoTutor help students learn. *International Journal of Artificial Intelligence in Education, 26*(1), 124–132. doi:10.100740593-015-0086-4

Graesser, A. C., Chipman, P., Haynes, B., & Olney, A. (2005). AutoTutor: An intelligent tutoring system with mixed-initiative dialogue. *IEEE Transactions on Education, 48*(4), 612–618. doi:10.1109/TE.2005.856149

Graesser, A. C., VanLehn, K., Rose, C. P., Jordan, P. W., & Harter, D. (2001). Intelligent tutoring systems with conversational dialogue. *AI Magazine, 22*(4), 39–51.

Graves, S. J., & Desai, C. M. (2006). Instruction via chat reference: Does co-browse help? *RSR. Reference Services Review, 34*(3), 340–357. doi:10.1108/00907320610685300

Greller, W., & Drachsler, H. (2012). Translating learning into Numbers: A generic framework for learning analytics. *Journal of Educational Technology & Society, 15*(3), 42–57.

Grinstein, G. (2003). *Which comes first, usability or utility?* IEEE Computer Society. doi:10.1109/VISUAL.2003.1250426

Griol, D., Baena, I., Molina, J. M., & de Miguel, A. S. (2014). A multimodal conversational agent for personalized language learning. In *Ambient intelligence-software and applications* (pp. 13–21). Springer. doi:10.1007/978-3-319-07596-9_2

Grudin, J., & Jacques, R. (2019). Chatbots, humbots, and the quest for artificial general intelligence. *Proceedings of the 2019 CHI Conference on Human Factors in Computing Systems*, (pp. 1–11). ACM. 10.1145/3290605.3300439

Grusky, M., Naaman, M., & Artzi, Y. (2018). Newsroom: A Dataset of 1.3 Million Summaries with Diverse Extractive Strategies. *Proceedings of the 2018 Conference of the North American Chapter of the Association for Computational Linguistics: Human Language Technologies*, (pp. 708–719). ACL. 10.18653/v1/N18-1065

Gull, S., Qureshi, J., & Syed, N. (2019). An indelible link between learning and technology. *Journal of Asian and African Social Science and Humanities, 5*(2), 58–73.

Gunning, D. (2017). Explainable artificial intelligence (xai). Defense Advanced Research Projects Agency (DARPA). *Nd Web, 2*, 2.

Guo, J. (2021). Shing: A Conversational Agent to Alert Customers of Suspected Online-payment Fraud with Empathetical Communication Skills, pp. 1-11. Association for Computing Machinery.

Haake, M., & Gulz, A. (2009). A look at the roles of look & roles in embodied pedagogical agents— A user preference perspective. *International Journal of Artificial Intelligence in Education, 19*, 39–71.

Habash, F. (2018). Unified guidelines and resources for arabic dialect orthography. In *Proceedings of the Eleventh International Conference on Language Resources and Evaluation*. ACL.

Hammad, R. (2018). *A hybrid e-learning framework: Process-based, semantically-enriched and service-oriented* [Doctoral dissertation, University of the West of England].

Hammad, R., Odeh, M., & Khan, Z. (2015). Towards a model-based approach to evaluate the effectiveness of e-learning. In *Proceeding of the 9th European Conference on IS Management and Evaluation ECIME* (pp. 111-119). Research Gate.

Han, X., Zhou, M., Turner, M. J., & Yeh, T. (2021). Designing effective interview chatbots: Automatic chatbot profiling and design suggestion generation for chatbot debugging. *In Proceedings of the 2021 CHI Conference on Human Factors in Computing Systems*, (pp. 1-15). ACM. 10.1145/3411764.3445569

Haristiani, N. (2019). Artificial intelligence (AI) chatbots as language learning medium: An inquiry. *Journal of Physics: Conference Series, 1387*(1), 2020. doi:10.1088/1742-6596/1387/1/012020

Haristiani, N., Danuwijaya, A. A., Rifai, M. M., & Sarila, H. (2019). Gengobot: A chatbot-based grammar application on mobile instant messaging as language learning medium. *Journal of Engineering Science and Technology, 14*, 3158–3173.

Haristiani, N., & Rifai, M. M. (2021). Chatbot-based application development and implementation as an autonomous language learning medium. *Indonesian Journal of Science & Technology, 6*(3), 561–576. doi:10.17509/ijost.v6i3.39150

Harley, J. M., Carter, C. K., Papaionnou, N., Bouchet, F., Landis, R. S., Azevedo, R., & Karabachian, L. (2016). Examining the predictive relationship between personality and emotion traits and students' agent-directed emotions: towards emotionally-adaptive agent-based learning environments. *User Modeling and User-Adapted Interaction, 26*(2-3), 177-219. https://link.springer.com/article/10.1007/s11257-016-9169-7

Harley, J. M., Carter, C. K., Papaionnou, N., Bouchet, F., Landis, R. S., Azevedo, R., & Karabachian, L. (2016). Examining the predictive relationship between personality and emotion traits and students' agent-directed emotions: Towards emotionally-adaptive agent-based learning environments. *User Modeling and User-Adapted Interaction, 26*(2-3), 177–219. doi:10.100711257-016-9169-7

Heffernan, N. T., & Croteau, E. A. (2004). Web-based evaluations showing differential learning for tutorial strategies employed by the Ms. Lindquist tutor. *Proceedings of the International Conference on Intelligent Tutoring Systems.*

Heller, B., Proctor, M., Mah, D., Jewell, L., & Cheung, B. (2005). Freudbot: An investigation of chatbot technology in distance education. In Proceedings of EdMedia + Innovate Learning. Association for the Advancement of Computing in Education (AACE).

Heo, M., & Lee, K. J. (2018). Chatbot as a new business communication tool: The case of Naver TalkTalk. *Business Communication Research and Practice, 1*(1), 41–45. doi:10.22682/bcrp.2018.1.1.41

He, T., Liu, J., Cho, K., Ott, M., Liu, B., Glass, J., & Peng, F. (2021). Analyzing the forgetting problem in the Pretrain-Finetuning of dialogue response models. In *Proceedings of the 16th Conference of the European Chapter of the Association for Computational Linguistics*, (pp. 1121-1133). Association for Computational Linguistics. 10.18653/v1/2021.eacl-main.95

Hien, H. T., Cuong, P.-N., Nam, L. N. H., Nhung, H. L. T. K., & Thang, L. D. (2018). Intelligent assistants in higher-education environments: The FITebot, a chatbot for administrative and learning support. In *Proceedings of the 9th International Symposium on Information and Communication Technology*, (pp. 69–76). ACM. 10.1145/3287921.3287937

Hijjawi, M., Bandar, Z., Crockett, K., & Mclean, D. (2014). ArabChat: An arabic conversational agent. In *2014 6th International Conference on Computer Science and Information Technology (CSIT)* (pp. 227-237). IEEE.

Hijjawi, M., Bandar, Z., & Crockett, K. (2016). The Enhanced Arabchat: An Arabic Conversational Agent. *International Journal of Advanced Computer Science and Applications*, 7(2), 7. doi:10.14569/IJACSA.2016.070247

Hirao, T., Okumura, M., Yasuda, N., & Isozaki, H. (2007). Supervised automatic evaluation for summarization with voted regression model. *Information Processing & Management*, 43(6), 1521–1535. doi:10.1016/j.ipm.2007.01.012

Hiremath, G., Hajare, A., Bhosale, P., Nanaware, R., & Wagh, K. S. (2018). Chatbot for education system. International Journal of Advance Research. *Ideas and Innovations in Technology*, 4(3), 37–43.

Hobert, S. (2019). How Are You, Chatbot? Evaluating Chatbots in Educational Settings – Results of a Literature Review. GI. doi:10.18420/DELFI2019_289

Hobert, S., & Meyer Von Wolff, R. (2019). Say Hello to Your New Automated Tutor -A Structured Literature Review on Pedagogical Conversational Agents. *Core*. https://core.ac.uk/download/pdf/301380749.pdf

Hobert, S., & Meyer von Wolff, R. (2019). *Say hello to your new automated tutor–a structured literature review on pedagogical conversational agents*. CORE.

Hobert, S. (2019). *How are you, chatbot? Evaluating chatbots in educational settings–results of a literature review*. DELFI.

Hochreiter, S., & Schmidhuber, J. (1997). Long Short-term Memory. *Neural Computation*, 9(8), 1735–1780. doi:10.1162/neco.1997.9.8.1735 PMID:9377276

Holmes, S. (2019). Usability testing of a healthcare chatbot: Can we use conventional methods to assess conversational user interfaces? In *Proceedings of the 31st European Conference on Cognitive Ergonomics (ECCE 2019)*. ACM. 10.1145/3335082.3335094

Holroyd, C. (2020). Technological innovation and building a 'super smart' society: Japan's vision of society 5.0. *Journal of Asian Public Policy*, 1–14.

Hornigold, T. (2019). This Chatbot has Over 660 Million Users—and It Wants to Be Their Best Friend. *Singularity Hub.* https://singularityhub.com/2019/07/14/this-chatbot-has-over-660-million-users-and-it-wants-to-be-their-best-friend/

Hsieh, S. W. (2011). Effects of cognitive styles on an MSN virtual learning companion system as an adjunct to classroom instructions. *Journal of Educational Technology & Society, 14*, 161–174.

Hsu, L. (2016). An empirical examination of efl learners' perceptual learning styles and acceptance of asr-based computer-assisted pronunciation training. *Computer Assisted Language Learning, 29*(5), 881–900. doi:10.1080/09588221.2015.1069747

Hu, T. (2018). Touch your heart: A tone-aware chatbot for customer care on social media, pp. 1-12. ACM.

Huang, J., Zhou, M., & Yang, D. (2018). *Exctracting chatbot knowledge from online discussion forums.* In 20th International Joint Conference on Artificial Intelligence, Hydera-bad, India.

Huang, W., Hew, K. F., & Fryer, L. K. (2022). Chatbots for language learning - Are they really useful? A systematic review of chatbot-supported language learning. *Journal of Computer Assisted Learning, 38*(1), 237–257. doi:10.1111/jcal.12610

Hum, H., He, X., & Li, D. (2018). From Eliza to XiaoIce: Challenges and opportunities with social chatbots. *Frontiers of Information Technology & Electronic Engineering, 19*, 10–26.

Hussain, S., Omid, A. S., & Nedal, A. (2019). A survey on conversational agents/chatbots classification and design techniques. *Workshops of the International Conference on Advanced Information Networking and Applications.* Springer.

Hussain, S., & Athula, G. (2018). Extending a conventional chatbot knowledge base to external knowledge source and introducing user based sessions for diabetes education. In *Proceedings of the 32nd International Conference on Advanced Information Networking and Applications Workshops,* (pp. 698-703). IEEE. 10.1109/WAINA.2018.00170

Hu, T., Xu, A., Liu, Z., You, Q., Guo, Y., Sinha, V., Luo, J., & Akkiraju, R. (2018). Touch Your Heart: A Tone-aware Chatbot for Customer Care on Social Media. *Proceedings of the 2018 CHI Conference on Human Factors in Computing Systems,* (pp. 1–12). ACM. 10.1145/3173574.3173989

Hutchinson, A. (2019). Facebook Messenger by the Numbers 2019. *Social Media Today.* https://www.socialmediatoday.com/news/facebook-messenger-by-the-numbers-2019-infographic/553809/

Hwang, G.-J., & Chang, C.-Y. (2021). A review of opportunities and challenges of chatbots in education. *Interactive Learning Environments,* 1–14.

IBM Research Editorial Staff. (2011, February 3). Knowing what it knows: selected nuances of Watson's strategy. IBM *Research Blog.* https://www.ibm.com/blogs/research/2011/02/knowing-what-it-knows-selected-nuances-of-watsons-strategy/

Ilamathi, K., & Banu, R. A., & Divya Priya, B. (2020). Integration of Intelligent Conversational Software or Chat-Bot. In *International Journal of Innovative Research in Science, Engineering and Technology*. http://www.ijirset.com/upload/2020/may/15_Integration_NC.PDF

Inostroza, R., Rusu, C., Roncagliolo, S., Jimenez, C., & Rusu, V. (2012). Usability heuristics for touchscreen-based mobile devices. In *2012 9th International Conference on Information Technology-New Generations*, Las Vegas, NV, USA, pp. 662–667. 10.1109/ITNG.2012.134

Insider Intelligence. (2022). Chatbot market in 2021: Stats, trends, and companies in the growing AI chatbot industry. *Business Insider.* https://www.businessinsider.com/chatbot-market-stats-trends

Insights, F. B. (2021, December 2). Global Chatbot Market: Presence of Large Companies in North America to Facilitate Growth, while Generating USD 1,953.3 Million by 2027, reports Fortune Business InsightsTM. *GlobeNewswire News Room.* https://www.globenewswire.com/news-release/2021/12/02/234474 3/0/en/Global-Chatbot-Market-Presence-of-Large-Companies-in- North-America-to-Facilitate-Growth-while-Generating-USD-1-95 3-3-Million-by-2027-reports-Fortune-Business-Insights.html

Ismail, M., & Ade-Ibijola, A. (2019). Lecturer's apprentice: A chatbot for assisting novice programmers. In *Proceedings of 2019 IEEE International Multidisciplinary Information Technology and Engineering Conference*, (pp. 1-8). IEEE. 10.1109/IMITEC45504.2019.9015857

ISTE. (2017). *ISTE standards for students.* ISTE. https://www.iste.org/standards/standards/ for-students

Jain, M., Kumar, P., Kota, R., & Patel, S. N. (2018). *Evaluating and Informing the Design of Chatbots.* . Association for Computing Machinery.

Jain, M., Kumar, P., Kota, R., & Patel, S. N. (2018). *Evaluating and Informing the Design of Chatbots.* Association for Computing Machinery.

Jain, M., Kumar, P., Kota, R., & Patel, S. N. (2018). Evaluating and informing the design of chatbots. *Proceedings of the 2018 Designing Interactive Systems Conference*, (pp. 895–906). ACM. 10.1145/3196709.3196735

James, R. (2021, February 11). Are Chatbots Vulnerable? Best Practices to Ensure Chatbots Security. *Medium.* https://chatbotslife.com/are-chatbots-vulnerable-best-practi ces-to-ensure-chatbots-security-d301b9f6ce17

Jia, J. (2003). *The Study of the Application of a Keywords-based Chatbot System on the Teaching of Foreign Languages.* Cornell University.

Jia, J. (2004). *The study of the application of a web-based chatbot system on the teaching of foreign languages.* In the Society for Information Technology & Teacher Education International Conference, Atlanta, GA, USA.

Jia, J. (2003). *The study of the application of a keywords-based chatbot system on the teaching of foreign languages.* Cornell University.

Jia, J. (2009). CSIEC: A computer assisted English learning chatbot based on textual knowledge and reasoning. *Knowledge-Based Systems*, *22*(4), 249–255. doi:10.1016/j.knosys.2008.09.001

Jurafsky, D., & Martin, J. (2021). Speech and language processing (3rd ed.). Stanford Press. https://web.stanford.edu/~jurafsky/slp3/

Jurafsky, D., & Martin, J. H. (2021). Speech and Language Processing. *Stanford Press*. https://web.stanford.edu/~jurafsky/slp3/

Jurafsky, D., & Martin, J. (2020). *Speech and Language Processing: An Introduction to Natural Language Processing* (Vol. 2). Computational Linguistics, and Speech Recognition.

Kaczorowska-Spychalska, D. (2019). Chatbots in marketing. *Management*, *23*(1).

Kaleem, M., Alobadi, O., O'Shea, J., & Crockett, K. (2016). *Framework for the formulation of metrics for conversational agent evaluation.* In RE-WOCHAT: Workshop on Collecting and Generating Resources for Chatbots and Conversational Agents-Development and Evaluation Workshop, Portorož, Slovenia.

Kannan, A., & Vinyals, O. (2017). Adversarial Evaluation of Dialogue Models. https://arxiv.org/abs/1701.08198

Kasthuri, E., & Balaji, S. (2021). A Chatbot for Changing Lifestyle in Education. *2021 Third International Conference On Intelligent Communication Technologies And Virtual Mobile Networks (ICICV).* IEEE. 10.1109/ICICV50876.2021.9388633

Kawasaki, M., Yamashita, N., Lee, Y.-C., & Nohara, K. (2020). Assessing Users' Mental Status from their Journaling Behavior through Chatbots. *Proceedings of the 20th ACM International Conference on Intelligent Virtual Agents (IVA '20)*, (pp. 1–8). ACM. 10.1145/3383652.3423870

Keierleber, M. (2022, April 13). Young and depressed? Try Woebot! The rise of mental health chatbots in the US. *The Guardian*. https://www.theguardian.com/us-news/2022/apr/13/chatbots-robot-therapists-youth-mental-health-crisis

Khan, S., & Rabbani, M. R. (2020). Chatbot as Islamic Finance Expert (CaIFE) When Finance Meets Artificial Intelligence. In *Proceedings of the 2020 4th International Symposium on Computer Science and Intelligent Control*, (pp. 1-5).

Kik. (2022). Poncho the Weathercat. *Kik*. https://www.kik.com/bots/poncho/

Kim, L. (2020, March 11). The Big List of the World's Most Popular Chatbots. *MobileMonkey*. https://mobilemonkey.com/blog/popular-chatbots

Kimmarita, L. (2022, August 24). Ministry to launch app, chatbot to help counter gender violence. *The Phnom Penh Post*. Www.phnompenhpost.com. https://www.phnompenhpost.com/national/ministry-launch-app-chatbot-help-counter-gender-violence

Kim, N.-Y. (2016). Effects of voice chat on EFL learners' speaking ability according to proficiency levels. *Multimedia-Assisted Language Learning, 19*(4), 63–88.

Kim, S. (2020). *Bot in the Bunch: Facilitating Group Chat Discussion by Improving Efficiency and Participation with a Chatbot.* . Association for Computing Machinery.

Kim, S., Lee, J., & Gweon, G. (2019). *Comparing Data from Chatbot and Web Surveys: Effects of Platform and Conversational Style on Survey Response Quality.* Association for Computing Machinery.

Kitaev, N., Kaiser, Ł., & Levskaya, A. (2020). Reformer: The Efficient Transformer. https://arxiv.org/abs/2001.04451

Kjuve, M., Følstad, A., Fostervold, K. I. & Brandtzaeg, P. B. (2022). A longitudinal study of human--chatbot relationships. *International Journal of Human-Computer Studies, 168*, 102903.

Kleoniki, A., Magkitouka, N., Tegos, S., & Demetriadis, S. (2012). Conversational agents in education: Using MentorChat to support students' dialogue. In *8th Pan-Hellenic Conference with International Participation "Information and Communication Technologies in Education"*, Volos, Greece.

Klopfenstein, L. C., Delpriori, S., Malatini, S., & Bogliolo, A. (2017, June). The rise of bots: A survey of conversational interfaces, patterns, and paradigms. In *Proceedings of the 2017 conference on designing interactive systems* (pp. 555-565). ACM. 10.1145/3064663.3064672

Knight, W. (2022, August 5). We Interviewed Meta's New AI Chatbot About … Itself. *Wired.* https://www.wired.com/story/blenderbot3-ai-chatbot-meta-interview/

Koehn, P., Hoang, H., Birch, A., Callison-Burch, C., Federico, M., Bertoldi, N., Cowan, B., Shen, W., Moran, C., Zens, R., Dyer, C., Bojar, O., Constantin, A., & Herbst, E. (2007). Moses: Open Source Toolkit for Statistical Machine Translation. *Proceedings of the 45th Annual Meeting of the Association for Computational Linguistics Companion*, (pp. 177–180). ACL. https://aclanthology.org/P07-2045

Ko, M. C., & Lin, Z. H. (2018). CardBot: A chatbot for business card management. In *Proceedings of the 23rd International Conference on Intelligent User Interfaces Companion*, (pp: 1–2). ACM. 10.1145/3180308.3180313

Kowatsch, T. (2017). *Text-based Healthcare Chatbots Supporting Patient and Health Professional Teams: Preliminary Results of a Randomized Controlled Trial on Childhood Obesity.* Paper presented at the Persuasive Embodies Conference on Intellifent Cirttual Agents. Stockholm, Sweeden.

Krassmann, A. L., Flach, J. M., Grando, A. R. C. D. S., Tarouco, L. M. R., & Bercht, M. (2019). A process for extracting knowledge base for chatbots from text corpora. In *IEEE Global Engineering Education Conference*, (pp. 322-329). IEEE. 10.1109/EDUCON.2019.8725064

Kruger, J.-L., & Steyn, F. (2013). Subtitles and Eye Tracking: Reading and Performance. *Reading Research Quarterly*, *49*(1), 105–120. doi:10.1002/rrq.59

Kryscinski, W., McCann, B., Xiong, C., & Socher, R. (2020). Evaluating the Factual Consistency of Abstractive Text Summarization. *Proceedings of the 2020 Conference on Empirical Methods in Natural Language Processing (EMNLP)*, (pp. 9332–9346). ACL. 10.18653/v1/2020.emnlp-main.750

Kuhail, M. A., Thomas, J., Alramlawi, S., Shah, S. J. H., & Thornquist, E. (2022, October). Interacting with a Chatbot-Based Advising System: Understanding the Effect of Chatbot Personality and User Gender on Behavior. In Informatics, 9(4), 81. MDPI.

Kuhail, M. A., Thomas, J., Alramlawi, S., Shah, S. J. H., & Thornquist, E. (2022b). Interacting with a Chatbot-Based Advising System: Understanding the Effect of Chatbot Personality and User Gender on Behavior. In Informatics, 9(4), 81. MDPI.

Kuhail, M. A., Al Katheeri, H., Negreiros, J., Seffah, A., & Alfandi, O. (2022). Engaging Students With a Chatbot-Based Academic Advising System. *International Journal of Human-Computer Interaction*, 1–27. doi:10.1080/10447318.2022.2074645

Kuhail, M. A., Alturki, N., Alramlawi, S., & Alhejori, K. (2022). Interacting with educational chatbots: A systematic review. *Education and Information Technologies*. Advance online publication. doi:10.100710639-022-11177-3

Kulkarni, C. E., Bernstein, M. S., & Klemmer, S. R. (2015). PeerStudio: rapid peer feedback emphasizes revision and improves performance. *In Proceedings of the second ACM conference on learning@ scale,* (pp. 75-84). ACM.

Kulkarni, P., Mahabaleshwarkar, A., Kulkarni, M., Sirsikar, N., & Gadgil, K. (2019). Conversational ai: An overview of methodologies, applications & future scope. In *2019 5th International Conference on Computing, Communication, Control and Automation (ICCUBEA)*, (pp. 1–7). IEEE.

Kumar, R., & Ali, M. (2008). *A Review on Chatbot Design and Implementation Techniques*. Research Gate.

Kusber, R. (2017). Chatbots–conversational UX platforms. In *Innovationen und Innovationsmanagement in der Finanzbranche* (pp. 231–244). Springer Gabler. doi:10.1007/978-3-658-15648-0_11

Lam, C. S. N., Chan, L. K., & See, C. Y. H. (2018). Converse, connect and consolidate–The development of an artificial intelligence chatbot for health sciences education. In *Frontiers in medical and health sciences education conference*. Bau Institute of Medical and Health Sciences Education, The University of Hong Kong.

Laranjo, L., Dunn, A. G., Tong, H. L., Kocaballi, A. B., Chen, J., Bashir, R., Surian, D., Gallego, B., Magrabi, F., Lau, A. Y. S., & Coiera, E. (2018). Conversational agents in healthcare: A systematic review. *Journal of the American Medical Informatics Association: JAMIA*, *25*(9), 1248–1258. https://doi.org/10.1093/jamia/ocy072

Learner, D. S. (2022, July 25). 7 Actionable Tips for Chatbot Security. *Data Science Learner*. https://www.datasciencelearner.com/actionable-tips-for-chatbot-security/

Lee, J. H., Yang, H., Shin, D., & Kim, H. (2020). Chatbots. *ELT Journal*, 74(3), 338–344. doi:10.1093/elt/ccaa035

Lee, J. Y., & Hwang, Y. (2022). A meta-analysis of the effects of using AI chatbots in Korean EFL education. *Studies in English Language & Literature*, 48(1), 213–243. doi:10.21087/nsell.2022.11.83.213

Lee, L.-K., Fung, Y.-C., Pun, Y.-W., Wong, K.-K., Yu, M. T.-Y., & Wu, N.-I. (2020). *Using a multiplatform chatbot as an onlinetutor in a university course. In 2020 international symposium on educational technology (ISET)*. IEEE.

Lee, Y. C., Yamashita, N., & Huang, Y. 2020. Designing a chatbot as a mediator for promoting deep self-disclosure to a real mental health professional. *Proceedings of the ACM on Human-Computer Interaction*, (pp. 1-27). ACM.

Lee, Y. C., Yamashita, N., & Huang, Y. 2021. Exploring the Effects of Incorporating Human Experts to Deliver Journaling Guidance through a Chatbot. *Proceedings of the ACM on Human-Computer Interaction*, (pp. 1-27). ACM.

Lee, Y.-C., Yamashita, N., Huang, Y., & Fu, W. (2020). *"I Hear You, I Feel You": Encouraging Deep Self-disclosure through a Chatbot*. Association for Computing Machinery.

Leonhardt, M., Tarouco, L. M. R., Vicari, R., Santos, E. R., & Da Silva, M. D. S. (2007). Using chatbots for network management training through problem-based oriented education. In *Proceedings of the Seventh IEEE International Conference on Advanced Learning Technologies*, (pp. 845-847). IEEE. 10.1109/ICALT.2007.275

Lester, J. C., Converse, S. A., Kahler, S. E., Barlow, S. T., Stone, B. A., & Bhogal, R. S. (1997). The persona effect: Affective impact of animated pedagogical agents. In *Proceedings of the ACMSIGCHI Conference on Human Factors in Computing Systems*, (pp. 359–366). ACM. 10.1145/258549.258797

Lewis, J. R. (1995). Computer system usability questionnaire. *International Journal of Human-Computer Interaction*.

Lewis, M., Liu, Y., Goyal, N., Ghazvininejad, M., Mohamed, A., Levy, O., Stoyanov, V., & Zettlemoyer, L. (2020). BART: Denoising Sequence-to-Sequence Pre-training for Natural Language Generation, Translation, and Comprehension. *Proceedings of the 58th Annual Meeting of the Association for Computational Linguistics*, (pp. 7871–7880). ACL. 10.18653/v1/2020.acl-main.703

Lin, C.-Y., & Hovy, E. (2003). Automatic Evaluation of Summaries Using N-gram Co-occurrence Statistics. *Proceedings of the 2003 Human Language Technology Conference of the North American Chapter of the Association for Computational Linguistics*, (pp. 150–157). ACL. https://aclanthology.org/N03-1020

Lin, M. P., & Chang, D. (2020). Enhancing Post-secondary Writers' Writing Skills with a Chatbot: A Mixed-Method Classroom Study. *Journal of Educational Technology & Society*, *23*, 78–92.

Lin, Y. H., & Tsai, T. (2019, December). A conversational assistant on mobile devices for primitive learners of computer programming. In *2019 IEEE International Conference on Engineering, Technology and Education (TALE)* (pp. 1-4). IEEE. 10.1109/TALE48000.2019.9226015

Lison, P., & Tiedemann, J. (2016). *Opensubtitles2016: Extracting large parallel corpora from movie and TV subtitles.* In 10th edition of the Language Resources and Evaluation Conference, Portorož, Slovenia.

Li, T. J.-J., Azaria, A., & Myers, B. A. (2017). SUGILITE: Creating Multimodal Smartphone Automation by Demonstration. *Proceedings of the 2017 CHI Conference on Human Factors in Computing Systems*, (pp. 6038–6049). ACM. 10.1145/3025453.3025483

Liu, Y., Muheidat, F., Papailler, K., & Prado, W. (n.d.). VR Meets AI Meets the Matrix: Using Embodied Conversational Agents for Experiential Learning. *Educause.* https://events.educause.edu/eli/annual-meeting/2022/agenda/vr-meets-ai-meets-the-matrix-using-embodied-conversational-agents-for-experiential-learning

Liu, M. (2018). *ReactionBot: Exploring the Effects of Expression-Triggered Emoji in Text Messages.* . Association for Computing Machinery.

Liu, Q., Liu, W., Yao, J., Liu, Y., & Pan, M. (2021). An Improved Method of Reservoir Facies Modeling Based on Generative Adversarial Networks. *Energies*, *14*(13), 3873. doi:10.3390/en14133873

Lokman, A. S., & Ameedeen, M. A. (2018). Modern chatbot systems: A technical review. *In Proceedings of the future technologies conference* (pp. 1012-1023). Springer.

Lombardi, M., Pascale, F., & Santaniello, D. (2019). An application for cultural heritage using a chatbot. In *Proceedings of the 2nd International Conference on Computer Applications & Information Security.* IEEE. 10.1109/CAIS.2019.8769525

Lowe, R., Noseworthy, M., Serban, I. V., Angelard-Gontier, N., Bengio, Y., & Pineau, J. (2018). Towards an Automatic Turing Test: Learning to Evaluate Dialogue Responses. https://arxiv.org/abs/1708.07149

Lu, Z., & Li, H. (2013). A Deep Architecture for Matching Short Texts. *Advances in Neural Information Processing Systems*, *26*. https://papers.nips.cc/paper/2013/hash/8a0e1141fd37fa5b98d5bb769ba1a7cc-Abstract.html

Lukovnikov, D., Fischer, A., & Lehmann, J. (2019). Pretrained Transformers for Simple Question Answering over Knowledge Graphs. In C. Ghidini, O. Hartig, M. Maleshkova, V. Svátek, I. Cruz, A. Hogan, J. Song, M. Lefrançois, & F. Gandon (eds.), The Semantic Web – ISWC 2019, (pp. 470–486). Springer International Publishing. doi:10.1007/978-3-030-30793-6_27

Lunden, I. (2016). Facebook opens analytics and FbStart to developers of the 34,000 bots on Messenger. *Tech Crunch.* https://techcrunch.com/2016/11/14/facebook-opens-analytics-and-fbstart-to-messengers-34000-bot-developers/

Lytras, M., Visvizi, A., Damiani, E., & Mathkour, H. (2019). The cognitive computing turn in education Prospects and application. *Computers in Human Behavior, 92,* 446–449. doi:10.1016/j.chb.2018.11.011

Mabunda, K., & Ade-Ibijola, A. (2019). Pathbot: An intelligent chatbot for guiding visitors and locating venues. In *Proceedings of 2019 IEEE 6th International Conference on Soft Computing & Machine Intelligence,* (pp: 160-168). IEEE. 10.1109/ISCMI47871.2019.9004411

Mageira, K., Pittou, D., Papasalouros, A., Kotis, K., Zangogianni, P., & Daradoumis, A. (2022). Educational AI chatbots for content and language integrated learning. *Applied Sciences (Basel, Switzerland), 12*(7), 3239. doi:10.3390/app12073239

Majumder, N. (2020). MIME: MIMicking Emotions for Empathetic Response Generation. *arXiv preprint arXiv:2010.01454.*

Makatchev, M., Fanaswala, I., Abdulsalam, A., Browning, B., Ghazzawi, W., Sakr, M., & Simmons, R. (2010). Dialogue patterns of an Arabic robot receptionist. In *2010 5th ACM/IEEE International Conference on Human-Robot Interaction (HRI)* (pp. 167-168). IEEE.

Masche, J., & Le, N.-T. (2017). A review of technologies for conversational systems. *International conference on computer science, applied mathematics and applications.* Springer.

Mateos-Sanchez, M., Melo, A. C., Blanco, L. S., & García, A. M. F. (2022). Chatbot, as educational and inclusive tool for people with intellectual disabilities. *Sustainability, 4*(3), 1520. doi:10.3390u14031520

Mathenge, R. (2022, June 29). Chatbot security measures you need to consider. *PrivacySavvy.* https://privacysavvy.com/security/business/chatbot-security/

Mathur, V. & Singh, A. (2018). *The rapidly changing landscape of conversational agents.* Cornell University.

Mavridis, N., AlDhaheri, A., AlDhaheri, L., Khanii, M., & AlDarmaki, N. (2011). Transforming IbnSina into an advanced multilingual interactive android robot. In 2011 IEEE GCC Conference and Exhibition (GCC) (pp. 120-123). IEEE. doi:10.1109/IEEEGCC.2011.5752467

Mayer, R. E. (2017). Using multimedia for e-learning. *Journal of Computer Assisted Learning, 33*(5), 403–423. doi:10.1111/jcal.12197

McCrae, R. R., & Costa, P. T. (1985). Updating Norman's «adequacy taxonomy»: Intelligence and personality dimensions in natural language and in questionnaires. *Journal of Personality and Social Psychology, 49*(3), 710–721. doi:10.1037/0022-3514.49.3.710 PMID:4045699

McCrae, R. R., & John, O. P. (1992). An introduction to the five-factor model and its applications. *Journal of Personality, 60*(2), 175–215. doi:10.1111/j.1467-6494.1992.tb00970.x PMID:1635039

Mckie, I. A. S., & Narayan, B. (2019). Enhancing the academic library experience with chatbots: An exploration of research and implications for practice. *Journal of the Australian Library and Information Association*, *68*(3), 268–277. doi:10.1080/24750158.2019.1611694

McNeal, M. L., & Newyear, D. (2013). Chapter 1: Introducing chatbots in libraries. Library Technolgy Reports, 49(8), 5-10.

McTear, M. (2021). *Conversational AI*. Morgan & Claypool.

McTear, M., Callejas, Z., & Griol, D. (2016). *The Conversational Interface*. Springer International Publishing. doi:10.1007/978-3-319-32967-3

McTear, M. (2020). Conversational ai: Dialogue systems, conversational agents, and chatbots. *Synthesis Lectures on Human Language Technologies*, *13*(3), 1–251. doi:10.1007/978-3-031-02176-3

Medeiros, L., Bosse, T., & Gerritsen, C. (2021). Can a Chatbot Comfort Humans? Studying the Impact of a Supportive Chatbot on Users' Self-Perceived Stress. *IEEE Transactions on Human-Machine Systems*, 343–353.

Medeiros, R. P., Ramalho, G. L., & Falcão, T. P. (2018). A systematic literature review on teaching and learning introductory programming in higher education. *IEEE Transactions on Education*, *62*(2), 77–90. doi:10.1109/TE.2018.2864133

Meffert, K. (2006). Supporting design patterns with annotations. In *13th Annual IEEE International Symposium and Workshop on Engineering of Computer-Based Systems (ECBS'06)*. (pp. 8). IEEE.

Mendez, S., Johanson, K., Martin Conley, V., Gosha, K., & Mack, A. (2020). Chatbots: Atoolto supplementthe future faculty mentoring of doctoral engineering students. *International Journal of Doctoral Studies*, *15*, 15. doi:10.28945/4579

Merchant, S. (2021, March 2). *The Best ChatBots For Behavioral Health*. AIM. https://www.aimblog.io/2021/03/02/these-chatbots-are-helping-with-mental-health-right-now/

Mesnil, G., Dauphin, Y., Yao, K., Bengio, Y., Deng, L., Hakkani-Tur, D., He, X., Heck, L., Tur, G., Yu, D., & Zweig, G. (2015). Using recurrent neural networks for slot filling in spoken language understanding. *IEEE/ACM Transactions on Audio, Speech, and Language Processing*, *23*(3), 530–539. doi:10.1109/TASLP.2014.2383614

Meyer von Wolff, R., & Hobert, S. (2019). Say Hello to Your New Automated Tutor – A Structured Literature Review on Pedagogical Conversational Agents, *Internationale Tagung Wirtschaftsinformatik*, *1*(14), 301-314. Tagungsband

Mikic-Fonte, F. A., Llamas-Nistal, M., & Caeiro-Rodríguez, M. (2018, October). Using a Chatterbot as a FAQ Assistant in a Course about Computers Architecture. In *2018 IEEE Frontiers in Education Conference (FIE)* (pp. 1-4). IEEE. 10.1109/FIE.2018.8659174

Mims, C. (2014). Advertising's New Frontier: Talk to the Bot. *Wall Street Journal*. https://www.wsj.com/articles/advertisings-new-frontier-talk-to-the-bot-1406493740

Mnasri, M. (2019). *Recent advances in conversational NLP: Towards the standardization of Chatbot building.* Cornell University.

Mnasri, M. (2019). *Recent advances in conversational NLP: Towards the standardization of Chatbot building.* Cornell University. https://arxiv.org/abs/1903.09025

Moher, D., Liberati, A., Tetzlaff, J., & Altman, D. G. (2009). The PRISMA Group (2009) Preferred reporting items for systematic reviews and meta-analyses: The PRISMA statement. *PLoS Medicine*, 6(7), e1000097. doi:10.1371/journal.pmed.1000097 PMID:19621072

Molnar, G., & Szuts, Z. (2018). The role of chatbots in formal education. In *Proceedings of the 2018 IEEE 16th International Symposium on Intelligent Systems and Informatics*, (pp. 197-202). IEEE. 10.1109/SISY.2018.8524609

Mondal, A., Dey, M., Das, D., Nagpal, S., & Garda, K. (2018). Chatbot: An automated conversation system for the educational domain. In *Proceedings of the International Joint Symposium on Artificial Intelligence and Natural Language Processing*, (pp. 1-5). IEEE. 10.1109/iSAI-NLP.2018.8692927

Mordor Intelligence. (2022). *Chatbot Market - Growth, Trends, Covid-19 Impact, And Forecasts (2022 - 2027).* Mordor Intelligence. https://www.mordorintelligence.com/industry-reports/chatbot-market

Moriuchi, E., Landers, M., Colton, D., & Hair, N. (2021). Engagement with chatbots versus augmented reality interactive technology in e-commerce. *Journal of Strategic Marketing*, 29(5), 375–389. doi:10.1080/0965254X.2020.1740766

Morris, R., Kouddous, K., Kshirsagar, R., & Schueller, S. (2018). Towards an artificially empathic conversational agent for mental health applications: System design and user perceptions. *Journal of Medical Internet Research*, 20(6), e10148.

Mou, Y., & Xu, K. (2017). The media inequality: Comparing the initial human-human and human-AI social interactions. *Computers in Human Behavior*, 72, 432–440. doi:10.1016/j.chb.2017.02.067

Murad, C., Munteanu, C., Cowan, B. R., & Clark, L. (2019). evolution or Evolution? Speech Interaction and HCI Design Guidelines. *IEEE Pervasive Computing*, 18(2), 33–45. doi:10.1109/MPRV.2019.2906991

Murad, C., Munteanu, C., Cowan, B. R., & Clark, L. (2019). Revolution or evolution? Speech interaction and HCI design guidelines. *IEEE Pervasive Computing*, 18(2), 33–45. https://doi.org/10.1109/MPRV.2019.2906991

Murad, D. F., Irsan, M., Akhirianto, P. M., Fernando, E., Murad, S. A., & Wijaya, M. H. (2019, July). Learning Support System using Chatbot in" Kejar C Package" Homeschooling Program. In *2019 International Conference on Information and Communications Technology (ICOIACT)* (pp. 32-37). IEEE. 10.1109/ICOIACT46704.2019.8938479

Naffi, N., Davidson, A., Boch, A., Nandaba, B. K., & Rougui, M. (2022). AI-powered chatbots, designed ethically, can support high-quality university teaching. *The Conversation.* https://theconversation.com/ai-powered-chatbots-designed-ethically-can-support-high-quality-university-teaching-172719

Naous, T., Hokayem, C., & Hajj, H. (2020). Empathy-driven Arabic conversational chatbot. *In Proceedings of the Fifth Arabic Natural Language Processing Workshop* (pp. 58-68). ACLA.

Nardi, B. A., & O'Day, V. (1996). Intelligent agents: What we learned at the library. *Libri, 46*(2), 59–88. doi:10.1515/libr.1996.46.2.59

Naseem, U., Razzak, I., Musial, K., & Imran, M. (2020). Transformer-based Deep Intelligent Contextual Embedding for Twitter sentiment analysis. *Future Generation Computer Systems, 113*, 58–69. doi:10.1016/j.future.2020.06.050

Nass, C. (1995). *Can computer personalities be human personalities?* Association for Computing Machinery.

Nathoo, A., Gangabissoon, T., & Bekaroo, G. (2019). Exploring the use of tangible user interfaces for teaching basic java programming concepts: A usability study. 2019 conference on next generation computing applications. NextComp.

Naveen Kumar, M., Chandar, P. C. L., Prasad, A. V., & Sumangali, K. (2016). Android based educational chatbot for visually impaired people. In *Proceedings of the IEEE International Conference on Computational Intelligence and Computing Research*, (pp. 1-4). IEEE.

Nazareno, D., de Melo, A., & Monteiro, I. T. (2021). Communication and personality: How COVID-19 government chatbots express themselves. *Proceedings of the XX Brazilian Symposium on Human Factors in Computing Systems*, (pp. 1–10). ACM. 10.1145/3472301.3484362

Ndukwe, I. G., Daniel, B. K., & Amadi, C. E. (2019, June). A machine learning grading system using chatbots. In *International conference on artificial intelligence in education* (pp. 365-368). Springer. 10.1007/978-3-030-23207-8_67

Neff, G., & Nagy, P. (2016). Automation, Algorithms, and Politics| Talking to Bots: Symbiotic Agency and the Case of Tay. *International Journal of Communication, 10*(0), 17. https://ijoc.org/index.php/ijoc/article/view/6277/1804

Negosanti, P. (2022, August 24). *Chatbots are revolutionizing the insurance industry.* PropertyCasualty360. https://www.propertycasualty360.com/2022/08/24/how-chatbots-are-revolutionizing-the-insurance-industry/?slreturn=2022072 5025922

Nenkova, A., & Passonneau, R. (2004). Evaluating Content Selection in Summarization: The Pyramid Method. *Proceedings of the Human Language Technology Conference of the North American Chapter of the Association for Computational Linguistics.* (pp. 145–152). ACL. https://aclanthology.org/N04-1019

Neves, A. M. M., Barros, F. A., & Hodges, C. (2006). IAIML: A mechanism to treat intentionality in AIML chatterbots. In *Proceedings of the International Conference on Tools with Artificial Intelligence*, (pp. 225-231). IEEE. 10.1109/ICTAI.2006.64

Newby, M., Nguyen, T. H., & Waring, T. S. (2014). Understanding customer relationship management technology adoption in small and medium-sized enterprises: An empirical study in the USA. *Journal of Enterprise Information Management.* doi:10.1108/JEIM-11-2012-0078

Ngai, E. W., Lee, M. C., Luo, M., Chan, P. S., & Liang, T. (2021). An intelligent knowledge-based chatbot for customer service. *Electronic Commerce Research and Applications*, *50*, 101098. doi:10.1016/j.elerap.2021.101098

Nguyen, H. D., Pham, V. T., Tran, D. A., & Le, T. T. (2019, October). Intelligent tutoring chatbot for solving mathematical problems in High-school. In *2019 11th International Conference on Knowledge and Systems Engineering (KSE)* (pp. 1-6). IEEE. 10.1109/KSE.2019.8919396

Nguyen, T., Le, A., Hoang, H., & Nguyen, T. (2021). NEU-chatbot: Chatbot for admission of National Economics University. *Computers And Education: Artificial Intelligence*, *2*, 100036. doi:10.1016/j.caeai.2021.100036

Nielsen Corporation. (2011) *State of the Media: Social Media Report Q3*. Nielsen. https://www.nielsen.com/insights/2011/social-mediareport-q3/, urldate = 2022-10-15

Nielsen, J. (1994). Enhancing the explanatory power of usability heuristics. In *Proceedings of the SIGCHI Conference on Human Factors in Computing Systems (CHI '94)* (pp. 152–158). ACM. doi:10.1145/191666.191729

Nielsen, J. (1994). *Usability Engineering*. Academic Press.

Nielsen, J., & Levy, J. (1994). Measuring usability: Preference vs. performance. *Communications of the ACM*, *4*(37), 66–75. doi:10.1145/175276.175282

Ni, L., Lu, C., Liu, N., & Liu, J. (2017). MANDY: Towards a Smart Primary Care Chatbot Application. In J. Chen, T. Theeramunkong, T. Supnithi, & X. Tang (Eds.), *Knowledge and Systems Sciences. Communications in Computer and Information Science.* Springer. doi:10.1007/978-981-10-6989-5_4

Nirala, K. K., Singh, N. K., & Purani, V. S. (2022). A survey on providing customer and public administration based services using AI: chatbot. *Multimedia Tools and Applications.* doi:10.1007/s11042-021-11458-y

Novak, T. P., & Hoffman, L. (2019). Relationship journeys in the internet of things: A new framework for understanding interactions between consumers and smart objects. *Journal of the Academy of Marketing Science*, *2*(47), 216–237. doi:10.100711747-018-0608-3

Nuruzzaman, M., & Hussain, O. K. (2018). A survey on chatbot implementation in customer service industry through deep neural networks. In *Proceedings of the IEEE 15th International Conference on e-Business Engineering*, (pp. 54-61). IEEE. 10.1109/ICEBE.2018.00019

Nurvembrianti, I., Arianti, N., & Noftalina, E. (2022). The use of Telegram chatbot application services as a means of communication in increasing satisfaction and knowledge of mothers who have toddlers. *Galore International Journal of Health Sciences and Research*, 7(1), 19–25. doi:10.52403/gijhsr.20220103

O'Brien, H. L., & Toms, G. (2010). The development and evaluation of a survey to measure user engagement. *Journal of the American Society for Information Science and Technology*, 61(1), 50–69. doi:10.1002/asi.21229

O'Leary, D. E. (2022). Massive data language models and conversational artificial intelligence: Emerging issues. *Intelligent Systems in Accounting, Finance & Management*, 29(3), 182–198. https://doi.org/10.1002/isaf.1522

Oh, K. J., Lee, D., Ko, B., & Choi, H.-J. (2017). *A chatbot for psychiatric counseling in mental healthcare service based on emotional dialogue analysis and sentence generation*. doi:10.1109/MDM.2017.64

Okonkwo, C. W., & Ade-Ibijola, A. (2020). Python-Bot: A Chatbot for Teaching Python Programming. *Engineering Letters, 29*(1).

Okonkwo, C. W., & Ade-Ibijola, A. (2021). Chatbots applications in education: A systematic review. *Computers and Education: Artificial Intelligence*, 2, 100033. doi:10.1016/j.caeai.2021.100033

Okuda, T., & Shoda, S. (2018). AI-based chatbot service for financial industry. *Fujitsu Scientific and Technical Journal*, 54(2), 4–8.

Ondáš, S., Pleva, M., & Hládek, D. (2019). How chatbots can be involved in the education process. In *2019 17th international conference on emerging elearning technologies and applications (ICETA)* (pp. 575–580). IEEE. 10.1109/ICETA48886.2019.9040095

Ong, R. J., Raof, R. A. A., Sudin, S., & Choong, K. Y. (2021). A Review of Chatbot development for Dynamic Web-based Knowledge Management System (KMS) in Small Scale Agriculture. *Journal of Physics: Conference Series*, 1755(1), 012051. https://doi.org/10.1088/1742-6596/1755/1/012051

Oudeyer, P.-Y., Gottlieb, J., & Lopes, M. (2016). Intrinsic motivation, curiosity, and learning: Theory and applications in educational technologies. In B. S. S. Knecht (Ed.), Progress in Brain Research: Vol. 229. *MotivationTheory, Neurobiology and Applications* (pp. 257–284). Elsevier. doi:10.1016/bs.pbr.2016.05.005

Pachamanova, D., Lo, V. S., & Gülpınar, N. (2020). Uncertainty representation and risk management for direct segmented marketing. *Journal of Marketing Management*, 36(1-2), 149–175. doi:10.1080/0267257X.2019.1707265

Papineni, K., Roukos, S., Ward, T., & Zhu, W.-J. (2002). Bleu: A Method for Automatic Evaluation of Machine Translation. *Proceedings of the 40th Annual Meeting of the Association for Computational Linguistics*, (pp. 311–318). ACM. 10.3115/1073083.1073135

Patel, S. (2019, August 21). 9 Excellent Benefits of Using Chatbots in Your Business. *REVE Chat*. https://www.revechat.com/blog/chatbot-business-benefits/

Patil, A., Marimuthu, K., & Niranchana, R. (2017). Comparative study of cloud platforms to develop a Chatbot. *IACSIT International Journal of Engineering and Technology*, 6(3), 57–61. doi:10.14419/ijet.v6i3.7628

Pears, M., Henderson, J., Bamidis, P., Pattichis, C., Karlgren, K., Wharrad, H., & Konstantinidis, S. (2021). Co-creation of chatbots as an educational resource: Training the trainers workshop. In *Proceedings of the 15th International Technology, Education and Development Conference*, (pp. 7808-7815). University of Nottingham.

Peng, Z., & Ma, X. (2019). A survey on construction and enhancement methods in service chatbots design. *CCF Transactions on Pervasive Computing and Interaction*, 1(3), 204–223. doi:10.100742486-019-00012-3

Pereira, M. J. & Luisa, C. (2013). *Just. Chat-a platform for processing information to be used in chatbots*. Semantic Scholar.

Perera, V. H., Senarathne, A. N., & Rupasinghe, L. (2019). Intelligent SOC Chatbot for Security Operation Center. *2019 International Conference on Advancements in Computing (ICAC)*. doi:10.1109/icac49085.2019.9103388

Pérez, J. Q. T. D. J. M. M. P., Daradoumis, T., & Puig, J. M. M. (2020). Rediscovering the use of chatbots in education: A systematic literature review. *Computer Applications in Engineering Education*, 28(6), 1549–1565. doi:10.1002/cae.22326

Pérez-Marín, D., & Pascual-Nieto, I. (2013). An exploratory study on how children interact with pedagogic conversational agents. *Behaviour & Information Technology*, 32(9), 955–964. doi:10.1080/0144929X.2012.687774

Peterson, B. (2017, October 29). I met Sophia, the word's first robot citizen, and the way she said goodbye nearly broke my heart. *Business Insider*. https://www.businessinsider.in/tech/i-met-sophia-the-words-first-robot-citizen-and-the-way-she-said-goodbye-nearly-broke-my-heart/articleshow/61322091.cms

Peyrard, M., Botschen, T., & Gurevych, I. (2017). Learning to Score System Summaries for Better Content Selection Evaluation. *Proceedings of the Workshop on New Frontiers in Summarization*, (pp. 74–84). ACL. 10.18653/v1/W17-4510

Pham, X., Pham, T., Nguyen, Q., Nguyen, T., & Cao, T. (2018). Chatbot as an Intelligent Personal Assistant for Mobile Language Learning. *Proceedings Of The 2018 2Nd International Conference On Education And E-Learning*. ACM. 10.1145/3291078.3291115

Piccolo, L., Mensio, M., & Alani, H. (2019). Chasing the Chatbots. In S. S. Bodrunova (Ed.), *Internet Science*. (pp. 157–169). Springer International Publishing.

Piltch, A. (2016, April 18). Talk is CHEAP: Why Chatbots will always be a waste of time. *Tom's Guide*. https://www.tomsguide.com/us/chatbots-waste-our-time,news-22562.html

Pinkwart, N., & Konert, J. (2019). How Are You, Chatbot? Evaluating Chatbots in Educational Settings -Results of a Literature Review, 259. *GI.* doi:10.18420/delfi2019_289

Popović, M. (2015). chrF: Character n-gram F-score for automatic MT evaluation. *Proceedings of the Tenth Workshop on Statistical Machine Translation*, (pp. 392–395). ACL. 10.18653/v1/W15-3049

Porcheron, M., Fischer, J. E., Reeves, S., & Sharples, S. (2018). Voice Interfaces in Everyday Life. Human Factors in Computing Systems (CHI '18), pp. 1-12.

Prendinger, H., & Ishizuka, M. (2005). The Empathic Companion: A Character-Based Interface That Addresses Users'affective States. *Applied Artificial Intelligence*, *19*(3-4), 267–285.

Press, G. (2022, April 24). *Practices that ensure the safety of chat bots*. WhatsApp Chatbot. https://wa-chatbot.com/practices-ensure-safety-chat-bots-your-company/

Przegalinska, A. K., Ciechanowski, L., Stróz, A., Gloor, P. A., & Mazurek, G. (2019). In bot we trust: A new methodology of chatbot performance measures. *Business Horizons*, *62*(6), 785–797. doi:10.1016/j.bushor.2019.08.005

Qin, C., Huang, W., & Hew, K. F. (2020). Using the community of inquiry framework to develop an educational chatbot: Lesson learned from a mobile instant messaging learning environment. In *Proceedings of the 28th international conference on computers in education*, (pp. 69-74). APSCE.

Racter,(1984). *The Policeman's Beard Is Half Constructed: Computer Prose and Poetry*. New York, Warner Books.

Radford, A., Narasimhan, K., Salimans, T., & Sutskever, I. (2018). *Improving language understanding by generative pre-training*. https://s3-us-west-2.amazonaws.com/openai-assets/research-covers/language-unsupervised/language_understanding_paper.pdf

Radford, A., Wu, J., Child, R., Luan, D., Amodei, D., & Sutskever, I. (2019). *Language Models are Unsupervised Multitask Learners*. Semantic Scholar.

Radziwill, N., & Benton, M. (2017). Evaluating quality of chatbots and intelligent conversational agents. Cornell University. https://arxiv.org/abs/1704.04579

Rafayet Ali, M., Sen, T., Kane, B., Bose, S., Carroll, T. M., Epstein, R. & Hoque, E. (2020). Novel Computational Linguistic Measures, Dialogue System, and the Development of SOPHIE: Standardized Online Patient for Healthcare Interaction Education. Cornell University.

Raj, S., Raj, K., & Karkal. (2019). *Building chatbots with Python*. Apress, doi:10.1007/978-1-4842-4096-0

Ramesh, K., Ravishankaran, S., Joshi, A., & Chandrasekaran, K. 2017. A survey of design techniques for conversational agents. In *International conference on information, communication and computing technology,* (pp. 336-350). Springer. 10.1007/978-981-10-6544-6_31

Ranoliya, B. R., Raghuwanshi, N., & Singh, S. (2017). Chatbot for university related FAQs. In *Proceedings of the International Conference on Advances in Computing, Communications and Informatics*, (pp. 1525-1530). IEEE.

Ranoliya, B. R., Raghuwanshi, N., & Singh, S. (2017, September). Chatbot for university related FAQs. In *2017 International Conference on Advances in Computing, Communications and Informatics (ICACCI)* (pp. 1525-1530). IEEE. 10.1109/ICACCI.2017.8126057

Rapp, A., Curti, L., & Boldi, A. (2021). The human side of human-chatbot interaction: A systematic literature review of ten years of research on text-based chatbots. *International Journal of Human-Computer Studies, 151,* 102630. doi:10.1016/j.ijhcs.2021.102630

RAPT & ArticuLab. (n.d.). *Overview.* ArticuLab, CMU. http://articulab.hcii.cs.cmu.edu/projects/rapt/

Reeves, B. & Nass, C. (1996). The media equation: How people treat computers, television, and new media like real people. *Cambridge, UK, 10,* 10.

Rei, R., Stewart, C., Farinha, A. C., & Lavie, A. (2020). COMET: A Neural Framework for MT Evaluation. *Proceedings of the 2020 Conference on Empirical Methods in Natural Language Processing (EMNLP)*, (pp. 2685–2702). ACL. 10.18653/v1/2020.emnlp-main.213

Rodrigo, M. M. T., Baker, R. S., Agapito, J., Nabos, J., Repalam, M. C., Reyes, S. S., & San Pedro, M. O. C. (2012). The efects of an interactive software agent on student afective dynamics while using; an intelligent tutoring system. *IEEE Transactions on Affective Computing, 3*(2), 224–236. doi:10.1109/T-AFFC.2011.41

Rohrig, C., & Heß, D. (2019). Omniman: A mobile assistive robot for intralogistics applications. *Engineering Letters, 27*(4), 893–900.

Roller, S., Dinan, E., Goyal, N., Ju, D., Williamson, M., Liu, Y., Xu, J., Ott, M., Shuster, K., Smith, E. M., Boureau, Y. L., & Weston, J. (2021). Recipes for building an open-domain chatbot. In *Proceedings of the 16th Conference of the European Chapter of the Association for Computational Linguistics*, (pp. 300–325). Association for Computational Linguistics.

Rooein, D. (2019, May). Data-driven edu chatbots. In *Companion Proceedings of The 2019 World Wide Web Conference* (pp. 46-49). ACM. 10.1145/3308560.3314191

Roos, R. (2018). *Chatbots in Education: A Passing Trend or a Valuable Pedagogical Tool?* [Master's Thesis, Uppsala University, Uppsala, Sweden].

Ruan, S., Jiang, L., Xu, Q., Liu, Z., Davis, G. M., Brunskill, E., & Landay, J. A. (2021). Englishbot: An ai-powered conversational system for second language learning. In *26th international conference on intelligent user interfaces* (pp. 434–444). ACM.

Ruan, S., Willis, A., Xu, Q., Davis, G. M., Jiang, L., Brunskill, E., & Landay, J. A. (2019). Bookbuddy: Turning digital materials into interactive foreign language lessons through a voice chatbot. In *Proceedings of the 6th 2019 ACM Conference on Learning at Scale.* ACM. 10.1145/3330430.3333643

Rubin, V. L., Chen, Y., & Thorimbert, L. M. (2010). Artificially intelligent conversational agents in libraries. *Library Hi Tech*, *28*(4), 496–522. doi:10.1108/07378831011096196

Rubio-Tamayo, J. L., Gertrudix Barrio, M., & García García, F. (2017). Immersive environments and virtual reality: Systematic review and advances in communication, interaction and simulation. *Multimodal Technologies and Interaction*, *4*(1), 21. doi:10.3390/mti1040021

Rybakova, M. (2020). 4 Evolving Technologies That Are Empowering Chatbots. *AI Authority*. https://aithority.com/guest-authors/4-evolving-technologies-that-are-empowering-chatbots/

Sai, A. B., Mohankumar, A. K., Arora, S., & Khapra, M. M. (2020). Improving Dialog Evaluation with a Multi-reference Adversarial Dataset and Large Scale Pretraining. *Transactions of the Association for Computational Linguistics*, *8*, 810–827. doi:10.1162/tacl_a_00347

Sandu, N., & Gide, E. (2019). Adoption of AI-Chatbots to enhance student learning experience in higher education in India. In *2019 18th International Conference on Information Technology Based Higher Education and Training (ITHET)*, pp. 1-5. IEEE. 10.1109/ITHET46829.2019.8937382

Sandu, N., & Gide, E. (2019, September). Adoption of AI-Chatbots to enhance student learning experience in higher education in India. In *2019 18th International Conference on Information Technology Based Higher Education and Training (ITHET)* (pp. 1-5). IEEE.

Satow, L. (2019). Lernen mit Chatbots und digitalin Assistenten. In A. Hohenstein & K. Wilbers (Eds.), *Handbuch E-Learning*. Wolters Kluwer.

Saxena, A. R. (2019, July 31). *Chatbot Security Framework: Everything you need to know about Chatbot security*. Medium. https://medium.com/@secxena/chatbot-security-framework-every thing-you-need-to-know-about-chatbot-security-243468f977b6

Schmidhuber, J. (1992). Learning to Control Fast-Weight Memories: An Alternative to Dynamic Recurrent Networks. *Neural Computation*, *4*(1), 131–139. doi:10.1162/neco.1992.4.1.131

See, A., Pappu, A., Saxena, R., Yerukola, A., & Manning, C. D. (2019). Do Massively Pretrained Language Models Make Better Storytellers? https://arxiv.org/abs/1909.10705 doi:10.18653/v1/K19-1079

Selig, J. (2022, March 24). Chatbot: What is a Chatbot? Why are Chatbots Important? *Expert.ai*. https://www.expert.ai/blog/chatbot/

Sellam, T., Das, D., & Parikh, A. P. (2020). BLEURT: Learning Robust Metrics for Text Generation. https://arxiv.org/abs/2004.04696 doi:10.18653/v1/2020.acl-main.704

Serban, I. V., Sankar, C., Germain, M., Zhang, S., Lin, Z., Subramanian, S., Kim, T., Pieper, M., Chandar, S., Ke, N. R., Rajeshwar, S., de Brebisson, A., Sotelo, J. M. R., Suhubdy, D., Michalski, V., Nguyen, A., Pineau, J., & Bengio, Y. (2017). A Deep Reinforcement Learning Chatbot. https://arxiv.org/abs/1709.02349

Serban, I. V., Sordoni, A., Bengio, Y., Courville, A., & Pineau, J. (2016). Building end-to-end dialogue systems using generative hierarchical neural network models. *Proceedings of the Thirtieth AAAI Conference on Artificial Intelligence*, (pp. 3776–3783). AAAI. 10.1609/aaai.v30i1.9883

Serenko, A., Bontis, N., & Detlor, B. (2007). End-user adoption of animated interface agents in everyday work applications. Behaviour &Amp. *Información Tecnológica*, *26*(2), 119–132. doi:10.1080/01449290500260538

Setlur, V., & Melanie, T. (2022). How do you Converse with an Analytical Chatbot? Revisiting Gricean Maxims for Designing Analytical Conversational Behavior. *In CHI Conference on Human Factors in Computing Systems*, (pp. 1-17). ACM.

Shagass, C., Roemer, R. A., & Amadeo, M. (1976). Eye-Tracking Performance and Engagement of Attention. *Archives of General Psychiatry*, *33*(1), 121–125. doi:10.1001/archpsyc.1976.01770010077015 PMID:1247358

Shah, H., Warwick, K., Vallverdú, J., & Wu, D. (2016). Can machines talk? Comparison of Eliza with modern dialogue systems. *Computers in Human Behavior*, *58*, 278–295. https://doi.org/10.1016/j.chb.2016.01.004

Shanbhag, A. (2020, September 28). Privacy And Security Considerations For Consumer-facing Chatbots. *BotCore*. https://botcore.ai/blog/chatbot-privacy-security/

Shang, L., Lu, Z., & Li, H. (2015). Neural Responding Machine for Short-Text Conversation. https://arxiv.org/abs/1503.02364 doi:10.3115/v1/P15-1152

Shangipour Ataei, T., Javdan, S., & Minaei-Bidgoli, B. (2020). Applying Transformers and Aspect-based Sentiment Analysis approaches on Sarcasm Detection. *Proceedings of the Second Workshop on Figurative Language Processing*, (pp. 67–71). ACL. doi:10.18653/v1/2020.figlang-1.9

Shang, L., Lu, Z., & Li, H. (2015). *Neural responding machine for short-text conversation.* Cornell University., doi:10.3115/v1/P15-1152

Shankar, V. (2018). How Artificial Intelligence (AI) is Reshaping Retailing. *Journal of Retailing*, *94*(4), VI–XI.

Shao, T., Guo, Y., Chen, H., & Hao, Z. (2019). Transformer-Based Neural Network for Answer Selection in Question Answering. *IEEE Access: Practical Innovations, Open Solutions*, *7*, 26146–26156. doi:10.1109/ACCESS.2019.2900753

Shawar, A. B., & Atwell, E. (2007). Chatbots: Are they Really Useful? *LDV-Forum – Band 22*(1), 29-49.

Shawar, B. A., & Atwell, E. (2007). Different measurements metrics to evaluate a chatbot system. In *Proceedings of the Workshop on Bridging the Gap: Academic and Industrial Research in Dialog Technologies*, (pp. 89–96). ACM. 10.3115/1556328.1556341

Shewan, D. (2022, April 22). 10 of the Most Innovative Chatbots on the Web. *WordStream*. https://www.wordstream.com/blog/ws/chatbots

Shin, D., Al-Imamy, S., & Hwang, Y. (2022). Cross-cultural differences in information processing of chatbot journalism: Chatbot news service as a cultural artifact. Cross Cultural &Amp. *Strategic Management*, *29*(3), 618–638. doi:10.1108/CCSM-06-2020-0125

Shin, D., Kim, H., Lee, J. H., & Yang, H. (2021). Exploring the use of an artificial intelligence chatbot as second language conversation partners. *Korean Journal of English Language and Linguistics*, *21*, 375–391.

Shi, W., Wang, X., Oh, Y. J., Zhang, J., Sahay, S., & Yu, Z. (2020). Effects of persuasive dialogues: Testing bot identities and inquiry strategies. *Proceedings of the 2020 CHI Conference on Human Factors in Computing Systems*, (pp. 1–13). ACM. 10.1145/3313831.3376843

Shneiderman, B. (2016). *Designing the user interface: strategies for effective human-computer interaction*. Pearson.

Shneiderman, B. (2020). Human-centered artificial intelligence: Reliable, safe & trustworthy. *International Journal of Human-Computer Interaction*, *36*(6), 495–504. doi:10.1080/1044731 8.2020.1741118

Shneiderman, B., Plaisant, C., Cohen, M., Jacobs, S., & Elmqvist, N. (2016). *Designing the user interface: Strategies for effective human-computer interaction* (6th ed.). Pearson.

Shukairy, A. (2018, May 9). Chatbots In Customer Service – Statistics and Trends [Infographic]. *The Invesp Blog: Conversion Rate Optimization Blog*. https://www.invespcro.com/blog/chatbots-customer-service/

Shumanov, M., & Johnson, L. (2021). Making conversations with chatbots more personalized. *Computers in Human Behavior*, *117*, 106627. doi:10.1016/j.chb.2020.106627

Silva, C. (2022, August 8). It Took Just One Weekend For Meta's New AI Chatbot To Become Racist. *Mashable India*. https://in.mashable.com/apps-and-software/36425/it-took-just-one-weekend-for-metas-new-ai-chatbot-to-become-racist

Sinclair, J. (Ed.). (2004). *How to use corpora in language teaching*. John Benjamins. doi:10.1075cl.12

Singh Gill, N. (2022, March 16). What are Chatbots and Why are they Important? *Xenonstack*. Www.xenonstack.com. https://www.xenonstack.com/insights/chatbots-applications

Sinha, S., Basak, S., Dey, Y., & Mondal, A. (2020). An educational chatbot for answering queries. In J. Mandal & D. Bhattacharya (Eds.), *Emerging Technology in Modelling and Graphics. Advances in Intelligent Systems and Computing, 937, 55-60*. Springer. doi:10.1007/978-981-13-7403-6_7

SiteLock. (2019). Chatbot Security Risks: What you need to know before starting an online chat – The SiteLock Blog. *Sitelock*. https://www.sitelock.com/blog/chatbot-security-risks/

Sjöström, J., Aghaee, N., Dahlin, M., & Ågerfalk, P. J. (2018). Designing chatbots for higher education practice. In *Proceedings of the International Conference on Information Systems Education and Research*, (pp. 1-10). Research Gate.

Sjöström, J., Aghaee, N., Dahlin, M., & Ågerfalk, P. J. (2018). *Designing chatbots for higher education practice.* Research Gate.

Skjuve, M., Følstad, A., Fostervold, K. I., & Brandtzaeg, P. B. (2021). My chatbot companion-a study of human-chatbot relationships. *International Journal of Human-Computer Studies, 149,* 102601. doi:10.1016/j.ijhcs.2021.102601

Slack. (2022). *Kyber.* Slack. https://slack.com/apps/A0EP69E58-kyber.

Smestad, T., & Volden, F. (n.d.). Chatbot Personalities Matters Improving the user experience of chatbot interfaces. *Conversations 2018.* Springer. https://conversations2018.files.wordpress.com/2018/10/conver sations_2018_paper_11_preprint1.pdf

Smestad, T. L., & Volden, F. (2019). Chatbot personalities matters: Improving the user experience of chatbot interfaces. In S. S. Bodrunova, O. Koltsova, A. Følstad, H. Halpin, P. Kolozaridi, L. Yuldashev, A. Smoliarova, & H. Niedermayer (Eds.), *Internet Science* (Vol. 11551, pp. 170–181). Springer International Publishing. doi:10.1007/978-3-030-17705-8_15

Smith-Griffin, J. (2022, January 18). 3 ways chatbots can support mental health in schools. *eSchool News.* https://www.eschoolnews.com/2022/01/18/3-ways-chatbots-can-s upport-mental-health-in-schools/2/

Smutny, P., & Schreiberova, P. (2020). Chatbots for learning: A review of educational chatbots for the Facebook Messenger. *Computers & Education, 151,* 103862. doi:10.1016/j.compedu.2020.103862

Snover, M. G., Madnani, N., Dorr, B., & Schwartz, R. (2009). TER-Plus: Paraphrase, semantic, and alignment enhancements to Translation Edit Rate. *Machine Translation, 23*(2–3), 117–127. doi:10.100710590-009-9062-9

Sojasingarayar, A. (2020). *Seq2Seq AI Chatbot with Attention Mechanism.* Academia. https://www.academia.edu/43262982/Seq2Seq_AI_Chatbot_with_Attention_Mechanism

Söllner, M., Bitzer, P., Janson, A., & Leimeister, J. M. (2017). Process is king: Evaluating the performance of technology-mediated learning in vocational software training. *Journal of Information Technology, 18*(2), 159.

Song, D., Oh, E. Y., & Rice, M. (2017, July). Interacting with a conversational agent system for educational purposes in online courses. In *2017 10th international conference on human system interactions (HSI)* (pp. 78-82). IEEE. 10.1109/HSI.2017.8005002

Song, Y., Li, C.-T., Nie, J.-Y., Zhang, M., Zhao, D., & Yan, R. (2018). An Ensemble of Retrieval-Based and Generation-Based Human-Computer Conversation Systems. *Proceedings of the Twenty-Seventh International Joint Conference on Artificial Intelligence,* (pp. 4382–4388). IJCAI. 10.24963/ijcai.2018/609

Sordoni, A., Galley, M., Auli, M., Brockett, C., Ji, Y., Mitchell, M., Nie, J.-Y., Gao, J., & Dolan, B. (2015). A Neural Network Approach to Context-Sensitive Generation of Conversational Responses. https://arxiv.org/abs/1506.06714 doi:10.3115/v1/N15-1020

Soto, C. J., Kronauer, A., & Liang, J. K. (2015). Five-factor model of personality. In S. K. Whitbourne (Ed.), *The Encyclopedia of Adulthood and Aging* (pp. 1–5). John Wiley & Sons, Inc. doi:10.1002/9781118521373.wbeaa014

Sree, V. K. C, K., G, S., & Rohan, R. (2019). Various Real Time Chat Bots and Their Applications in Human Life. *International Journal of Recent Technology and Engineering, 8*(4), 3461–3467. doi:10.35940/ijrte.d6902.118419

Sreelakshmi, A. S., Abhinaya, S. B., Nair, A., & Nirmala, S. J. (2019). A question answering and quiz generation chatbot for education. In 2019 Grace Hopper Celebration India (GHCI) (pp. 1-6). IEEE. doi:10.1109/GHCI47972.2019.9071832

Sreelakshmi, A. S., Abhinaya, S. B., Nair, A., & Nirmala, S. J. (2019, November). A question answering and quiz generation chatbot for education. In *2019 Grace Hopper Celebration India (GHCI)* (pp. 1-6). IEEE.

Srivastava, B., Rossi, F., Usmani, S., & Bernagozzi, M. (2020). Personalized Chatbot Trustworthiness Ratings. *IEEE Transactions On Technology And Society, 1*(4), 184–192. doi:10.1109/TTS.2020.3023919

Stanojević, M., & Sima'an, K. (2014). BEER: BEtter Evaluation as Ranking. *Proceedings of the Ninth Workshop on Statistical Machine Translation*, (pp. 414–419). ACL. 10.3115/v1/W14-3354

Statista.com. (2023). *Size of the chatbot market worldwide in 2016 and 2025.* https://www.statista.com/statistics/656596/worldwide-chatbot-market/

Straits Research. (2022, June 29). Chatbot Market Growth is projected to reach USD 3.62 Billion by 2030, growing at a CAGR of 23.9%: Straits Research. *GlobeNewswire News Room.* https://www.globenewswire.com/news-release/2022/06/29/2471371/0/en/Chatbot-Market-Growth-is-projected-to-reach-USD-3-62-Billion-by-2030-growing-at-a-CAGR-of-23-9-Straits-Research.html

Strigér, A. (2017). *End-to-End Trainable Chatbot for Restaurant Recommendations.* KTH. https://www.diva-portal.org/smash/get/diva2:1139496/FULLTEXT01.pdf

Strijbos, J. W., Martens, R. L., & Jochems, W. M. G. (2004). Designing for interaction: Six steps to designing computer-supported group-based learning. *Computers & Education, 24*(4), 403–424. doi:10.1016/j.compedu.2003.10.004

Suebsombut, P., Sureephong, P., Sekhari, A., Chernbumroong, S., & Bouras, A. (2022). Chatbot application to support smart agriculture in Thailand. In *Proceedings of Joint International Conference on Digital Arts, Media and Technology with ECTI Northern Section Conference on Electrical, Electronics, Computer and Telecommunications Engineering*, (pp. 364-367). IEEE. 10.1109/ECTIDAMTNCON53731.2022.9720318

Sugisaki, K., & Bleiker, A. (2020). Usability guidelines and evaluation criteria for conversational user interfaces - a heuristic and linguistic approach. In *MuC'20: Proceedings of the Conference on Mensch Und Computer* (pp. 309–319). ACM.

Sugisaki, K., & Bleiker, A. 2020. Usability guidelines and evaluation criteria for conversational user interfaces: a heuristic and linguistic approach, 309--319. ACM. doi:10.1145/3404983.3405505

Suleman, R. M., Mizoguchi, R., & Ikeda, M. (2016). A new perspective of negotiation-based dialog to enhance metacognitive skills in the context of open learner models. *International Journal of Artificial Intelligence in Education, 26*(4), 1069–1115. doi:10.100740593-016-0118-8

Sun, C., Baradel, F., Murphy, K., & Schmid, C. (2019). Learning Video Representations using Contrastive Bidirectional Transformer. https://arxiv.org/abs/1906.05743

Sutcliffe, A. & Gault, B., 2004. Heuristic evaluation of virtual reality applications.. *Interacting with computers, 16*(4), 831-849.

Svenningsson, N., & Faraon, M. (2019). Artificial intelligence in conversational agents: A study of factors related to perceived humanness in chatbots. *Proceedings of the 2019 2nd Artificial Intelligence and Cloud Computing Conference,* (pp. 151–161). ACM. 10.1145/3375959.3375973

Tao, C., Mou, L., Zhao, D., & Yan, R. (2017). RUBER: An Unsupervised Method for Automatic Evaluation of Open-Domain Dialog Systems. *Proceedings of the AAAI Conference on Artificial Intelligence, 32.* AAAI. 10.1609/aaai.v32i1.11321

Tegos, S., Psathas, G., Tsiatsos, T., Katsanos, C., Karakostas, A., Tsibanis, C., & Demetriadis, S. (2020). Enriching synchronous collaboration in online courses with confgurable conversational agents. In *International Conference on Intelligent Tutoring Systems* (pp. 284–294). Springer. 10.1007/978-3-030-49663-0_34

Tegos, S., Demetriadis, S., & Karakostas, A. (2015). Promoting academically productive talk with conversational agent interventions in collaborative learning settings. *Computers & Education, 87,* 309–325.

Tenney, I., Das, D., & Pavlick, E. (2019). BERT Rediscovers the Classical NLP Pipeline. https://arxiv.org/abs/1905.05950 doi:10.18653/v1/P19-1452

Tettelin, T. (2022, June 24). How to build a chatbot in just 10 steps. *Medium.* https://tesstettelin.medium.com/how-to-build-a-chatbot-in-just-10-steps-a9f74e12c601

Thompson, B., & Post, M. (2020). Paraphrase Generation as Zero-Shot Multilingual Translation: Disentangling Semantic Similarity from Lexical and Syntactic Diversity https://arxiv.org/abs/2008.04935

Thorat, S. A., & Jadhav, V. (2020). A review on implementation issues of rule-based chatbot systems. *Proceedings of the International Conference on Innovative Computing \& Communications (ICICC).* SSRN. 10.2139srn.3567047

Timpe-Laughlin, V., Sydorenko, T., & Daurio, P. (2020). Using spoken dialogue technology for l2 speaking practice: What do teachers think? *Computer Assisted Language Learning*, 1–24.

Todd, S. (2022). The Employee Experience Advantage – Jacob Morgan. *Open Sourced Workplace*. https://opensourcedworkplace.com/news/the-employee-experience-advantage-jacob-morgan

Top 10 Benefits of Using AI Chatbots in your Business. (n.d.). AgreeYa Solutions. https://agreeya.com/whitepaper/top-10-benefits-of-using-ai-chatbots-in-your-business/

Toxtli, C., Monroy-Hernández, A., & Cranshaw, J. (2018). *Understanding chatbot-mediated task management.* . Association for Computing Machinery.

Toxtli, C., Monroy-Hernández, A., & Cranshaw, J. (2018). *Understanding Chatbot-mediated Task Management.* . Association for Computing Machinery.

Trivialworks Solutions Pvt Ltd. (2018). Trivialworks.com. https://trivialworks.com/amazon-alexa/

Troussas, C., Krouska, A., & Virvou, M. (2017, November). Integrating an adjusted conversational agent into a mobile-assisted language learning application. In *IEEE 29th International Conference on Tools with Artificial Intelligence (ICTAI)* (pp. 1153-1157). IEEE. 10.1109/ICTAI.2017.00176

Tsai, P. (2019). Beyond self-directed computer-assisted pronunciation learning: A qualitative investigation of a collaborative approach. *Computer Assisted Language Learning*, *32*(7), 713–744. doi:10.1080/09588221.2019.1614069

Tung, L. (2022, August 8). Meta warns its new chatbot may forget that it's a bot. *ZDNET*. https://www.zdnet.com/article/meta-warns-its-new-chatbot-may-not-tell-you-the-truth/

Tur, G., & Deng, L. (2011). Intent Determination and Spoken Utterance Classification. *Spoken Language Understanding*, 93–118. doi:10.1002/9781119992691.ch4

Turing, A. M. (1950). Computing machinery and intelligence. *Mind*, *59*(236), 433–460. doi:10.1093/mind/LIX.236.433

Turing, A. M. (1950). Computing Machinery and Intelligence. *Mind*, *LIX*(236), 433–460. https://doi.org/10.1093/mind/lix.236.433

Ucedavélez, T., & Morana, M. M. (2015). *Risk Centric Threat Modeling Process for Attack Simulation and Threat Analysis. Hoboken.* John Wiley & Sons, Inc.

UCI Libraries Reference Department. (2012, September 17). *Retrieved from Policies and procedures: Reference Statistics Category Definitions:* UCI. http://staff.lib.uci.edu/refstats-docs.php

Ureta, J., & Rivera, J. P. (2018). *Using chatbots to teach stem related research concepts t o high school students.* Research Gate.

Vaish, A. (2022, August 23). AI: How the Rise Of Chatbot Is Powering a Futuristic Present? *Entrepreneur*. https://www.entrepreneur.com/article/433939

van der Meij, H., van der Meij, J., & Harmsen, R. (2015). Animated pedagogical agents effects on enhancing student motivation and learning in a science inquiry learning environment. *Educational Technology Research and Development*, *63*(3), 381–403. doi:10.100711423-015-9378-5

Vanichvasin, P. (2021). Chatbot development as a digital learning tool to increase students' research knowledge. *International Education Studies*, *14*(2), 44–53. doi:10.5539/ies.v14n2p44

Vantage Research Market. (2022, March 17). Top Trends Driving the Global Healthcare Chatbots Market | Size Will Cross USD 431.47 Million by 2028. *GlobeNewswire News Room*. https://www.globenewswire.com/en/news-release/2022/03/17/240 4993/0/en/Top-Trends-Driving-the-Global-Healthcare-Chatbots-Market-Size-Will-Cross-USD-431-47-Million-by-2028-Global-Rep ort-by-Vantage-Market-Research.html

Vaswani, A., Shazeer, N., Parmar, N., Uszkoreit, J., Jones, L., Gomez, A. N., Kaiser, L., & Polosukhin, I. (2017). Attention Is All You Need. https://arxiv.org/abs/1706.03762

Venable, J. R., Pries-Heje, J., & Baskerville, R. L. (2017). *Choosing a design science research methodology*. AISEL.

Verasius, A., Sano, D., Imanuel, T. D., Calista, M. I., Nindito, H., & Condrobimo, A. R. (2018). The application of AGNES algorithm to optimize knowledge base for tourism chatbot. In *Proceedings of the International Conference on Information Management and Technology*, (pp. 65-68). Semantic Scholar.

Verleger, M., & Pembridge, J. (2018). A Pilot Study Integrating an AI-driven Chatbot in an Introductory Programming Course. *2018 IEEE Frontiers In Education Conference (FIE)*. IEEE. 10.1109/FIE.2018.8659282

Vetter, M. (2002). Quality aspects of bots. In *Software Quality and Software Testing in Internet Times* (pp. 165–184). Springer Berlin Heidelberg. doi:10.1007/978-3-642-56333-1_11

Vinyals, O., & Le, Q. (2015). A Neural Conversational Model. https://arxiv.org/abs/1506.05869

Voroneckis, R. (2019, January 30). Main benefits of using a Chatbot for your business. *Medium*. https://towardsdatascience.com/main-benefits-of-using-a-chat bot-for-your-business-b4ad00f02fb

Wallace, R. (2003). *The elements of AIML style*, 139. Alice AI Foundation.

Wallace, R. (2001). *The Elements of AIML Style*. ALICE A.I Foundation.

Wang, H., Tan, M., Yu, M., Chang, S., Wang, D., Xu, K., Guo, X., & Potdar, S. (2019). Extracting Multiple-Relations in One-Pass with Pre-Trained Transformers. https://arxiv.org/abs/1902.01030 doi:10.18653/v1/P19-1132

Wang, Q., Li, B., Xiao, T., Zhu, J., Li, C., Wong, D. F., & Chao, L. S. (2019). Learning Deep Transformer Models for Machine Translation. https://arxiv.org/abs/1906.01787 doi:10.18653/v1/P19-1176

Wang, L. (2021). Cass: Towards building a social-support chatbot for online health community. *Proceedings of the ACM on Human-Computer Interaction*, (pp. 1-31). ACM.

Wang, W., & Siau, K. (2018). Living with Artificial Intelligence–Developing a Theory on Trust in Health Chatbots. In *Proceedings of the Sixteenth Annual Pre-ICIS Workshop on HCI Research in MIS* (pp. 1-5). Association for Information Systems.

Wegerif, R. (2004). The role of educational software as a support for teaching and learning conversations. *Computers & Education*, *43*(1–2), 179–191. doi:10.1016/j.compedu.2003.12.012

Weizenbaum, J. (1966). Eliza – a computer program for the study of natural language communication between man and machine. *Communications of the ACM*, *9*(1), 36–45.

Weizenbaum, J. (1966). ELIZA—A computer program for the study of natural language communication between man and machine. *Communications of the ACM*, *9*(1), 36–45. doi:10.1145/365153.365168

Weizenbaum, J. (1983). ELIZA— A computer program for the study of natural language communication between man and machine. *Communications of the ACM*, *26*(1), 23 28. doi:10.1145/357980.357991

Westerman, D., Cross, A. C., & Lindmark, P. G. (2019). I believe in a thing called bot: Perceptions of the humanness of chatbots. *Communication Studies*, *70*(3), 295–312. doi:10.1080/1051097 4.2018.1557233

What are the Advantages and Disadvantages of Chatbots in Business ? (2020, April 20). GeeksforGeeks. https://www.geeksforgeeks.org/what-are-the-advantages-and-di sadvantages-of-chatbots-in-business/

What Are The Benefits of Chatbots? 2021 Chatbot Guide. (n.d.). Whisbi. Retrieved August 27, 2022, from https://www.whisbi.com/guides/chatbot/benefits/#:~:text=They %20Improve%20Customer%20Experience&text=Conversational%20sal es%20and%20marketing%20help

What are the privacy and security issues associated with chatbots ? (n.d.). Tutorialspoint. Www.tutorialspoint.com. https://www.tutorialspoint.com/what-are-the-privacy-and-secu rity-issues-associated-with-chatbots

Wilcox, B. (2014). Winning the Loebner's. https://www. gamasutra.com/blogs/BruceWilcox/20141020/228091/ Winning_the_Loebners.php

Winkler, R., & Soellner, M. (2018). Unleashing the potential of chatbots in education: A state-of-the-art analysis. In *Academy of Management Annual Meeting Proceedings*. Academy of Management. 10.5465/AMBPP.2018.15903abstract

Winkler, R., & Söllner, M. (2018). Unleashing the potential of chatbots in education: A state-of-the-art analysis. *In Academy of Management Annual Meeting*. AOM.

Winkler, R., Hobert, S., Salovaara, A., & Söllner, M., & Leimeister, Jan Marco (2020). Sara, the lecturer: Improving learning in online education with a scafolding-based conversational agent. In *Proceedings of the 2020 CHI conference on human factors in computing systems* (pp. 1–14). ACM. 10.1145/3313831.3376781

Wollny, S., Schneider, J., Di Mitri, D., Weidlich, J., Rittberger, M., & Drachsler, H. (2021). Are we there yet? -A systematic literature review on chatbots in education. *Frontiers in artificial intelligence, 4.*

Wollny, S., Schneider, J., Di Mitri, D., Weidlich, J., Rittberger, M., & Drachsler, H. (2021). Are we there yet? - A systematic literature review on chatbots in education. *Frontiers in Artificial Intelligence, 4*, 654924. doi:10.3389/frai.2021.654924 PMID:34337392

Xiao, Z., Zhou, M. X., Chen, W., Yang, H., & Chi, C. (2020). If I hear you correctly: Building and evaluating interview chatbots with active listening skills. *Proceedings of the 2020 CHI Conference on Human Factors in Computing Systems*, (pp. 1–14). ACM. 10.1145/3313831.3376131

Xiao, Z., Zhou, M. X., Liao, Q. V., Mark, G., Chi, C., Chen, W., & Yang, H. (2020). Tell Me About Yourself: Using an AI-Powered Chatbot to Conduct Conversational Surveys with Open-ended Questions. *ACM Transactions on Computer-Human Interaction, 27*(3), 1–37. doi:10.1145/3381804

Xu, A. (2017). A new chatbot for customer service on social media. *Proceedings of the 2017 CHI conference on human factors in computing systems*, (pp. 3506–3510). ACM. 10.1145/3025453.3025496

Xu, L., Sanders, L., Li, K., & Chow, J. C. (2021). Chatbot for health care and oncology applications using artificial intelligence and machine learning: Systematic review. *JMIR Cancer, 7*(4), e27850. doi:10.2196/27850 PMID:34847056

Yadav, D., Malik, P., Dabas, K., & Singh, P. (2019). Feedpal: Understanding opportunities for chatbots in breastfeeding education of women in India. *Proceedings of the ACM on Human-Computer Interaction*, (pp. 1-30). ACM. 10.1145/3359272

Yang, H. C., & Zapata-Rivera, D. (2010). Interlanguage pragmatics with a pedagogical agent: The request game. *Computer Assisted Language Learning, 23*(5), 395–412. doi:10.1080/0958 8221.2010.520274

Yang, S., & Evans, C. (2019, November). Opportunities and challenges in using AI chatbots in higher education. In *Proceedings of the 2019 3rd International Conference on Education and E-Learning* (pp. 79-83). 10.1145/3371647.3371659

Yang, X., Li, H., Ni, L., & Li, T. (2021). Application of artificial intelligence in precision marketing. *Journal of Organizational and End User Computing, 33*(4), 209–219. doi:10.4018/JOEUC.20210701.oa10

Yan, J. N., Gu, Z., Lin, H., & Rzeszotarski, J. M. (2020). Silva: Interactively Assessing Machine Learning Fairness Using Causality. *Proceedings of the 2020 CHI Conference on Human Factors in Computing Systems*, (pp. 1–13). ACM. 10.1145/3313831.3376447

Yan, Z., Duan, N., Bao, J., Chen, P., Zhou, M., Li, Z., & Zhou, J. (2016). DocChat: An Information Retrieval Approach for Chatbot Engines Using Unstructured Documents. *Proceedings of the 54th Annual Meeting of the Association for Computational Linguistics* (Volume 1, pp. 516–525). ACL. 10.18653/v1/P16-1049

Yen, C., & Chiang, M.-C. (2021). Trust me, if you can: A study on the factors that influence consumers' purchase intention triggered by chatbots based on brain image evidence and self-reported assessments. *Behaviour & Information Technology*, *40*(11), 1177–1194. doi:10.1080/0144929X.2020.1743362

Young, S., Gašić, M., Thomson, B., & Williams, J. D. (2013). POMDP-Based Statistical Spoken Dialog Systems: A Review. *Proceedings of the IEEE*, *101*(5), 1160–1179. doi:10.1109/JPROC.2012.2225812

Yu, S., Chen, Y., & Zaidi, H. (2020). A Financial Service Chatbot based on Deep Bidirectional Transformers. https://arxiv.org/abs/2003.04987

Yuan, W., Neubig, G., & Liu, P. (2021). BARTSCORE: Evaluating Generated Text as Text Generation. Cornell University.

Yuen, M. (2022). Chatbot market in 2022: Stats, trends, and companies in the growing AI chatbot industry. *Insider Intelligence*. https://www.insiderintelligence.com/insights/chatbot-market-stats-trends/

Zaki, M. (2017). Corpus-based teaching in the Arabic classroom: Theoretical and practical perspectives. *International Journal of Applied Linguistics*, *27*(2), 514–541. doi:10.1111/ijal.12159

Zakos, J., & Capper, L. (2008). CLIVE—An artificially intelligent chat robot for conversational language practice. In *SETN 2008: Artificial Intelligence: Theories, Models and Applications* (pp. 437–442). Springer. doi:10.1007/978-3-540-87881-0_46

Zanzotto, F. M. (2019). *Human-in-the-loop Artificial Intelligence*. ACM.

Zarouali, B., Van den Broeck, E., Walrave, M., & Poels, K. (2018). Predicting consumer responses to a chatbot on Facebook. *Cyberpsychology, Behavior, and Social Networking*, *21*(8), 491–497. doi:10.1089/cyber.2017.0518 PMID:30036074

Zemcik, M. T. (2019). A brief history of chatbots. *DEStech Transactions on Computer Science and Engineering, 10*.

Zemčík, T. (2019). A Brief History of Chatbots. *DEStech Transactions on Computer Science and Engineering*. doi:10.12783/dtcse/aicae2019/31439

Zhang, T., Kishore, V., Wu, F., Weinberger, K. Q., & Artzi, Y. (2020). BERTScore: Evaluating Text Generation with BERT. https://arxiv.org/abs/1904.09675

Zhang, Z., Li, J., Zhu, P., Zhao, H., & Liu, G. (2018). Modelling Multi-turn Conversation with Deep Utterance Aggregation. https://arxiv.org/abs/1806.09102

Zhang, C., Ré, C., Cafarella, M., De Sa, C., Ratner, A., Shin, J., Wang, F., & Wu, S. (2017). Deepdive: Declarative knowledge base construction. *Communications of the ACM*, *6*(5), 93–102. doi:10.1145/3060586

Zhao, W., Peyrard, M., Liu, F., Gao, Y., Meyer, C. M., & Eger, S. (2019). MoverScore: Text Generation Evaluating with Contextualized Embeddings and Earth Mover Distance. https://arxiv.org/abs/1909.02622 doi:10.18653/v1/D19-1053

Zheng, Q. (2022). UX Research on Conversational Human-AI Interaction: A Literature Review of the ACM Digital Library. *Proceedings of the 2022 CHI Conference on Human Factors in Computing Systems (CHI '22)*. ACM. 10.1145/3491102.3501855

Zheng, Q. (2022). *X Research on Conversational Human-AI Interaction: A Literature Review of the ACM Digital Library.* . Association for Computing Machinery.

Zhou, M. X., Mark, G., Li, J., & Yang, H. (2019). Trusting virtual agents: The effect of personality. *ACM Transactions on Interactive Intelligent Systems*, *9*(2–3), 1–36. doi:10.1145/3232077

Zubair Khan, M., & Mahamat Yassin, S. (2021). *SeerahBot: An Arabic Chatbot About Prophet's Biography. International Journal of Innovative Research in Computer Science & Technology.* IJIRCST.

Compilation of References

About the Contributors

Mohammad Amin Kuhail received a Ph.D. in software development from the IT University of Copenhagen, Denmark, and an M.Sc. degree in software engineering from the University of York, UK. He served as an Assistant Teaching Professor with the University of Missouri–Kansas City (UMKC), USA, for six years. In 2019, he joined Zayed University, serving as an Assistant Professor. Dr. Kuhail won the teaching award at UMKC in 2018 and received several research grants. Moreover, Dr. Kuhail is currently a reviewer at several journals and conferences, including ITICSE, IEEE Access, and MDPI Informatics. Dr. Kuhail is the founder and developer of a personal-financing system named "Organic Budget". Dr. Kuhail is a Computer Scientist and a Software Engineer with a diverse skill set that spans web development, object-oriented programming, algorithms, and usability. His research interests include human-computer interaction, educational technology, IT education, and smart city.

Bayan Abu Shawar holds a BSc and a Master degree in Computer Science from University of Jordan, and a PhD from the School of Computing at University of Leeds. Currently she is an Associate Professor in the Cybersecurity Department in the Faculty of Engineering at AL Ain University. Before Joining AL Ain University, she was an Associate Professor at Arab Open University in Jordan. Her research interests include Chatbots, Natural Language Intelligent, Information Retrieval, Artificial Intelligent, e-Learning, Question Answering systems, and Learning Management Systems.

Rawad Hammad is a Co-Director for Smart Health Centre, Programme Leader for MSc Computing Course, and MSc Digital Education Course, Technology Enhanced Learning Research Group Leader, and a Senior Lecturer in Computer Science and Digital Technologies at the University of East London. Rawad has an extensive experience in Software Engineering, Technology Enhanced Learning (TEL), Artificial Intelligence in Education, and Smart Health research and practice. Rawad contributed to and led various international projects, published research articles and has been involved in various conference programme committees including EC-TEL, LAK, AIED and BUSTECH. Moreover, Rawad is supervising postgraduate students, currently 5 PhD students in addition to a varied number of MSc students. Rawad is an executive committee member of the International Society of Artificial Intelligence in Education (AIED) and a committee member of different research bodies, and conferences including EC-TEL, LAK, AI for Post-COVID Education, and Networks in Education. In 2018, he received his PhD in Software Engineering from the University of the West of England (UWE). In 2010, he received his MSc in Cognitive Computing from Goldsmiths University of London. He led numerous international projects such as TRANSFER and SmartTech which include partnerships with different universities, research centres, and governmental institutes from different countries including Japan, Germany, Finland and the Middle East. Prior to coming to the University of East London, Rawad was a Senior Education Solutions Researcher/Analyst at King's College London; a Researcher at the Centre for Complex Cooperative Systems at the University of the West of England.

* * *

Alice Ashcroft is a final year PhD candidate studying the effect of gendered language in software development processes at Lancaster University.

Angela Ashcroft has two years of experience designing interactions for a Chatbot and is currently studying for a Masters in Marketing.

Belem Barbosa received her PhD in Business and Management Studies – Specialisation in Marketing and Strategy from the University of Porto, Portugal. She is Assistant Professor at the School of Economics and Management of the University of Porto. She is full researcher at GOVCOPP, the Research Unit of Governance, Competitiveness, and Public Policies, and Invited Researcher at cef.up Center for Economics and Finance at the University of Porto. Her research interests lie primarily in the areas of digital marketing and consumer behavior.

Guendalina Caldarini is a Natural Language Processing Engineer and researcher. Her research is focused on Natural Language Generation, Conditional Text Generation and Dialogue Modeling.

Marta Ferreira earned her Master in Marketing from the University of Porto. She is a marketing practitioner. Her main research interests are communication and digital marketing.

Masood Ghayoomi received his PhD degree in Computational Linguistics from Berlin Freie University, Berlin, Germany in 2014, and M.S. degree in Computational Linguistics from Nancy2 University, Nancy, France and Saarland University, Saarbrücken, Germany, in 2009. Currently he is a faculty member at the Institute for Humanities and Cultural Studies. His research interests include Computational Linguistics, Natural Language Processing, Machine Learning, Corpus Linguistics, Syntax and Lexical Semantics.

Michael Hammond received his Ph.D. in linguistics from UCLA in 1984. He is currently a full professor in the Department of Linguistics at the University of Arizona. He also has appointments in Cognitive Science, Second Language Acquisition and Teaching, and Cognition and Neural Systems. His research, published in numerous journal articles, chapters and books, has been supported by grants from NIH, NSF, and others. His work has focused on phonology (the sound system of natural language) and morphology (how words are constructed) with particular attention on English, Welsh, and Scottish Gaelic. He has approached these issues using traditional linguistic language elicitation techniques, but also experimentally, computationally, and using poetry and language games as data. He's done psycholinguistic work on speech perception, learnability, and the relationship of grammar to language processing.

Elsayed Issa is currently a Ph.D. candidate specializing in Arabic linguistics at the School of Middle Eastern and North African Studies (MENAS) at the University of Arizona. He obtained an M.A. degree in Machine Translation from Alexandria University in Egypt, and an M.S. degree from the Human Language Technology (HLT) program at the Linguistics Department at the University of Arizona. His research interests include phonology, morphology, natural language processing, machine learning, blended learning, and education technology. http://u.arizona.edu/~elsayedissa/.886e8034-6263-4c70-b6a3-638b76972776

Sardar Jaf has strong research interest in Artificial Intelligence, Data Science, Cybersecurity and Pedagogical research. He has been serving as technical committee member for a number of national and international conferences and journals. His teaching roles include the deliver of a range of Computer Science subjects to undergraduate and postgraduate students, and he has supervised students at undergraduate, postgraduate and PhD levels. Dr. Jaf is a Fellow of the Higher Education Academy and a member of the Association for Computational Linguistics.

Sana A. Khan is currently pursuing her graduate studies in Computer Engineering from the American University of Sharjah, Sharjah, United Arab Emirates. She received her B.S. degree in Electrical Engineering from Abu Dhabi University, Abu Dhabi, United Arab Emirates, in 2018. Sana has been working as a Researcher throughout multiple universities in the region.

S. Uma is Professor in the Department of Computer Science and Engineering at Hindusthan College of Engineering and Technology, Coimbatore, Tamil Nadu, India. She received her B.E., degree in Computer Science and Engineering (CSE) in First Class with Distinction from P.S.G. College of Technology, M.S.,(By Res.,)., degree from Anna University, Chennai, Tamil Nadu. She received her Ph.D., in the faculty of Information and Communication Engineering from Anna University, Chennai with High Commendation. She has 32 years of academic experience and organized many National and International seminars, workshops and conferences. She has published more than 100 research papers in National and International Conferences, Journals, Book Chapters, Patents and Books. She is a potential reviewer of International Journals and Member of Professional Bodies like ISTE, CSI, IEEE, IAENG, etc., She is a recipient of "Bharath Jyoti", "Certificate of Excellence" and "Best Citizen of India" Awards. Her research interests are pattern recognition and analysis of nonlinear time series data, AI and digital analytics.

Index

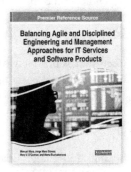

Ensure Quality Research is Introduced to the Academic Community

Become an Evaluator for IGI Global Authored Book Projects

Premier Reference Source

Stabilizing Currency and Preserving Economic Sovereignty Using the Grondona System

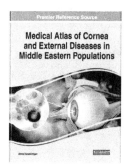

Premier Reference Source

Medical Atlas of Cornea and External Diseases in Middle Eastern Populations

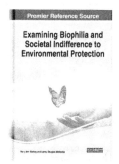

Premier Reference Source

Examining Biophilia and Societal Indifference to Environmental Protection

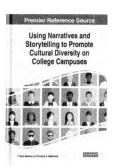

Premier Reference Source

Using Narratives and Storytelling to Promote Cultural Diversity on College Campuses

The overall success of an authored book project is dependent on quality and timely manuscript evaluations.

Applications and Inquiries may be sent to:
development@igi-global.com

Applicants must have a doctorate (or equivalent degree) as well as publishing, research, and reviewing experience. Authored Book Evaluators are appointed for one-year terms and are expected to complete at least three evaluations per term. Upon successful completion of this term, evaluators can be considered for an additional term.

If you have a colleague that may be interested in this opportunity, we encourage you to share this information with them.

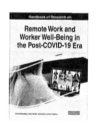

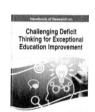